# DAYTIME SHOOTING STAR

★ ★★
★ ★

Story & Art by
Mika Yamamori

★5★

# CONTENTS

## STORY THUS FAR

Suzume Yosano is a first-year in high school. Born in the country, she grew up living a free and easy life. Due to family circumstances, she was forced to transfer to a school in Tokyo. Lost on her first day in the city, she is found by a man who later turns out to be her homeroom teacher, Mr. Shishio. Suzume gradually develops feelings for him.

The appearance of Shishio's ex-girlfriend Tsubomi, and Shishio's everyday words and actions, soon have Suzume declaring her love to him, though he turns her down. But Shishio keeps sending mixed messages, which leave Suzume confused. When Suzume explains this, he tells her he enjoys being with her. Suzume tries to feel satisfied just knowing that he feels that way.

With the start of a new semester, Suzume aims to turn things around by volunteering for the Cultural Festival Committee. She tries to suppress her feelings for Shishio, but his attitude toward her seems to have changed...

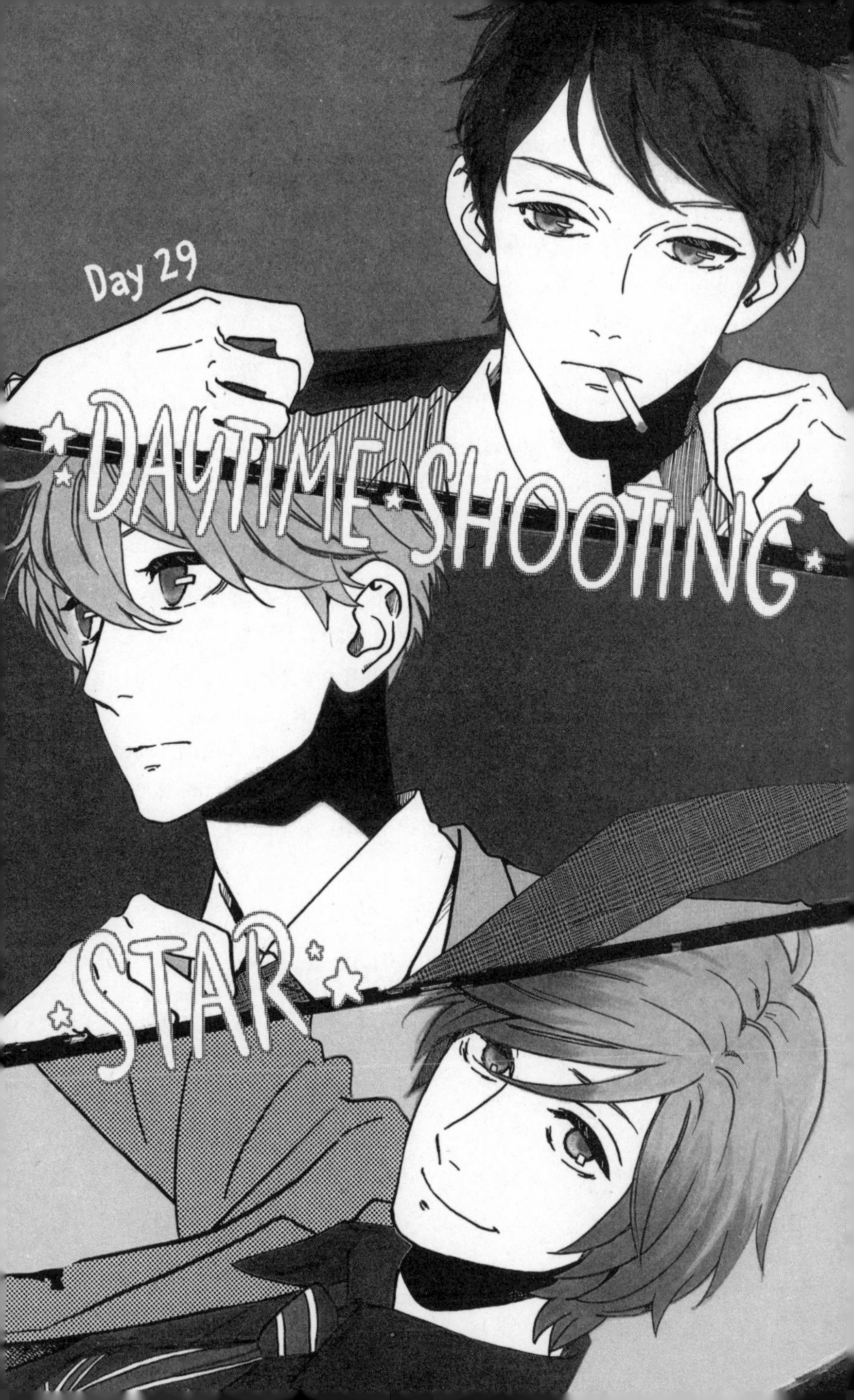
Day 29
DAYTIME SHOOTING STAR

# And so...

Oh my! What's this? We've hit *Daytime Shooting Star* volume 5 already!! In a way, this volume marks the first junction in this series.

I've been a nervous wreck up until this point...and I think I will continue to be until the story reaches its conclusion. We still have a ways to go, but I hope you will stay with me to the end to see what our heroine and the other characters will do, and how they will grow.

On a side note, Ms. K, the editor who had been with me since my debut, was transferred out of *Margaret Comics*. The announcement came as quite a shock to me. Thank you very much for everything! Without Ms. K, I don't think I would be where I am today. Good luck in your new job! I will do my best with the help of Ms. U (a young woman with great legs)!! I hope you will keep an eye on me! Oops, this has suddenly turned into a letter to Ms. K (LOL)!! Oh dear.

Well...

# Anyway, I hope you all enjoy volume 5 of *Daytime Shooting Star*!!

Mika

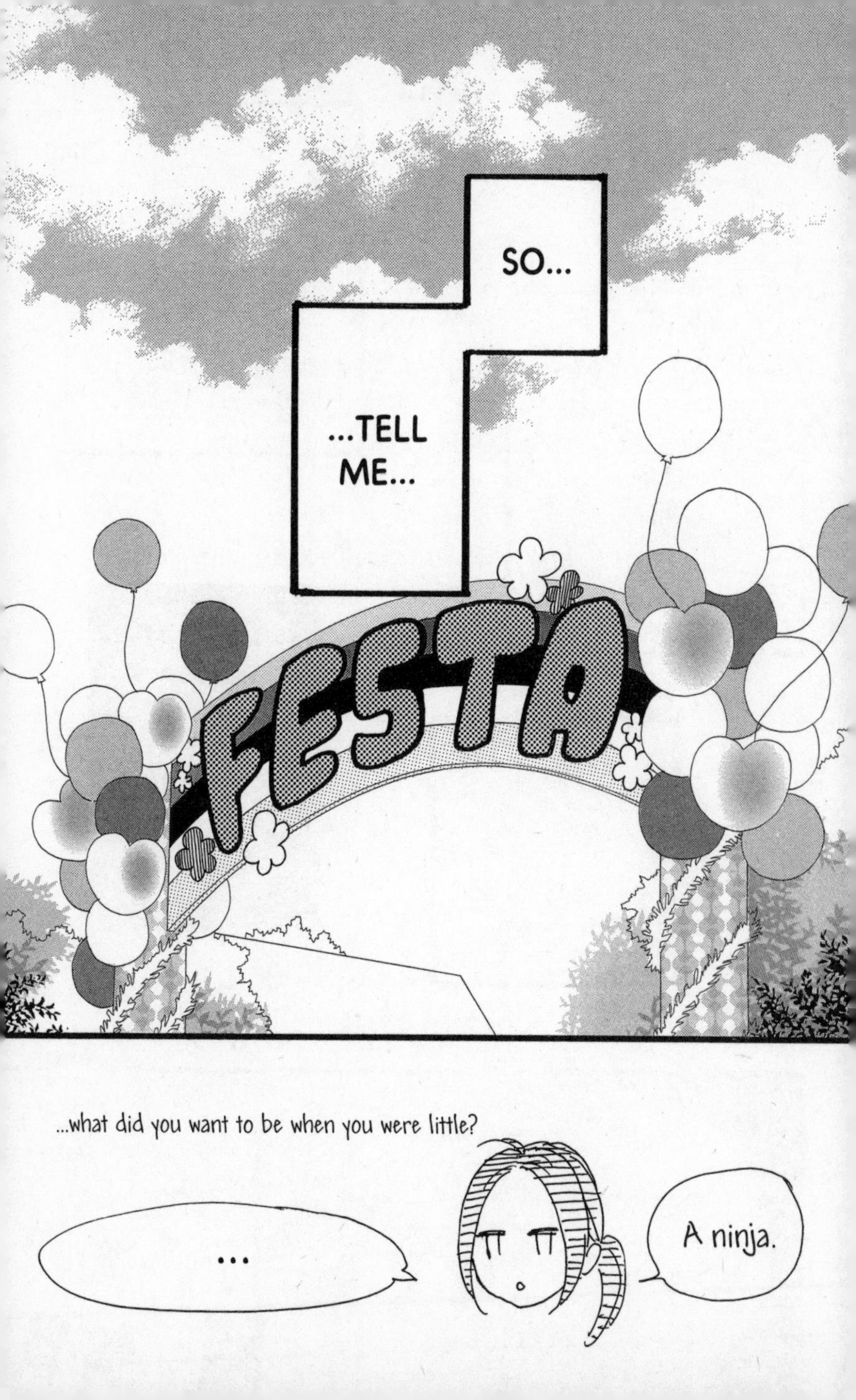
SO...
...TELL ME...
FESTA
...what did you want to be when you were little?
A ninja.
...

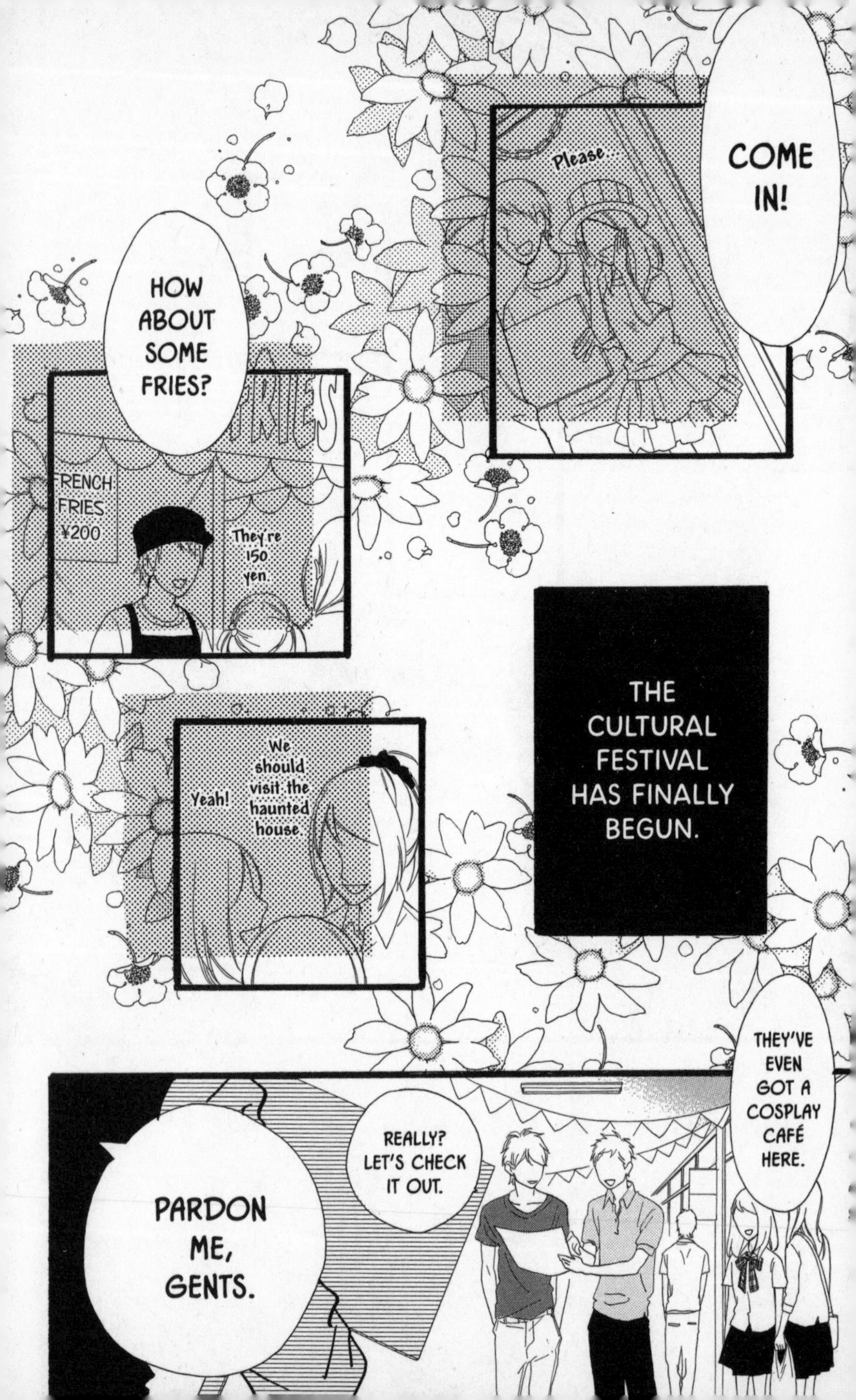
COME IN!
Please...
HOW ABOUT SOME FRIES?
FRIES
FRENCH FRIES ¥200
They're 150 yen.
THE CULTURAL FESTIVAL HAS FINALLY BEGUN.
We should visit the haunted house.
Yeah!
THEY'VE EVEN GOT A COSPLAY CAFÉ HERE.
REALLY? LET'S CHECK IT OUT.
PARDON ME, GENTS.

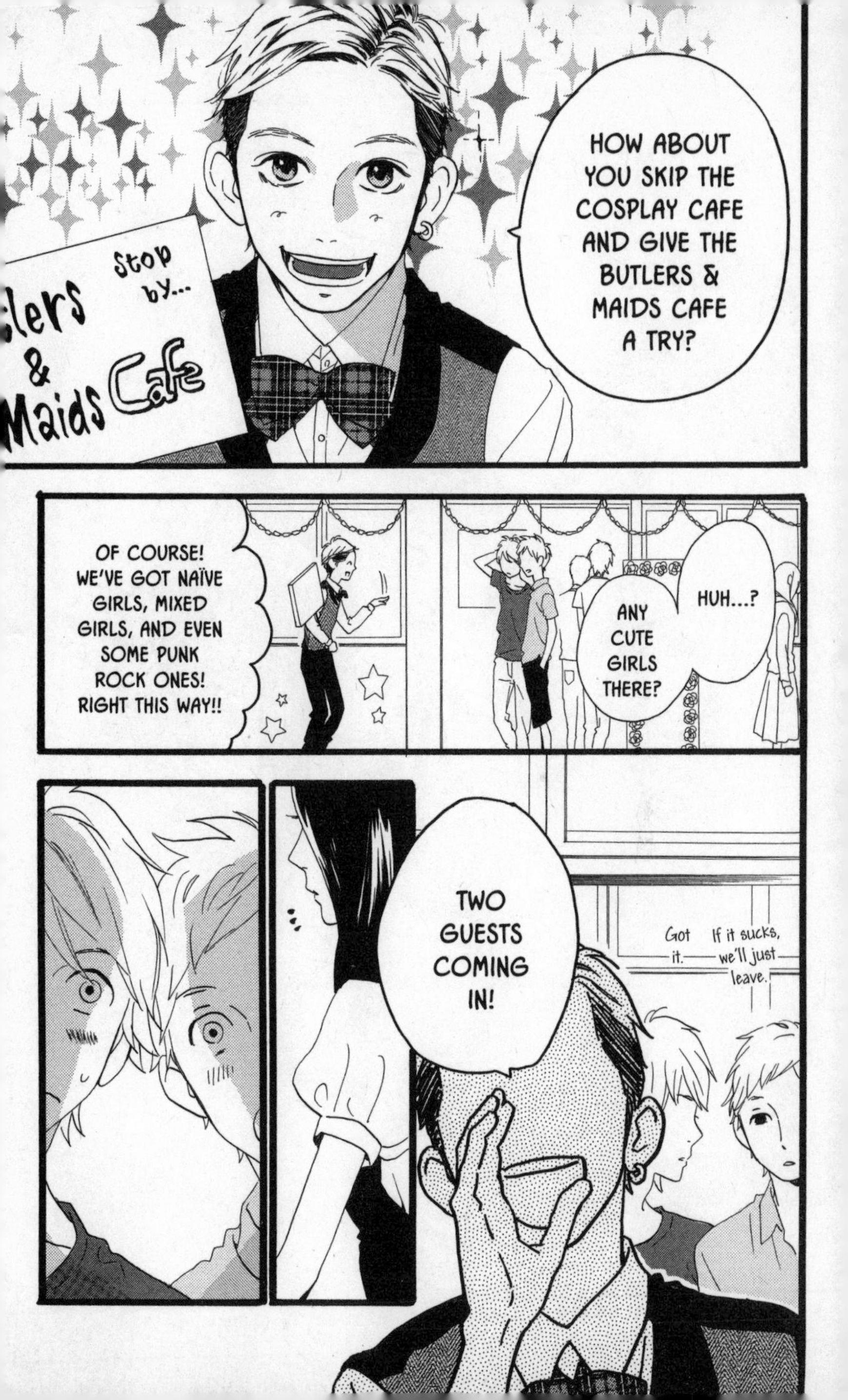
HOW ABOUT YOU SKIP THE COSPLAY CAFE AND GIVE THE BUTLERS & MAIDS CAFE A TRY?
Stop by...
lers & Maids Cafe
HUH...?
ANY CUTE GIRLS THERE?
OF COURSE! WE'VE GOT NAÏVE GIRLS, MIXED GIRLS, AND EVEN SOME PUNK ROCK ONES! RIGHT THIS WAY!!
If it sucks, we'll just leave.
Got it.
TWO GUESTS COMING IN!

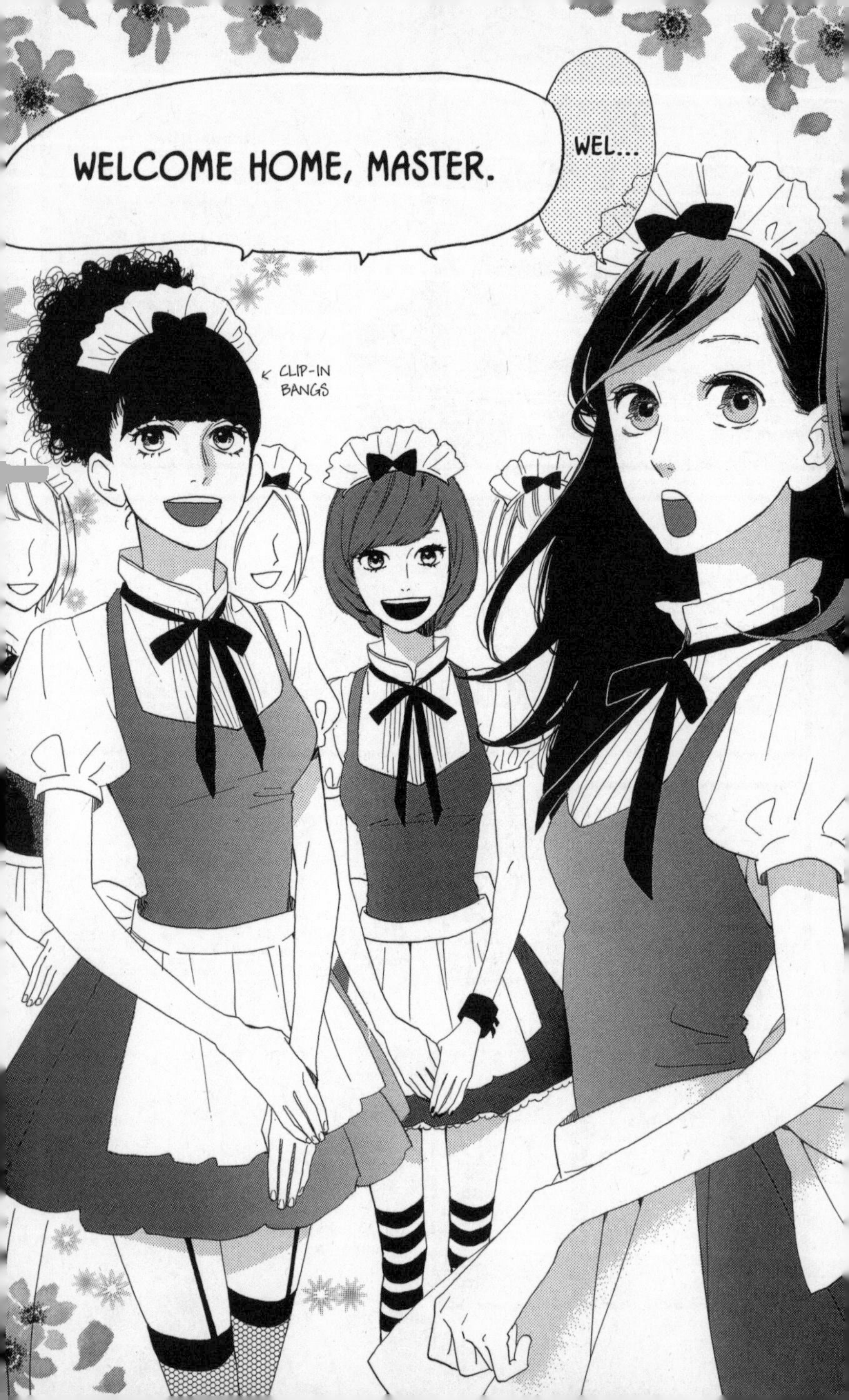
WEL...
WELCOME HOME, MASTER.
CLIP-IN BANGS

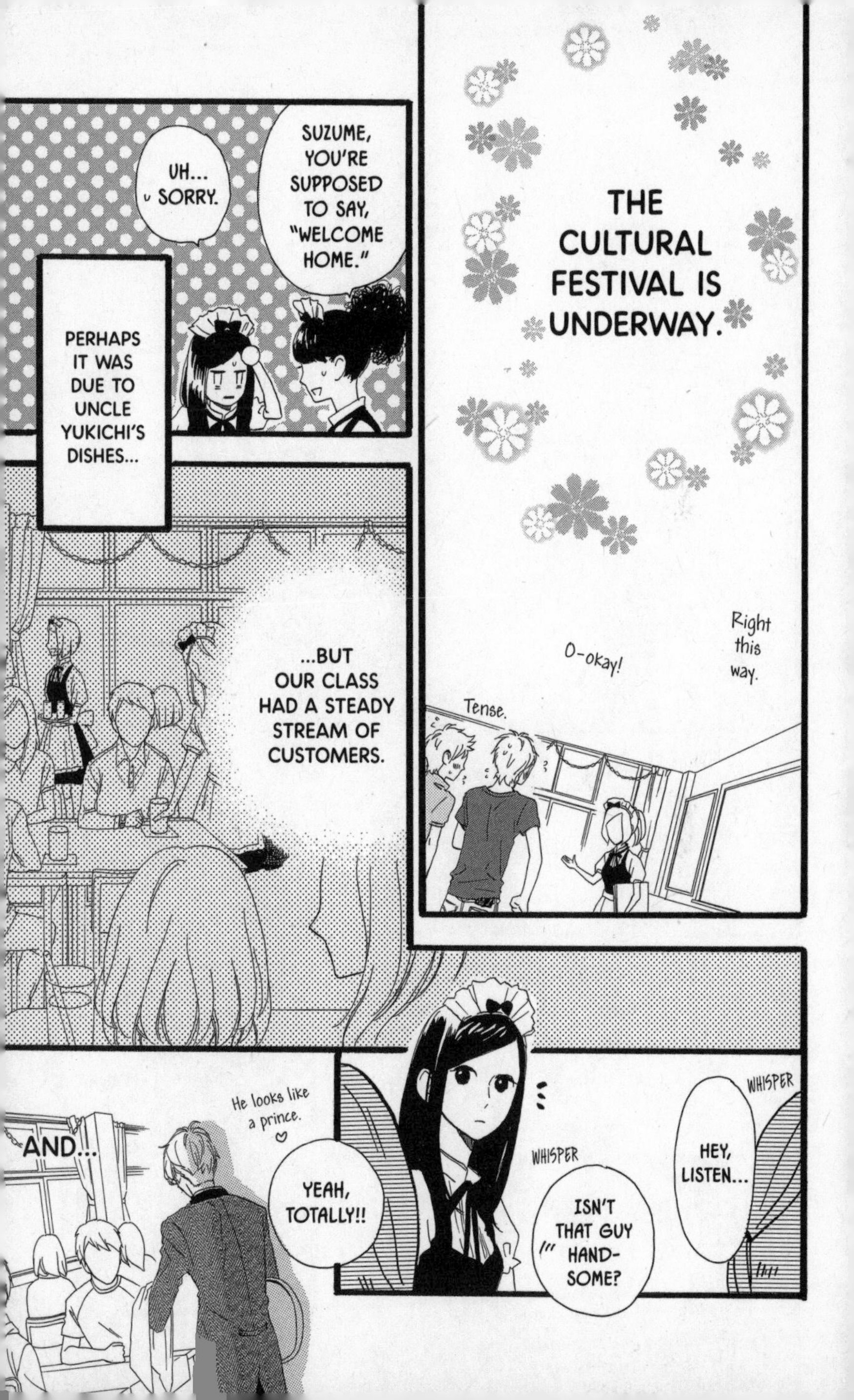
THE CULTURAL FESTIVAL IS UNDERWAY.
Right this way.
O-okay!
Tense.
SUZUME, YOU'RE SUPPOSED TO SAY, "WELCOME HOME."
UH... SORRY.
PERHAPS IT WAS DUE TO UNCLE YUKICHI'S DISHES...
...BUT OUR CLASS HAD A STEADY STREAM OF CUSTOMERS.
WHISPER
HEY, LISTEN...
WHISPER
ISN'T THAT GUY HANDSOME?
YEAH, TOTALLY!!
He looks like a prince.
AND...

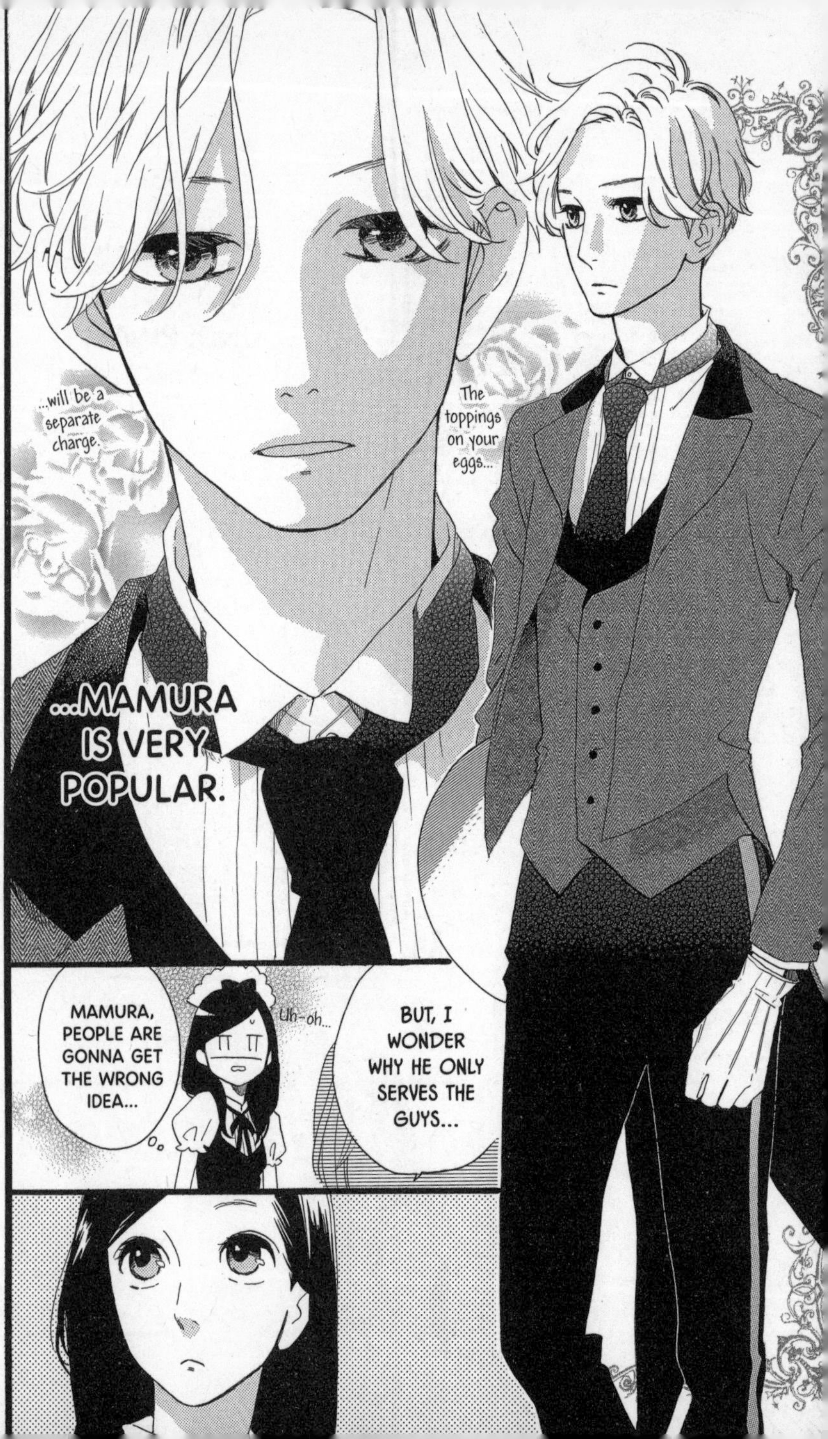
The toppings on your eggs...
...will be a separate charge.
...MAMURA IS VERY POPULAR.
BUT, I WONDER WHY HE ONLY SERVES THE GUYS...
Uh-oh...
MAMURA, PEOPLE ARE GONNA GET THE WRONG IDEA...

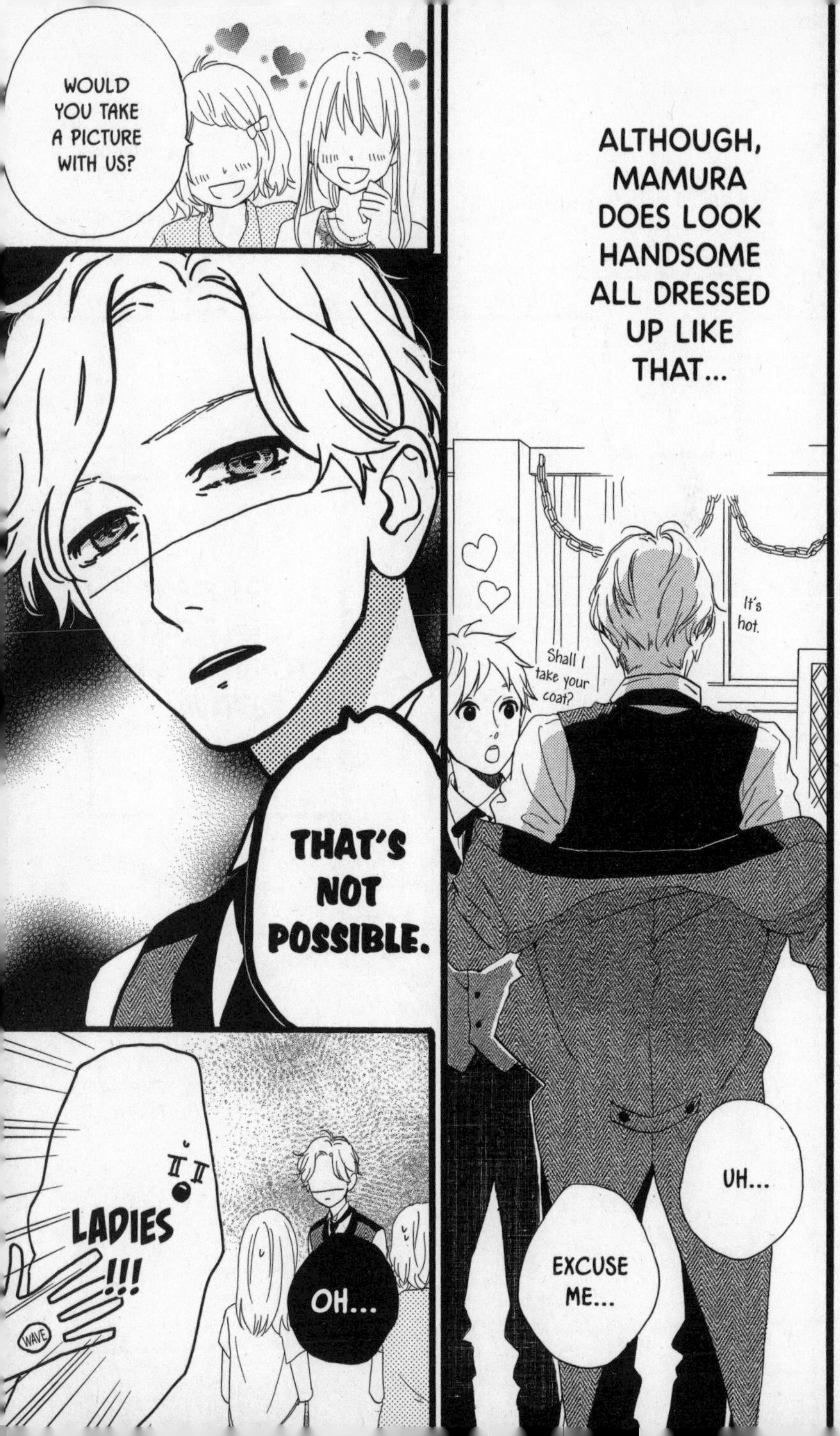
ALTHOUGH, MAMURA DOES LOOK HANDSOME ALL DRESSED UP LIKE THAT...
It's hot.
Shall I take your coat?
UH...
EXCUSE ME...
WOULD YOU TAKE A PICTURE WITH US?
THAT'S NOT POSSIBLE.
OH...
LADIES!!!
WAVE

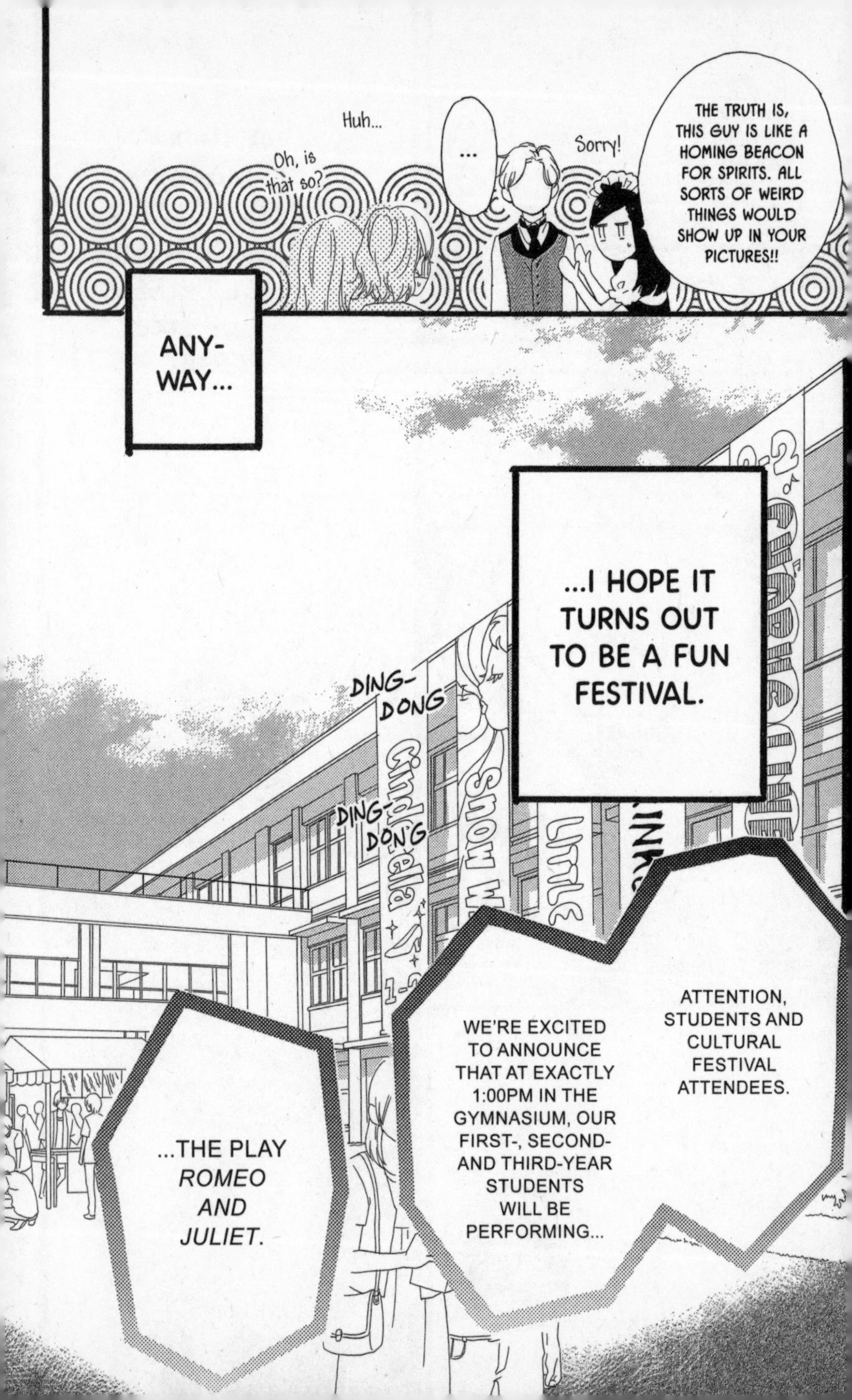
THE TRUTH IS, THIS GUY IS LIKE A HOMING BEACON FOR SPIRITS. ALL SORTS OF WEIRD THINGS WOULD SHOW UP IN YOUR PICTURES!!
Sorry!
...
Huh...
Oh, is that so?
ANY-WAY...
...I HOPE IT TURNS OUT TO BE A FUN FESTIVAL.
DING-DONG
DING-DONG
ATTENTION, STUDENTS AND CULTURAL FESTIVAL ATTENDEES.
WE'RE EXCITED TO ANNOUNCE THAT AT EXACTLY 1:00PM IN THE GYMNASIUM, OUR FIRST-, SECOND- AND THIRD-YEAR STUDENTS WILL BE PERFORMING...
...THE PLAY *ROMEO AND JULIET*.

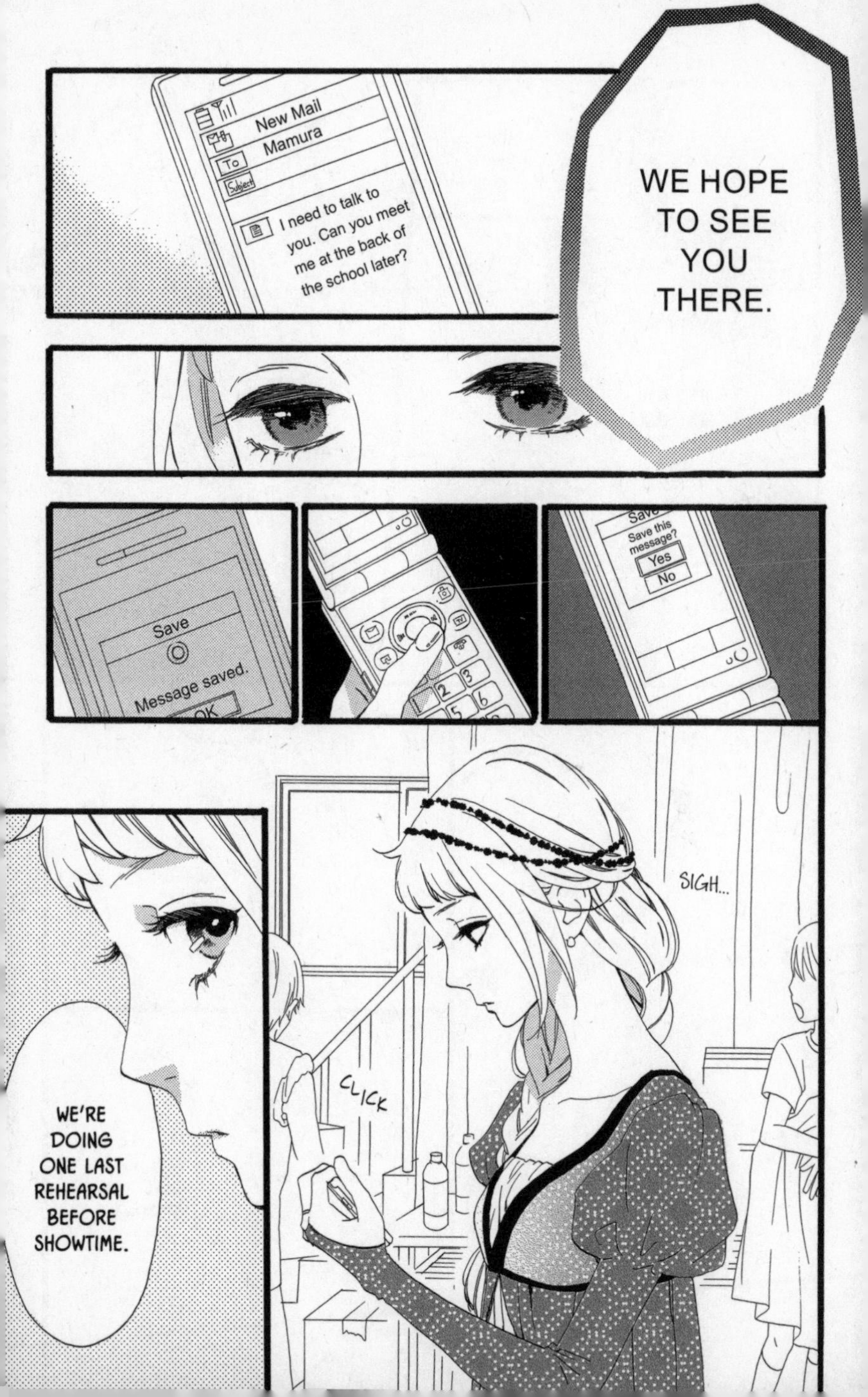
WE HOPE TO SEE YOU THERE.
New Mail
To
Mamura
Subject
I need to talk to you. Can you meet me at the back of the school later?
Save this message?
Yes
No
Save
Message saved.
SIGH...
CLICK
WE'RE DOING ONE LAST REHEARSAL BEFORE SHOWTIME.

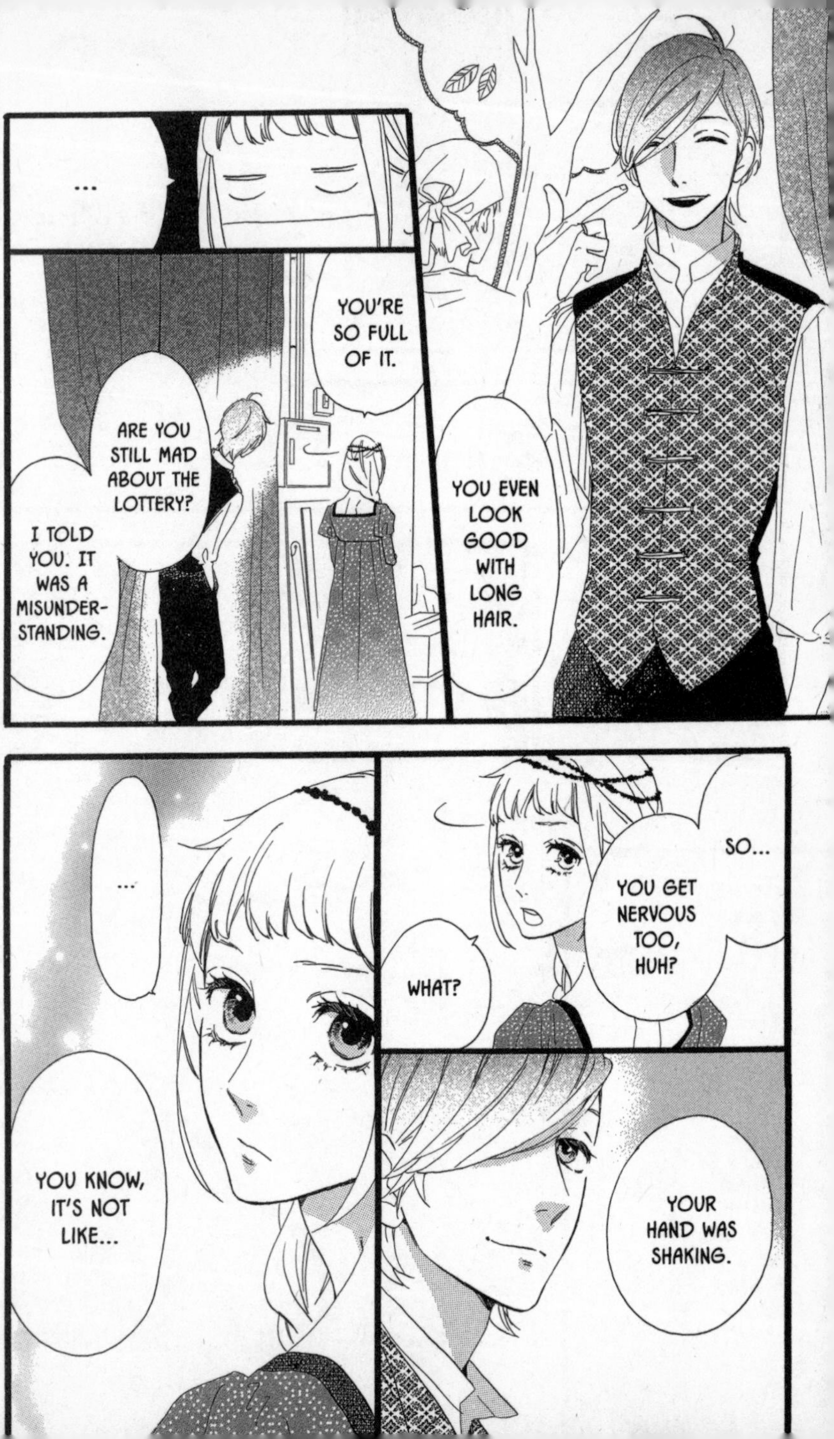
YOU EVEN LOOK GOOD WITH LONG HAIR.
...
YOU'RE SO FULL OF IT.
ARE YOU STILL MAD ABOUT THE LOTTERY?
I TOLD YOU. IT WAS A MISUNDER-STANDING.
SO...
YOU GET NERVOUS TOO, HUH?
WHAT?
YOUR HAND WAS SHAKING.
...
YOU KNOW, IT'S NOT LIKE...

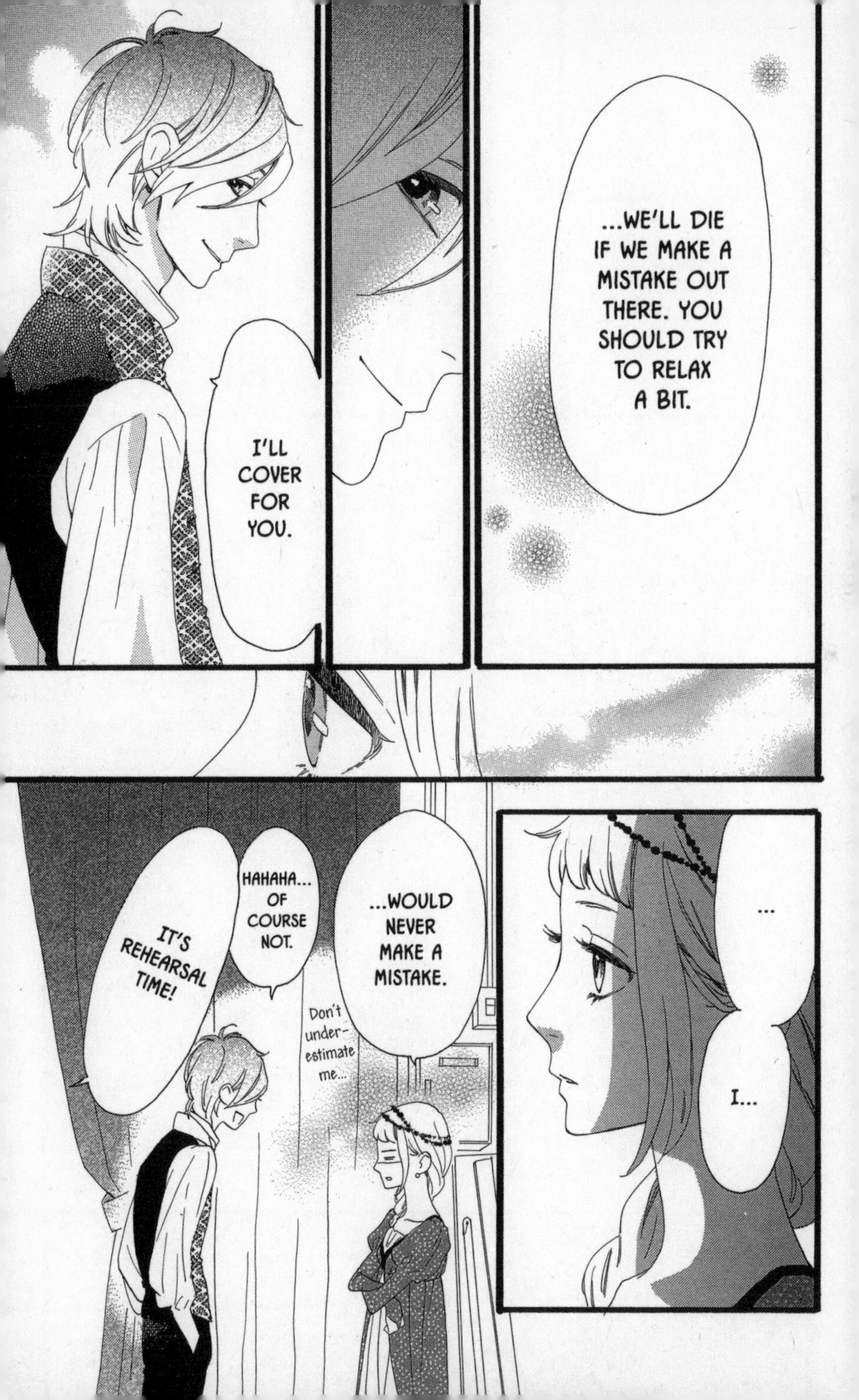
...WE'LL DIE IF WE MAKE A MISTAKE OUT THERE. YOU SHOULD TRY TO RELAX A BIT.
I'LL COVER FOR YOU.
...
I...
...WOULD NEVER MAKE A MISTAKE.
Don't under-estimate me...
HAHAHA... OF COURSE NOT.
IT'S REHEARSAL TIME!

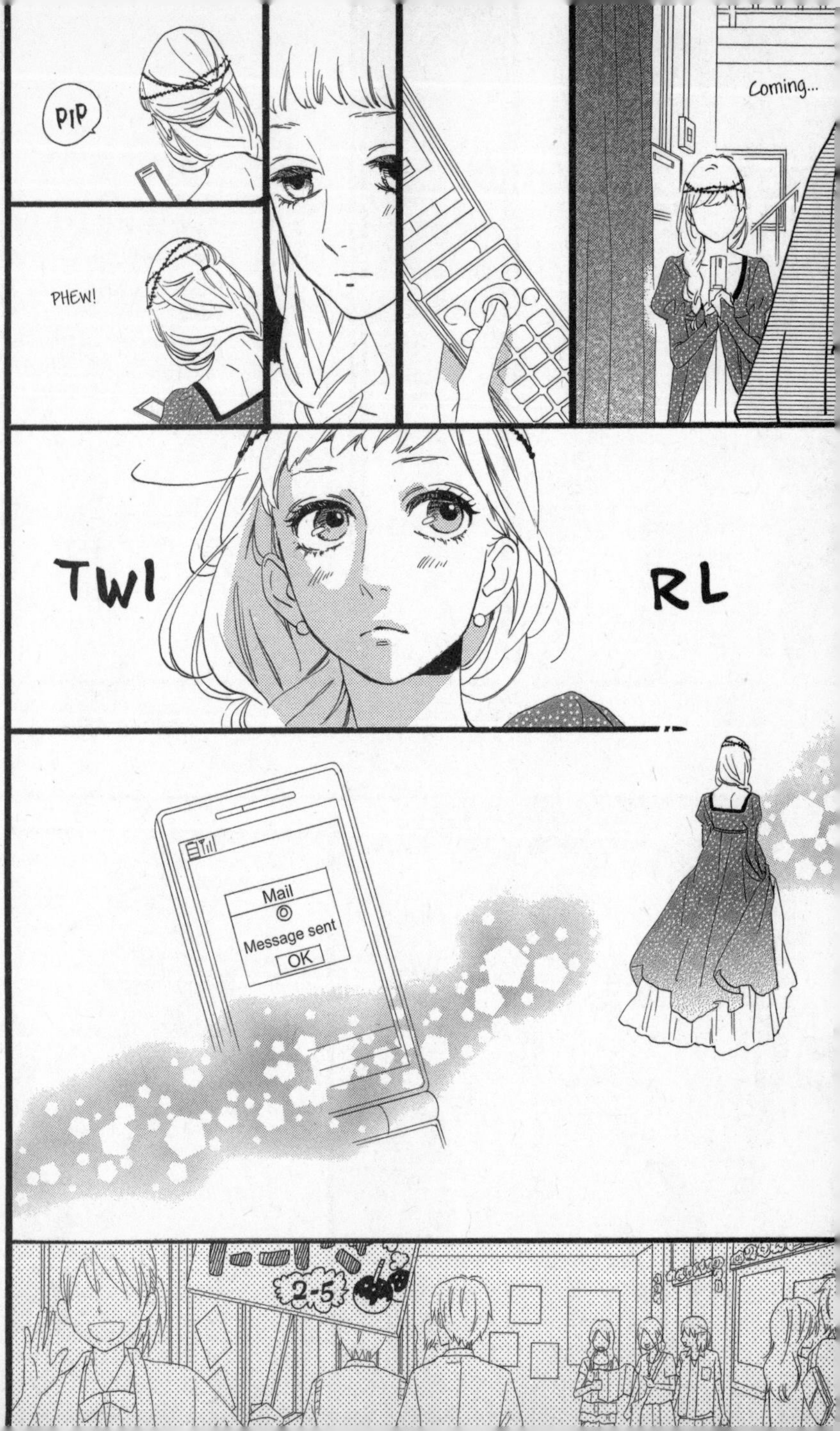
Coming...
PIP
PHEW!
TWI RL
Mail
Message sent
OK
2-5

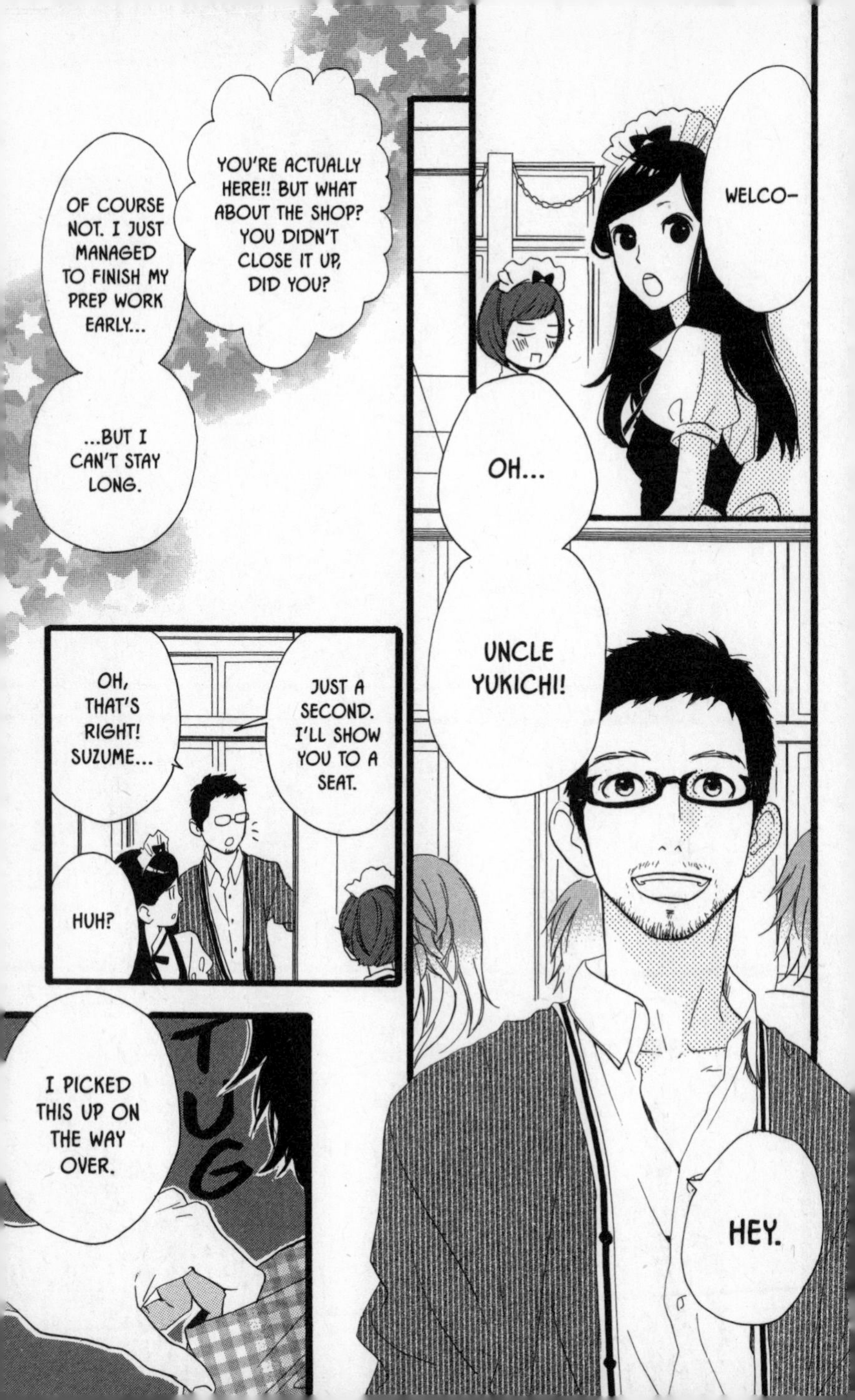
WELCO-
OH...
UNCLE YUKICHI!
HEY.
YOU'RE ACTUALLY HERE!! BUT WHAT ABOUT THE SHOP? YOU DIDN'T CLOSE IT UP, DID YOU?
OF COURSE NOT. I JUST MANAGED TO FINISH MY PREP WORK EARLY...
...BUT I CAN'T STAY LONG.
JUST A SECOND. I'LL SHOW YOU TO A SEAT.
OH, THAT'S RIGHT! SUZUME...
HUH?
TUG
I PICKED THIS UP ON THE WAY OVER.

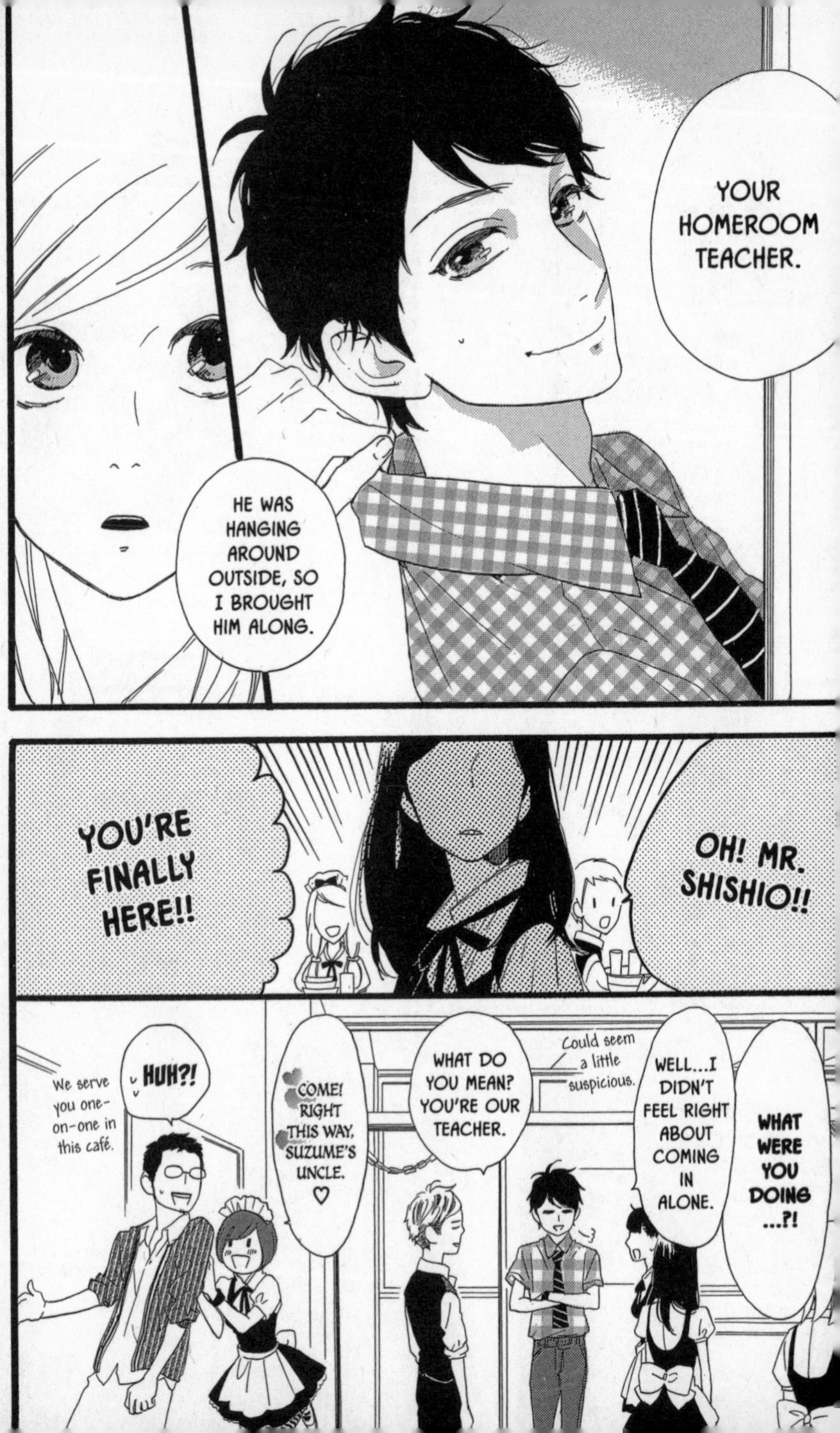
YOUR HOMEROOM TEACHER.
HE WAS HANGING AROUND OUTSIDE, SO I BROUGHT HIM ALONG.
OH! MR. SHISHIO!!
YOU'RE FINALLY HERE!!
WHAT WERE YOU DOING ...?!
WELL...I DIDN'T FEEL RIGHT ABOUT COMING IN ALONE.
Could seem a little suspicious.
WHAT DO YOU MEAN? YOU'RE OUR TEACHER.
COME! RIGHT THIS WAY, SUZUME'S UNCLE. ♡
HUH?!
We serve you one-on-one in this café.

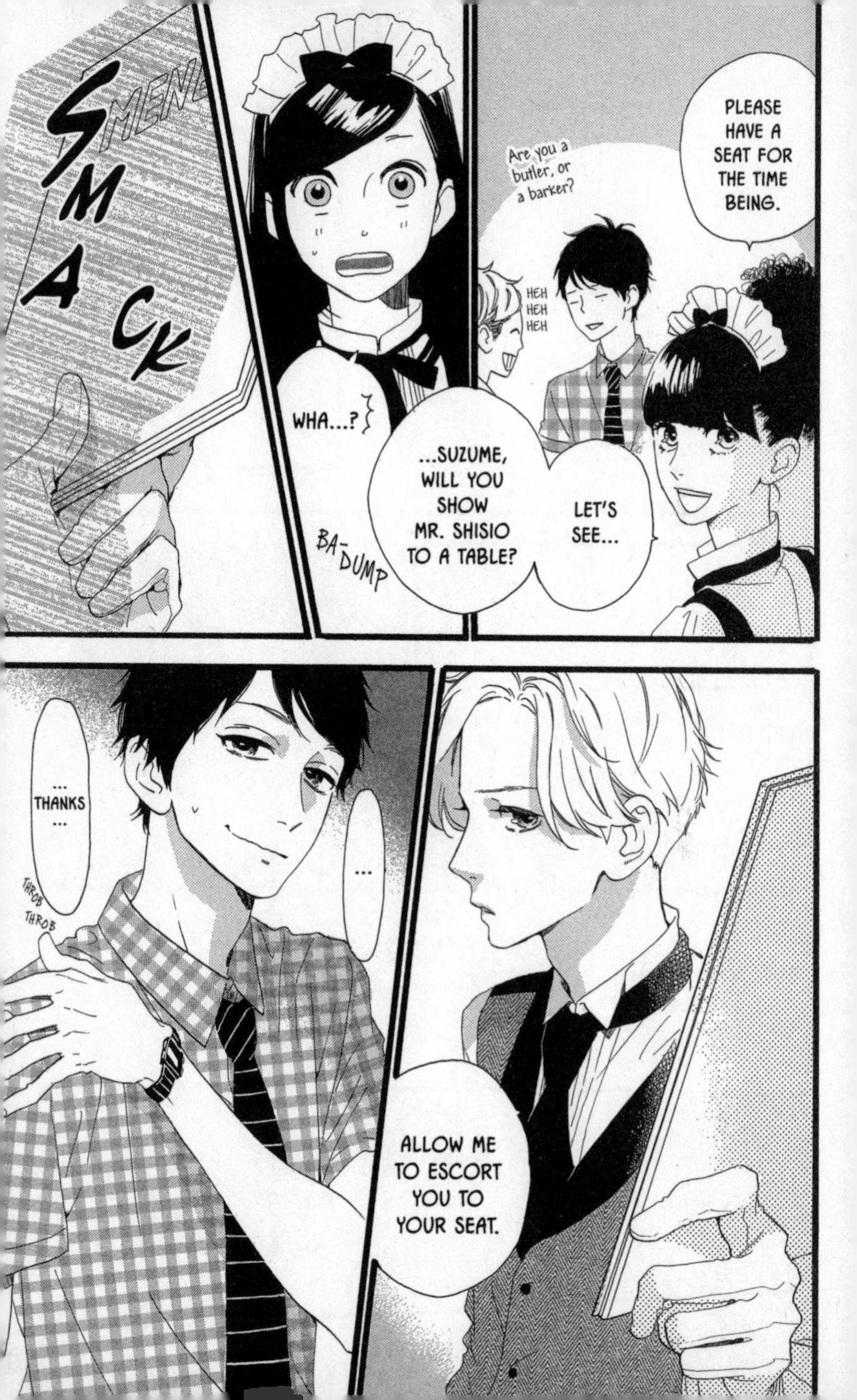
PLEASE HAVE A SEAT FOR THE TIME BEING.
Are you a butler, or a barker?
HEH HEH HEH
LET'S SEE...
...SUZUME, WILL YOU SHOW MR. SHISIO TO A TABLE?
WHA...?
BA-DUMP
SMACK
ALLOW ME TO ESCORT YOU TO YOUR SEAT.
...
...THANKS...
THROB THROB

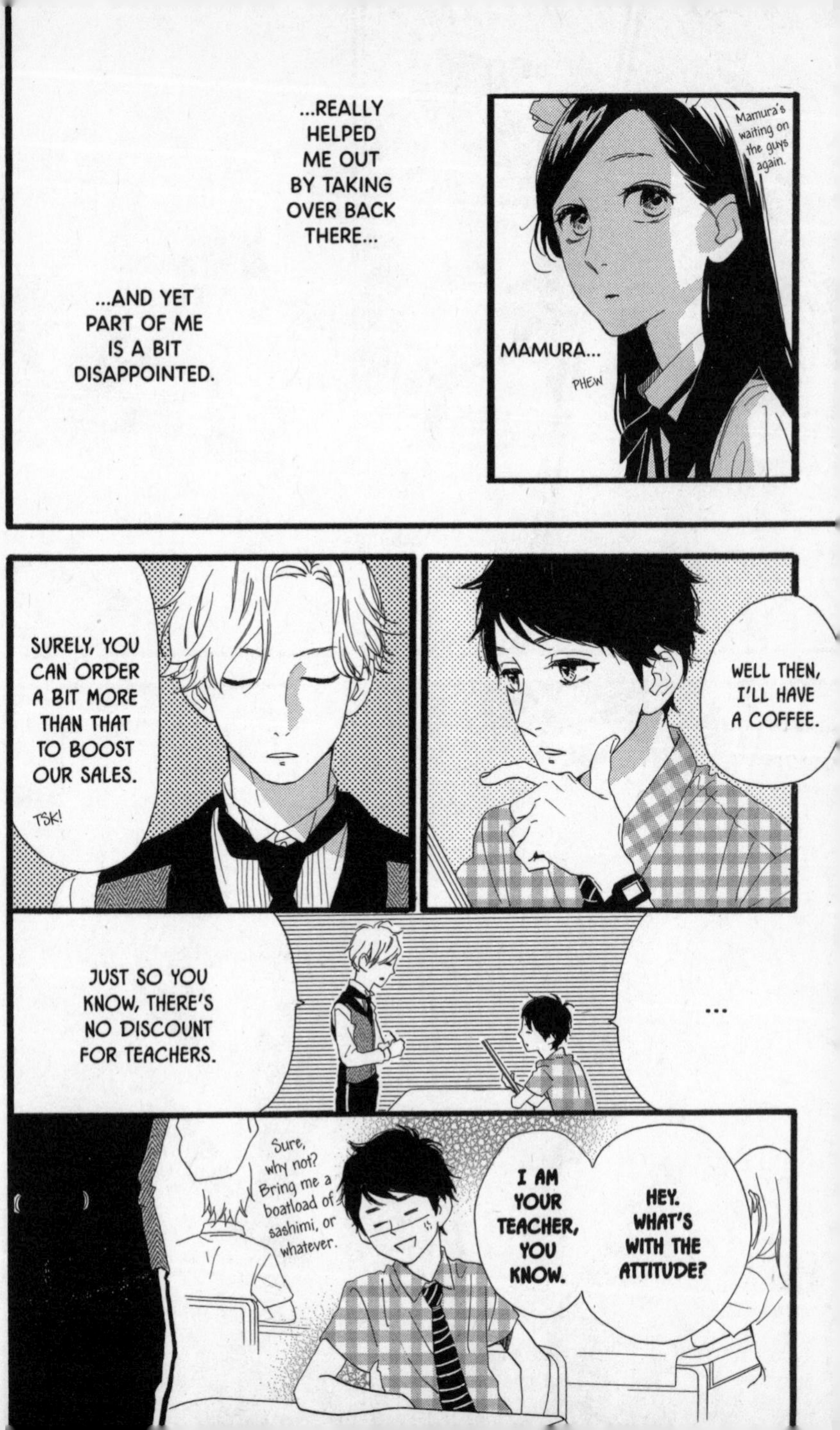
Mamura's waiting on the guys again.
MAMURA...
PHEW
...REALLY HELPED ME OUT BY TAKING OVER BACK THERE...
...AND YET PART OF ME IS A BIT DISAPPOINTED.
WELL THEN, I'LL HAVE A COFFEE.
SURELY, YOU CAN ORDER A BIT MORE THAN THAT TO BOOST OUR SALES.
TSK!
...
JUST SO YOU KNOW, THERE'S NO DISCOUNT FOR TEACHERS.
HEY. WHAT'S WITH THE ATTITUDE?
I AM YOUR TEACHER, YOU KNOW.
Sure, why not? Bring me a boatload of sashimi, or whatever.

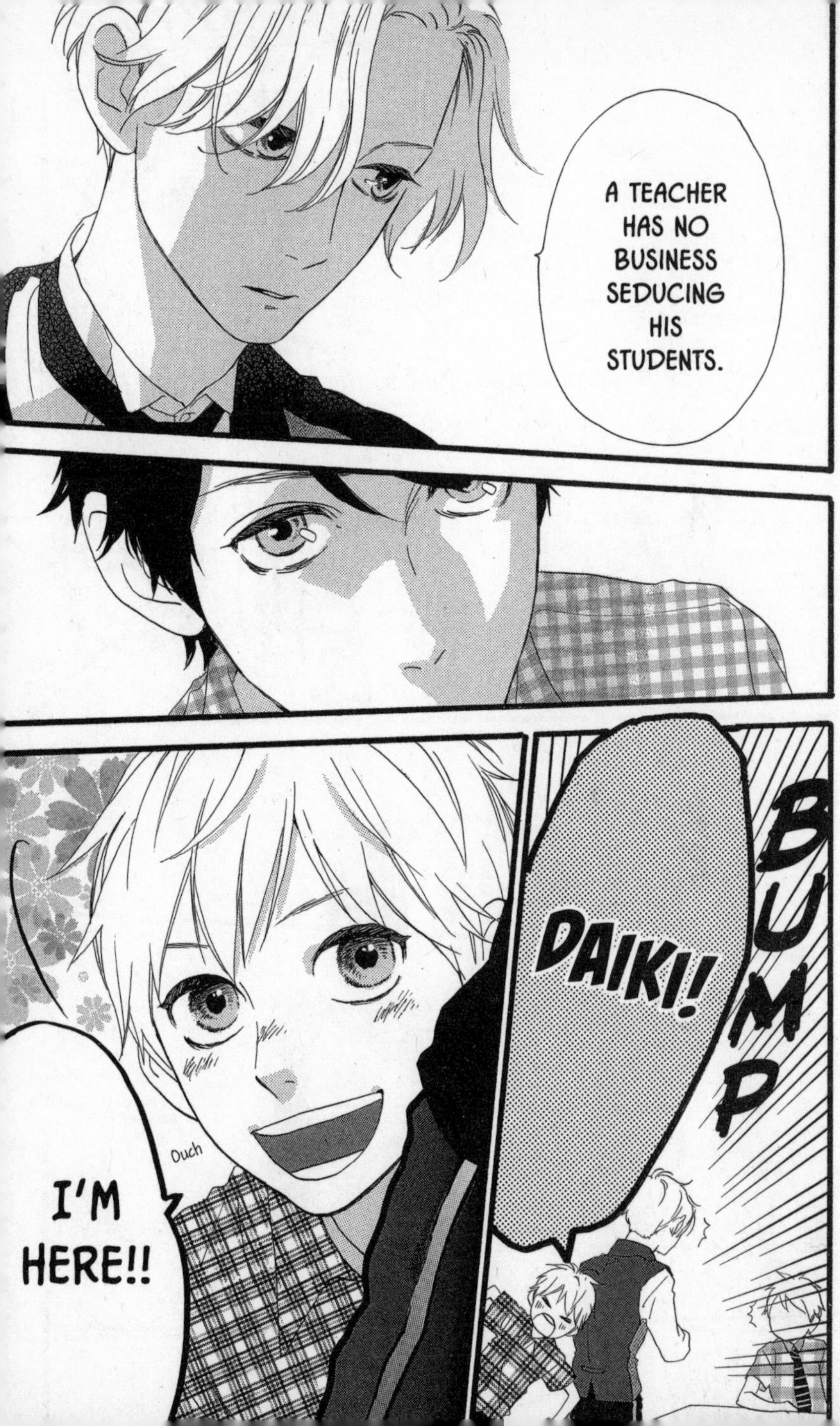
A TEACHER HAS NO BUSINESS SEDUCING HIS STUDENTS.
BUMP
DAIKI!!
Ouch
I'M HERE!!

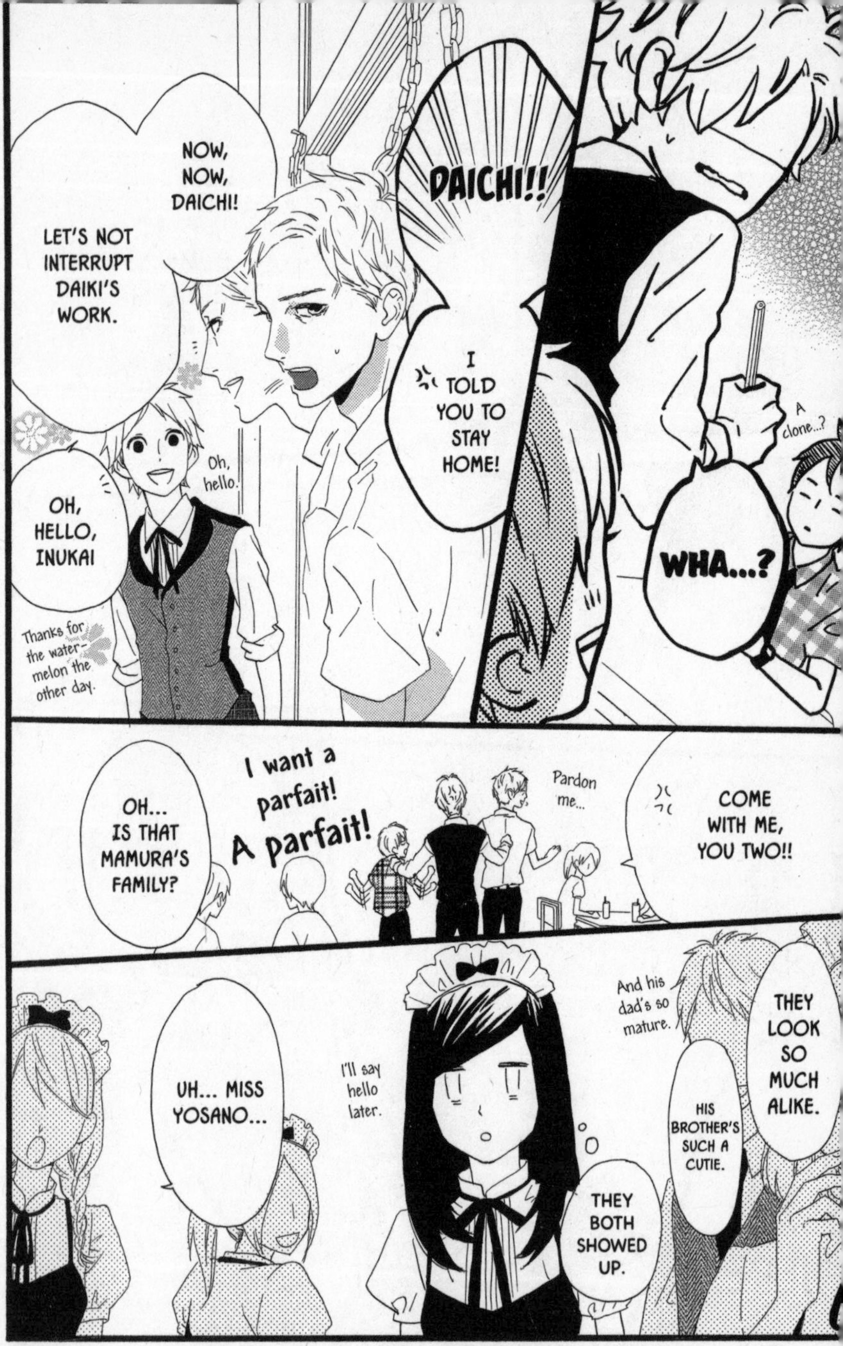
DAICHI!!
I TOLD YOU TO STAY HOME!
WHA...?
A clone...?
NOW, NOW, DAICHI!
LET'S NOT INTERRUPT DAIKI'S WORK.
Oh, hello.
OH, HELLO, INUKAI
Thanks for the watermelon the other day.
COME WITH ME, YOU TWO!!
Pardon me...
I want a parfait! A parfait!
OH... IS THAT MAMURA'S FAMILY?
THEY LOOK SO MUCH ALIKE.
And his dad's so mature.
HIS BROTHER'S SUCH A CUTIE.
THEY BOTH SHOWED UP.
I'll say hello later.
UH... MISS YOSANO...

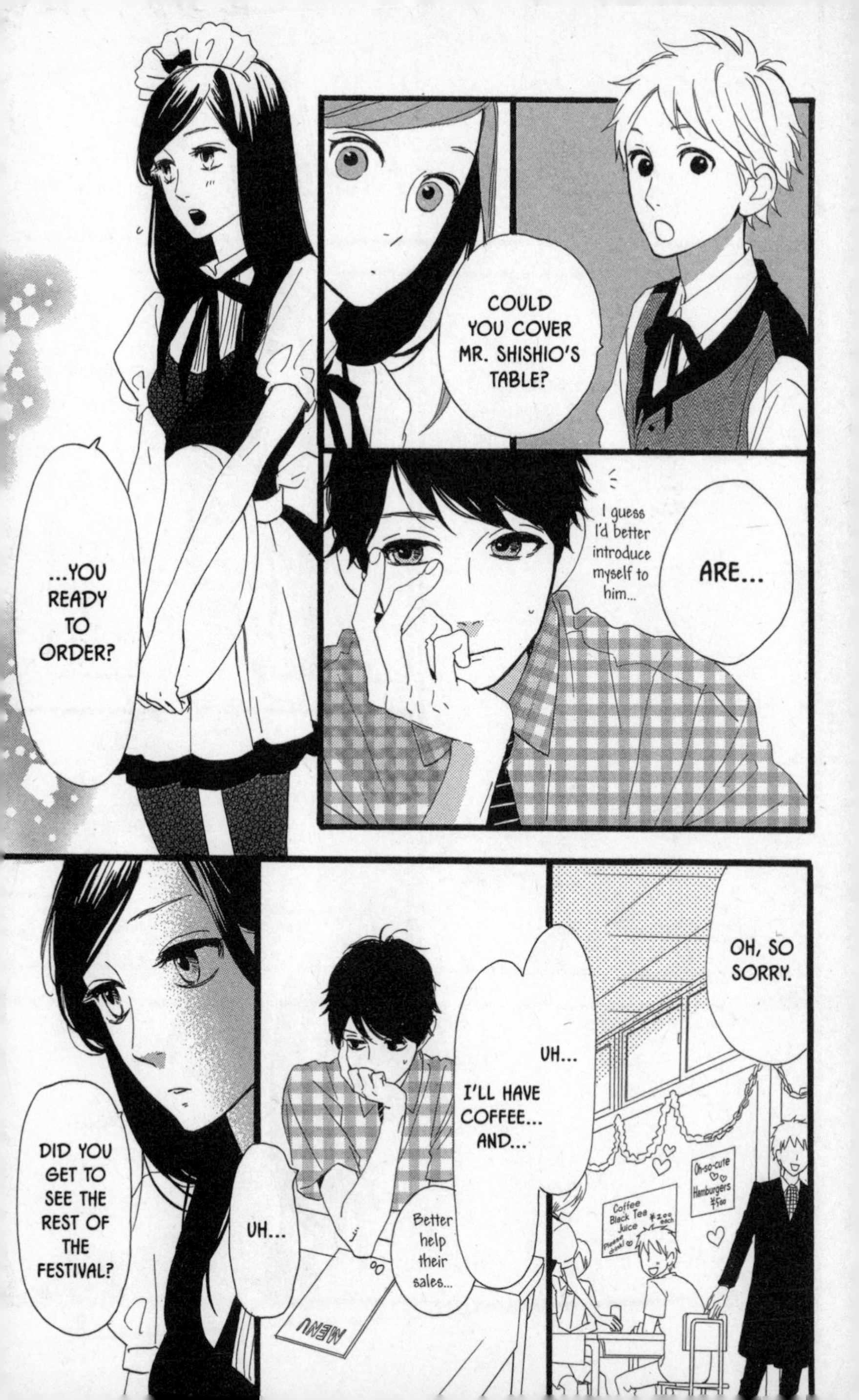
COULD YOU COVER MR. SHISHIO'S TABLE?
ARE...
I guess I'd better introduce myself to him...
...YOU READY TO ORDER?
OH, SO SORRY.
Oh-so-cute Hamburgers
Coffee Black Tea Juice
UH...
I'LL HAVE COFFEE... AND...
Better help their sales...
UH...
DID YOU GET TO SEE THE REST OF THE FESTIVAL?
MENU

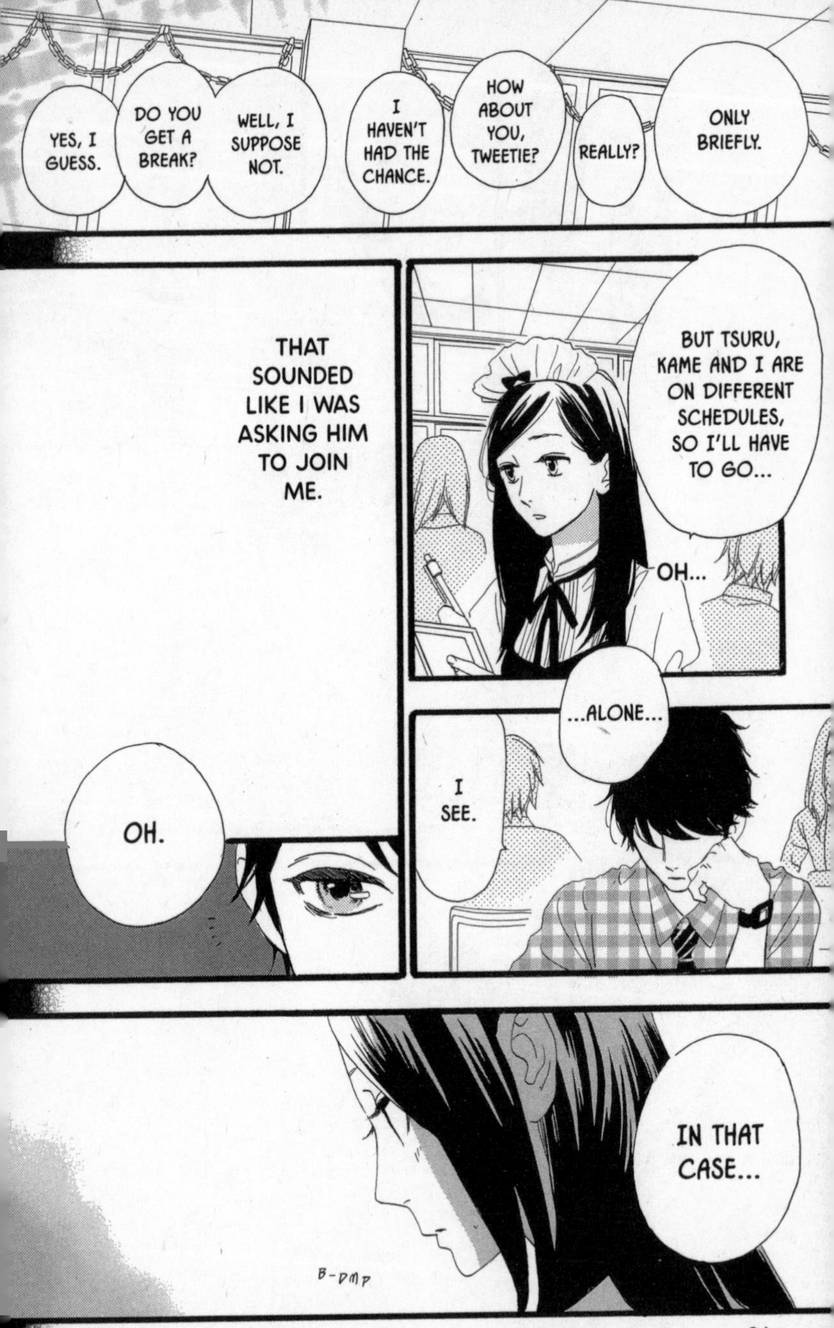
ONLY BRIEFLY.
REALLY?
HOW ABOUT YOU, TWEETIE?
I HAVEN'T HAD THE CHANCE.
WELL, I SUPPOSE NOT.
DO YOU GET A BREAK?
YES, I GUESS.
BUT TSURU, KAME AND I ARE ON DIFFERENT SCHEDULES, SO I'LL HAVE TO GO...
OH...
...ALONE...
I SEE.
THAT SOUNDED LIKE I WAS ASKING HIM TO JOIN ME.
OH.
IN THAT CASE...
B-DMP

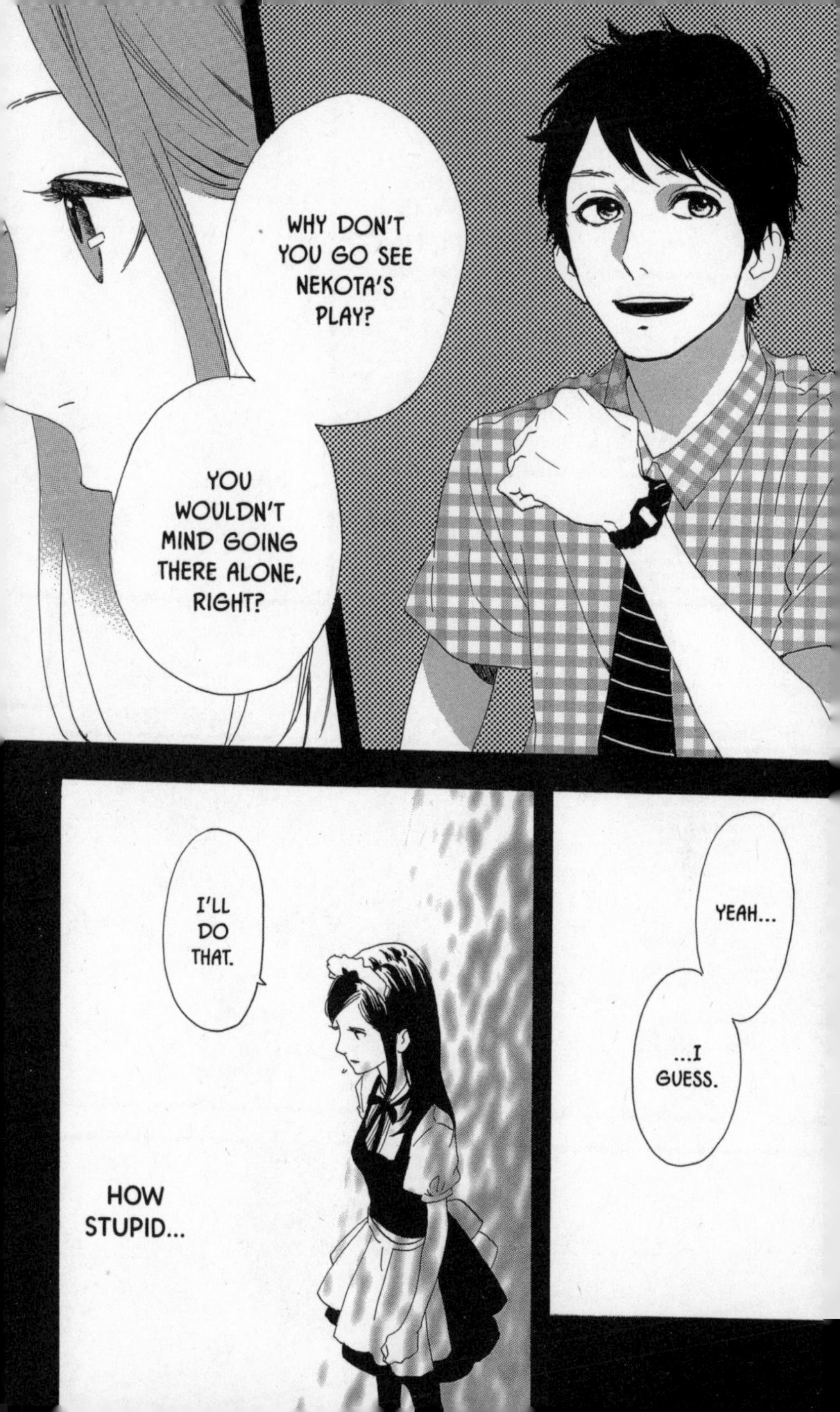
WHY DON'T YOU GO SEE NEKOTA'S PLAY?
YOU WOULDN'T MIND GOING THERE ALONE, RIGHT?
YEAH...
...I GUESS.
I'LL DO THAT.
HOW STUPID...

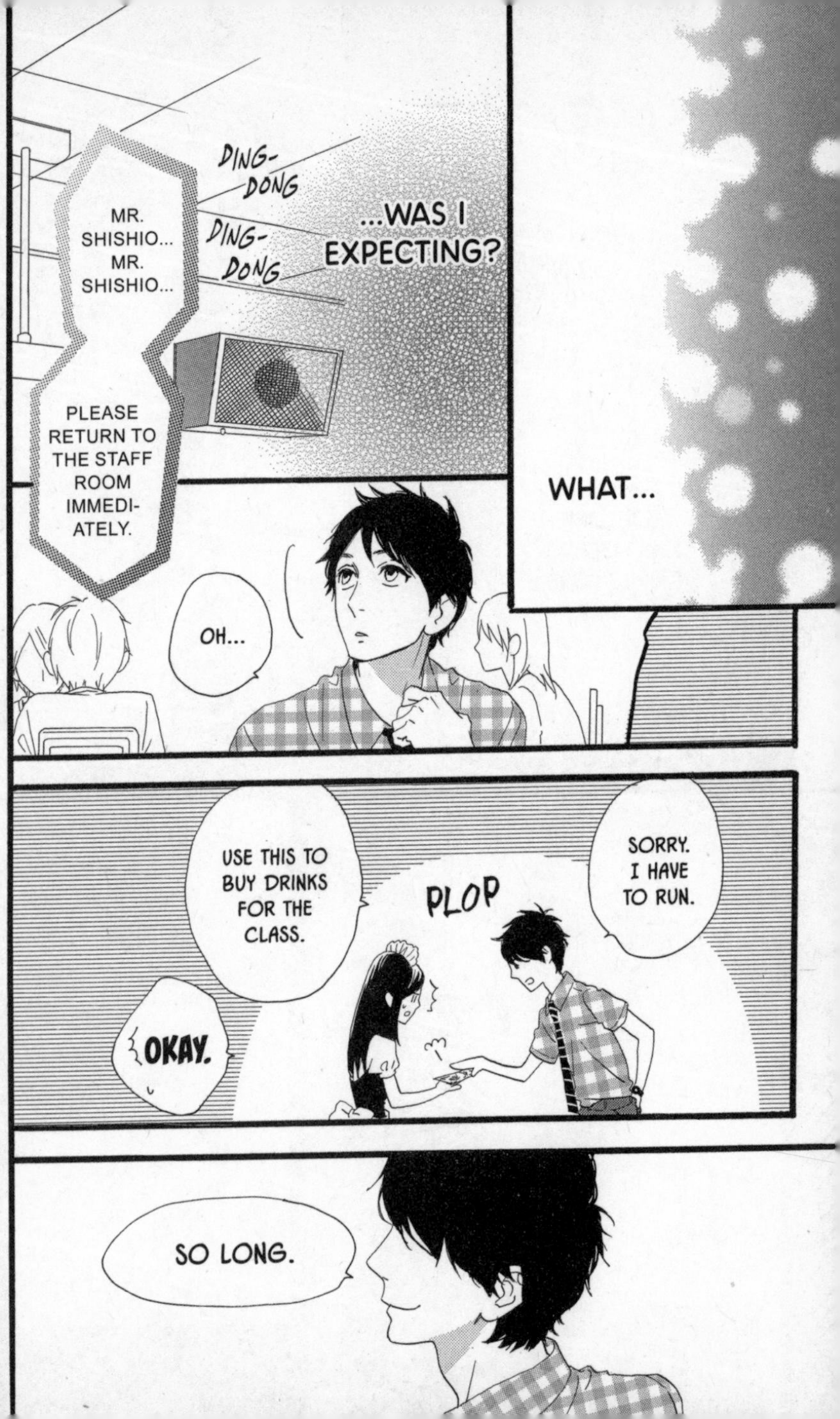
WHAT...
...WAS I EXPECTING?
DING-DONG
DING-DONG
MR. SHISHIO... MR. SHISHIO...
PLEASE RETURN TO THE STAFF ROOM IMMEDIATELY.
OH...
SORRY. I HAVE TO RUN.
PLOP
USE THIS TO BUY DRINKS FOR THE CLASS.
OKAY.
SO LONG.

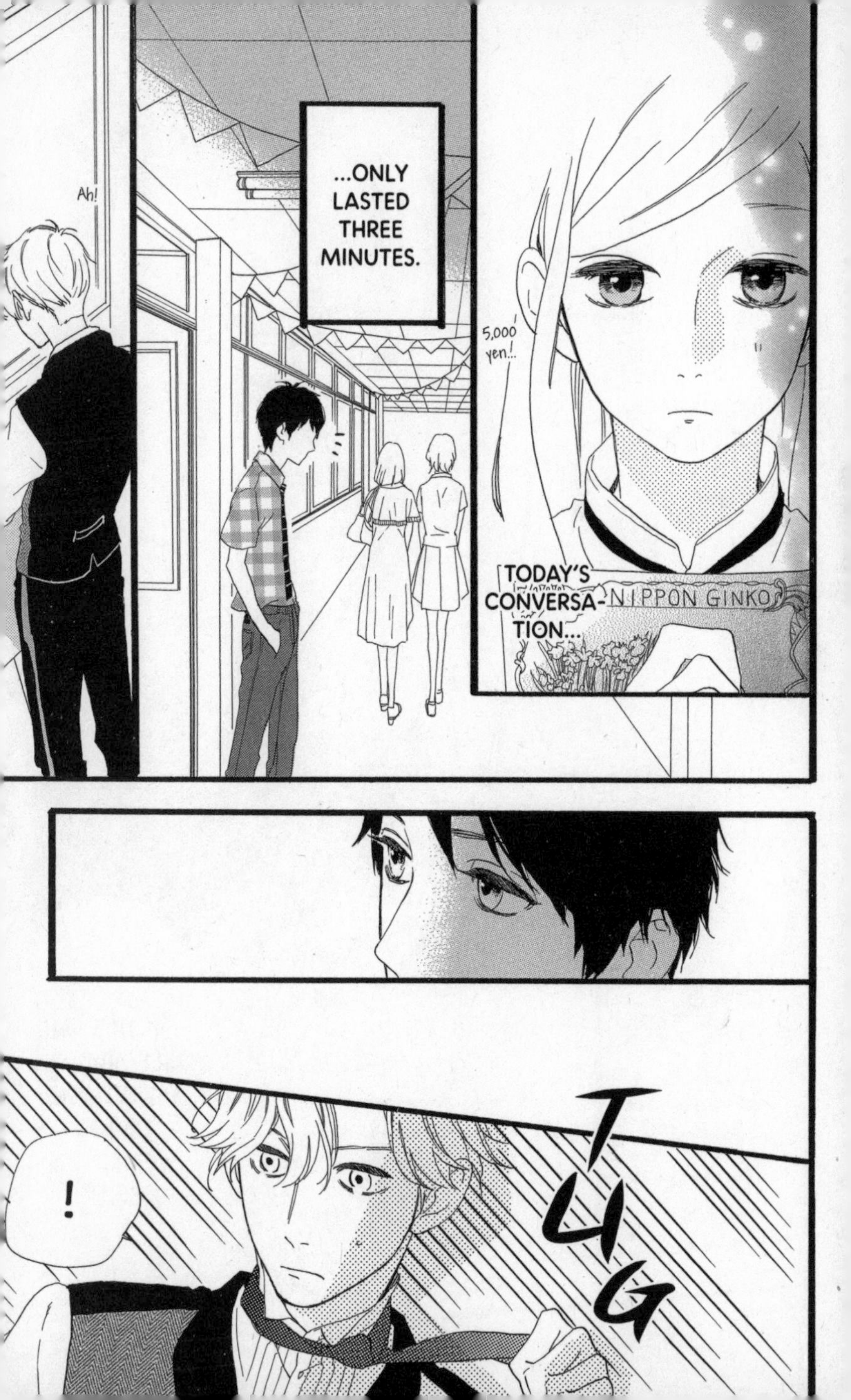
5,000 yen!!
NIPPON GINKO
TODAY'S CONVERSA-TION...
...ONLY LASTED THREE MINUTES.
Ah!
TUG
!

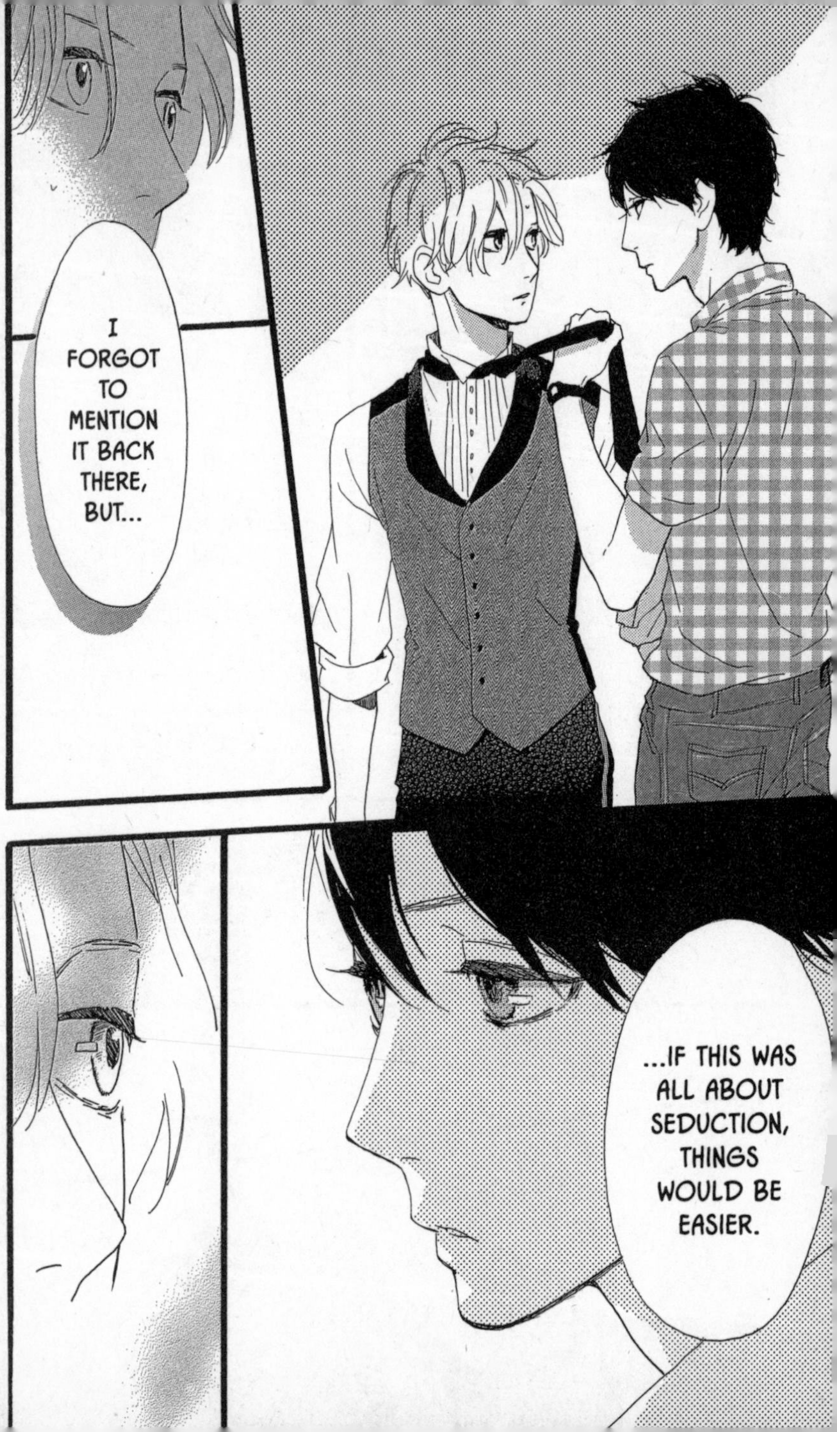
I FORGOT TO MENTION IT BACK THERE, BUT...
...IF THIS WAS ALL ABOUT SEDUCTION, THINGS WOULD BE EASIER.

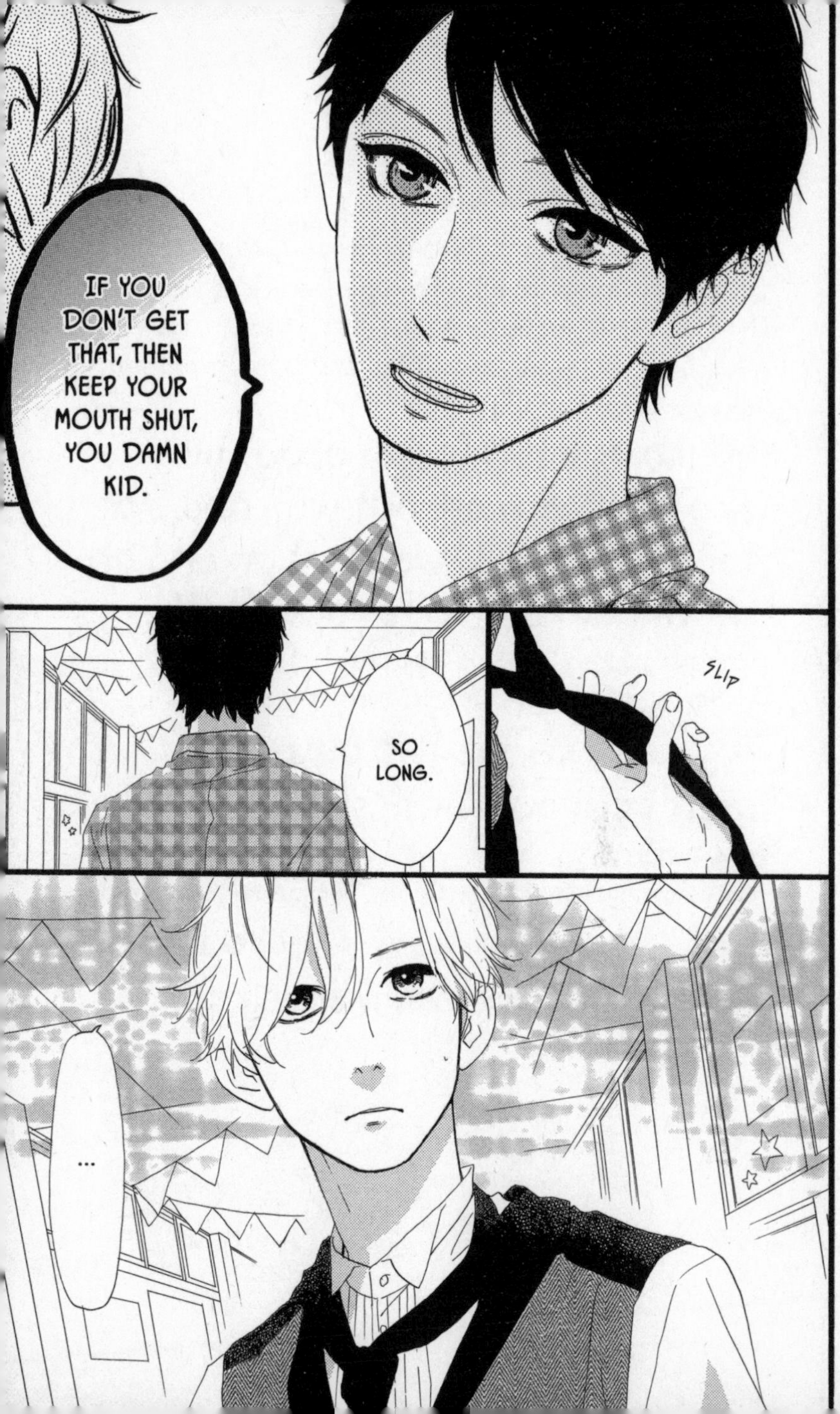
IF YOU DON'T GET THAT, THEN KEEP YOUR MOUTH SHUT, YOU DAMN KID.
SLIP
SO LONG.
...

# And so...

The other week, Momoko Koda of *Bessatsu Margaret* and I took part in a citywide singles event! I guess we've finally hit that point in our lives... Anyway, I put on a skirt, even though I'm not used to wearing one, and eagerly joined the crowd. It did not go well.

**We completely forgot about the two guys we were out with and, hot toddies in hand, we went on and on about our passion for our jobs!!**

Momoko sat there crushing a pickled plum in her drink!! It's no use. Whether it's a singles event or a party with prospective husbands, **the two of us just aren't cut out for this!!!**

And another thing...the two guys didn't know we were manga artists, so they were completely lost. (We just said we worked part time.) We exchanged contact information, **but we haven't heard from them since.**

What?! That's strange.

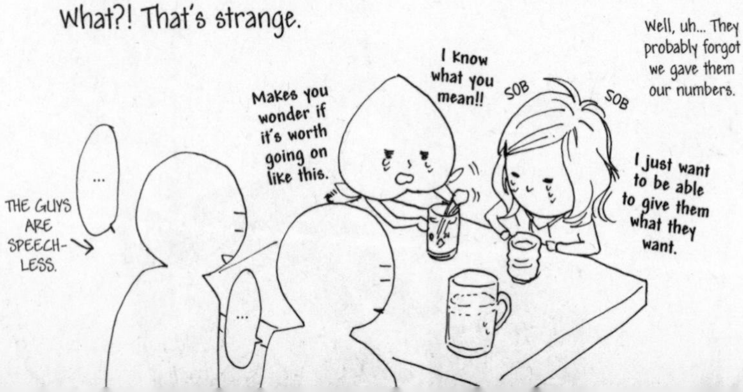
Well, uh... They probably forgot we gave them our numbers.
I just want to be able to give them what they want.
SOB
SOB
I know what you mean!!
Makes you wonder if it's worth going on like this.
...
...
THE GUYS ARE SPEECHLESS.

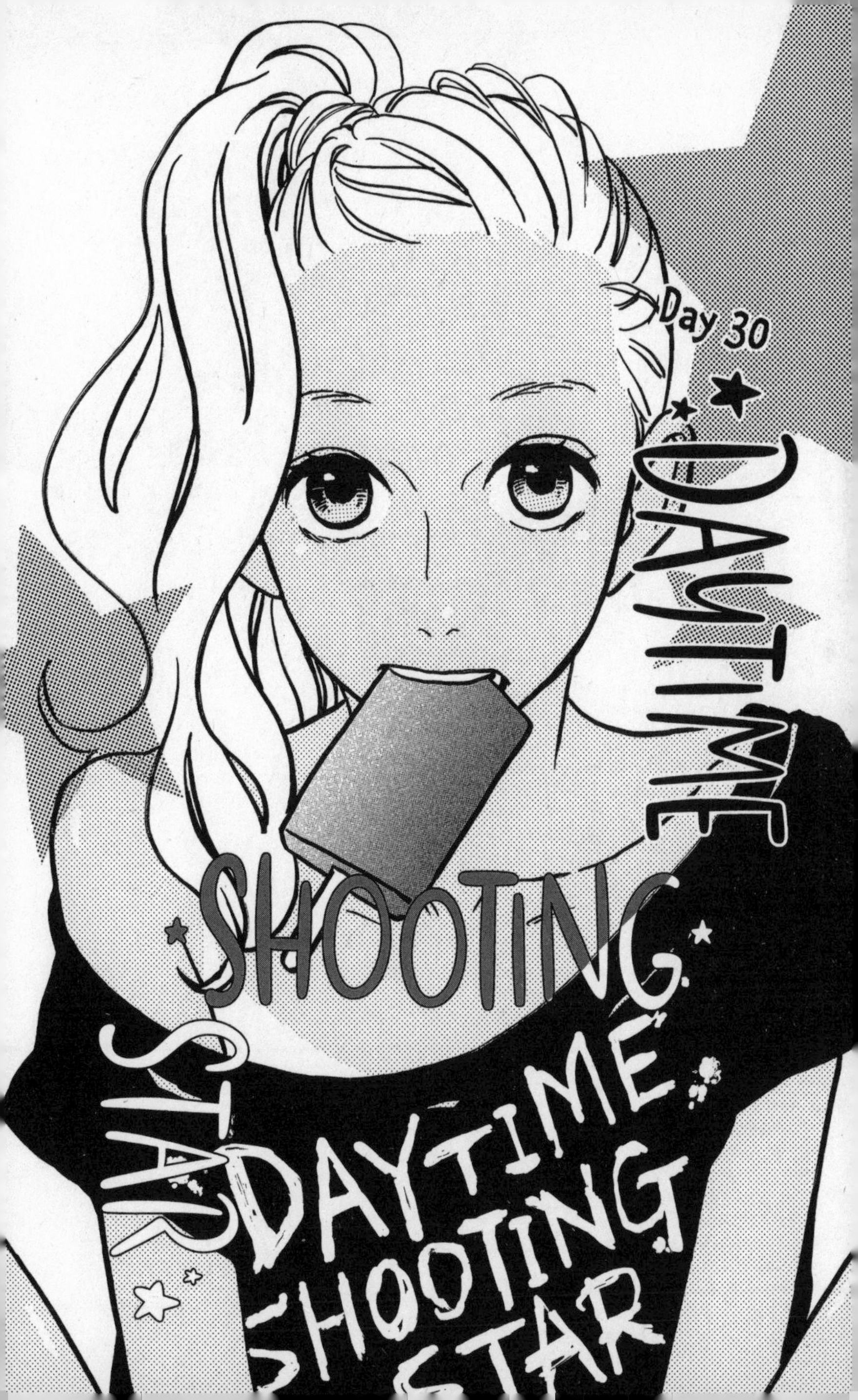
Day 30
DAYTIME SHOOTING STAR
DAYTIME
SHOOTING
STAR

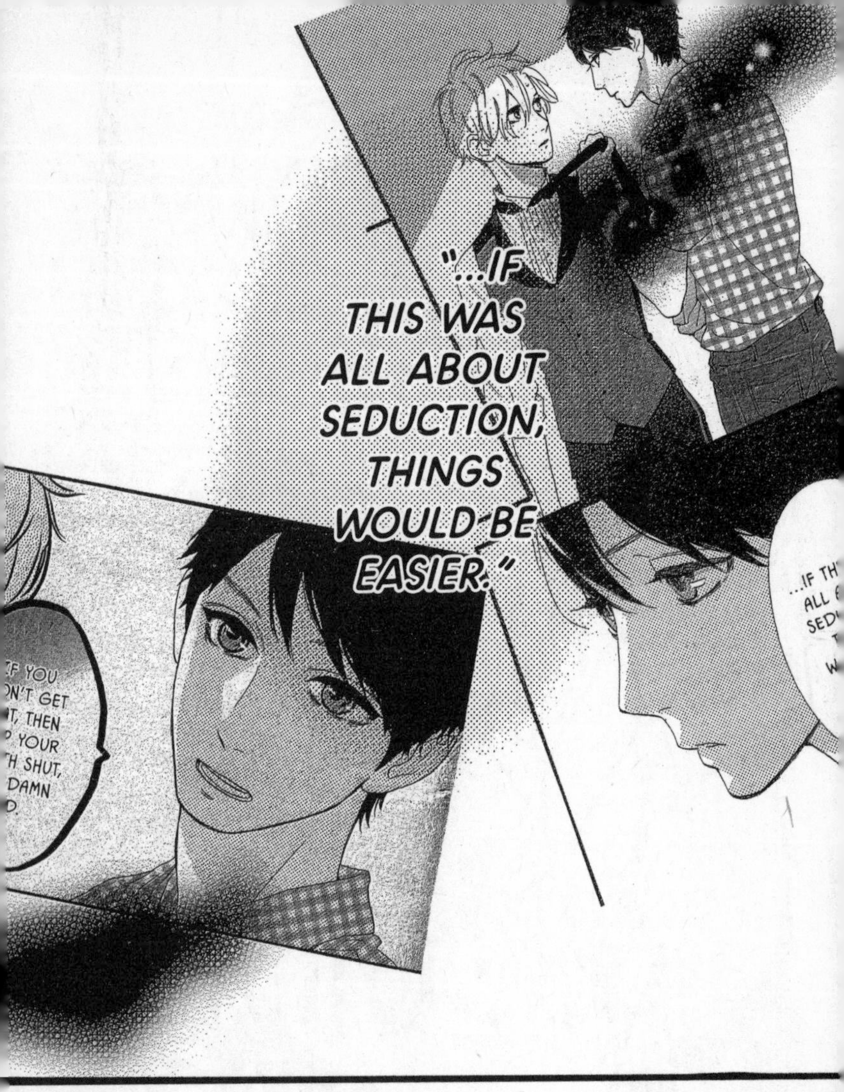
"...IF THIS WAS ALL ABOUT SEDUCTION, THINGS WOULD BE EASIER."

Yuyuka talking to herself.

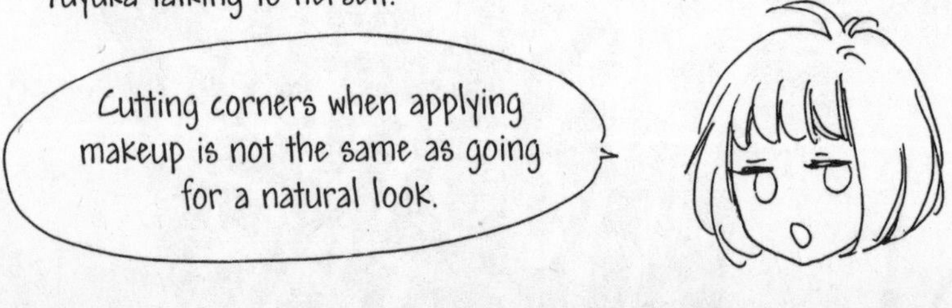
Cutting corners when applying makeup is not the same as going for a natural look.

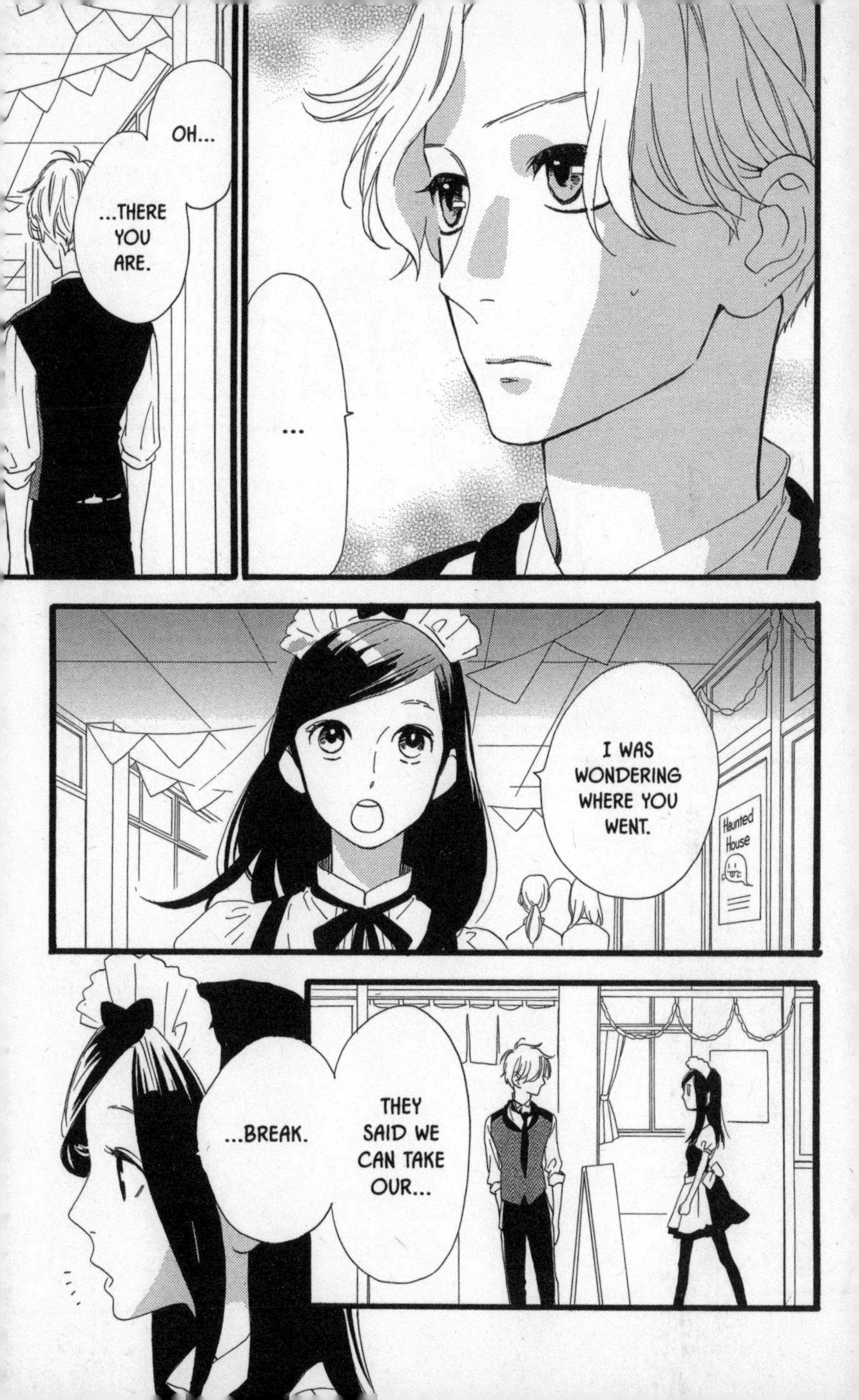
...
OH...
...THERE YOU ARE.
I WAS WONDERING WHERE YOU WENT.
Haunted House
THEY SAID WE CAN TAKE OUR...
...BREAK.

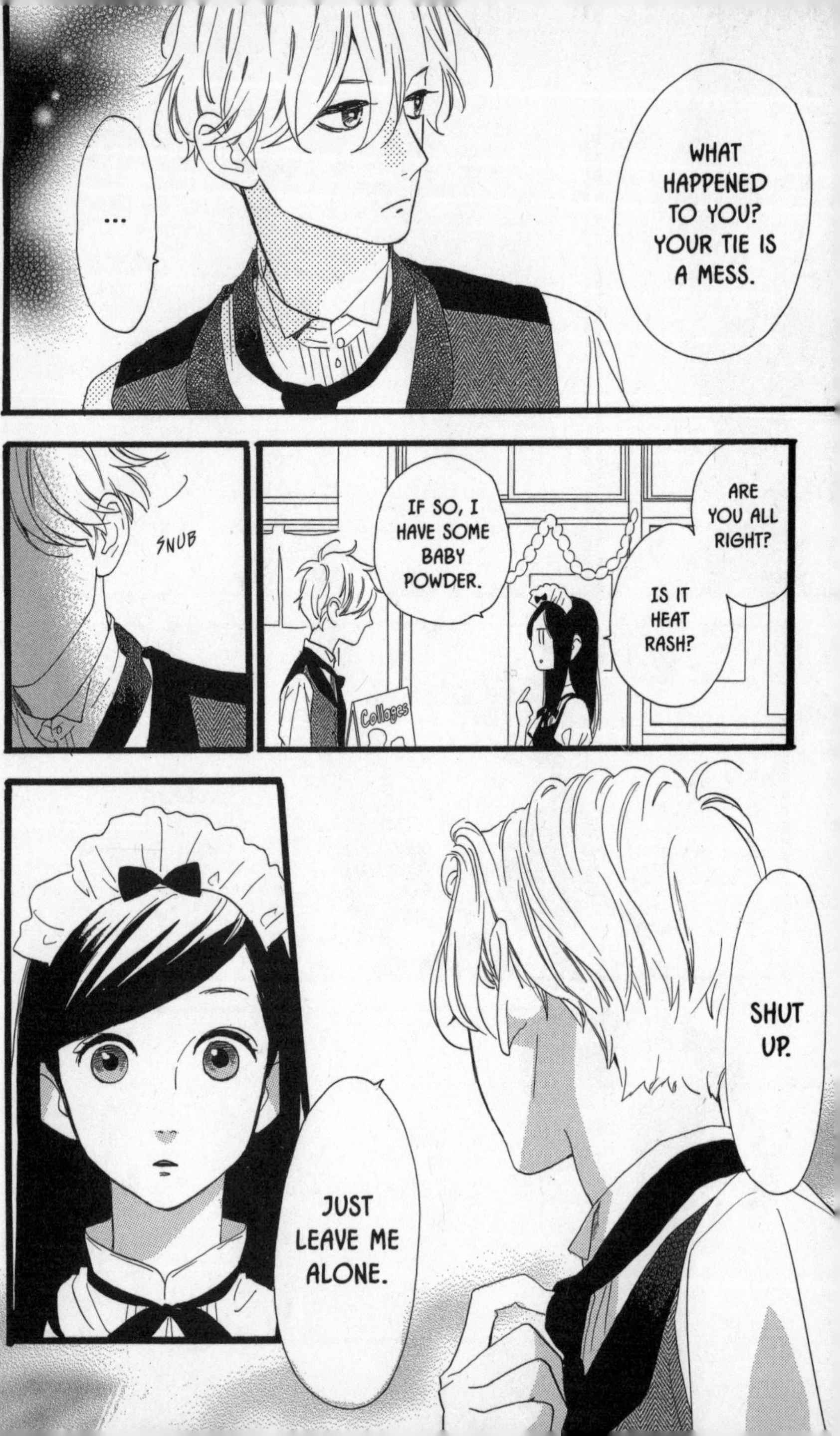
WHAT HAPPENED TO YOU? YOUR TIE IS A MESS.
...
ARE YOU ALL RIGHT?
IS IT HEAT RASH?
IF SO, I HAVE SOME BABY POWDER.
Collages
SNUB
SHUT UP.
JUST LEAVE ME ALONE.

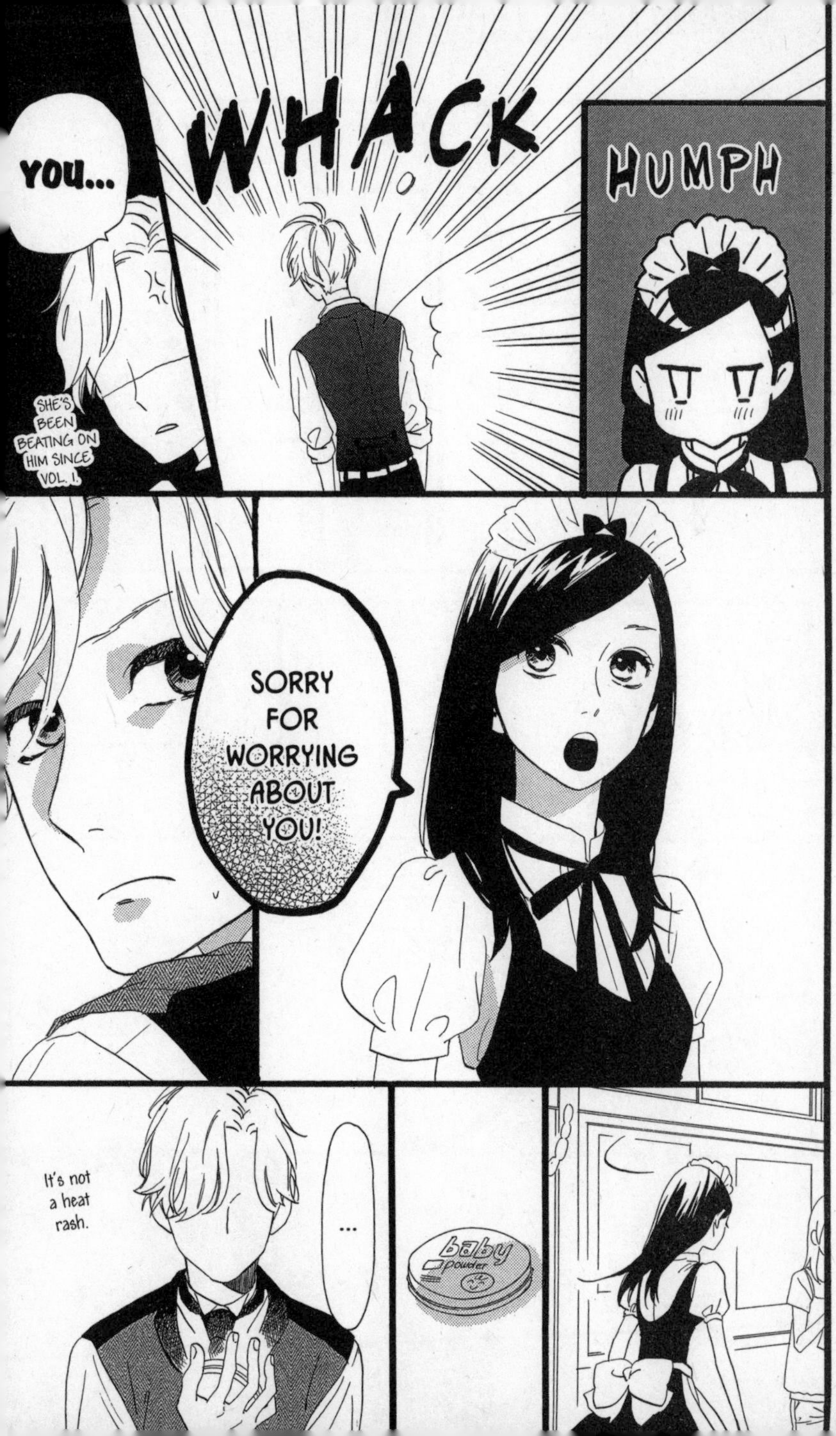
HUMPH
WHACK
YOU...
SHE'S BEEN BEATING ON HIM SINCE VOL. 1.
SORRY FOR WORRYING ABOUT YOU!
baby powder
...
It's not a heat rash.

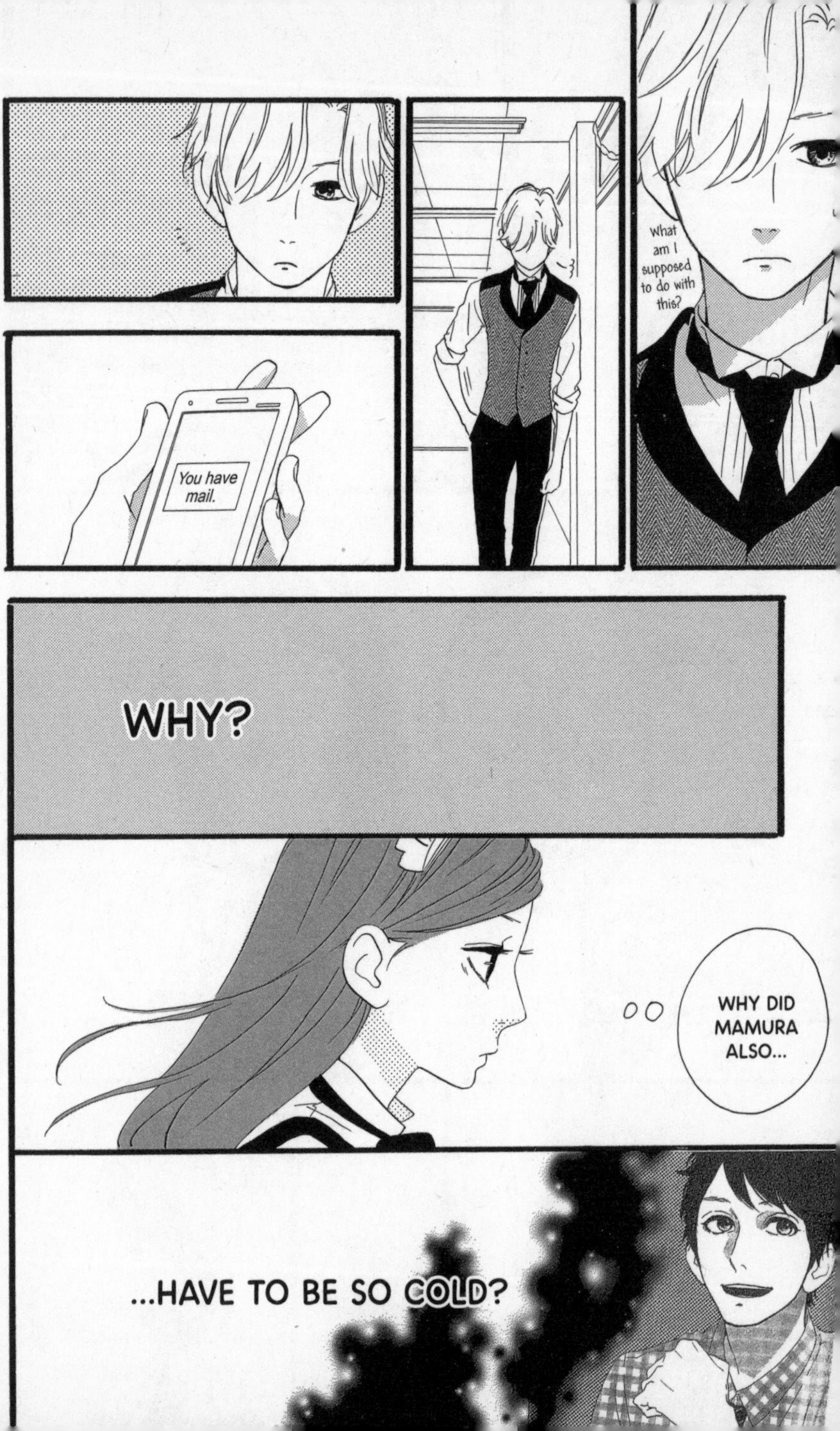
What am I supposed to do with this?
You have mail.
WHY?
WHY DID MAMURA ALSO...
...HAVE TO BE SO COLD?

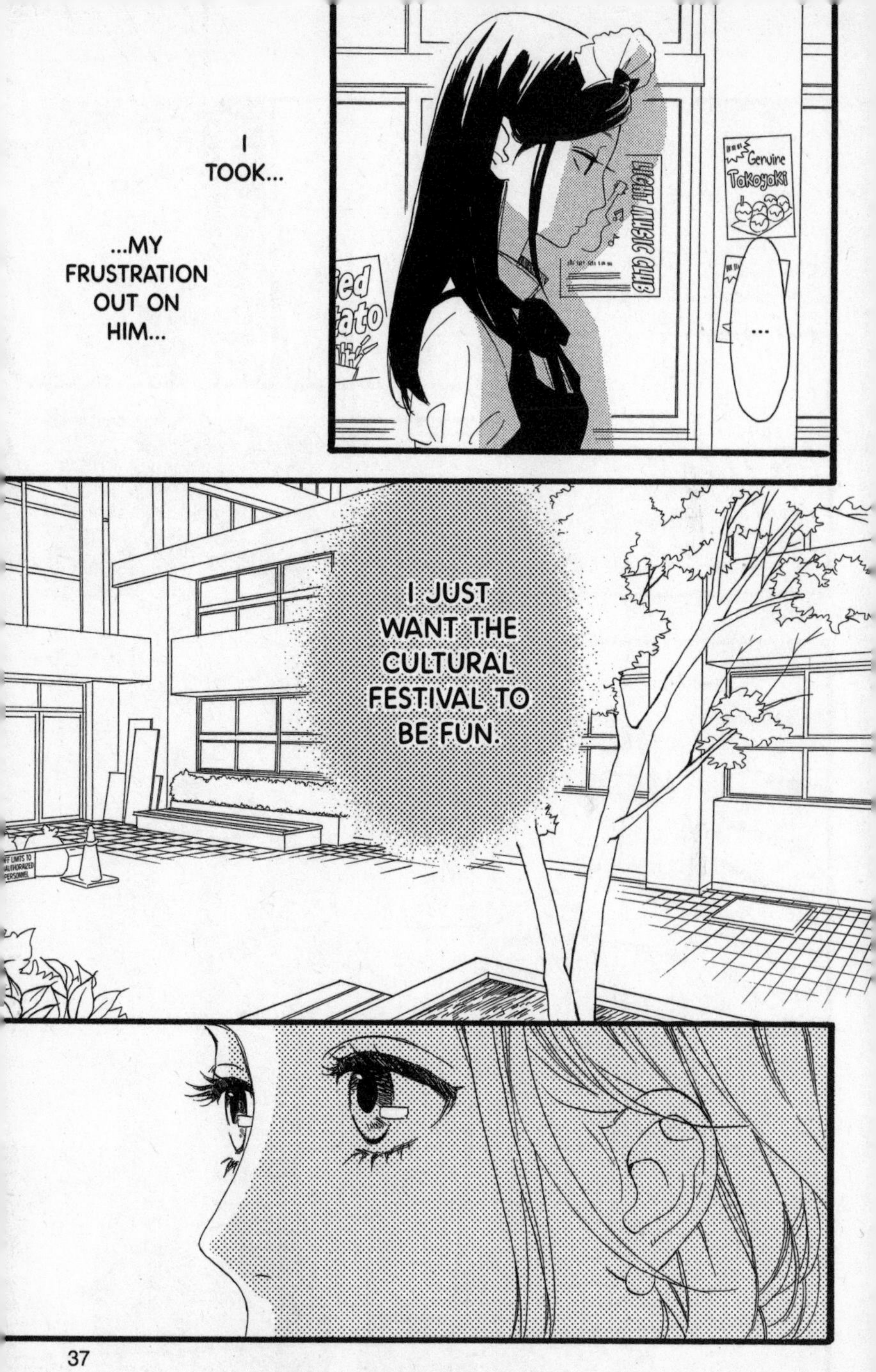
Genuine Takoyaki
LIGHT MUSIC CLUB
...
I TOOK...
...MY FRUSTRATION OUT ON HIM...
I JUST WANT THE CULTURAL FESTIVAL TO BE FUN.

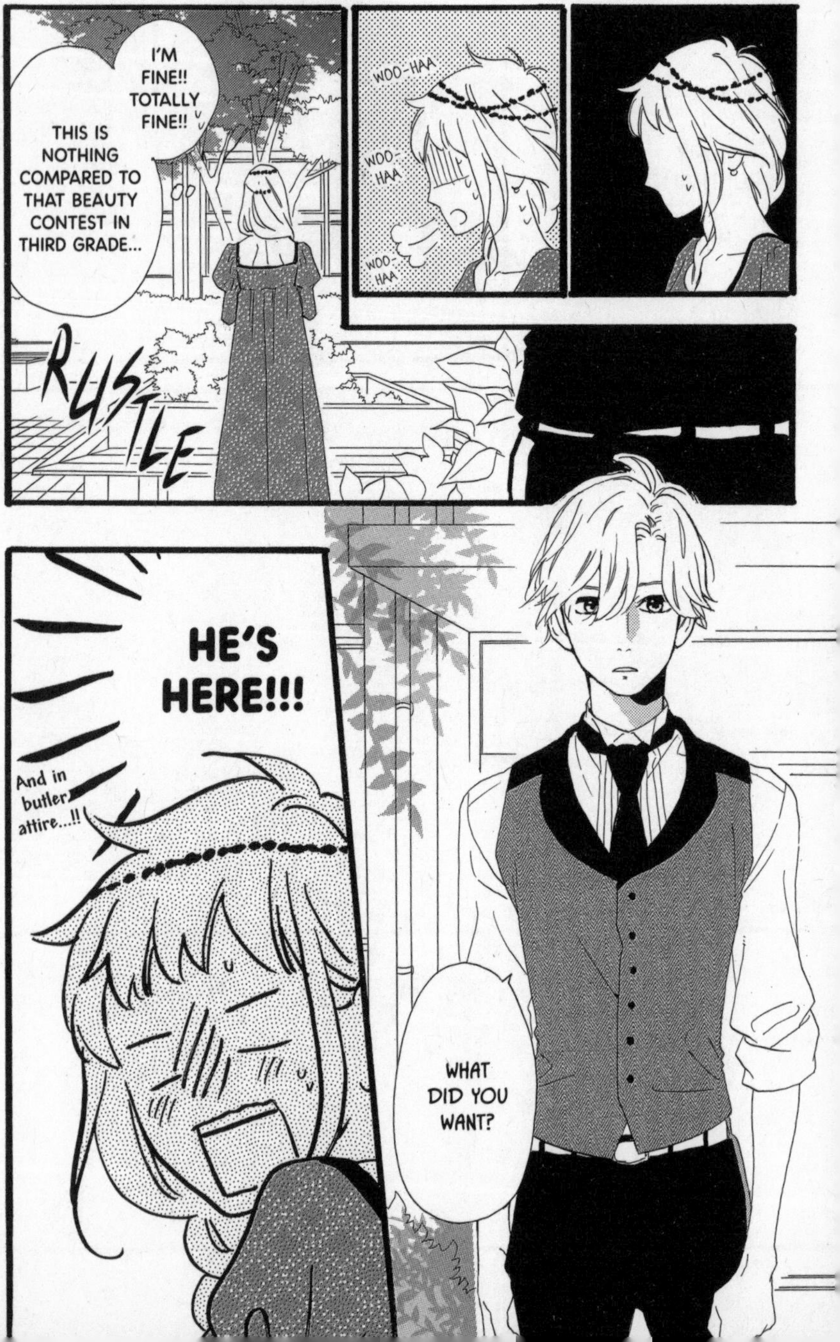
WOO-HAA
WOO-HAA
WOO-HAA
I'M FINE!! TOTALLY FINE!!
THIS IS NOTHING COMPARED TO THAT BEAUTY CONTEST IN THIRD GRADE...
RUSTLE
WHAT DID YOU WANT?
HE'S HERE!!!
And in butler attire...!!

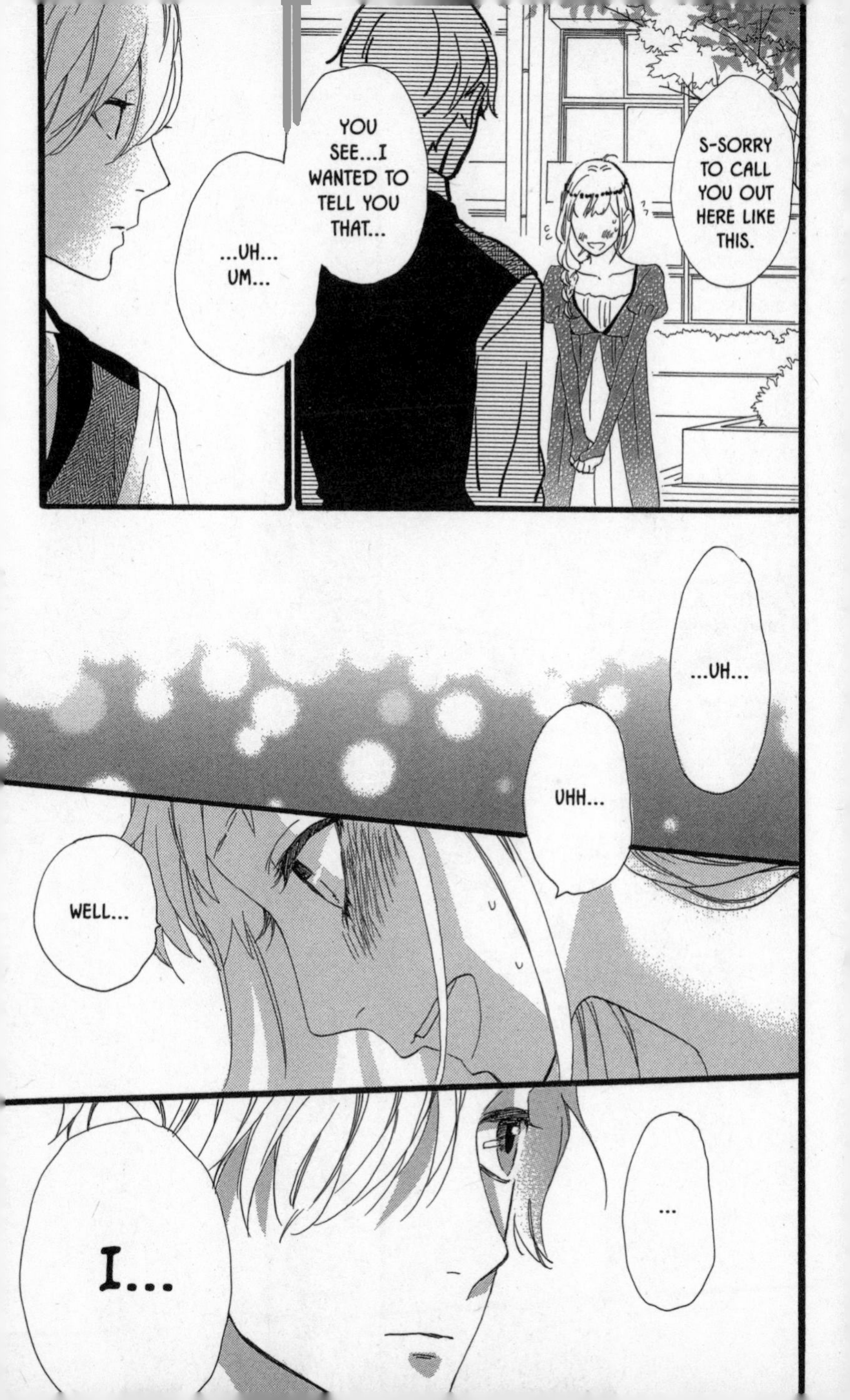
S-SORRY TO CALL YOU OUT HERE LIKE THIS.
YOU SEE...I WANTED TO TELL YOU THAT...
...UH... UM...
...UH...
UHH...
WELL...
...
I...

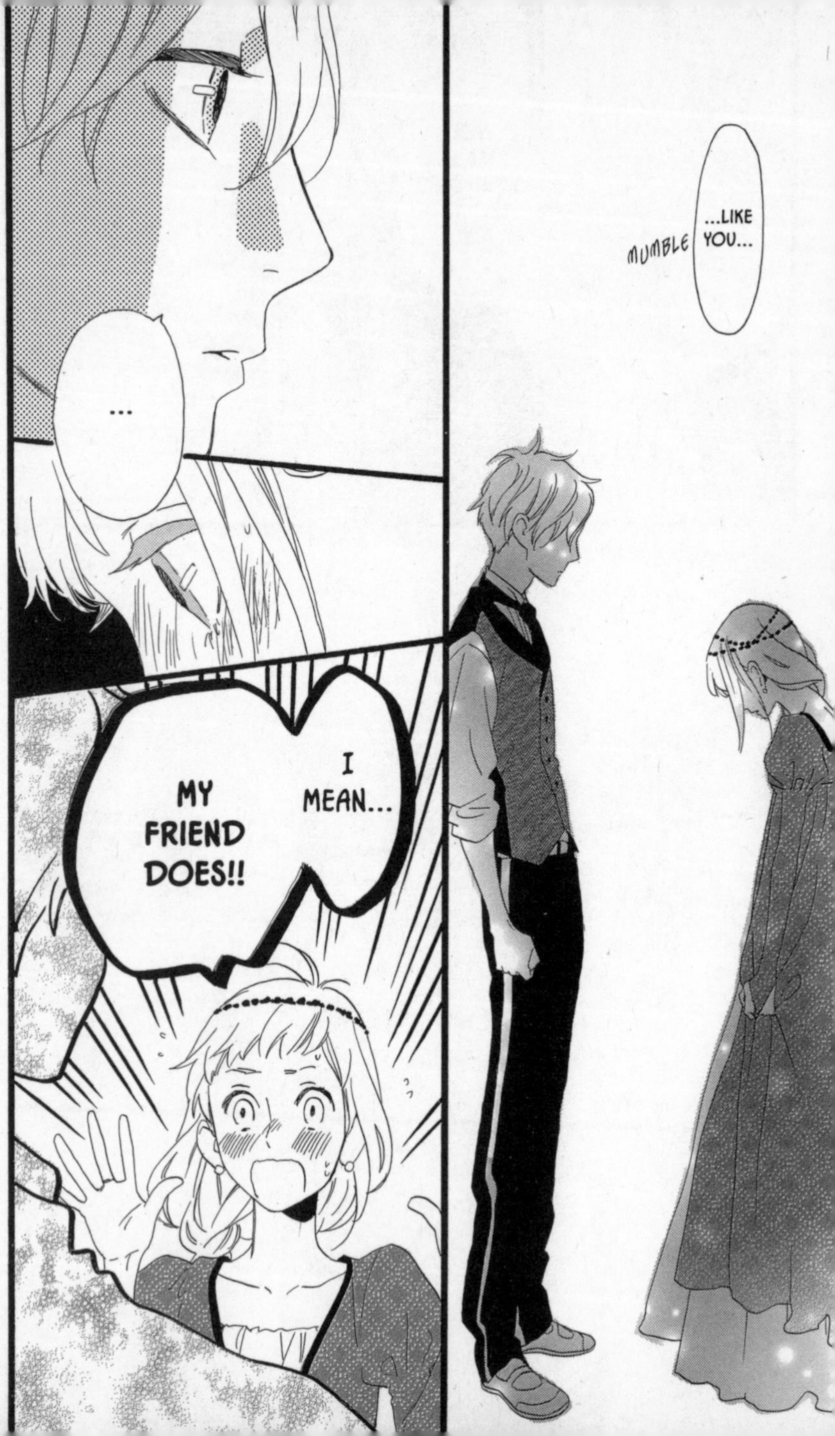
MUMBLE
...LIKE YOU...
...
I MEAN... MY FRIEND DOES!!

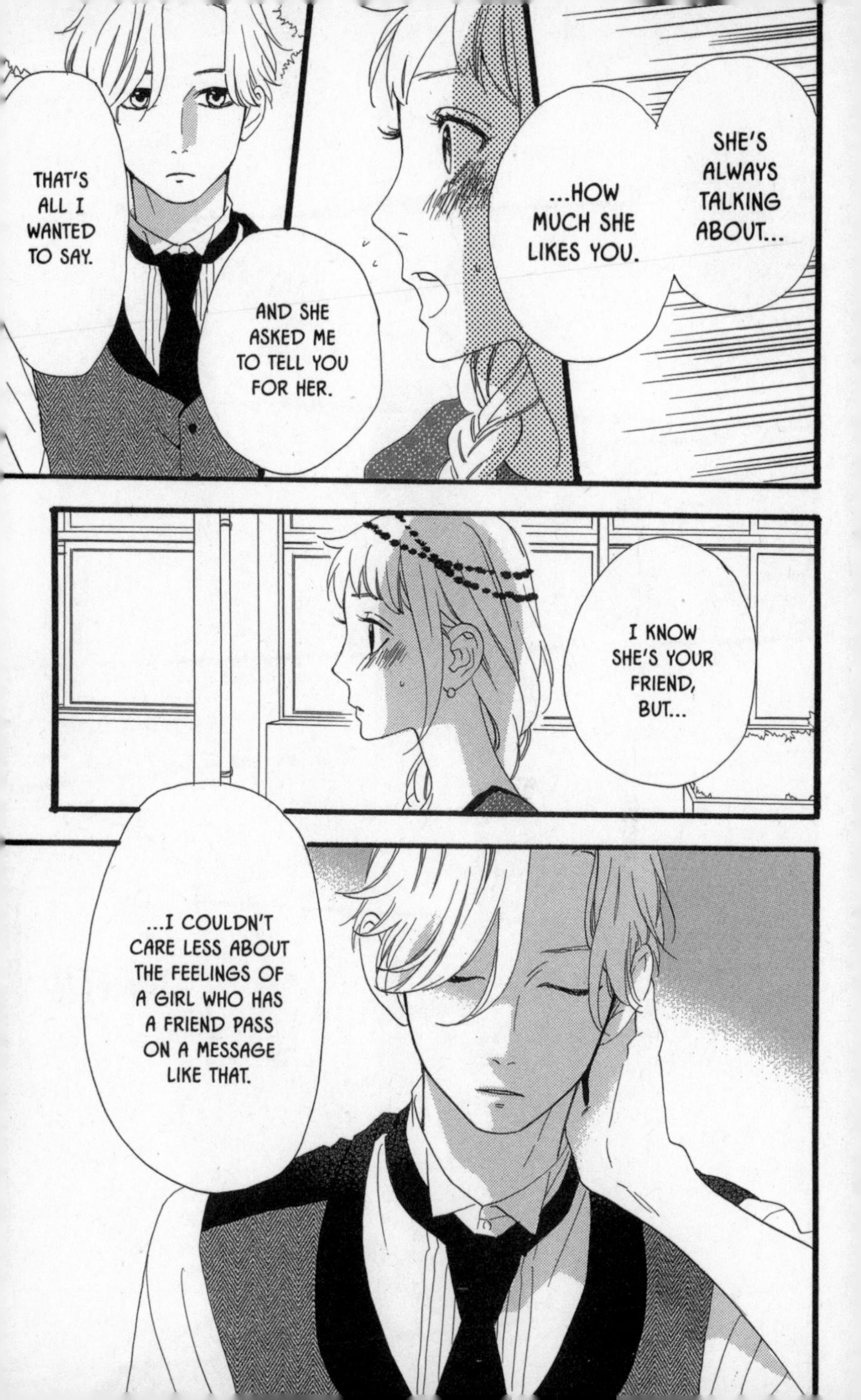
SHE'S ALWAYS TALKING ABOUT...
...HOW MUCH SHE LIKES YOU.
AND SHE ASKED ME TO TELL YOU FOR HER.
THAT'S ALL I WANTED TO SAY.
I KNOW SHE'S YOUR FRIEND, BUT...
...I COULDN'T CARE LESS ABOUT THE FEELINGS OF A GIRL WHO HAS A FRIEND PASS ON A MESSAGE LIKE THAT.

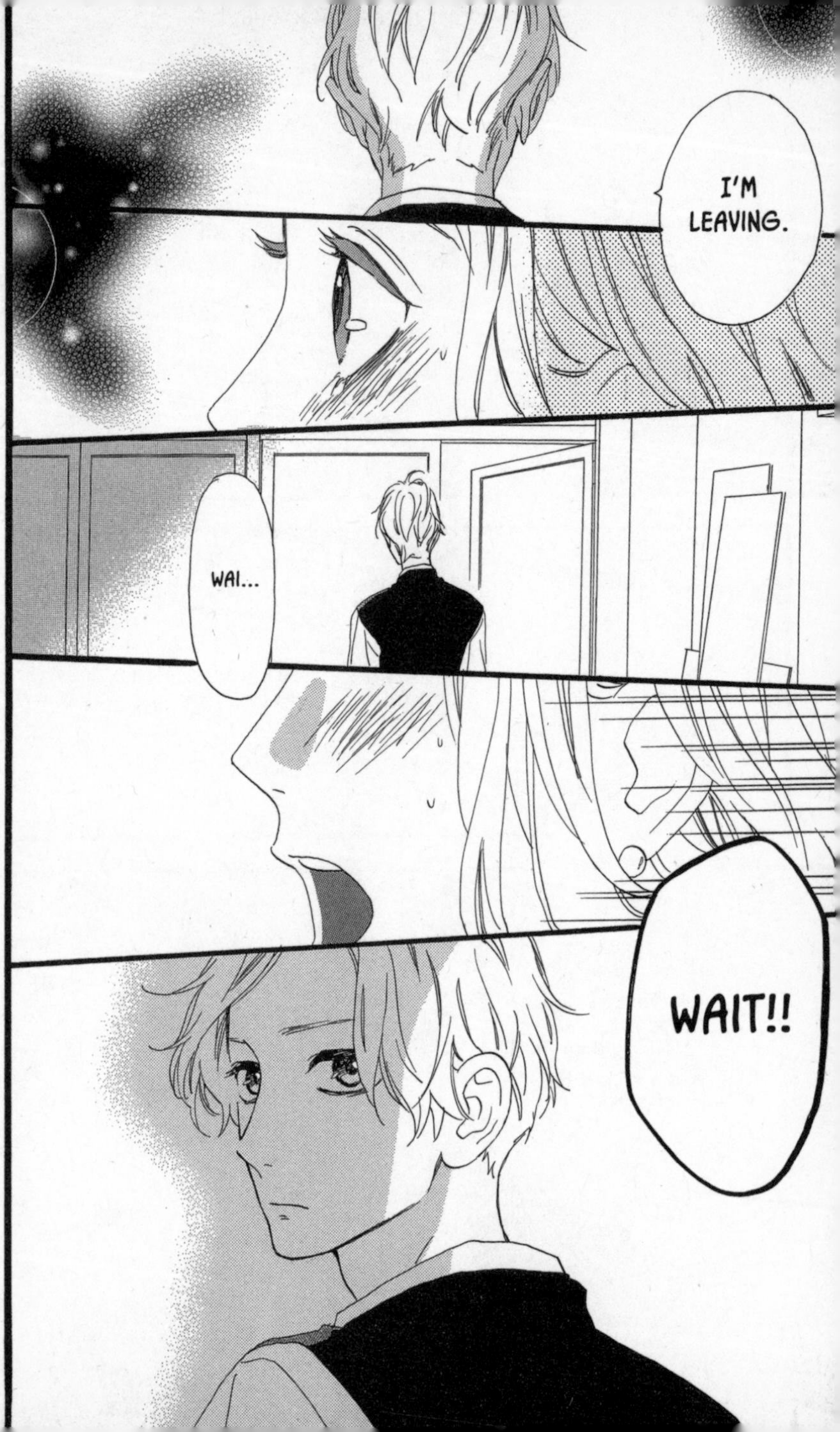
I'M LEAVING.
WAI...
WAIT!!

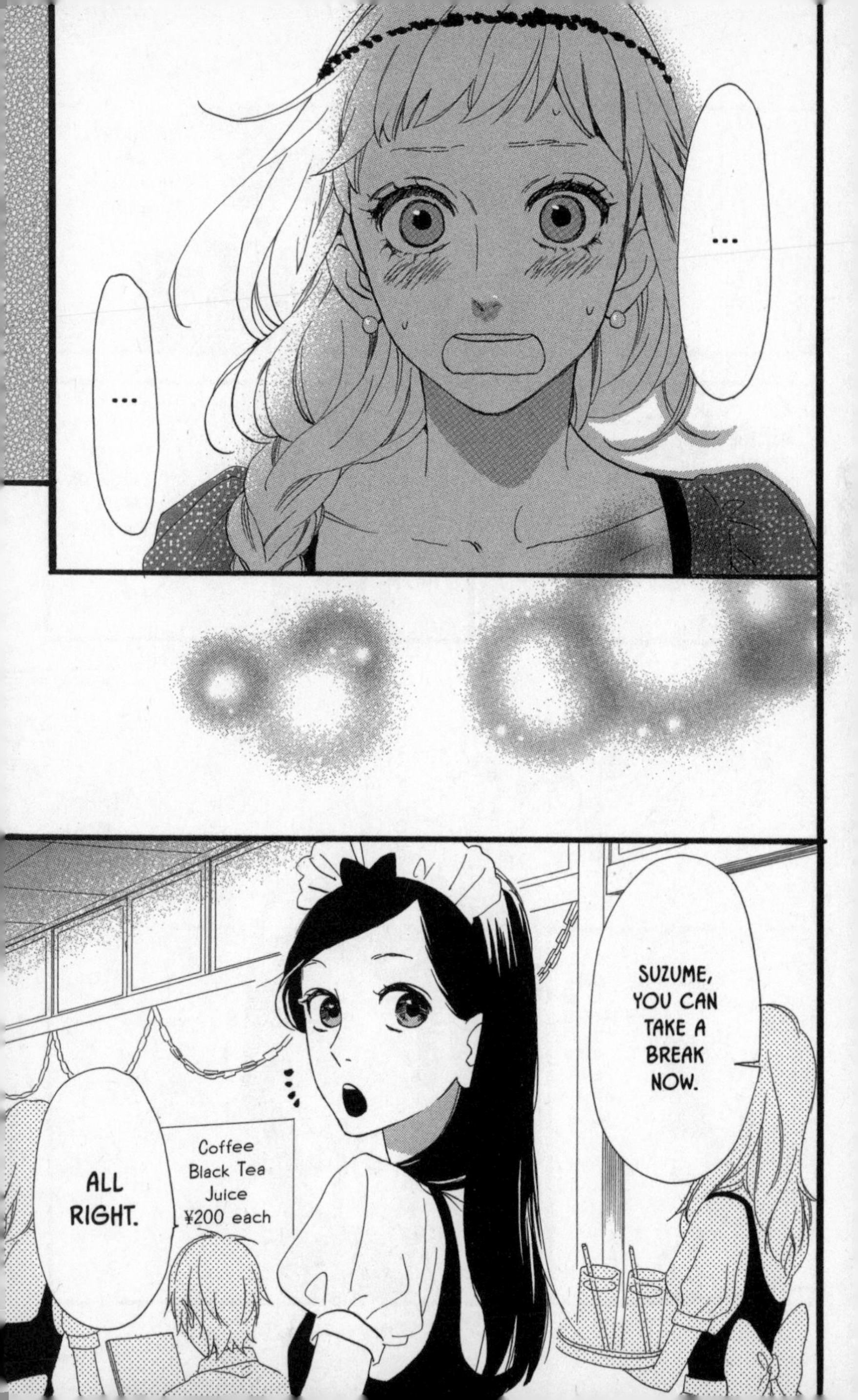
...
...
SUZUME, YOU CAN TAKE A BREAK NOW.
Coffee
Black Tea
Juice
¥200 each
ALL RIGHT.

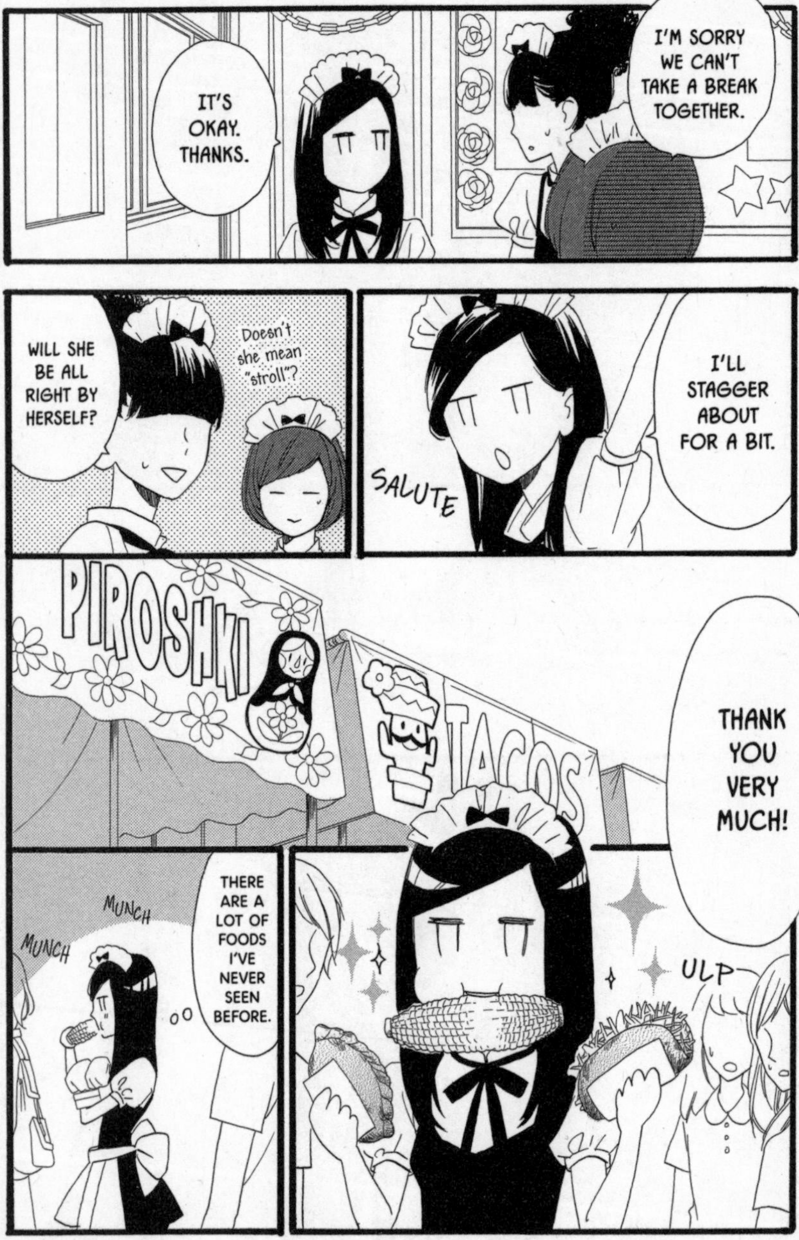
I'M SORRY WE CAN'T TAKE A BREAK TOGETHER.
IT'S OKAY. THANKS.
I'LL STAGGER ABOUT FOR A BIT.
SALUTE
Doesn't she mean "stroll"?
WILL SHE BE ALL RIGHT BY HERSELF?
THANK YOU VERY MUCH!
TACOS
PIROSHKI
ULP
THERE ARE A LOT OF FOODS I'VE NEVER SEEN BEFORE.
MUNCH
MUNCH

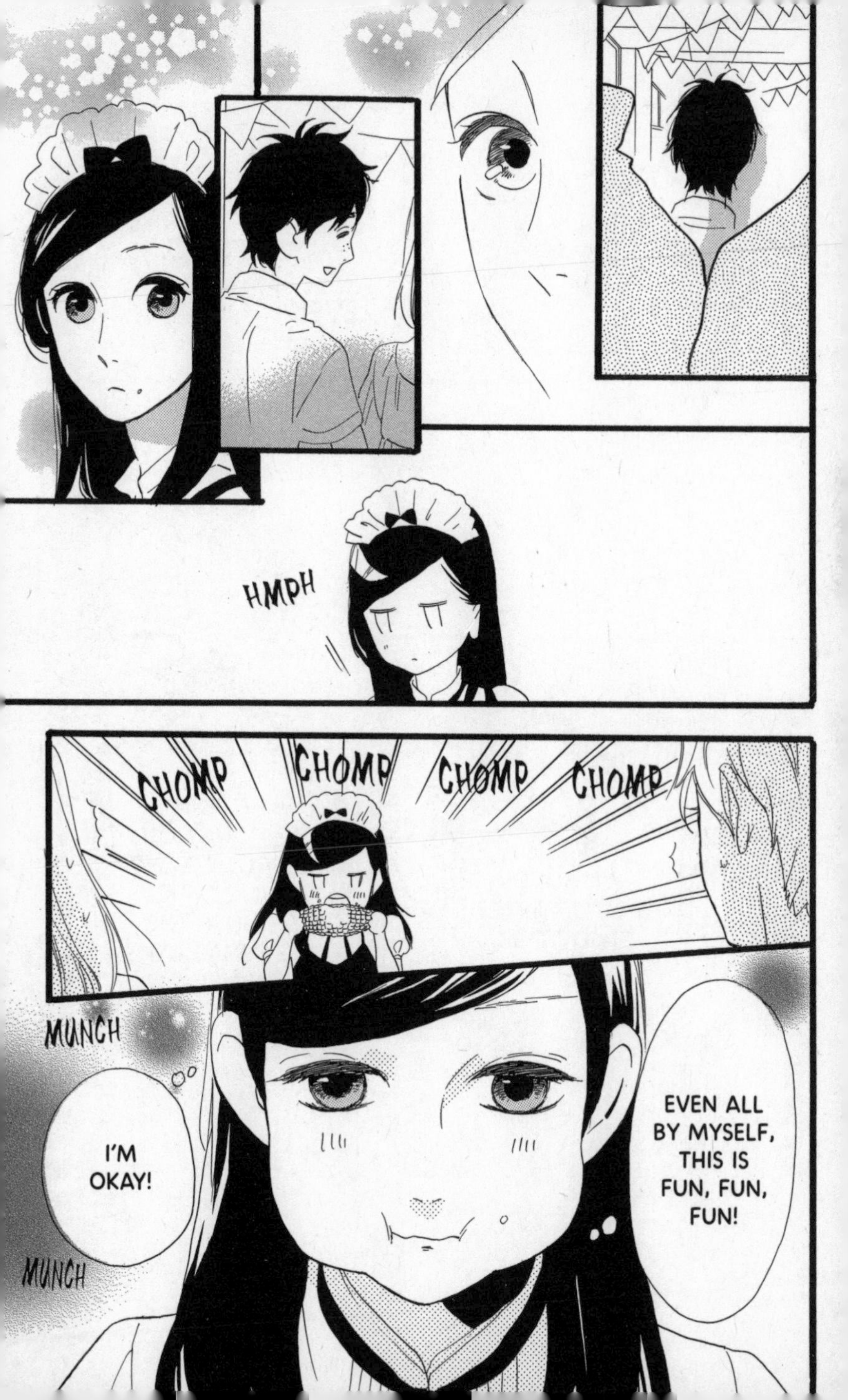
HMPH
CHOMP
CHOMP
CHOMP
CHOMP
EVEN ALL BY MYSELF, THIS IS FUN, FUN, FUN!
MUNCH
I'M OKAY!
MUNCH

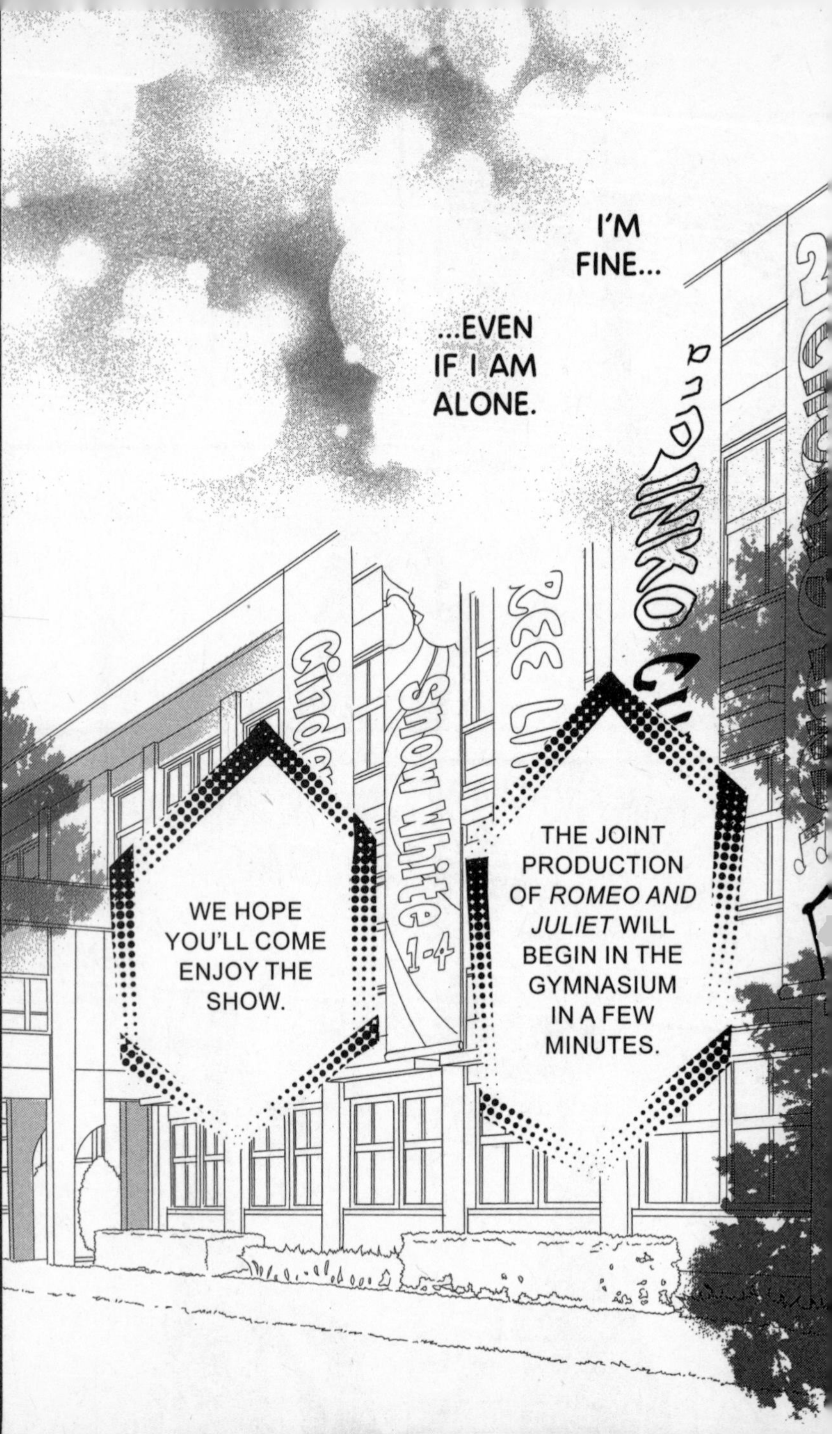
I'M FINE...
...EVEN IF I AM ALONE.
THE JOINT PRODUCTION OF *ROMEO AND JULIET* WILL BEGIN IN THE GYMNASIUM IN A FEW MINUTES.
Snow White 1-4
WE HOPE YOU'LL COME ENJOY THE SHOW.

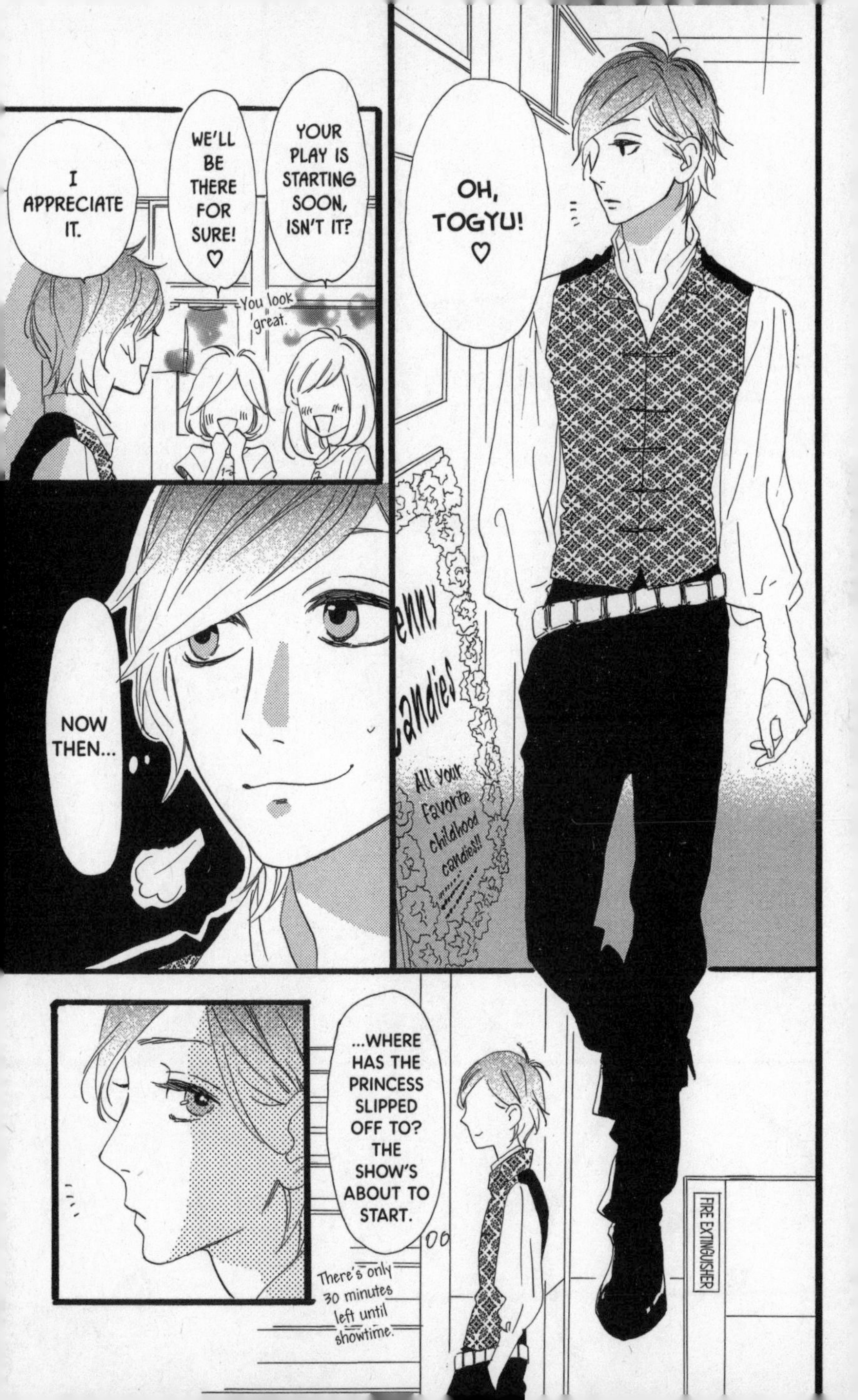
OH, TOGYU! ♡
Candies
All your favorite childhood candies!!
YOUR PLAY IS STARTING SOON, ISN'T IT?
WE'LL BE THERE FOR SURE! ♡
I APPRECIATE IT.
You look great.
NOW THEN...
...WHERE HAS THE PRINCESS SLIPPED OFF TO? THE SHOW'S ABOUT TO START.
There's only 30 minutes left until showtime.
FIRE EXTINGUISHER

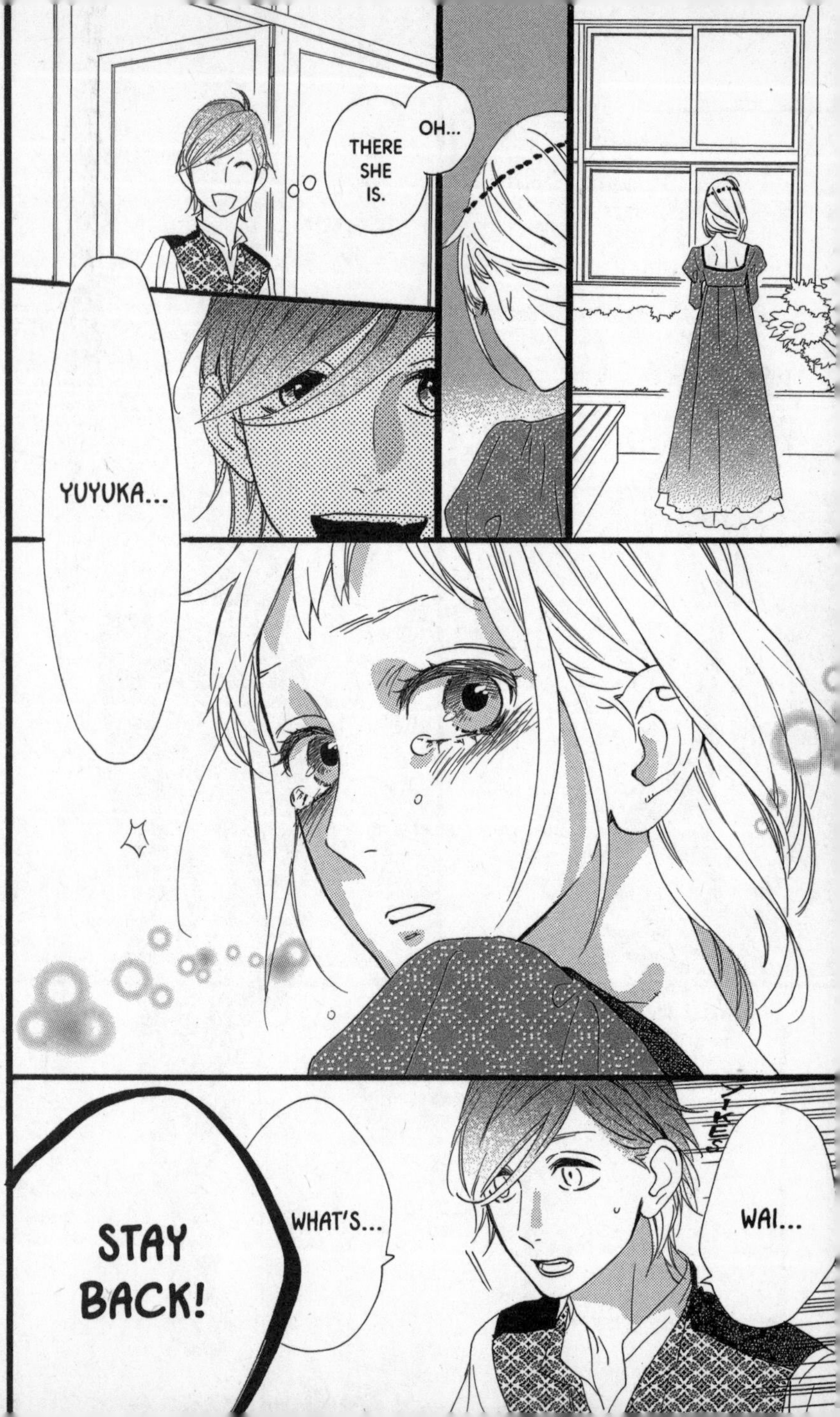
OH... THERE SHE IS.
YUYUKA...
WAI...
YIKES
WHAT'S...
STAY BACK!

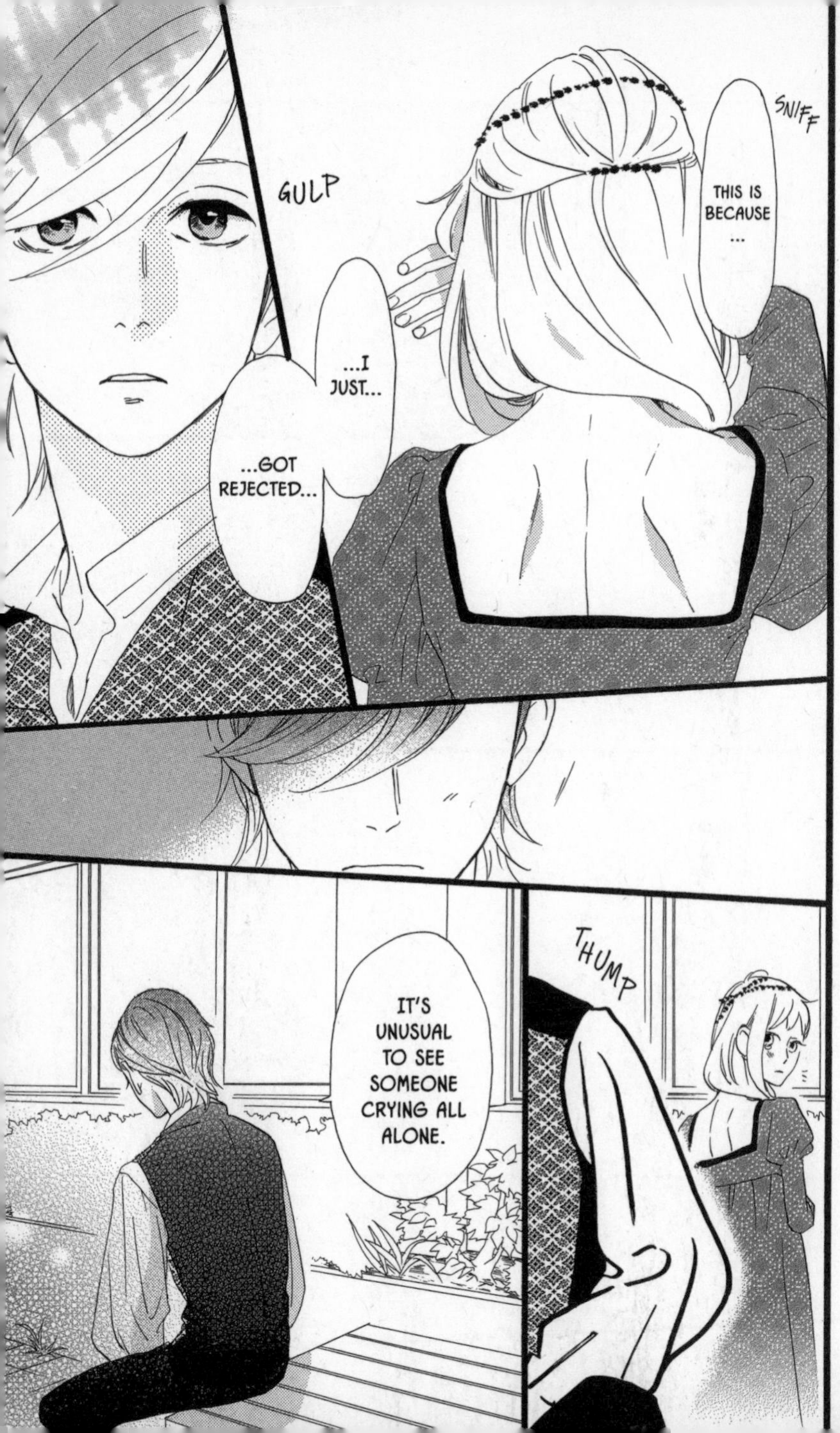
SNIFF
THIS IS BECAUSE ...
...I JUST...
...GOT REJECTED...
GULP
THUMP
IT'S UNUSUAL TO SEE SOMEONE CRYING ALL ALONE.

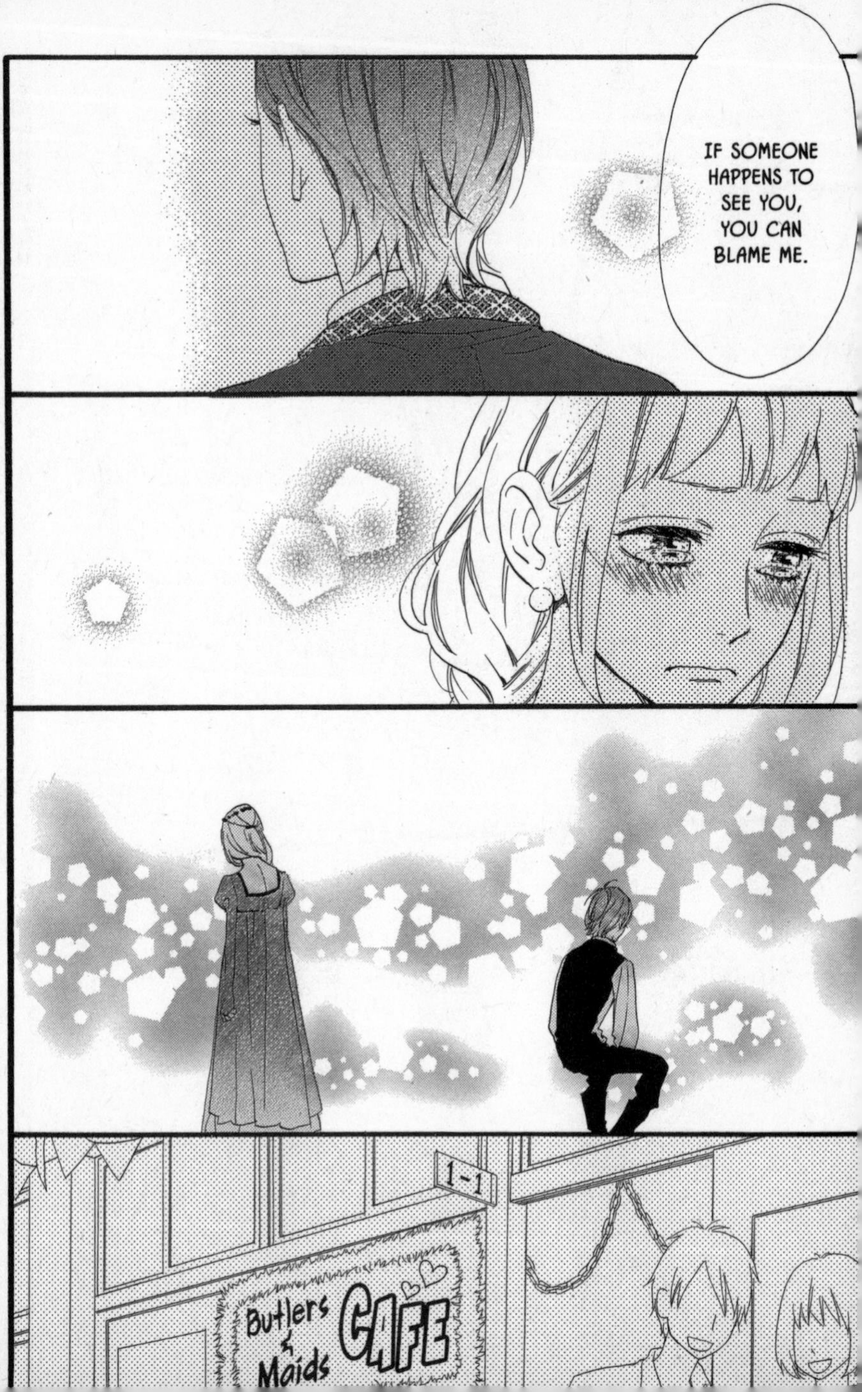

IF SOMEONE HAPPENS TO SEE YOU, YOU CAN BLAME ME.
1-1
Butlers & Maids
CAFE

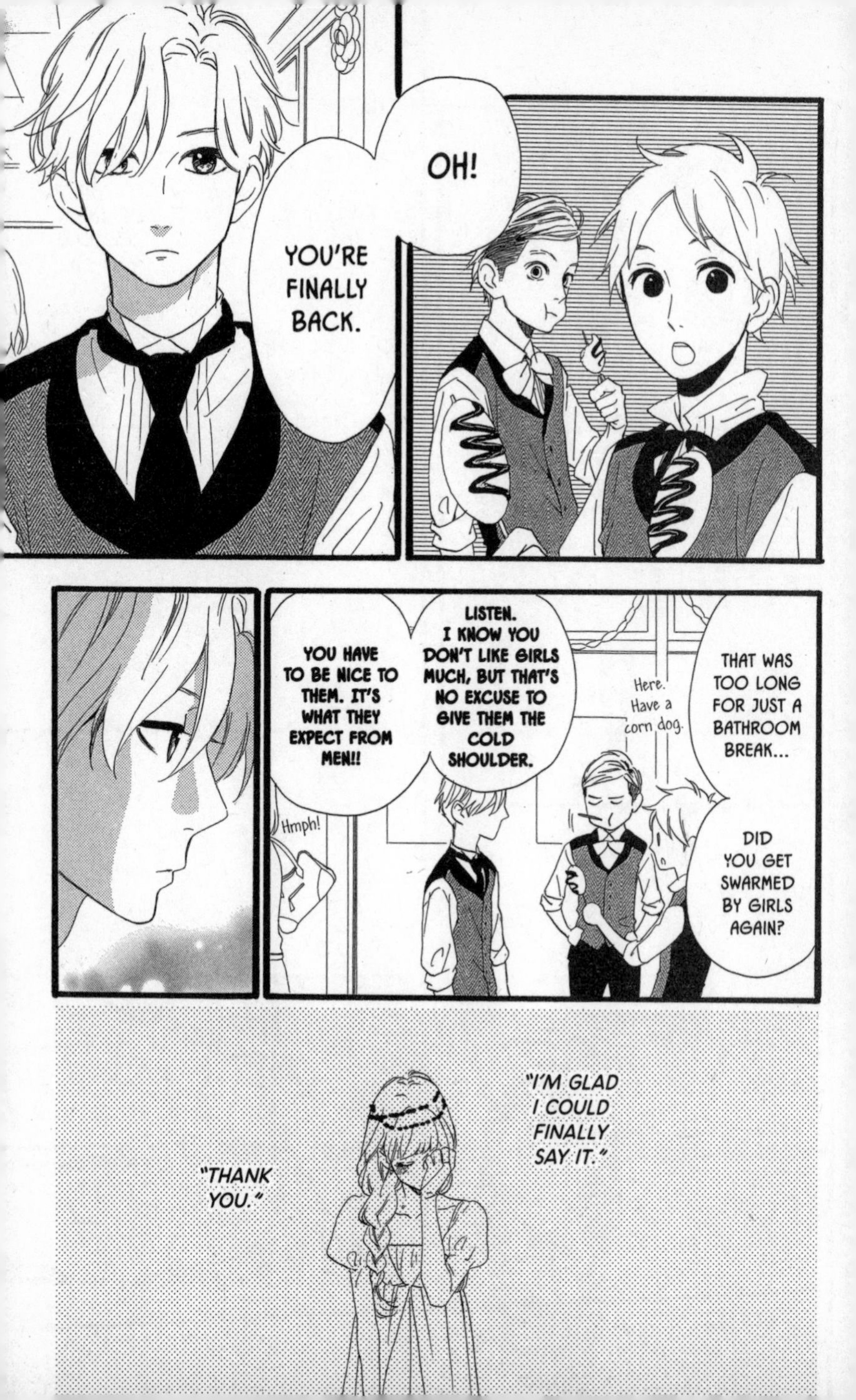
OH!
YOU'RE FINALLY BACK.
THAT WAS TOO LONG FOR JUST A BATHROOM BREAK...
DID YOU GET SWARMED BY GIRLS AGAIN?
Here. Have a corn dog.
LISTEN. I KNOW YOU DON'T LIKE GIRLS MUCH, BUT THAT'S NO EXCUSE TO GIVE THEM THE COLD SHOULDER.
YOU HAVE TO BE NICE TO THEM. IT'S WHAT THEY EXPECT FROM MEN!!
Hmph!
"I'M GLAD I COULD FINALLY SAY IT."
"THANK YOU."

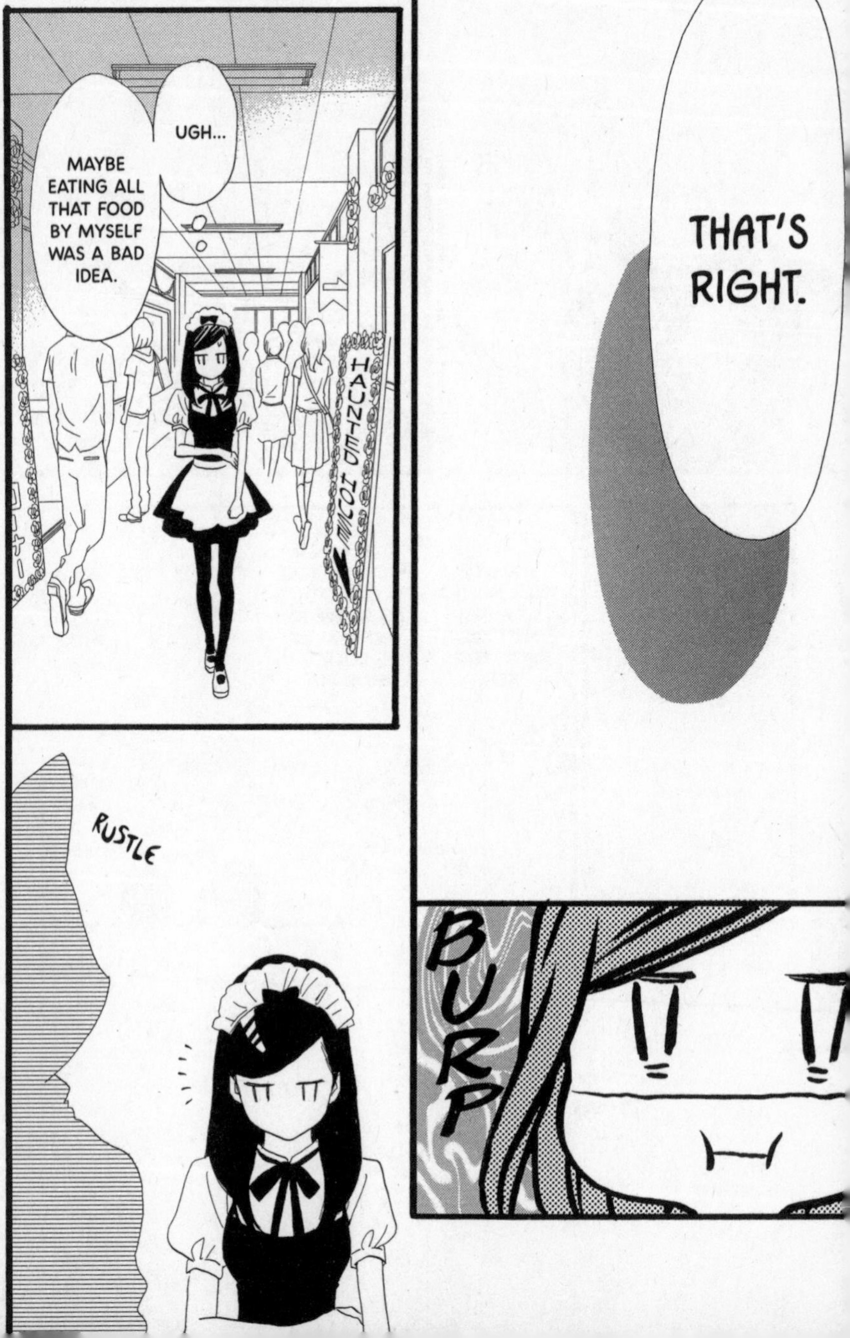
THAT'S RIGHT.
BURP
UGH...
MAYBE EATING ALL THAT FOOD BY MYSELF WAS A BAD IDEA.
HAUNTED HOUSE
RUSTLE

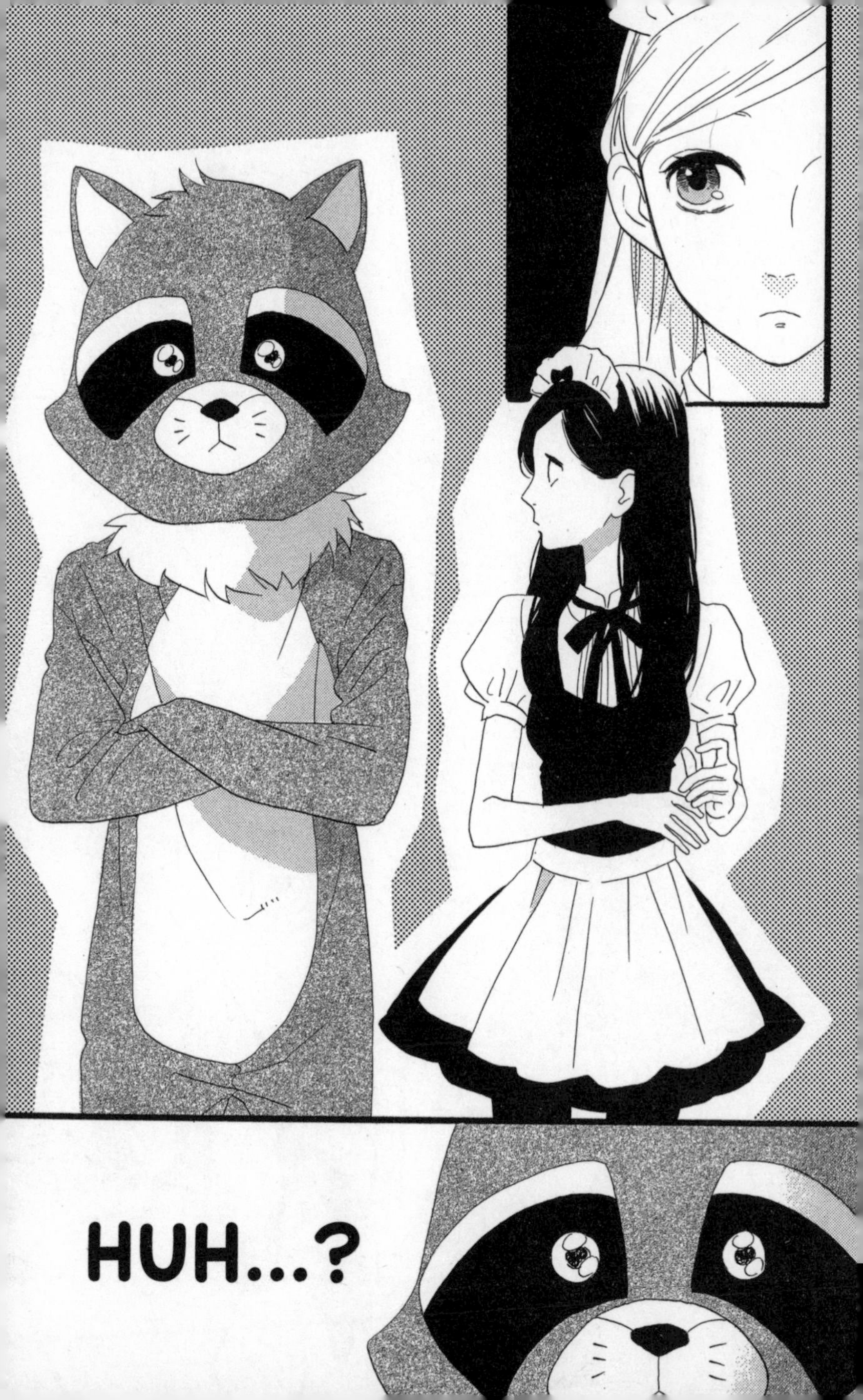
HUH...?

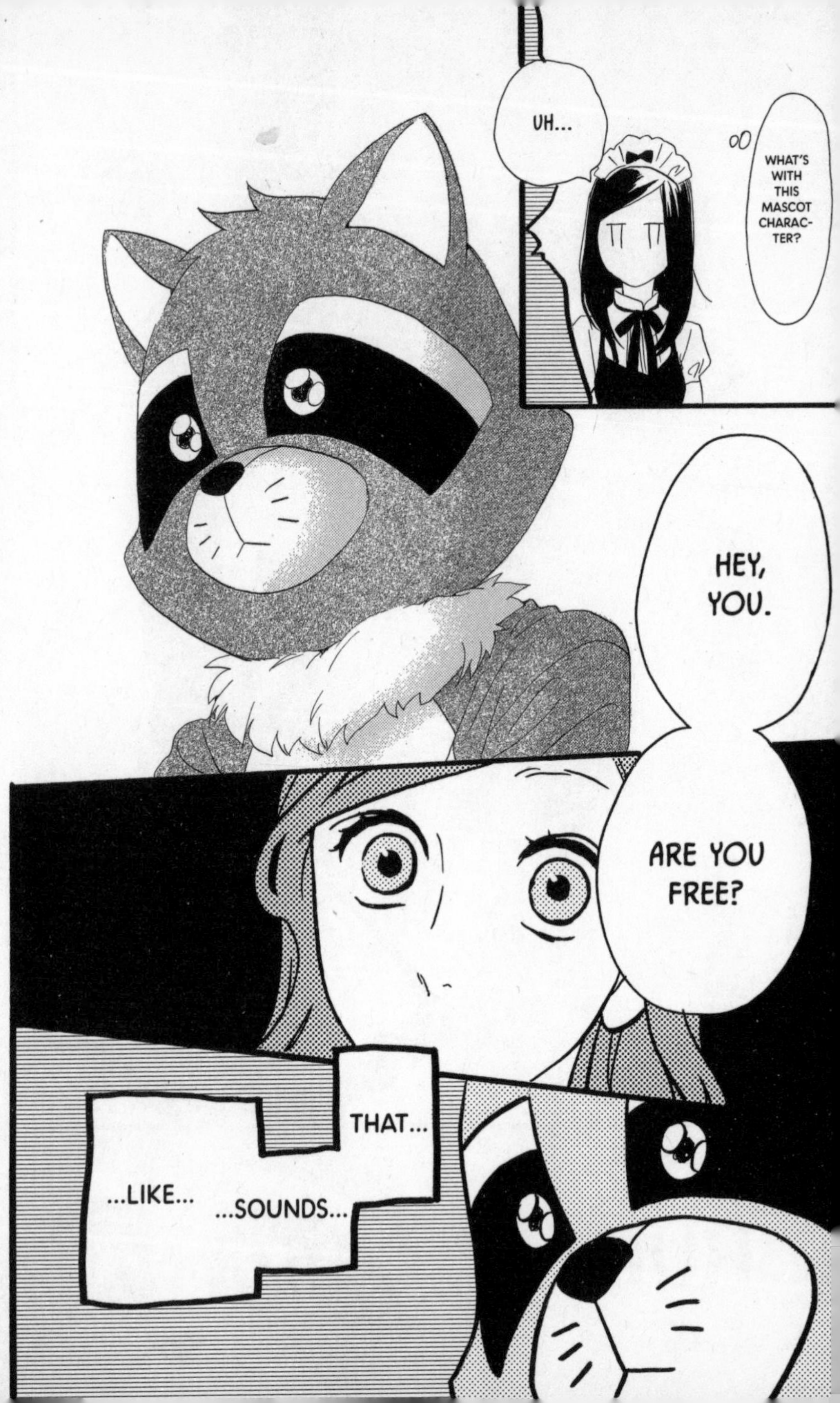
UH...
WHAT'S WITH THIS MASCOT CHARACTER?
HEY, YOU.
ARE YOU FREE?
THAT...
...SOUNDS...
...LIKE...

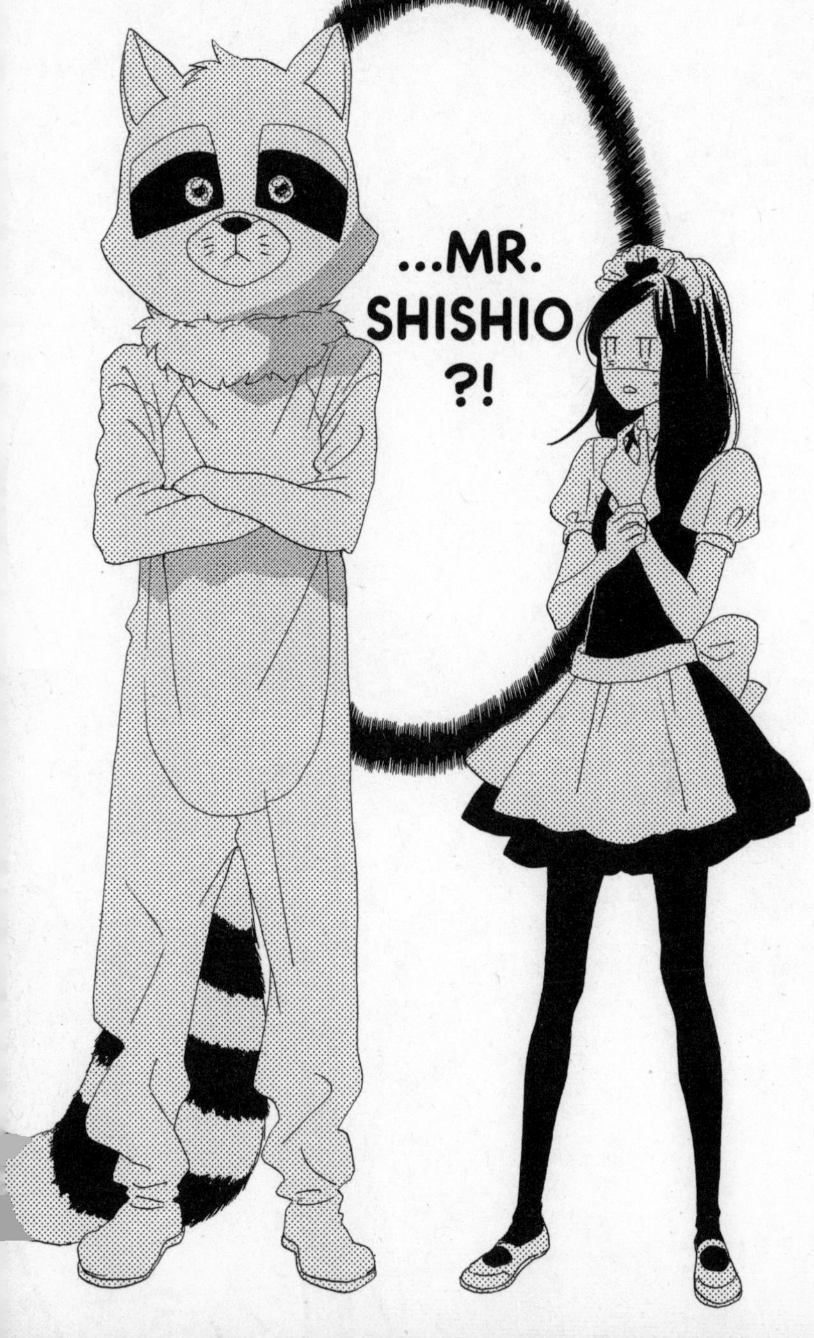
...MR.
SHISHIO
?!

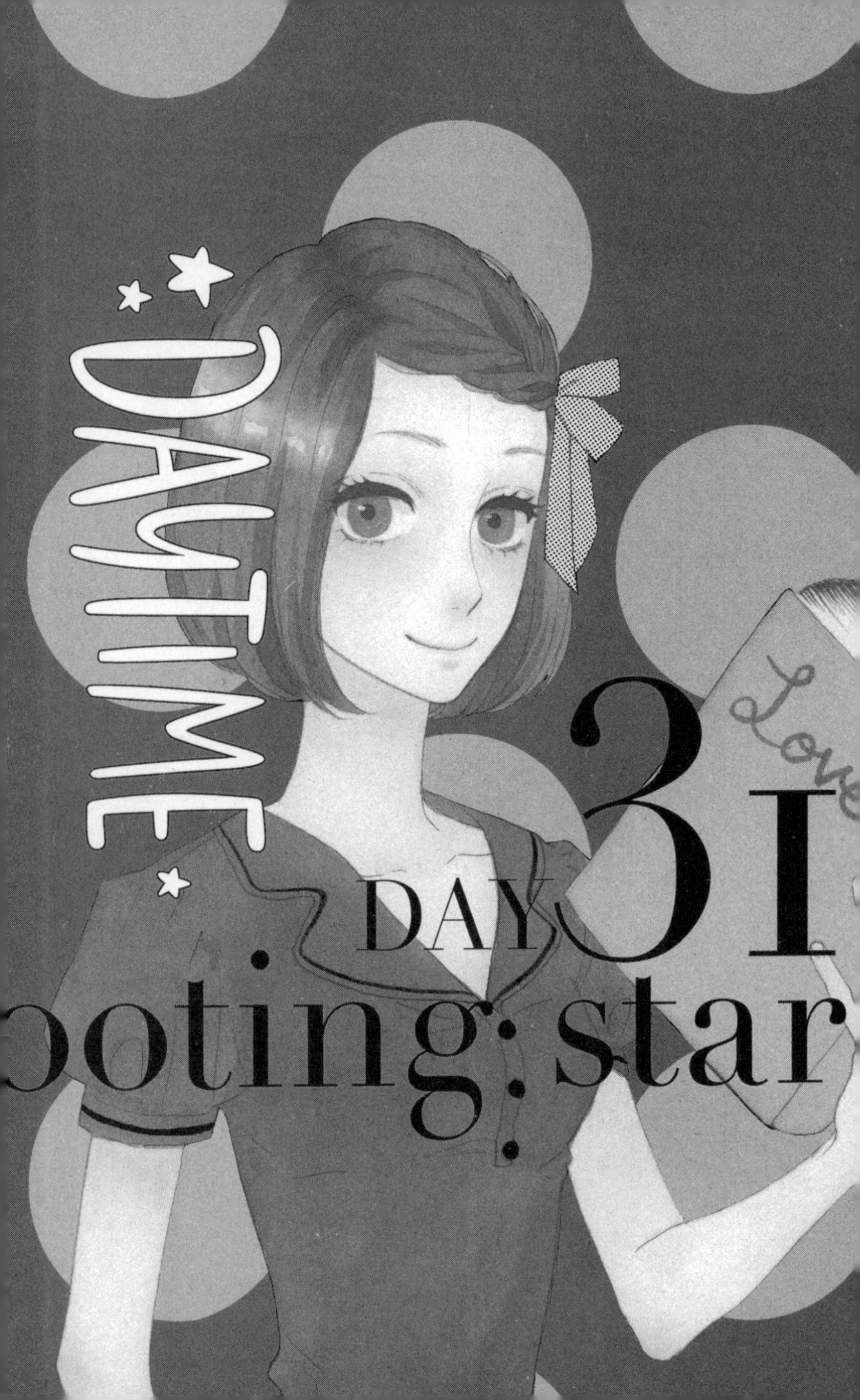

DAYTIME
DAY 31
Love

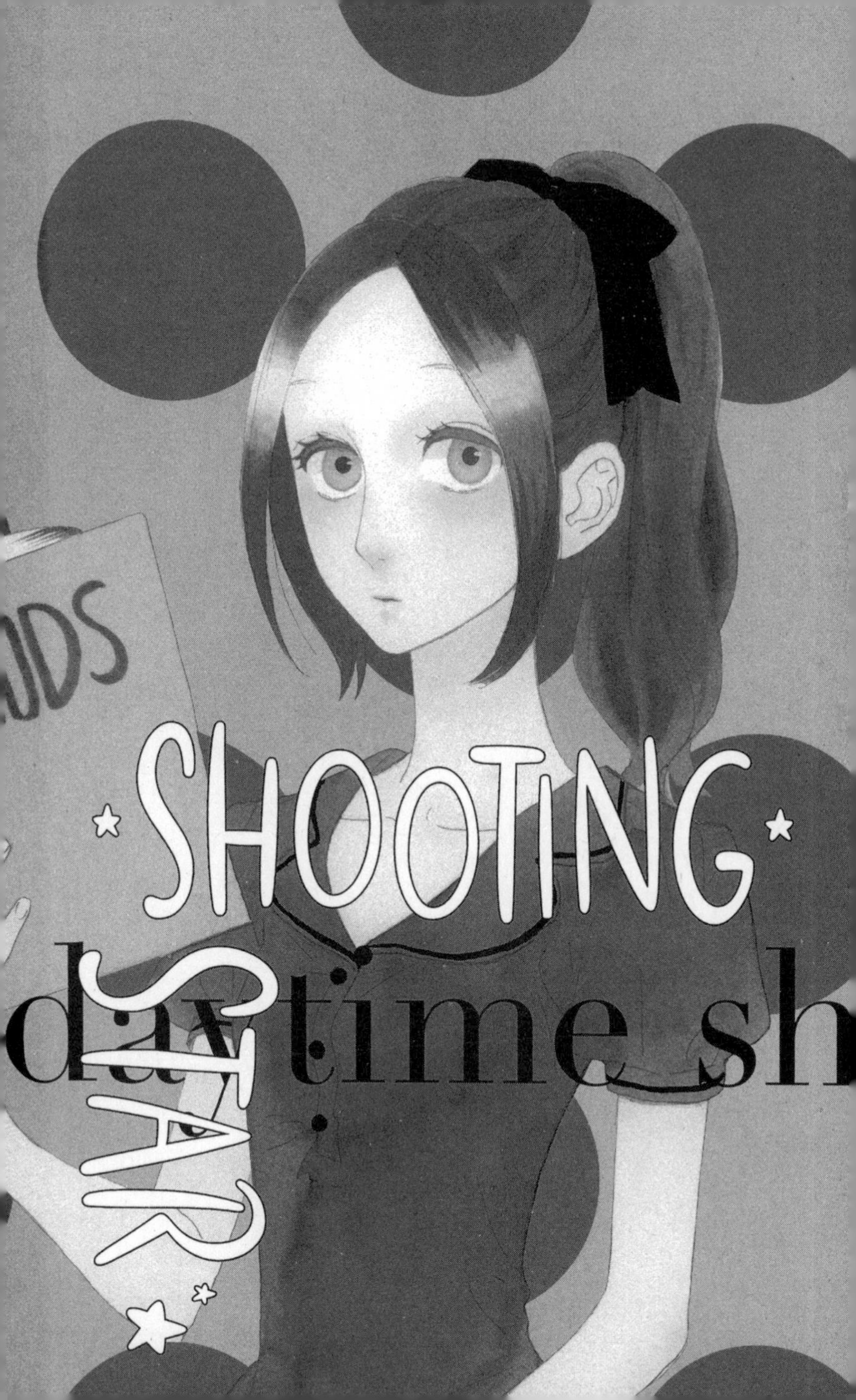
SHOOTING STAR
daytime sh

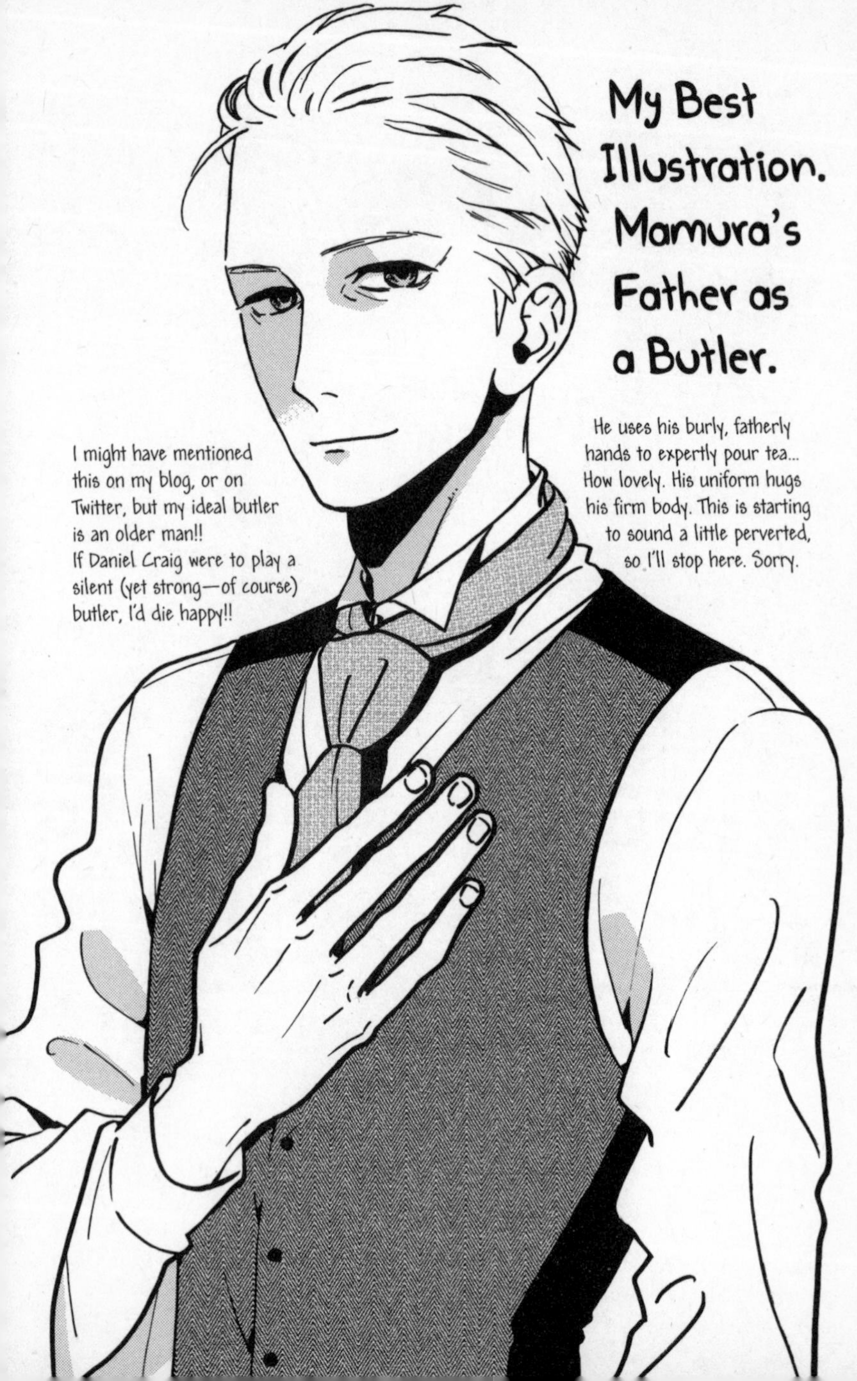
My Best Illustration. Mamura's Father as a Butler.
He uses his burly, fatherly hands to expertly pour tea... How lovely. His uniform hugs his firm body. This is starting to sound a little perverted, so I'll stop here. Sorry.
I might have mentioned this on my blog, or on Twitter, but my ideal butler is an older man!! If Daniel Craig were to play a silent (yet strong—of course) butler, I'd die happy!!

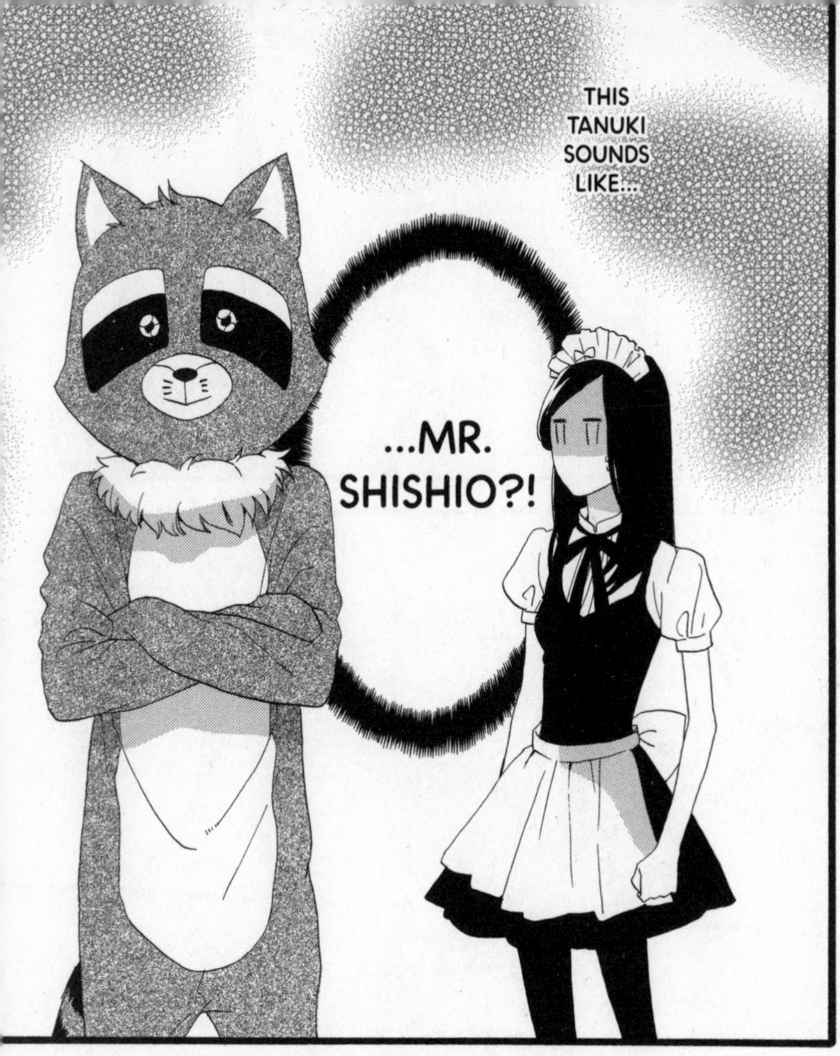
THIS TANUKI SOUNDS LIKE...
...MR. SHISHIO?!

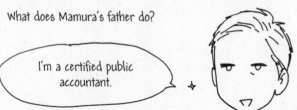

What does Mamura's father do?

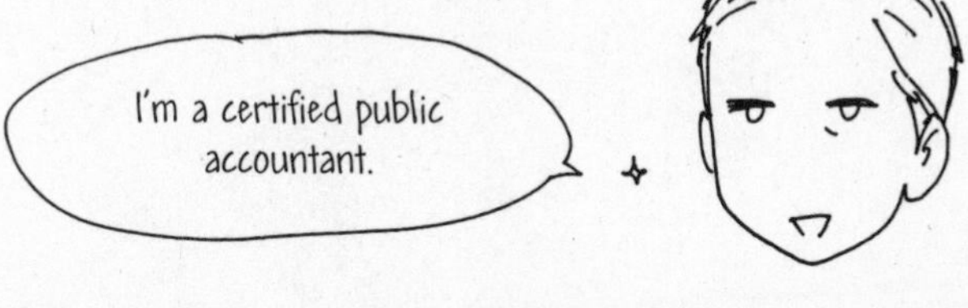
I'm a certified public accountant.

Seems about right.

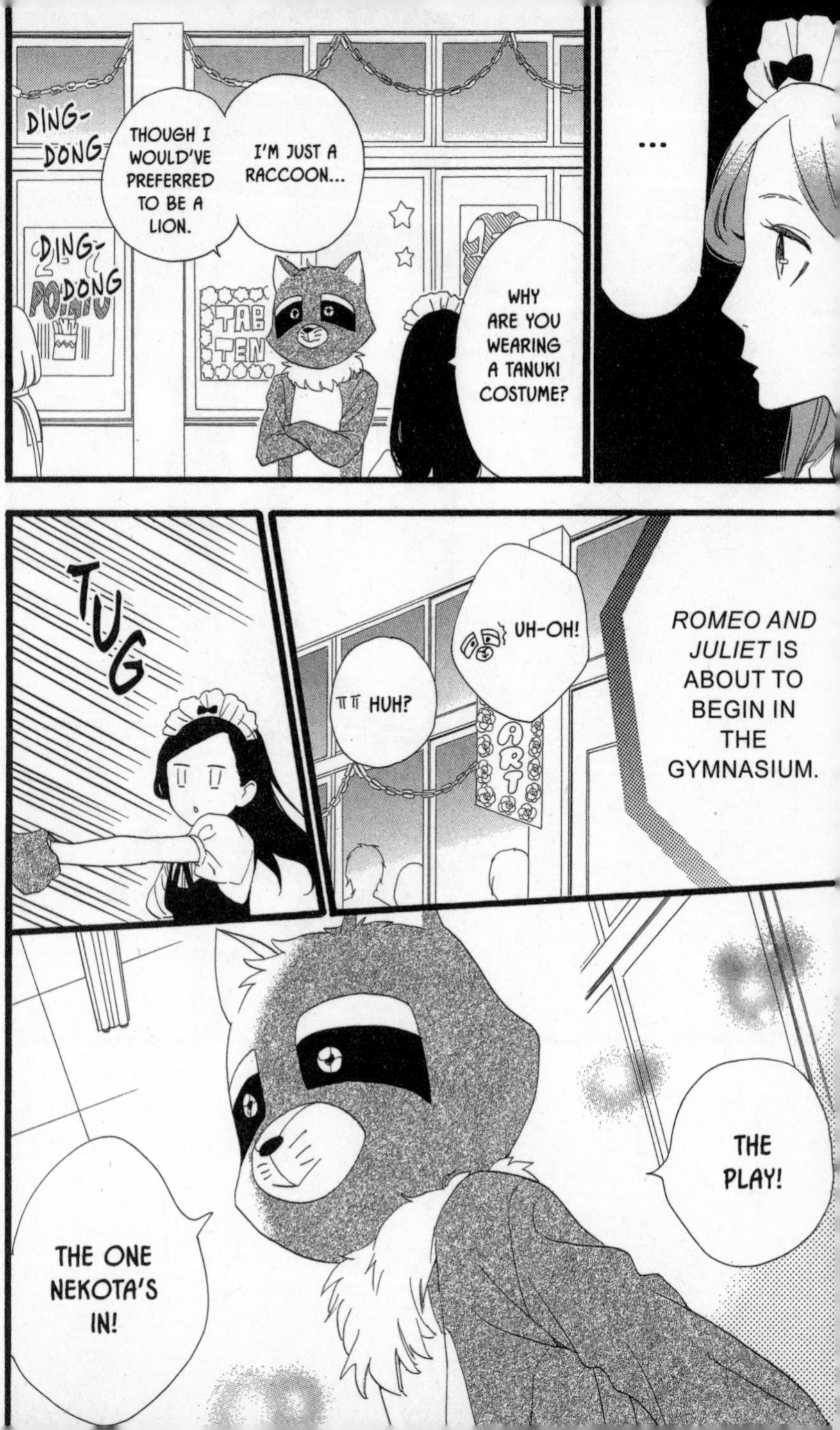
...
WHY ARE YOU WEARING A TANUKI COSTUME?
I'M JUST A RACCOON...
THOUGH I WOULD'VE PREFERRED TO BE A LION.
TAB TEN
DING-DONG
DING-DONG
*ROMEO AND JULIET* IS ABOUT TO BEGIN IN THE GYMNASIUM.
UH-OH!
ART
HUH?
TUG
THE PLAY!
THE ONE NEKOTA'S IN!

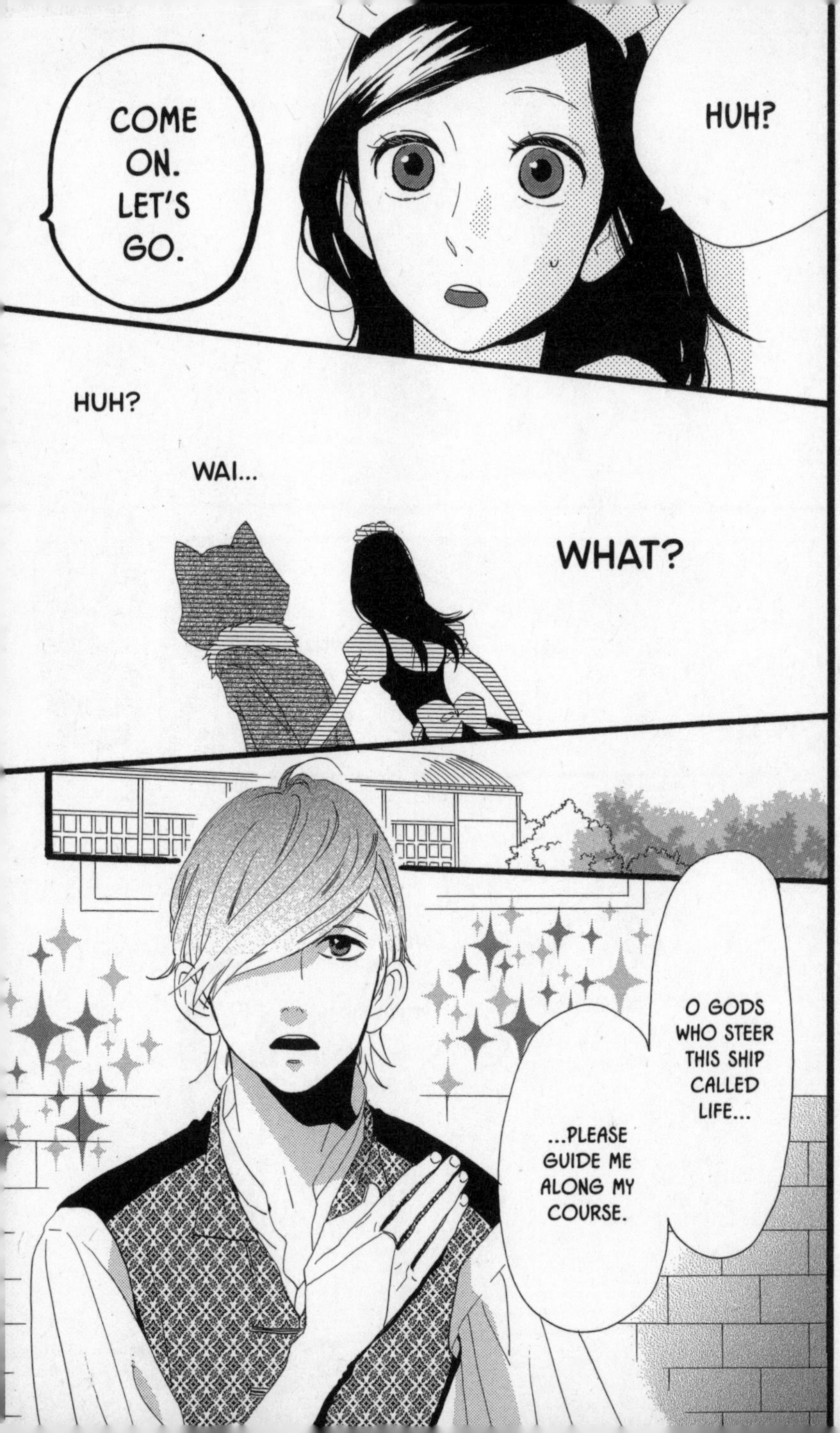
HUH?
COME ON. LET'S GO.
HUH?
WAI...
WHAT?
O GODS WHO STEER THIS SHIP CALLED LIFE...
...PLEASE GUIDE ME ALONG MY COURSE.

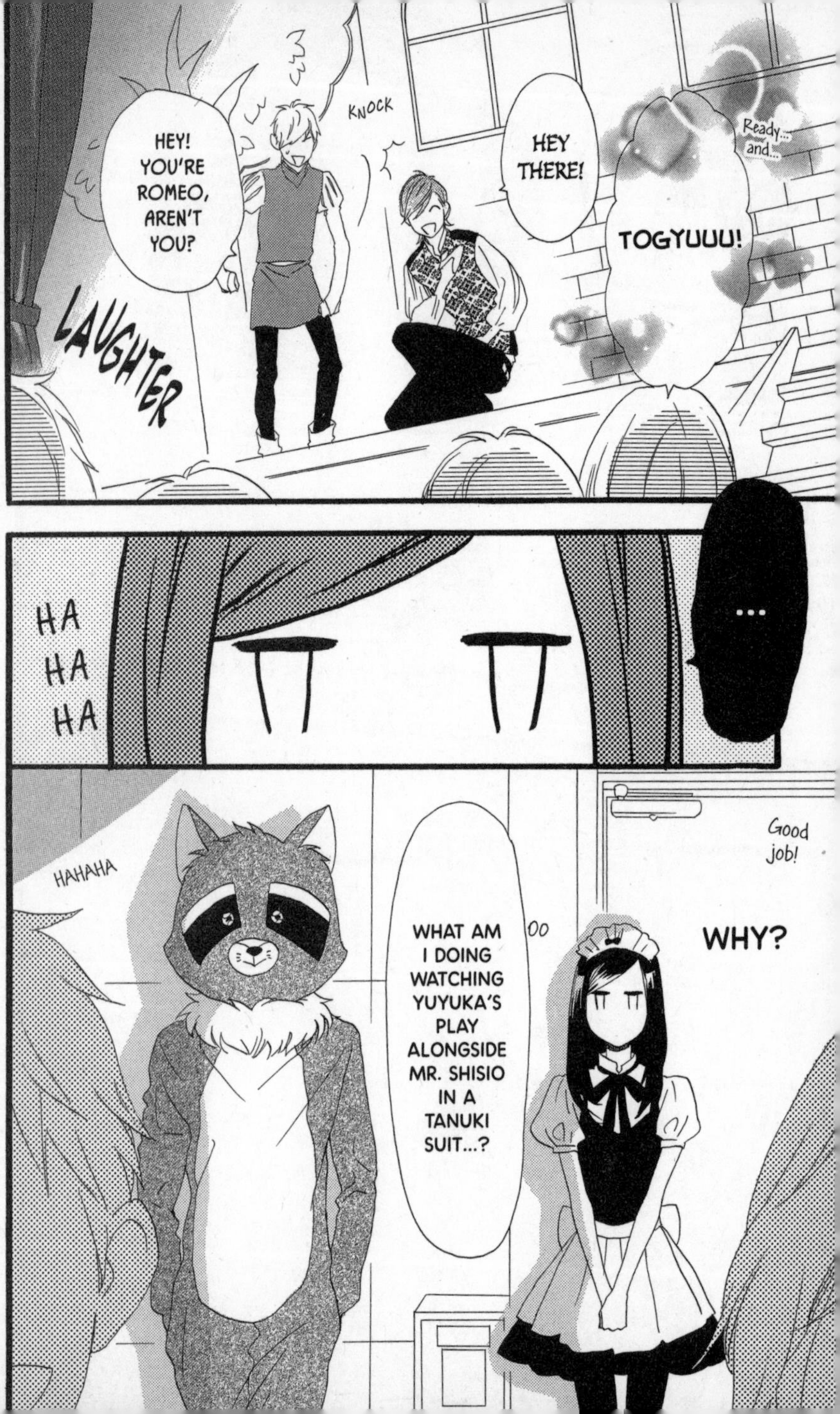
Ready... and...
TOGYUUU!
HEY THERE!
KNOCK
HEY! YOU'RE ROMEO, AREN'T YOU?
LAUGHTER
...
HA HA HA
Good job!
WHY?
WHAT AM I DOING WATCHING YUYUKA'S PLAY ALONGSIDE MR. SHISIO IN A TANUKI SUIT...?
HAHAHA

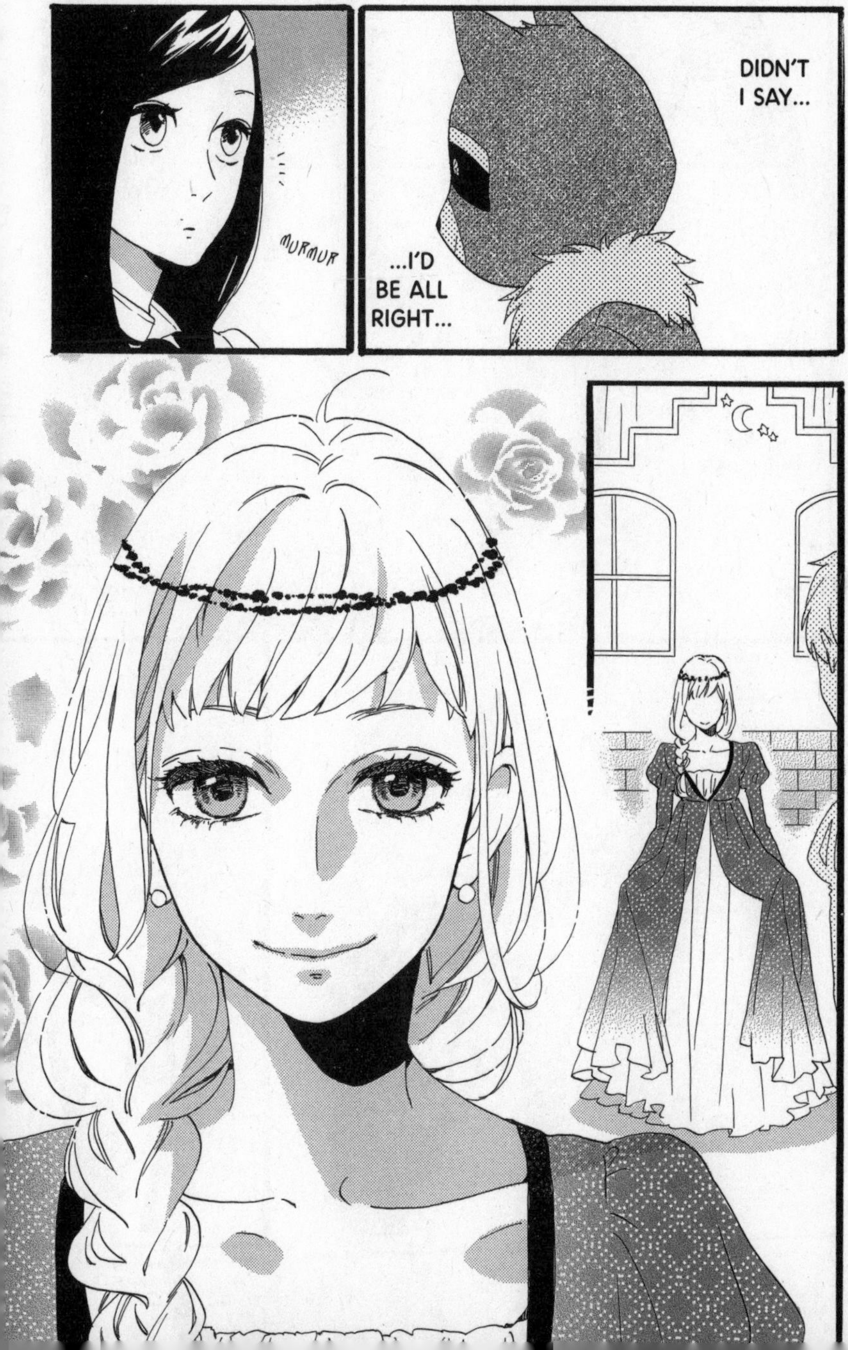
DIDN'T I SAY...
...I'D BE ALL RIGHT...
MURMUR

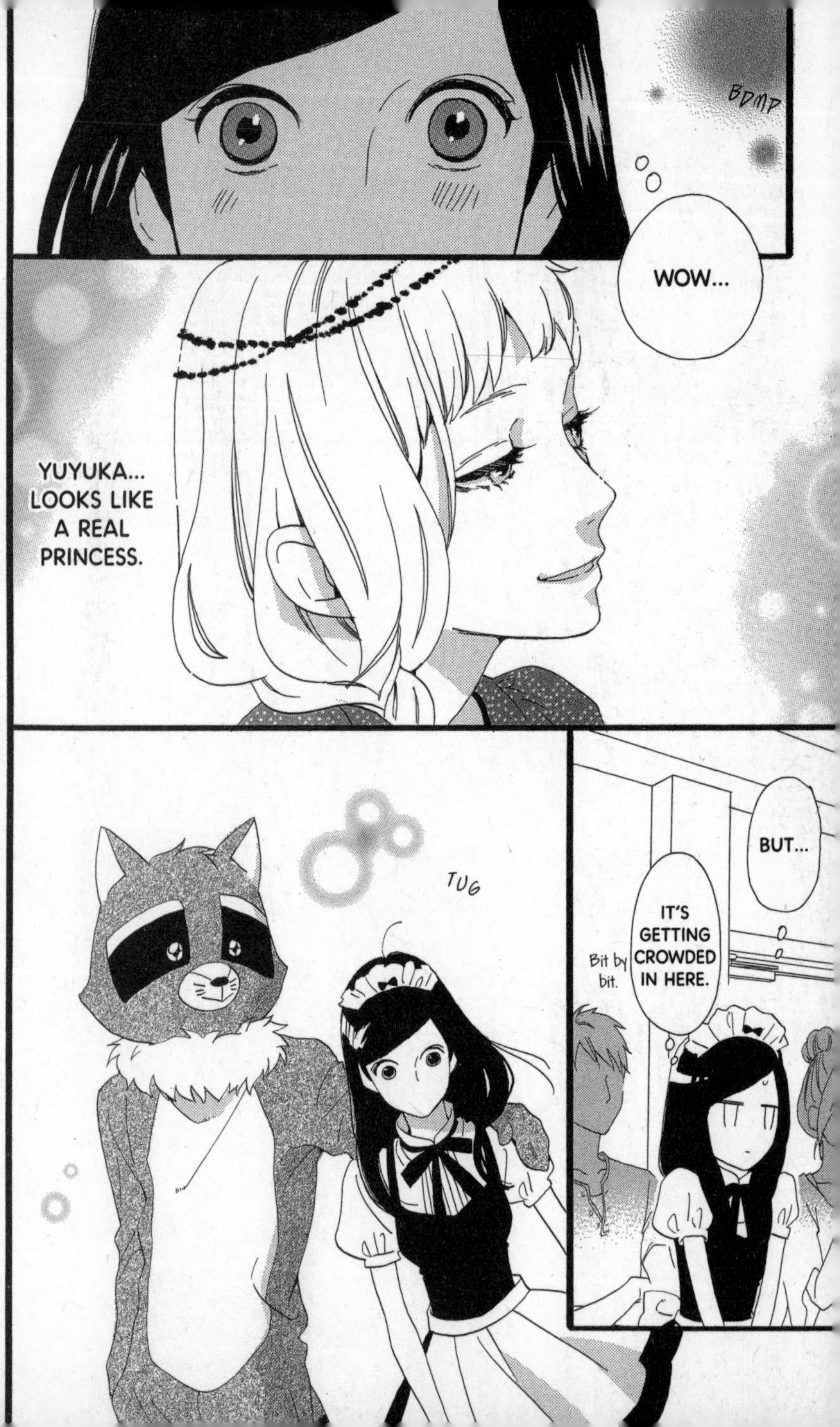
BDMP
WOW...
YUYUKA... LOOKS LIKE A REAL PRINCESS.
BUT...
IT'S GETTING CROWDED IN HERE.
Bit by bit.
TUG

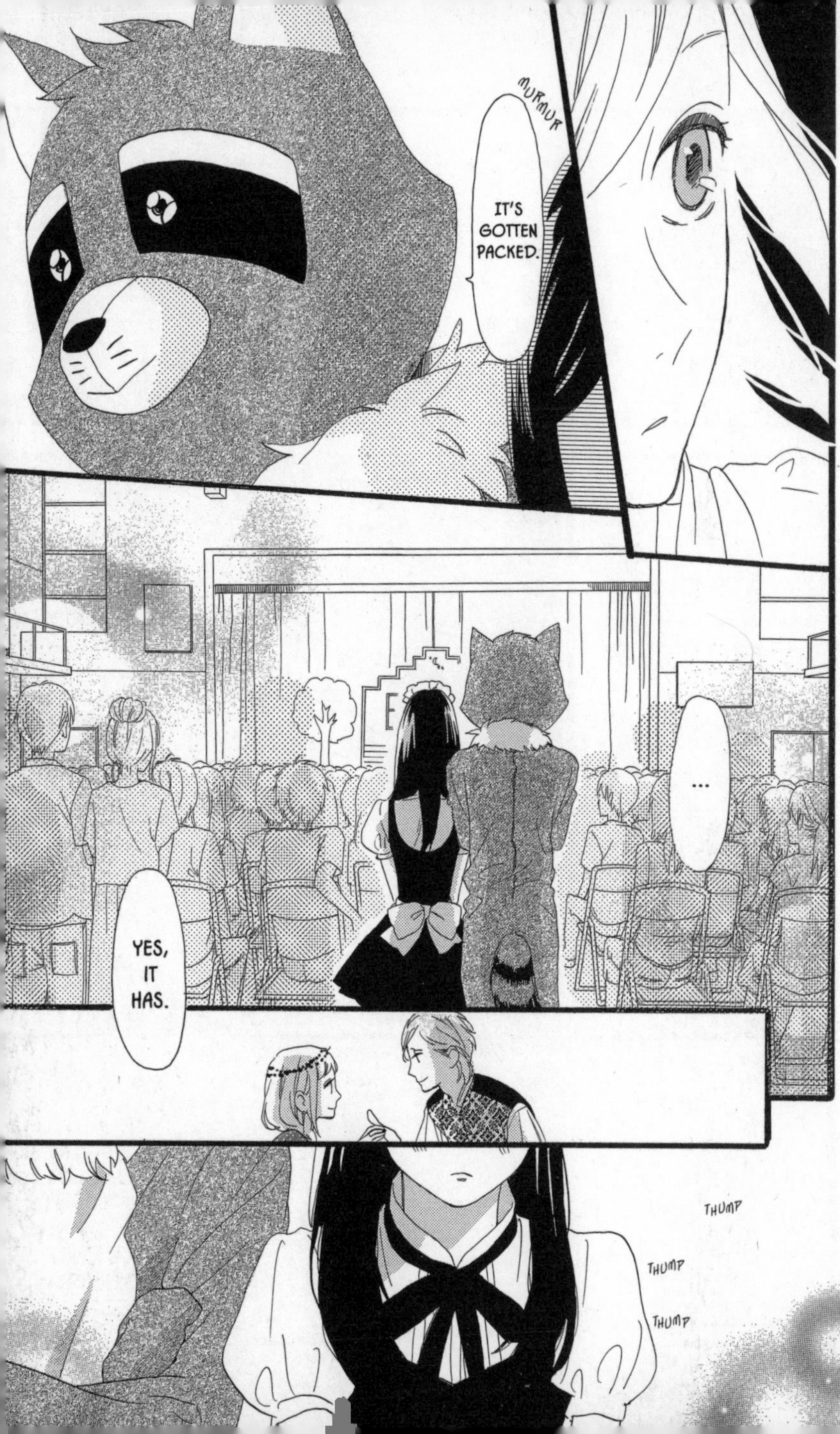

MURMUR
IT'S GOTTEN PACKED.
...
YES, IT HAS.
THUMP
THUMP
THUMP

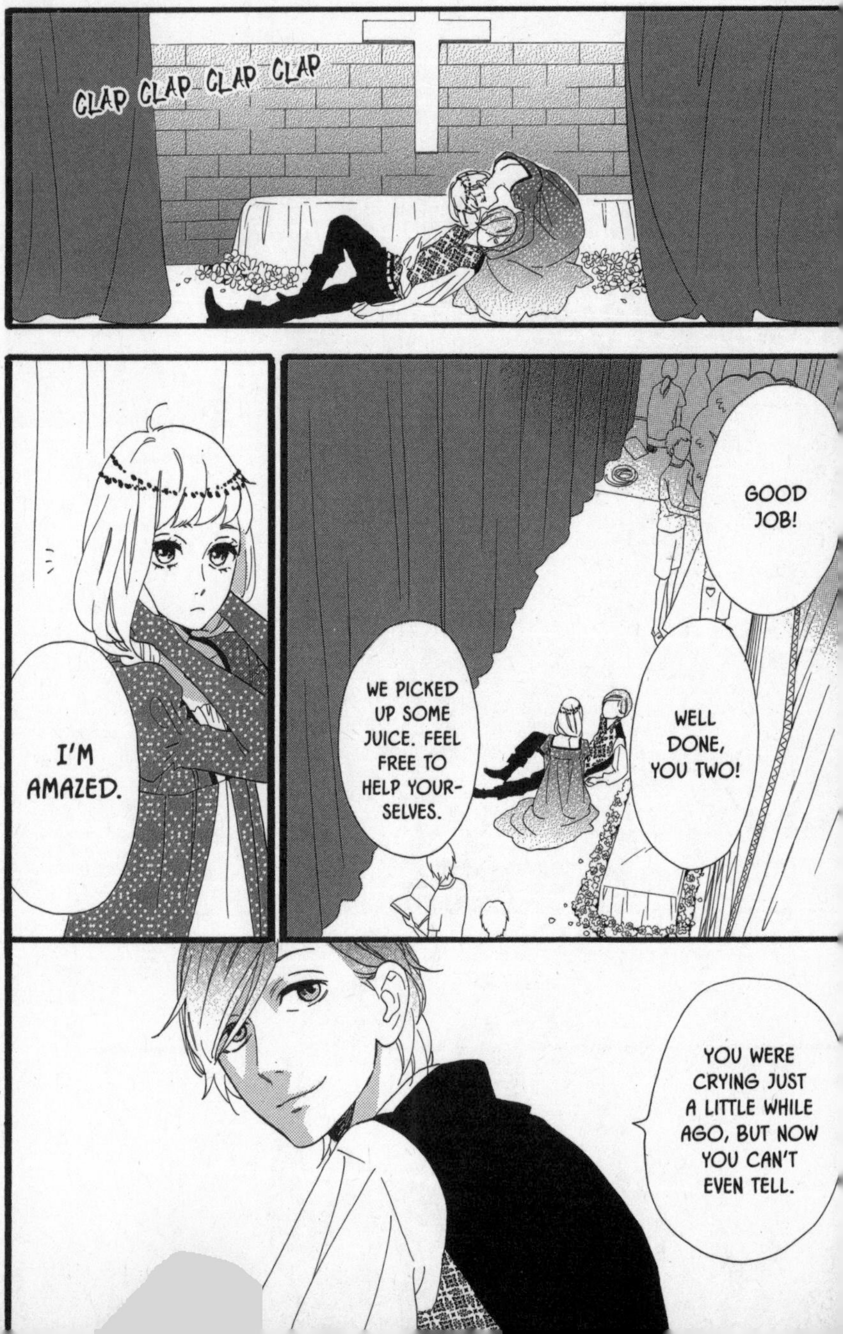
CLAP CLAP CLAP CLAP
GOOD JOB!
WELL DONE, YOU TWO!
WE PICKED UP SOME JUICE. FEEL FREE TO HELP YOUR-SELVES.
I'M AMAZED.
YOU WERE CRYING JUST A LITTLE WHILE AGO, BUT NOW YOU CAN'T EVEN TELL.

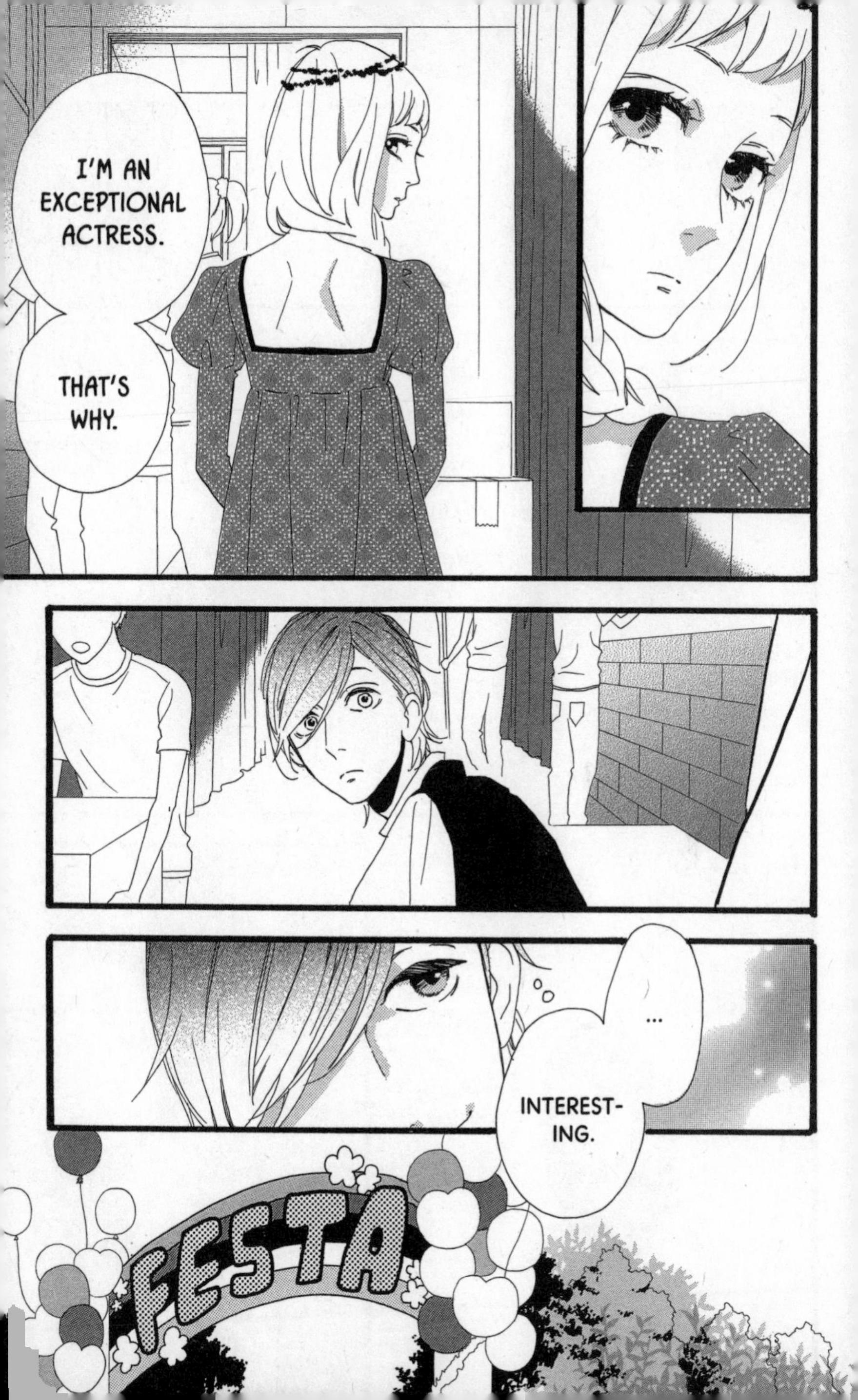
I'M AN EXCEPTIONAL ACTRESS.
THAT'S WHY.
...
INTERESTING.
FESTA

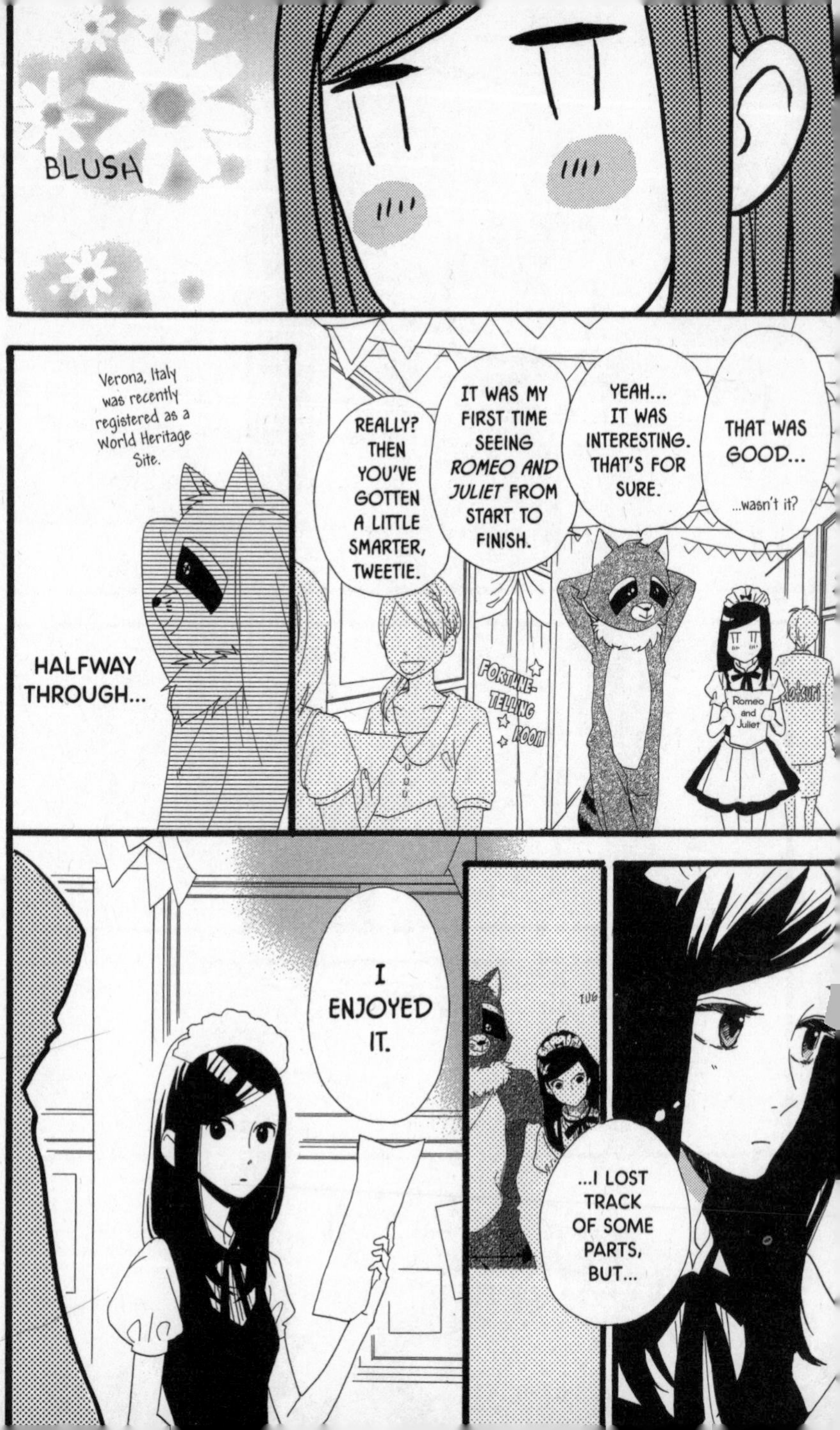
BLUSH
THAT WAS GOOD...
...wasn't it?
YEAH... IT WAS INTERESTING. THAT'S FOR SURE.
IT WAS MY FIRST TIME SEEING *ROMEO AND JULIET* FROM START TO FINISH.
REALLY? THEN YOU'VE GOTTEN A LITTLE SMARTER, TWEETIE.
Romeo and Juliet
FORTUNE-TELLING ROOM
Verona, Italy was recently registered as a World Heritage Site.
HALFWAY THROUGH...
TUG
...I LOST TRACK OF SOME PARTS, BUT...
I ENJOYED IT.

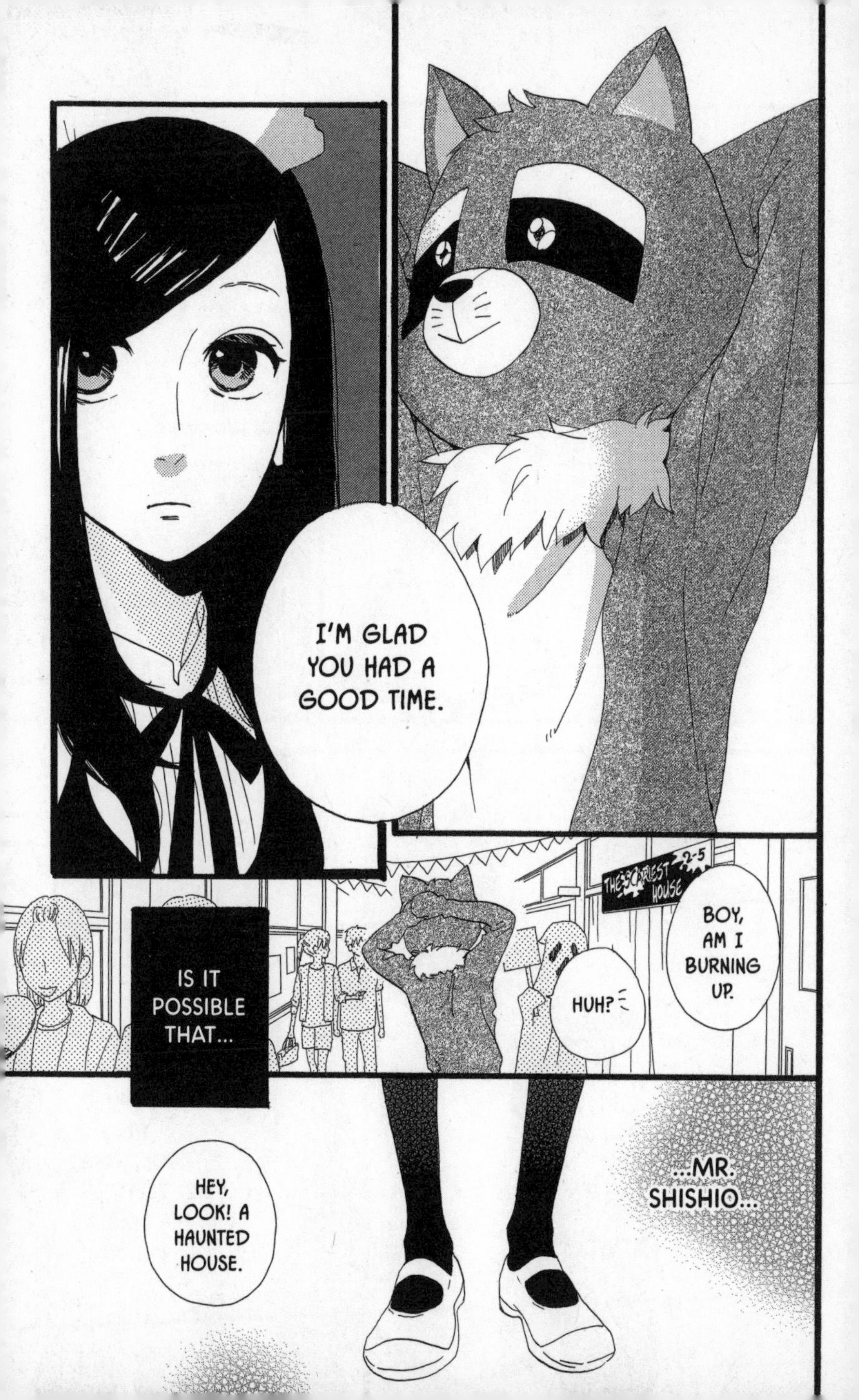
I'M GLAD YOU HAD A GOOD TIME.
2-5
HOUSE
BOY, AM I BURNING UP.
HUH?
IS IT POSSIBLE THAT...
...MR. SHISHIO...
HEY, LOOK! A HAUNTED HOUSE.

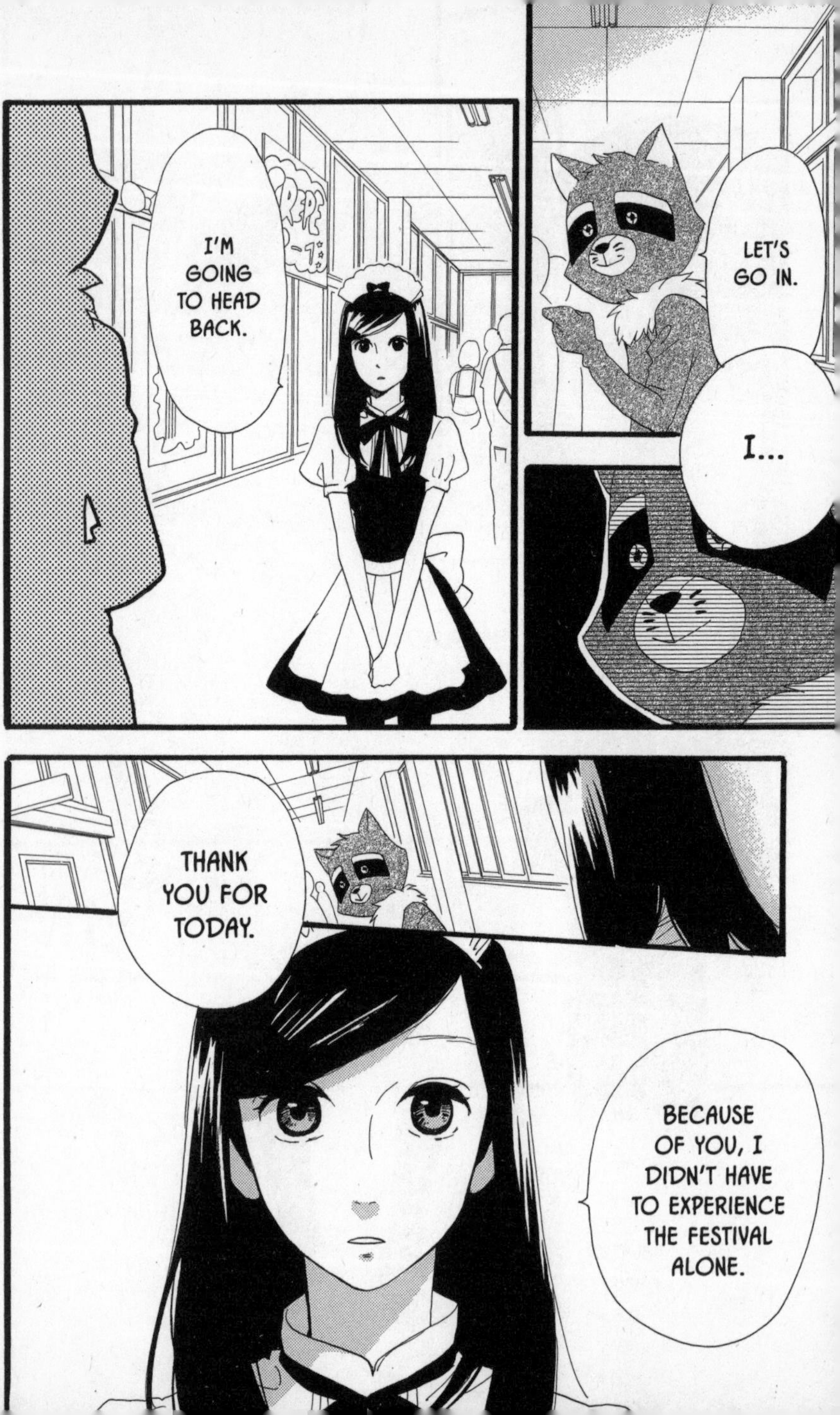
LET'S GO IN.
I...
I'M GOING TO HEAD BACK.
THANK YOU FOR TODAY.
BECAUSE OF YOU, I DIDN'T HAVE TO EXPERIENCE THE FESTIVAL ALONE.

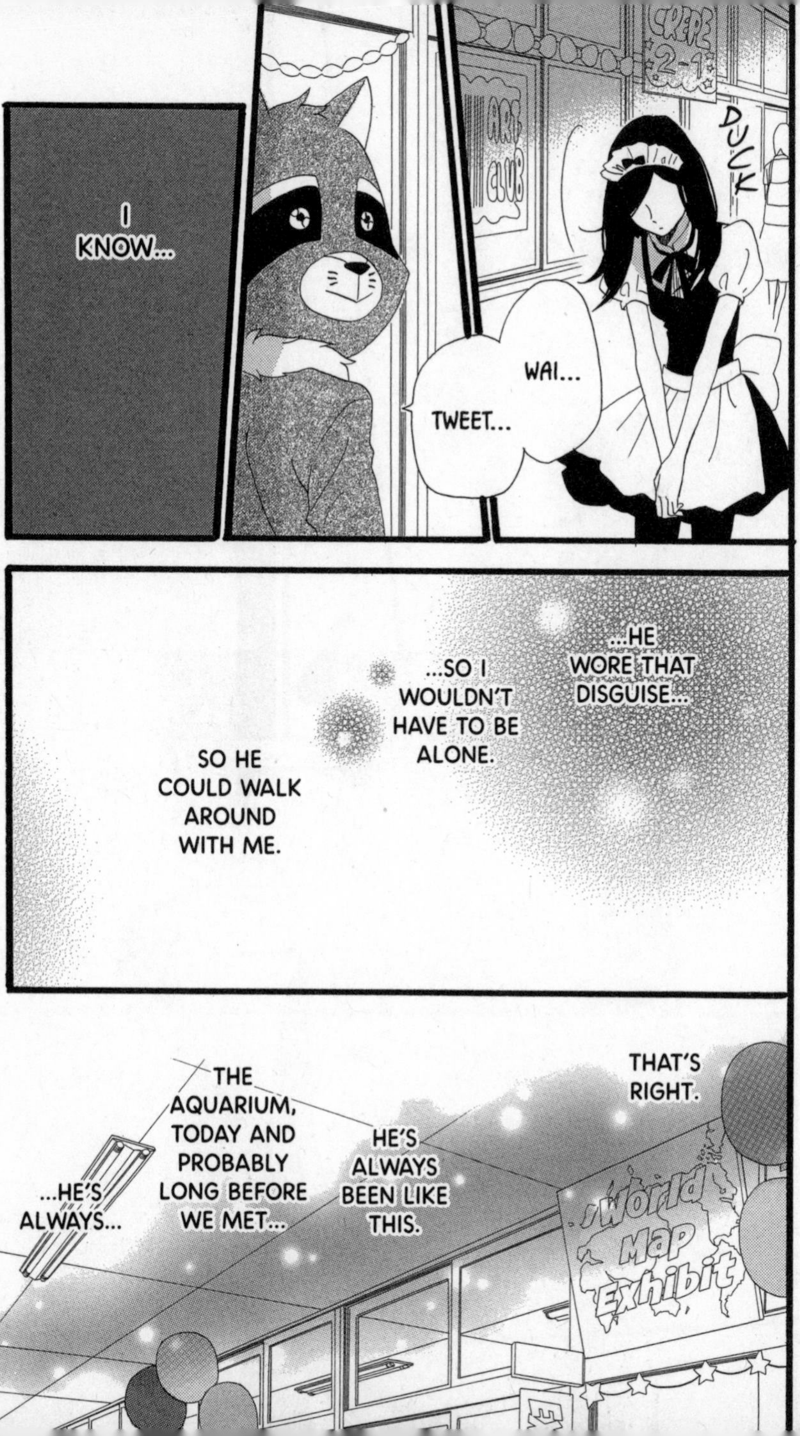
CREPE 2-1
ART CLUB
DUCK
WAI... TWEET...
I KNOW...
...HE WORE THAT DISGUISE...
...SO I WOULDN'T HAVE TO BE ALONE.
SO HE COULD WALK AROUND WITH ME.
THAT'S RIGHT.
HE'S ALWAYS BEEN LIKE THIS.
THE AQUARIUM, TODAY AND PROBABLY LONG BEFORE WE MET...
...HE'S ALWAYS...
World Map Exhibit

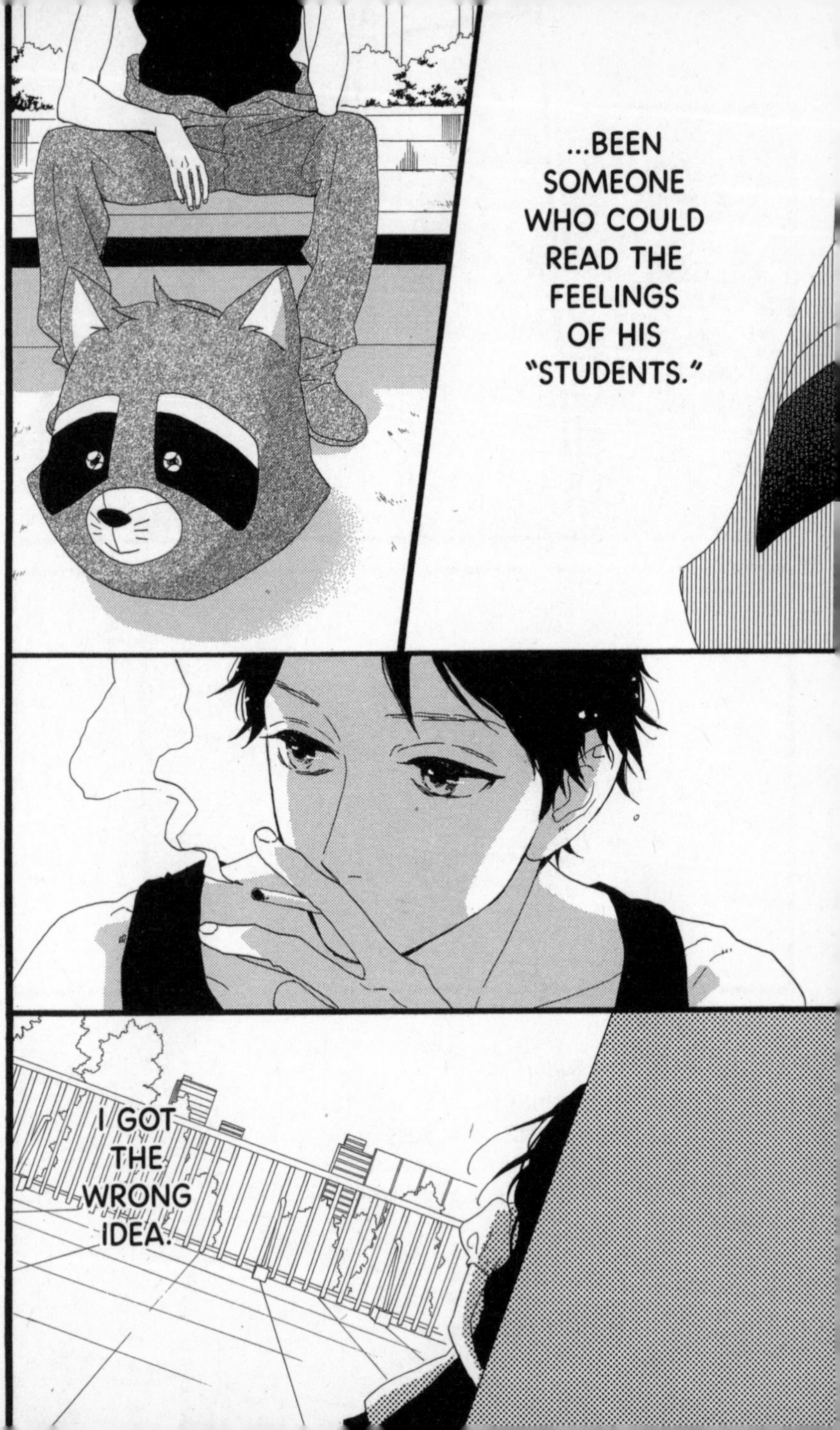
...BEEN SOMEONE WHO COULD READ THE FEELINGS OF HIS "STUDENTS."
I GOT THE WRONG IDEA.

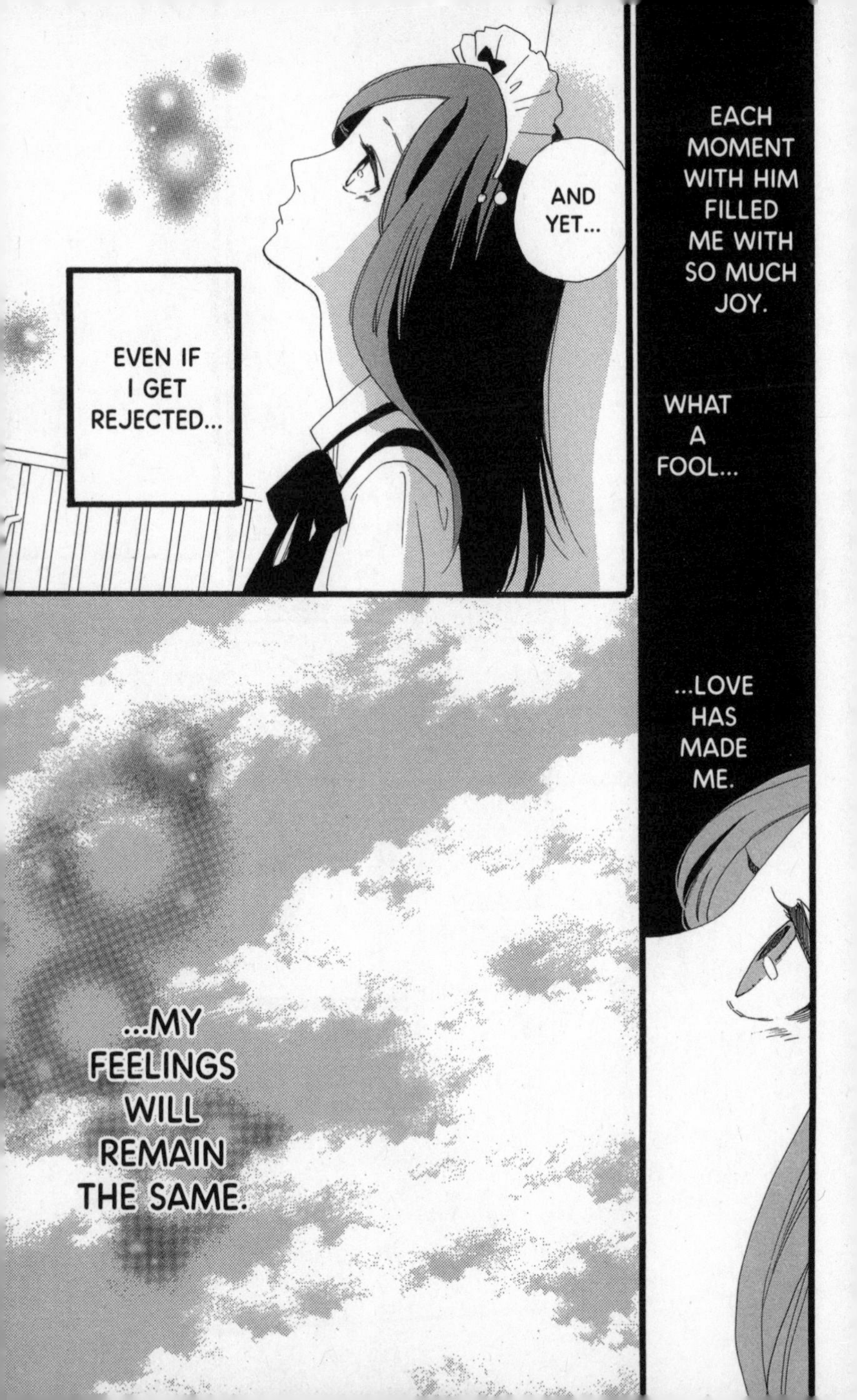
EACH MOMENT WITH HIM FILLED ME WITH SO MUCH JOY.
WHAT A FOOL...
...LOVE HAS MADE ME.
AND YET...
EVEN IF I GET REJECTED...
...MY FEELINGS WILL REMAIN THE SAME.

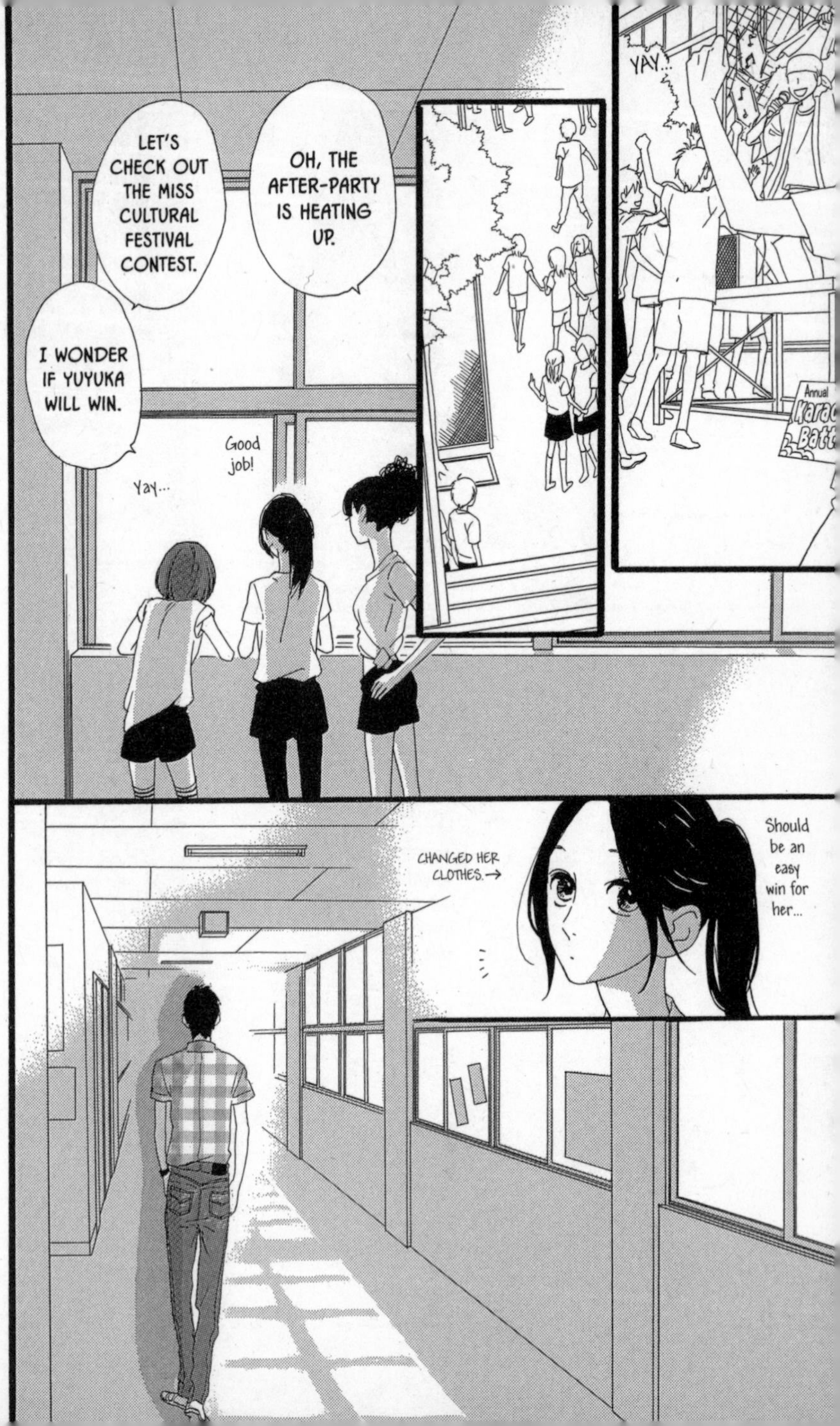

YAY...
Annual
OH, THE AFTER-PARTY IS HEATING UP.
LET'S CHECK OUT THE MISS CULTURAL FESTIVAL CONTEST.
I WONDER IF YUYUKA WILL WIN.
Good job!
Yay...
Should be an easy win for her...
CHANGED HER CLOTHES.→

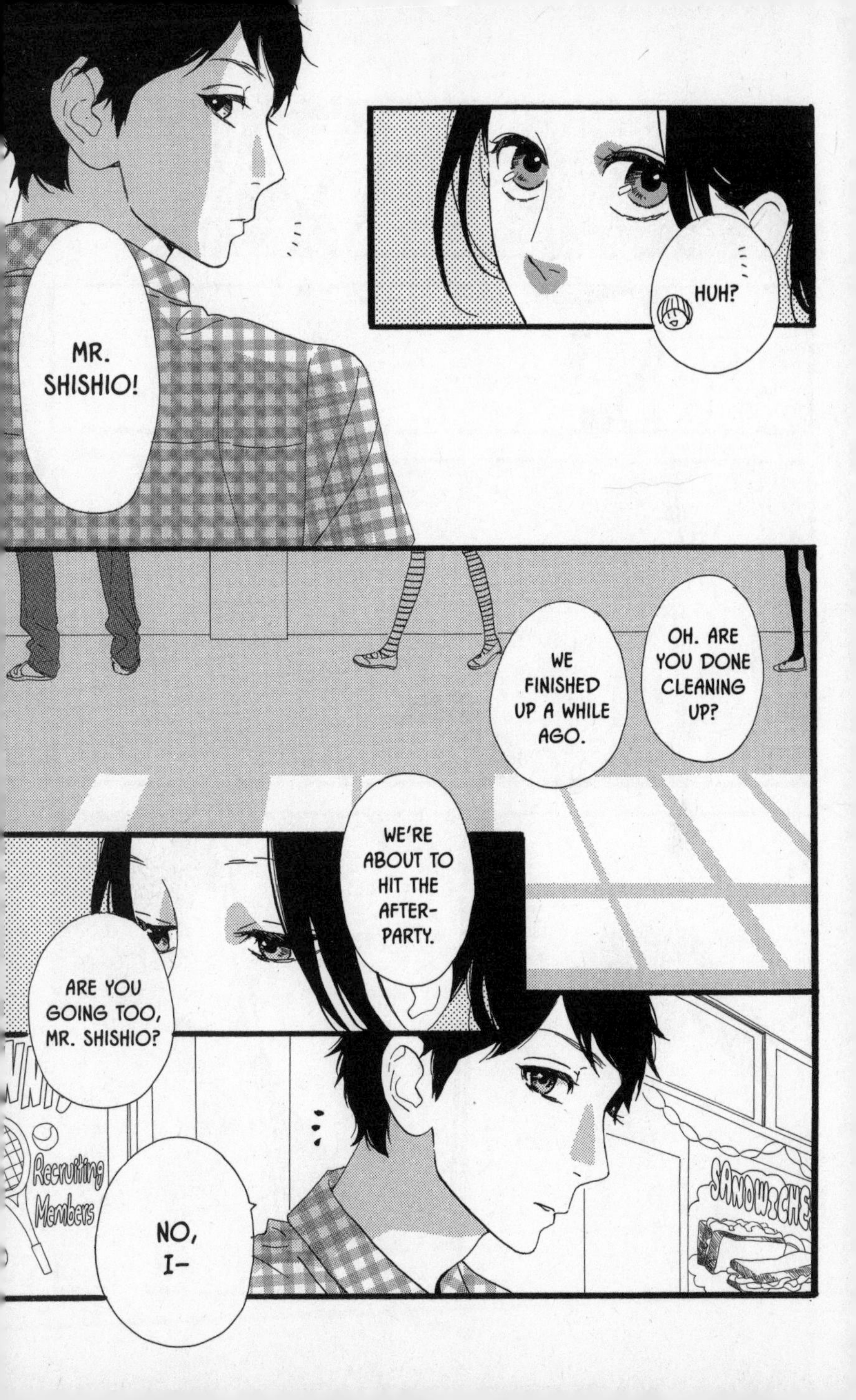
HUH?
MR. SHISHIO!
OH. ARE YOU DONE CLEANING UP?
WE FINISHED UP A WHILE AGO.
WE'RE ABOUT TO HIT THE AFTER-PARTY.
ARE YOU GOING TOO, MR. SHISHIO?
SANDWICHE
Recruiting Members
NO, I–

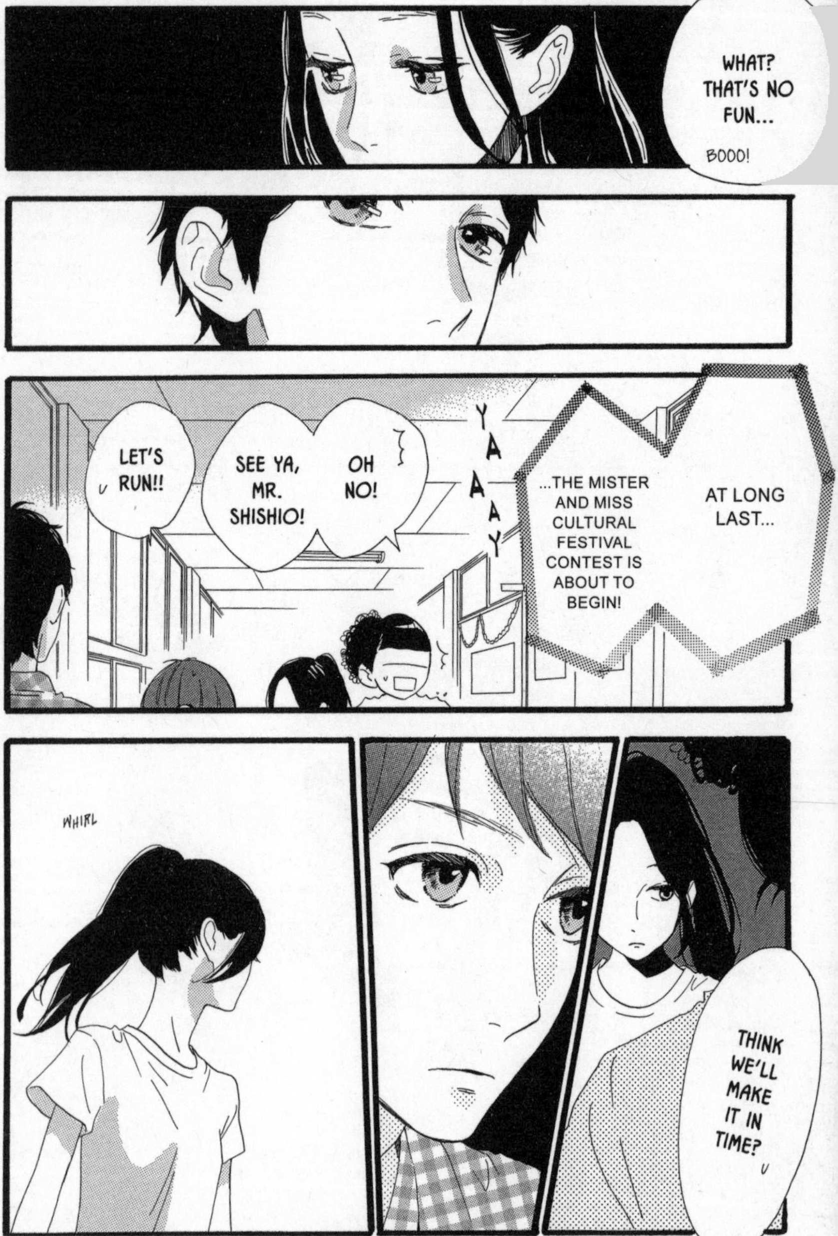
WHAT? THAT'S NO FUN...
BOOO!
AT LONG LAST...
...THE MISTER AND MISS CULTURAL FESTIVAL CONTEST IS ABOUT TO BEGIN!
YAAAY
OH NO!
SEE YA, MR. SHISHIO!
LET'S RUN!!
THINK WE'LL MAKE IT IN TIME?
WHIRL

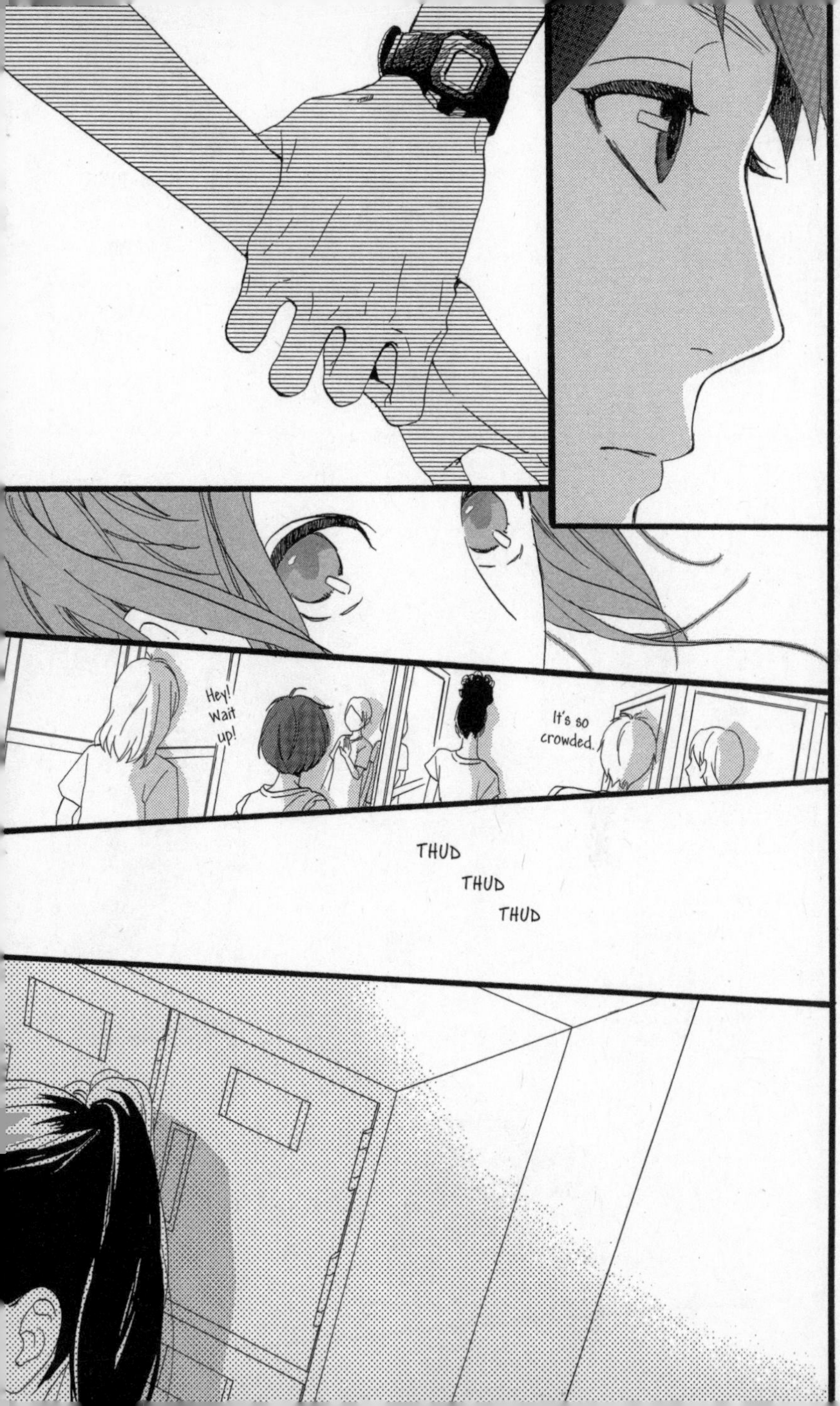
It's so crowded.
Hey! Wait up!
THUD
THUD
THUD

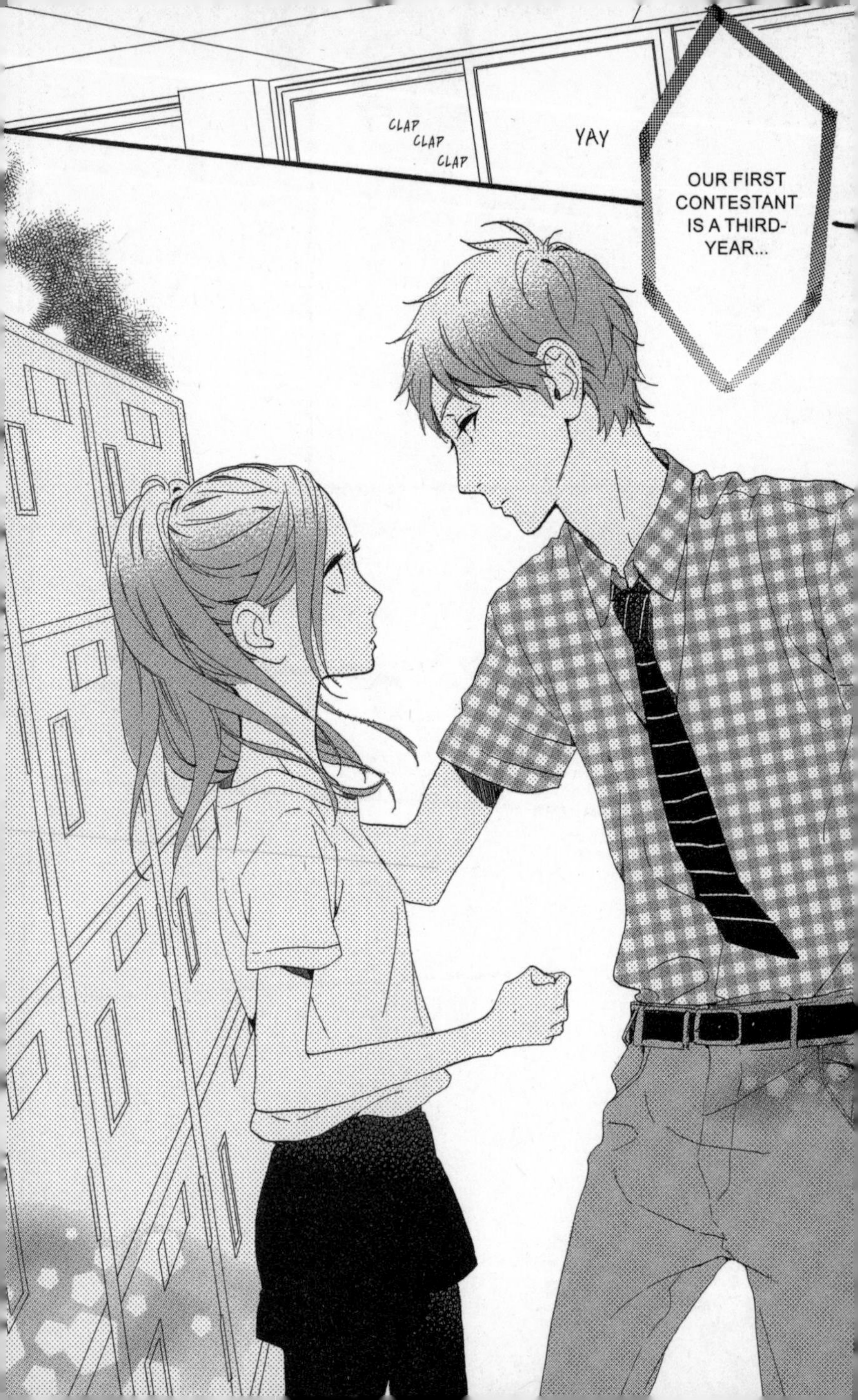
OUR FIRST CONTESTANT IS A THIRD-YEAR...
YAY
CLAP CLAP CLAP

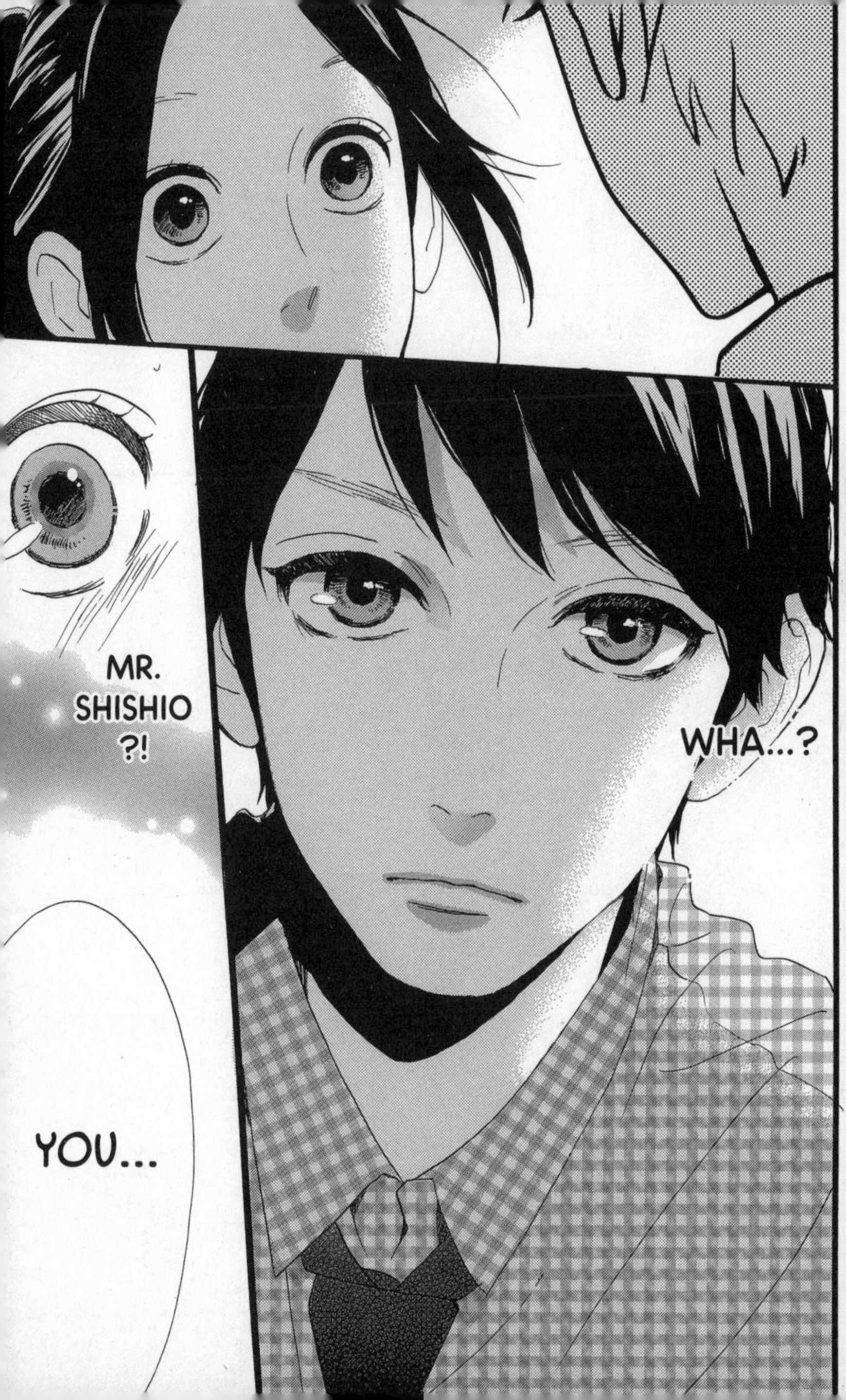
WHA...?
MR. SHISHIO ?!
YOU...

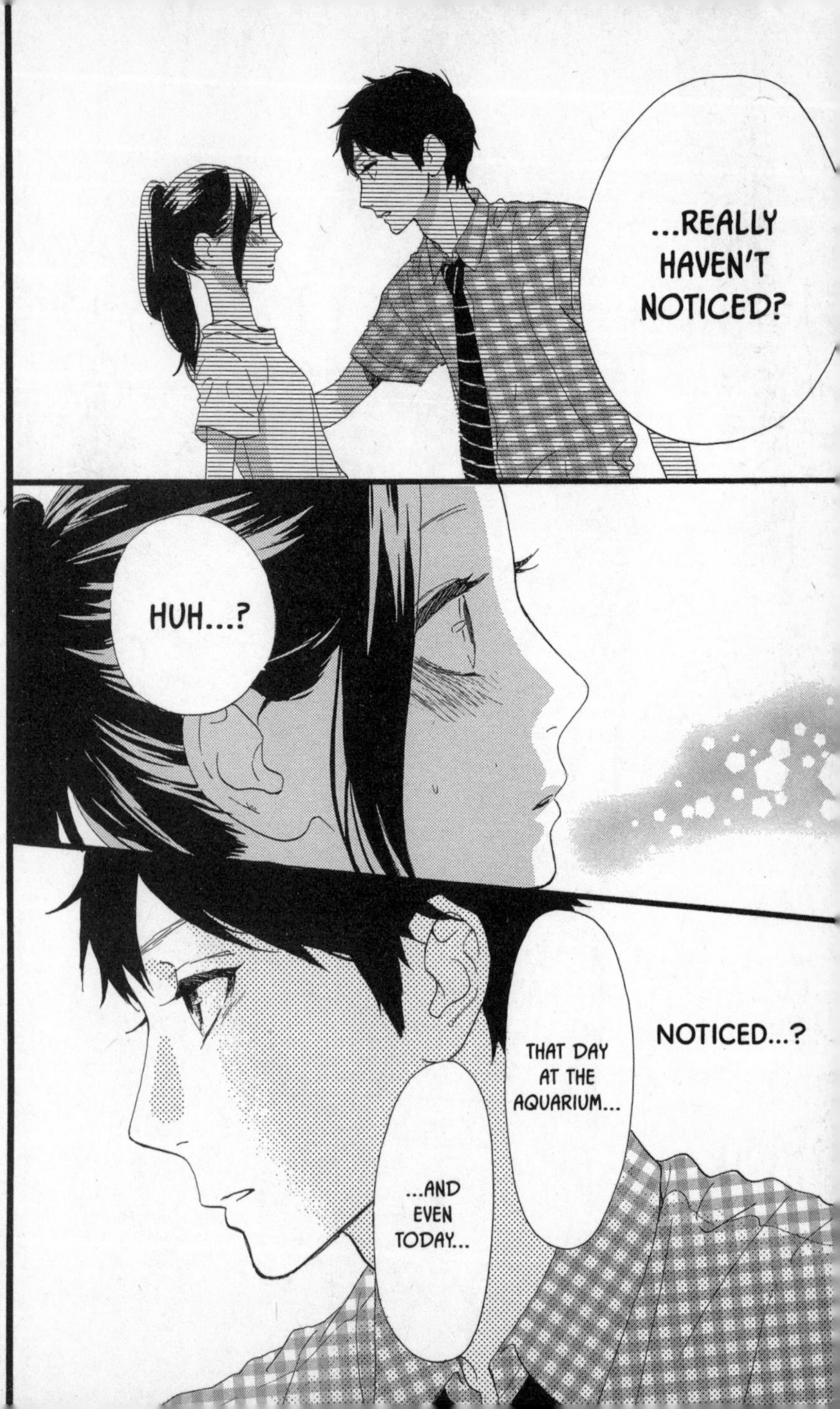
...REALLY HAVEN'T NOTICED?
HUH...?
NOTICED...?
THAT DAY AT THE AQUARIUM...
...AND EVEN TODAY...

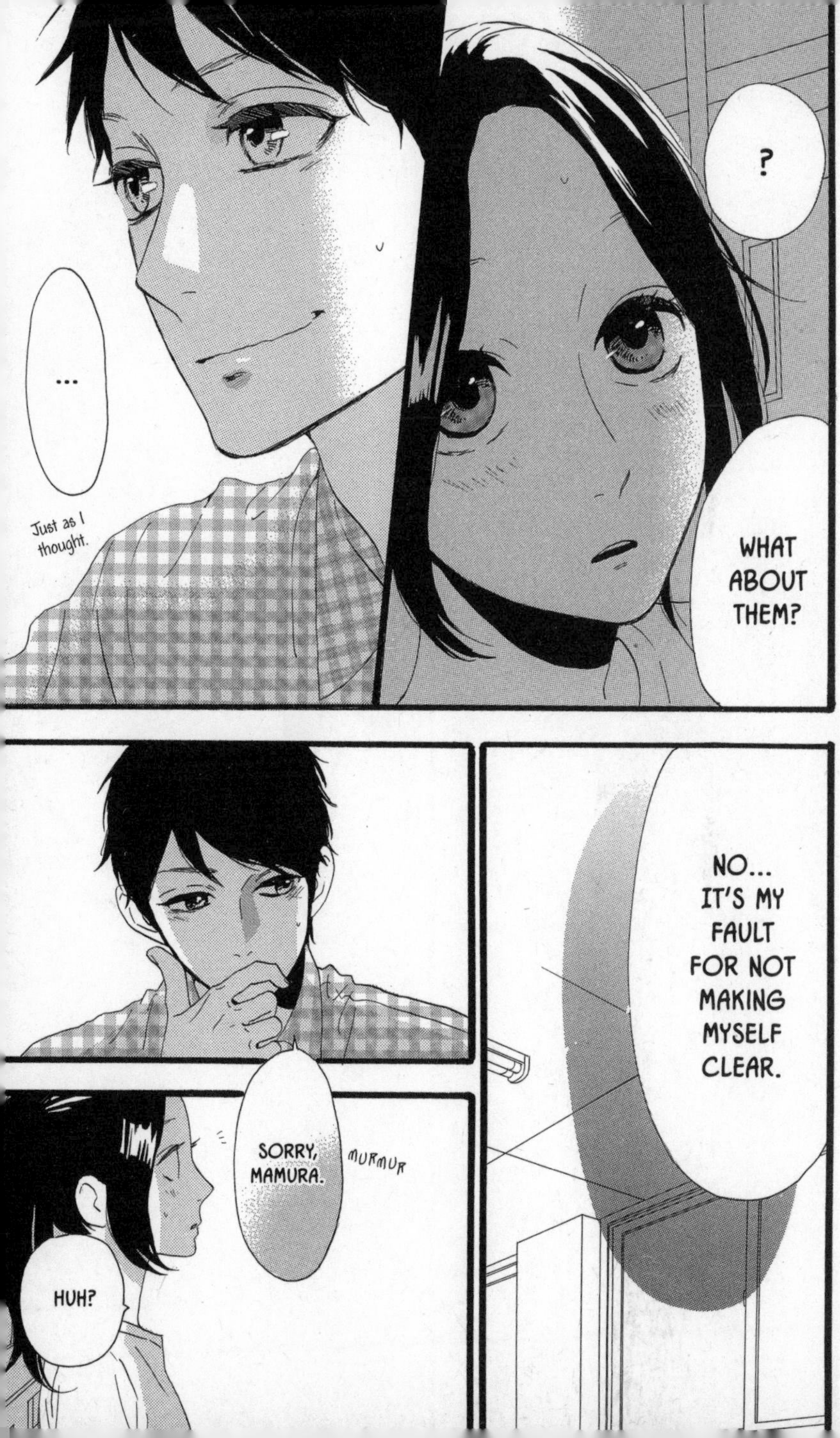
?
WHAT ABOUT THEM?
...
Just as I thought.
NO... IT'S MY FAULT FOR NOT MAKING MYSELF CLEAR.
SORRY, MAMURA.
MURMUR
HUH?

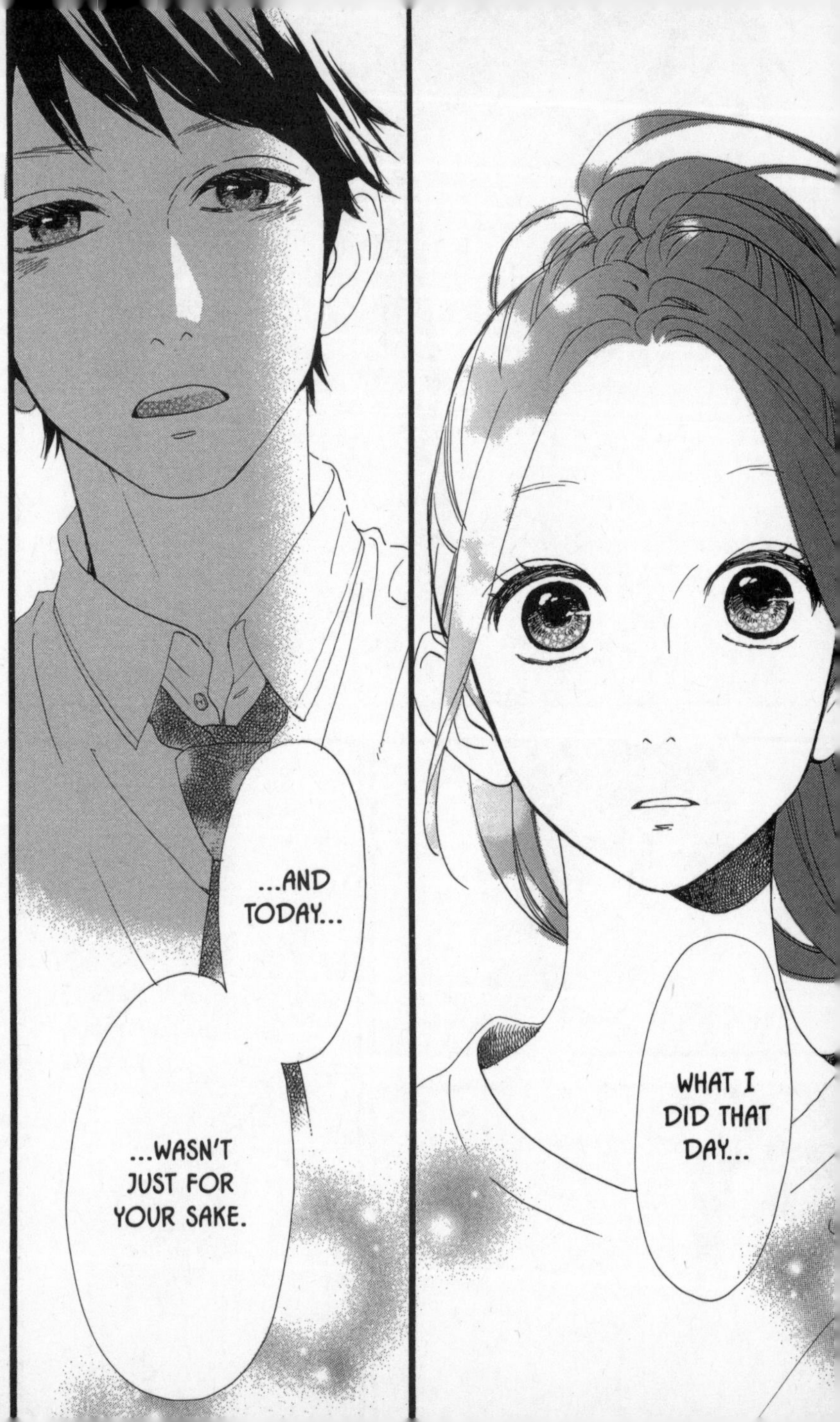
WHAT I DID THAT DAY...
...AND TODAY...
...WASN'T JUST FOR YOUR SAKE.

I WANTED...
...TO BE WITH YOU.

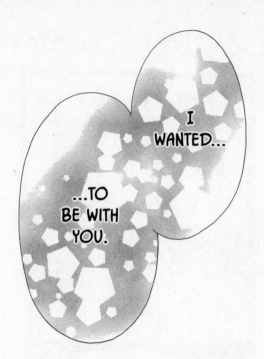

# Daytime Theater

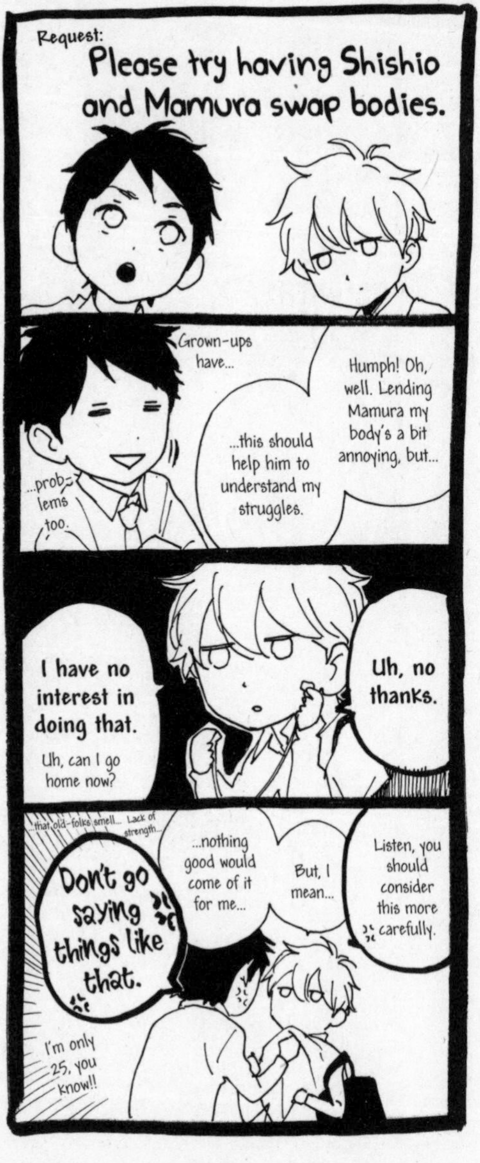
Request:
Please try having Shishio and Mamura swap bodies.
Humph! Oh, well. Lending Mamura my body's a bit annoying, but...
...this should help him to understand my struggles.
Grown-ups have...
...prob-lems too.
Uh, no thanks.
I have no interest in doing that.
Uh, can I go home now?
Listen, you should consider this more carefully.
But, I mean...
...nothing good would come of it for me...
...that old-folks smell... Lack of strength...
Don't go saying things like that.
I'm only 25, you know!!

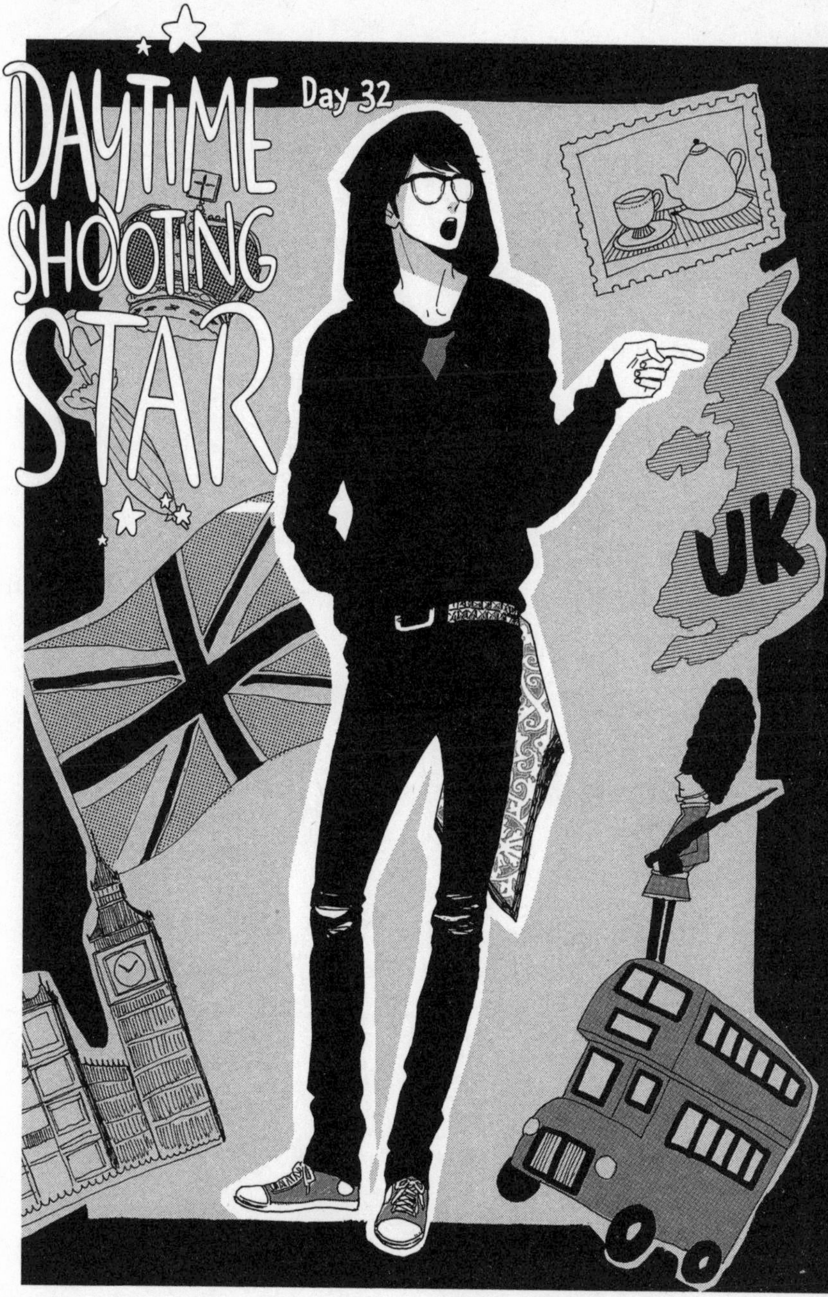
DAYTIME SHOOTING STAR
Day 32
UK

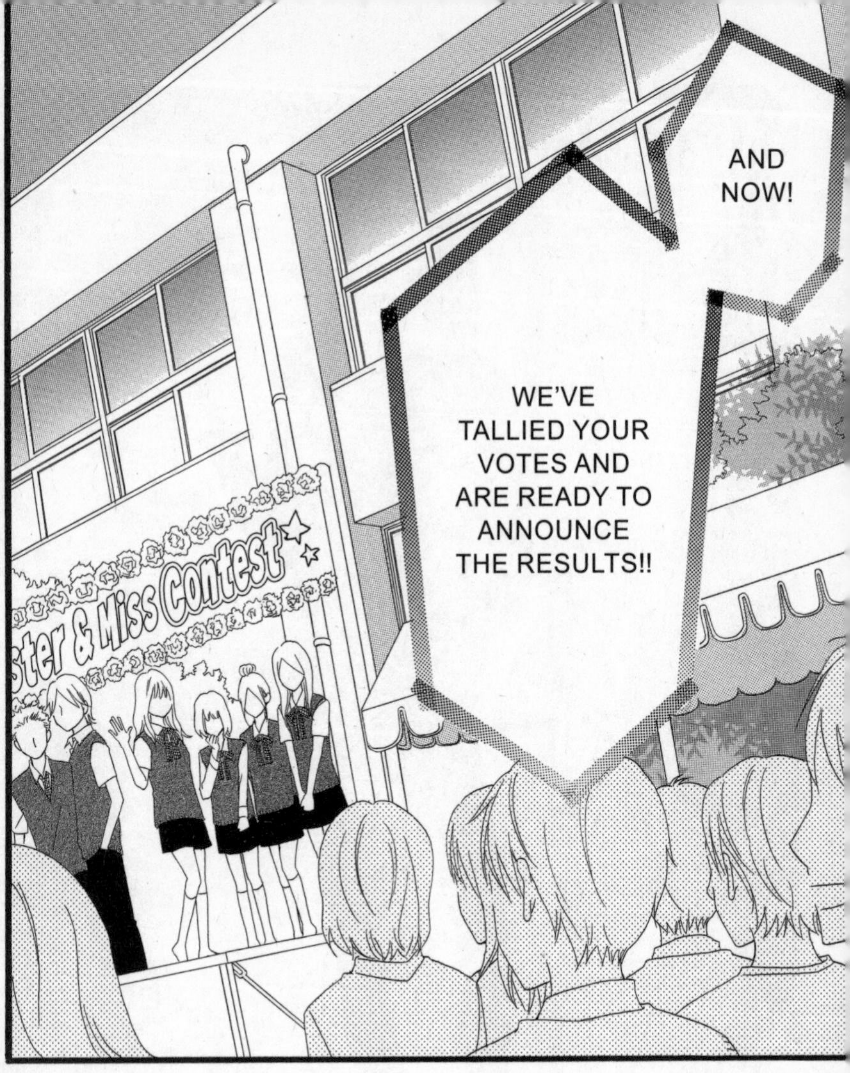
AND NOW!
WE'VE TALLIED YOUR VOTES AND ARE READY TO ANNOUNCE THE RESULTS!!
ster & Miss Contest

What kind of music do you listen to, Mamura?

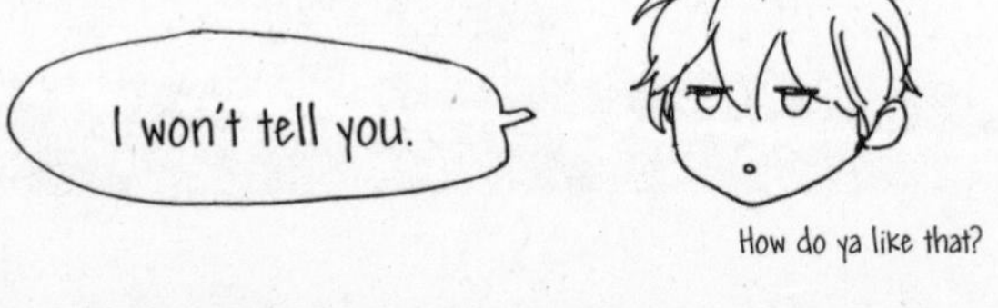
I won't tell you.

How do ya like that?

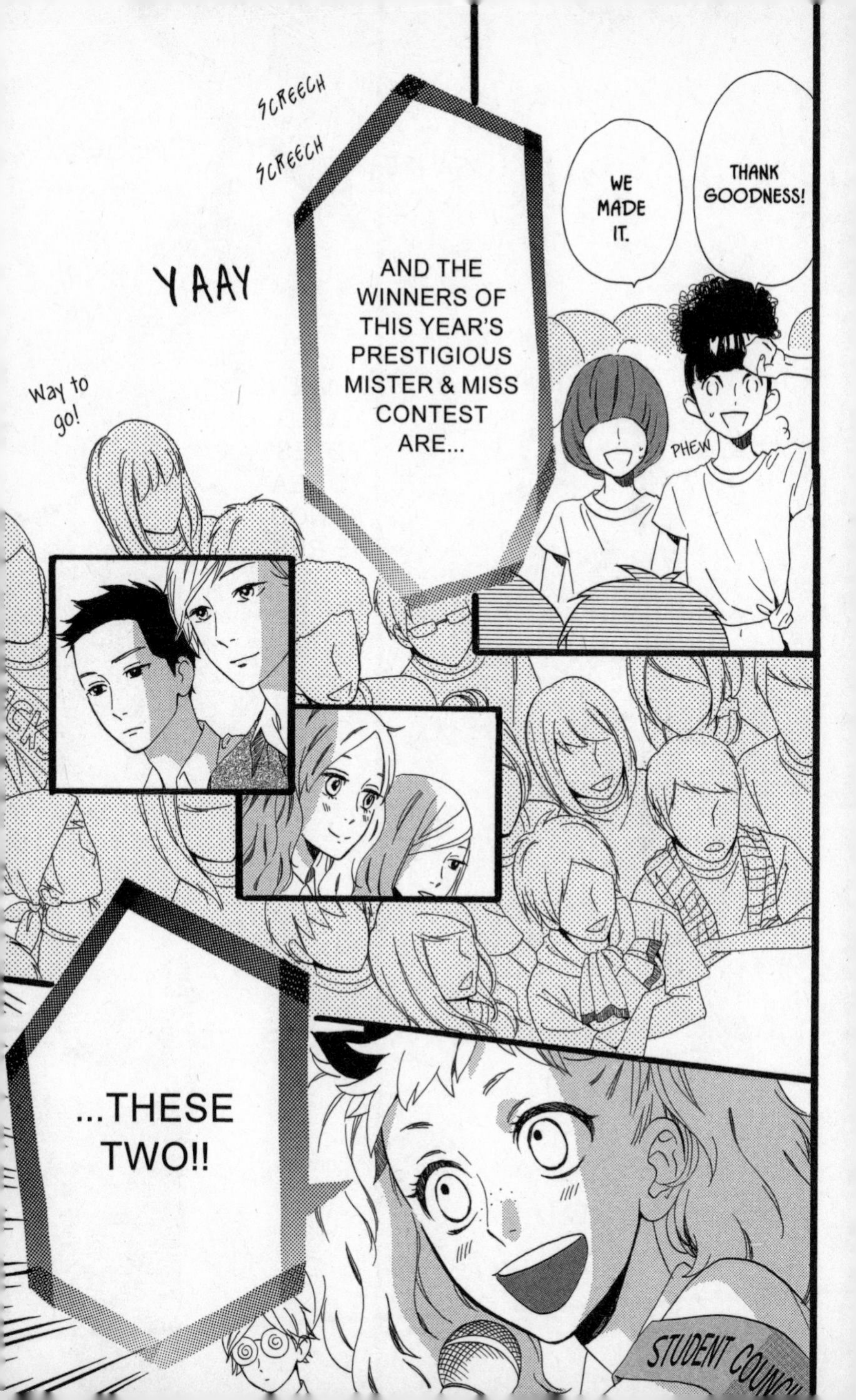

THANK GOODNESS!
WE MADE IT.
PHEW
SCREECH
SCREECH
AND THE WINNERS OF THIS YEAR'S PRESTIGIOUS MISTER & MISS CONTEST ARE...
YAAY
Way to go!
...THESE TWO!!
STUDENT COUN

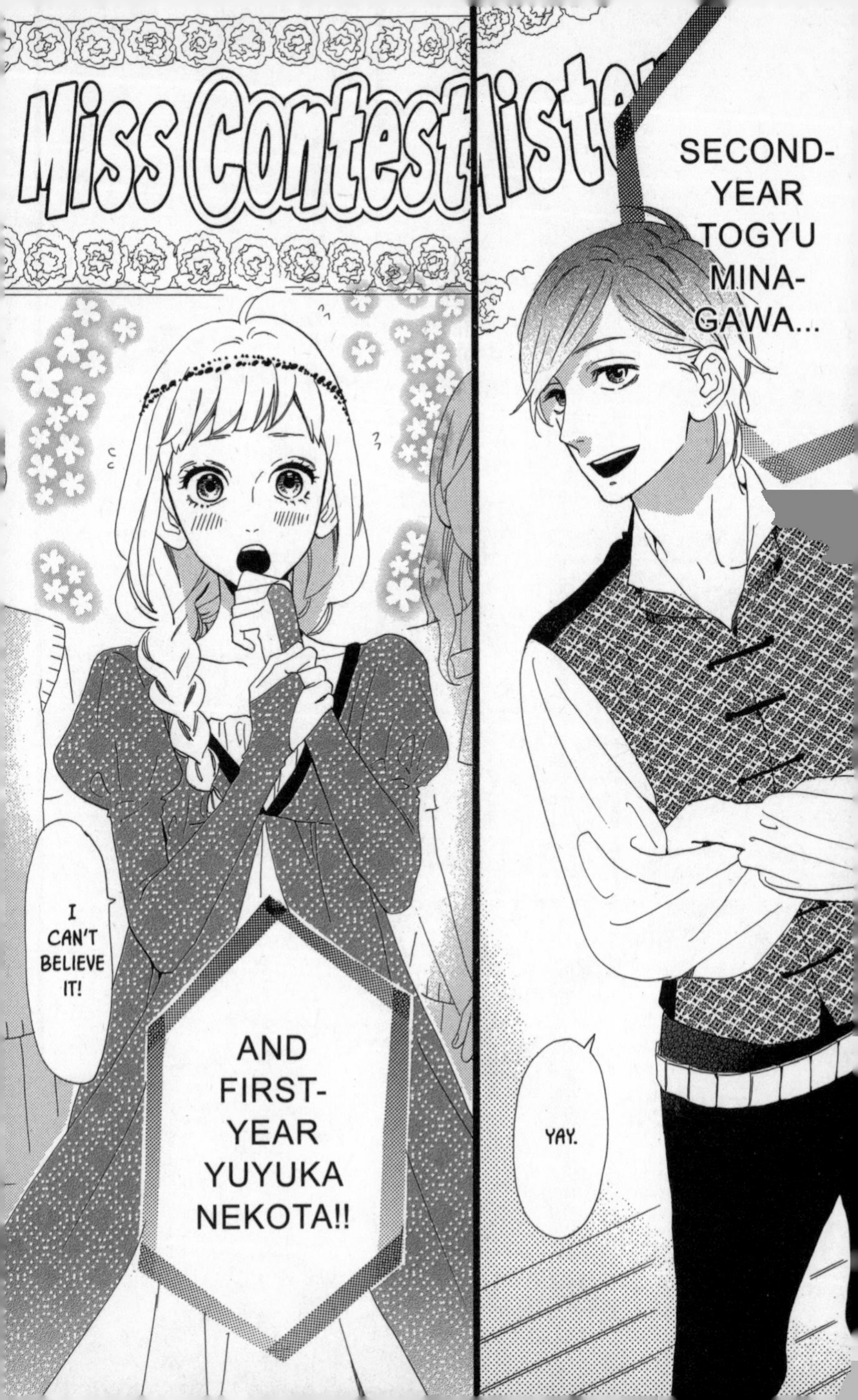
Miss Contest
SECOND-YEAR TOGYU MINAGAWA...
YAY.
AND FIRST-YEAR YUYUKA NEKOTA!!
I CAN'T BELIEVE IT!

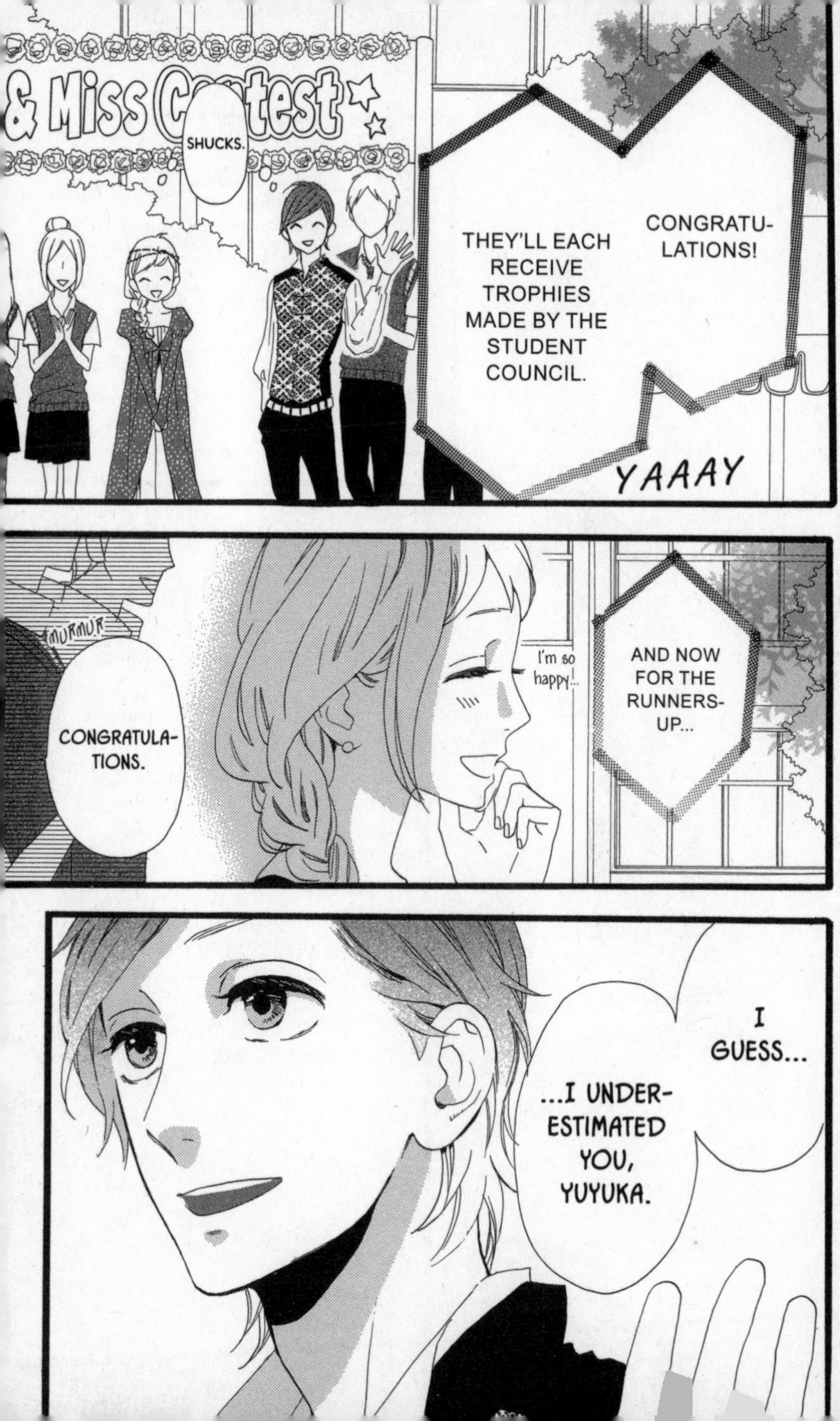
CONGRATU-LATIONS!
THEY'LL EACH RECEIVE TROPHIES MADE BY THE STUDENT COUNCIL.
YAAAY
& Miss
SHUCKS.
AND NOW FOR THE RUNNERS-UP...
I'm so happy!..
MURMUR
CONGRATULA-TIONS.
I GUESS...
...I UNDER-ESTIMATED YOU, YUYUKA.

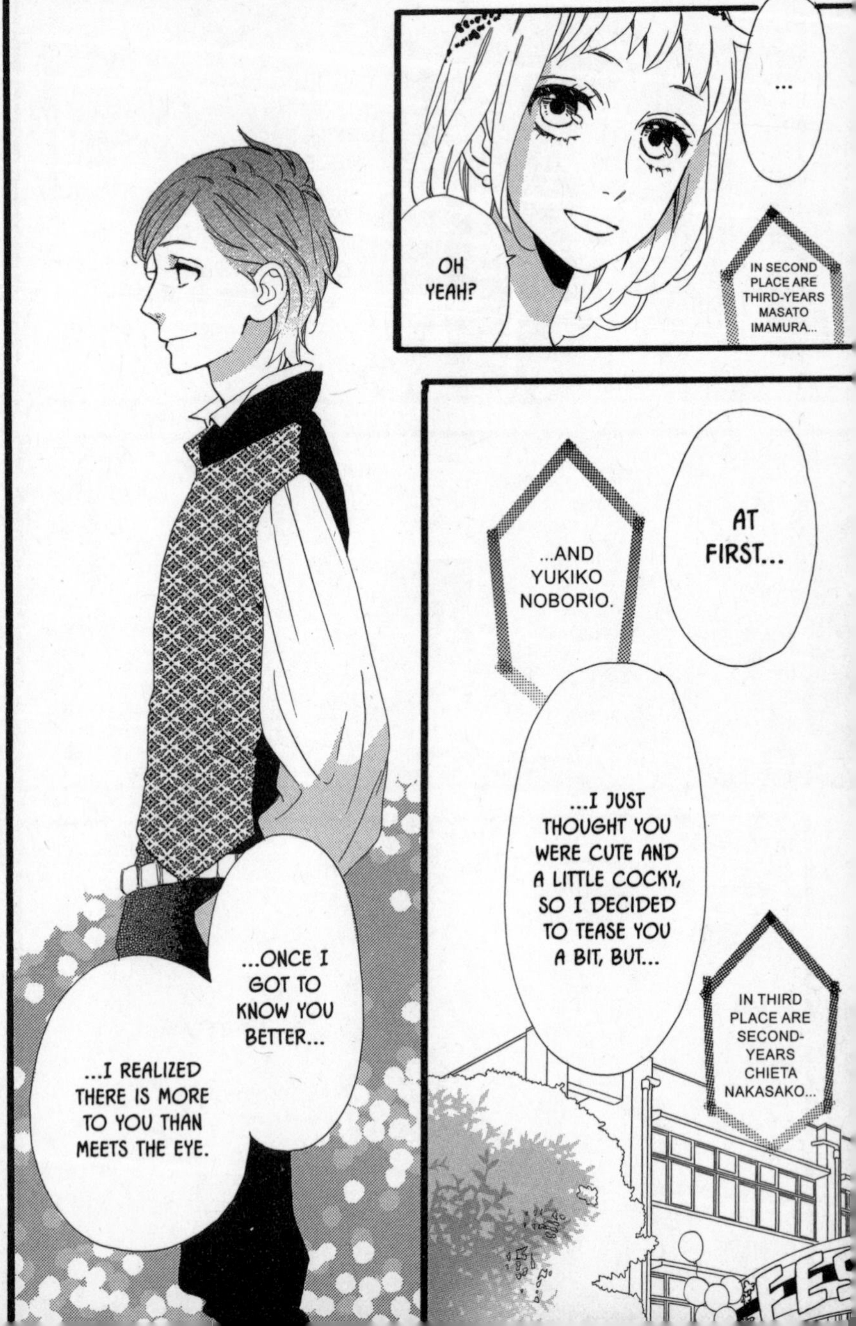
...
IN SECOND PLACE ARE THIRD-YEARS MASATO IMAMURA...
OH YEAH?
AT FIRST...
...I JUST THOUGHT YOU WERE CUTE AND A LITTLE COCKY, SO I DECIDED TO TEASE YOU A BIT, BUT...
IN THIRD PLACE ARE SECOND-YEARS CHIETA NAKASAKO...
...AND YUKIKO NOBORIO.
...ONCE I GOT TO KNOW YOU BETTER...
...I REALIZED THERE IS MORE TO YOU THAN MEETS THE EYE.

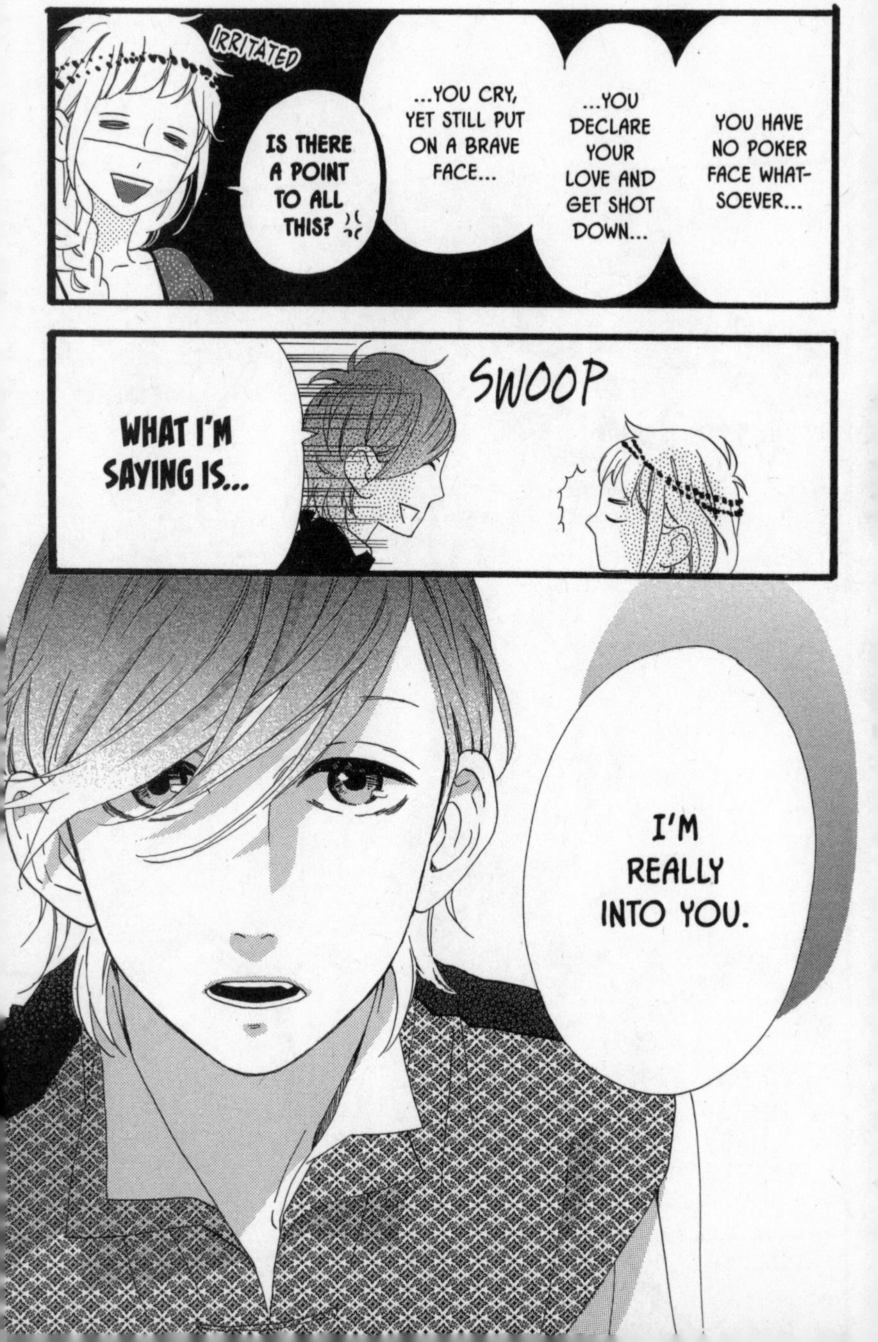
YOU HAVE NO POKER FACE WHAT-SOEVER...
...YOU DECLARE YOUR LOVE AND GET SHOT DOWN...
...YOU CRY, YET STILL PUT ON A BRAVE FACE...
IS THERE A POINT TO ALL THIS?
IRRITATED
SWOOP
WHAT I'M SAYING IS...
I'M REALLY INTO YOU.

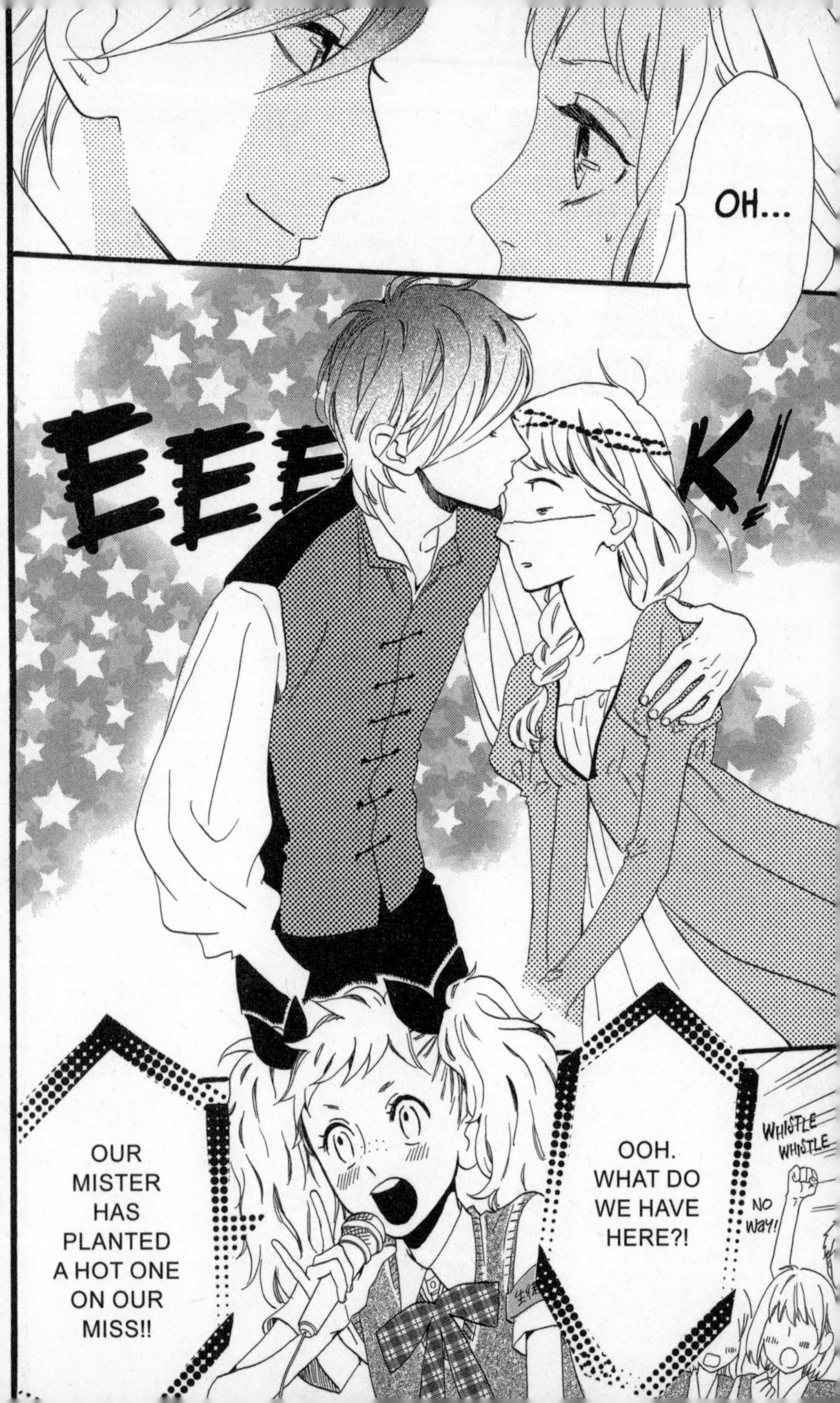
OH...
EEEK!
OOH. WHAT DO WE HAVE HERE?!
OUR MISTER HAS PLANTED A HOT ONE ON OUR MISS!!
WHISTLE WHISTLE
NO WAY!

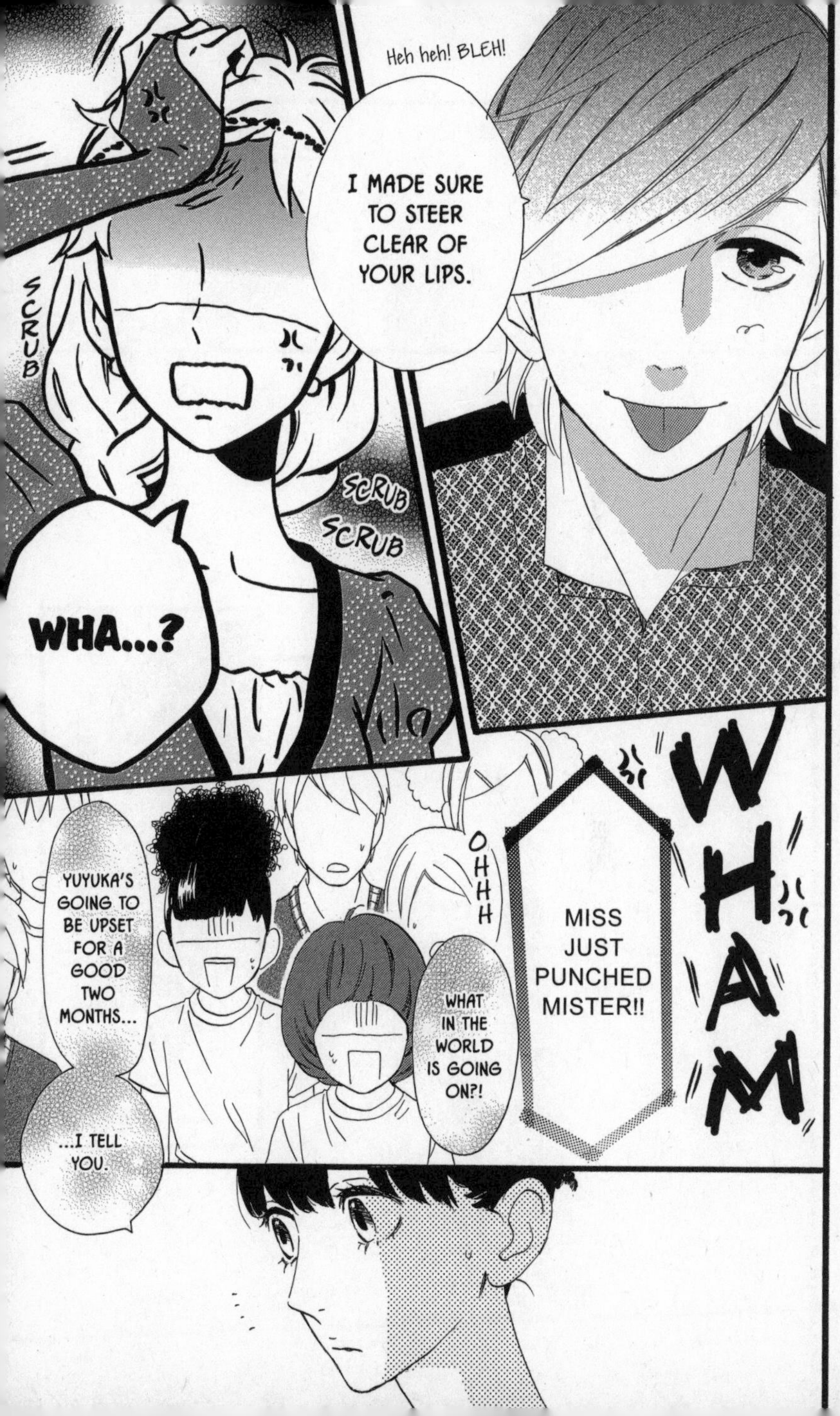
Heh heh! BLEH!
I MADE SURE TO STEER CLEAR OF YOUR LIPS.
SCRUB
WHA...?
SCRUB
SCRUB
WHAM
MISS JUST PUNCHED MISTER!!
OHHH
WHAT IN THE WORLD IS GOING ON?!
YUYUKA'S GOING TO BE UPSET FOR A GOOD TWO MONTHS...
...I TELL YOU.

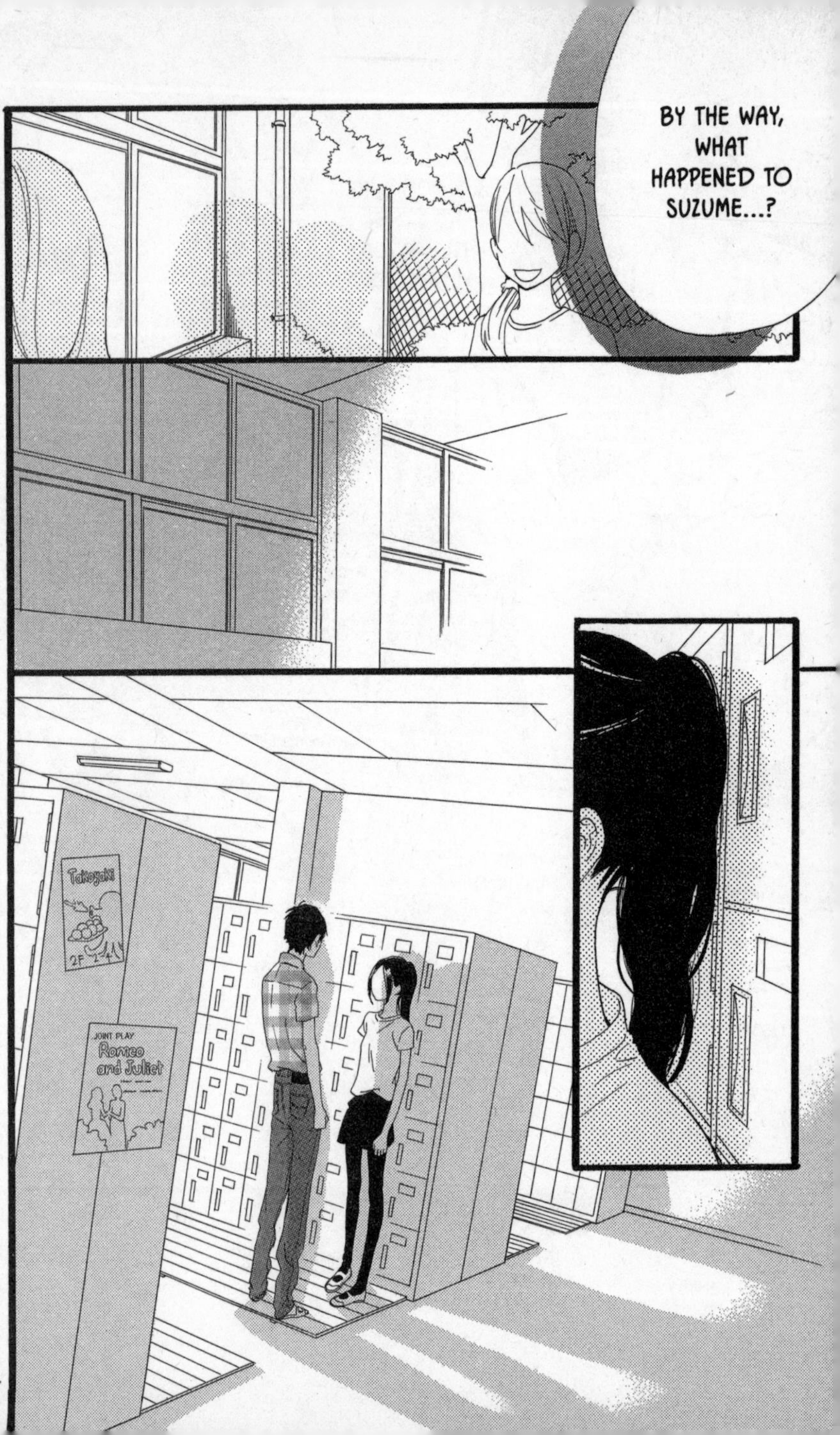
BY THE WAY, WHAT HAPPENED TO SUZUME...?
Takoyaki
JOINT PLAY
Romeo and Juliet

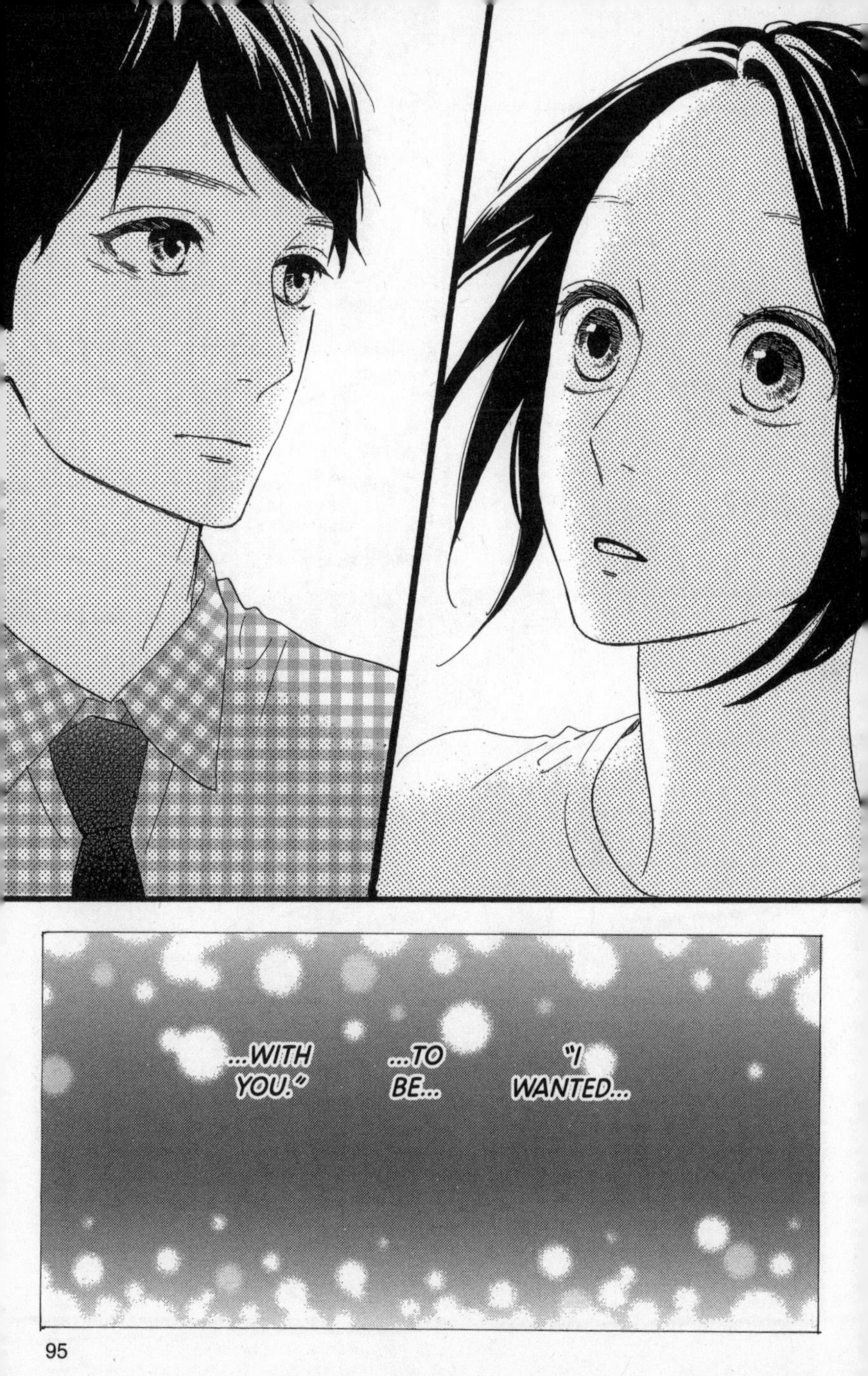
"I
WANTED...
...TO
BE...
...WITH
YOU."

I wanted to be with yo
I wanted to b... ...with yo
I wante...
I want...
I war...
I war...
I wa...
I wa...
I wa...
I w...
I war... n... ...y...
I war... h... ...yo
I wan... h... ...yo
wanted to y... ...yo
I wanted to ...yo
I wanted t... ...vo

Turn around about five times.

I'M NOT SURE I GET WHAT YOU MEAN.

WHY?

AFTER ALL...

WELL...

...THAT'S...

...YOU'RE SAYING...

...ALMOST LIKE...

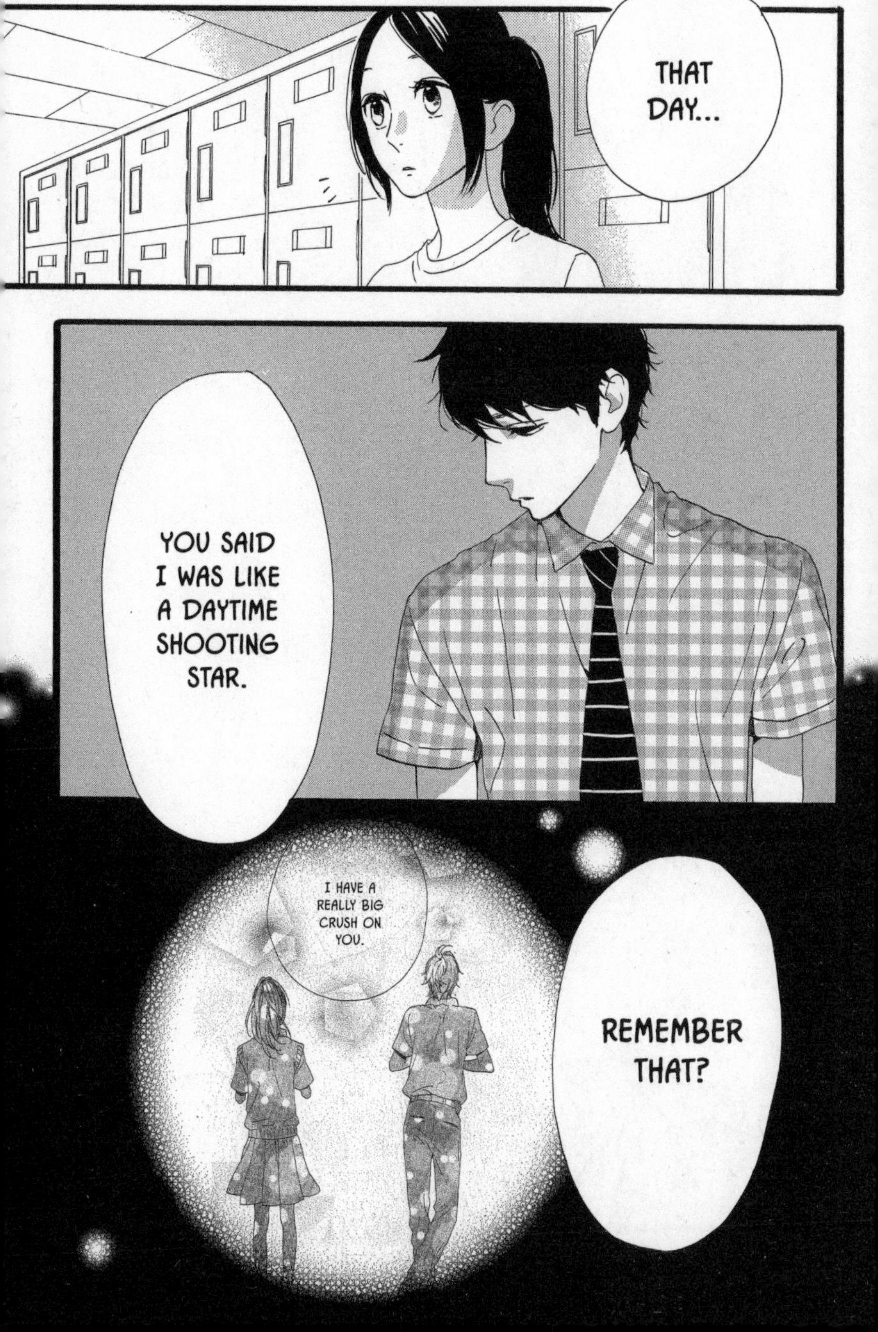
THAT DAY...
YOU SAID I WAS LIKE A DAYTIME SHOOTING STAR.
REMEMBER THAT?
I HAVE A REALLY BIG CRUSH ON YOU.

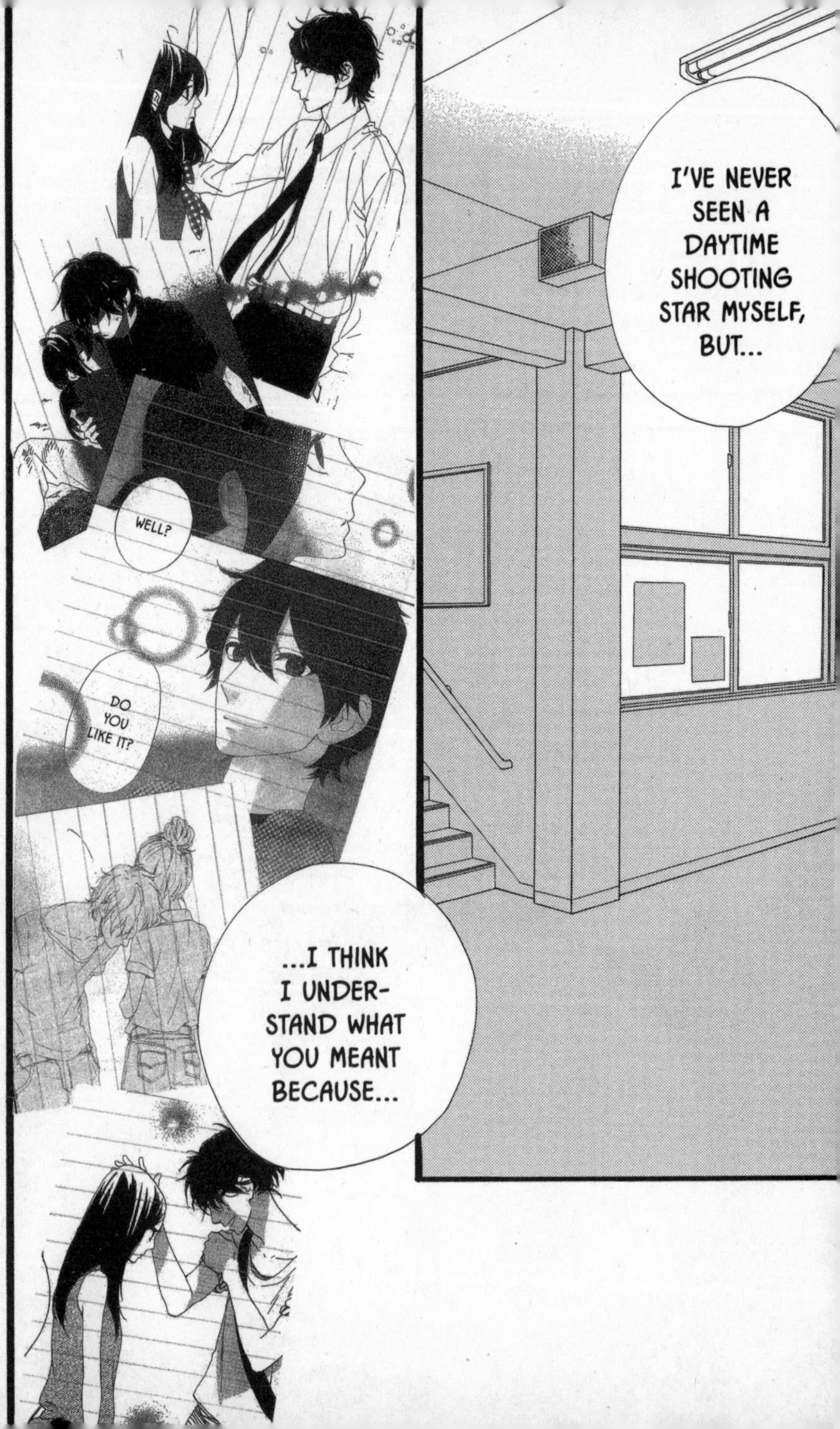
I'VE NEVER SEEN A DAYTIME SHOOTING STAR MYSELF, BUT...
...I THINK I UNDER-STAND WHAT YOU MEANT BECAUSE...
WELL?
DO YOU LIKE IT?

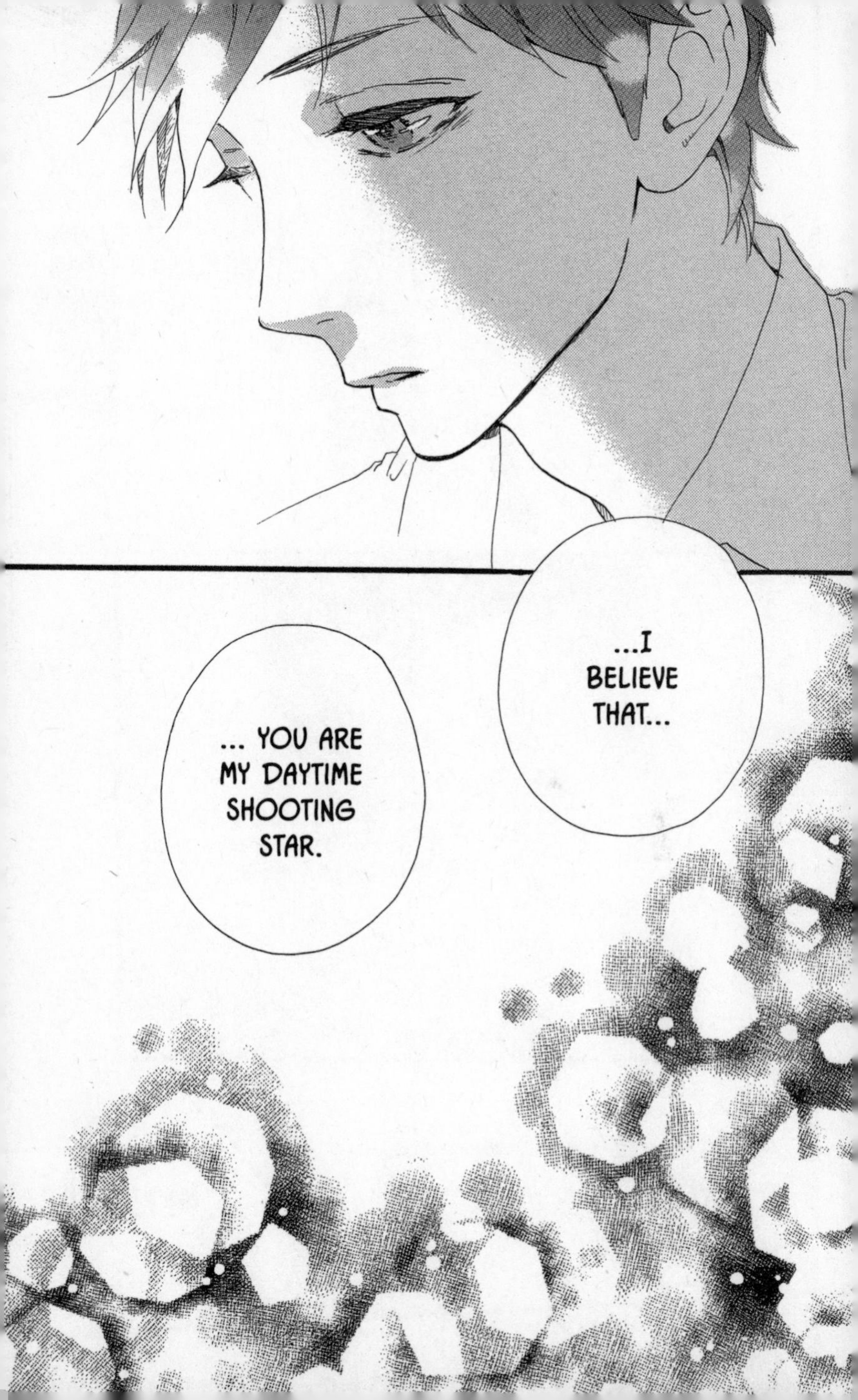
...I BELIEVE THAT...
... YOU ARE MY DAYTIME SHOOTING STAR.

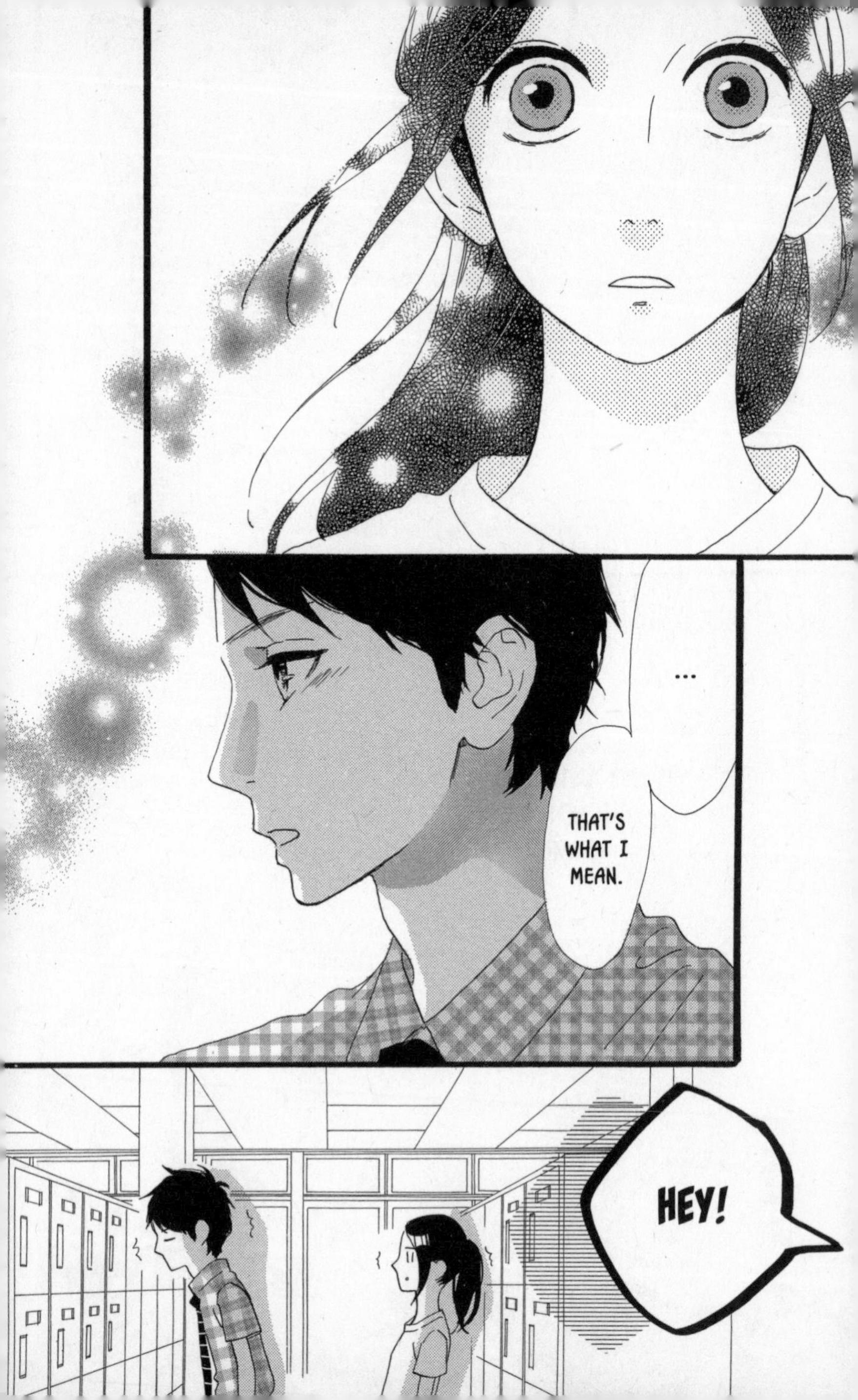
...
THAT'S WHAT I MEAN.
HEY!

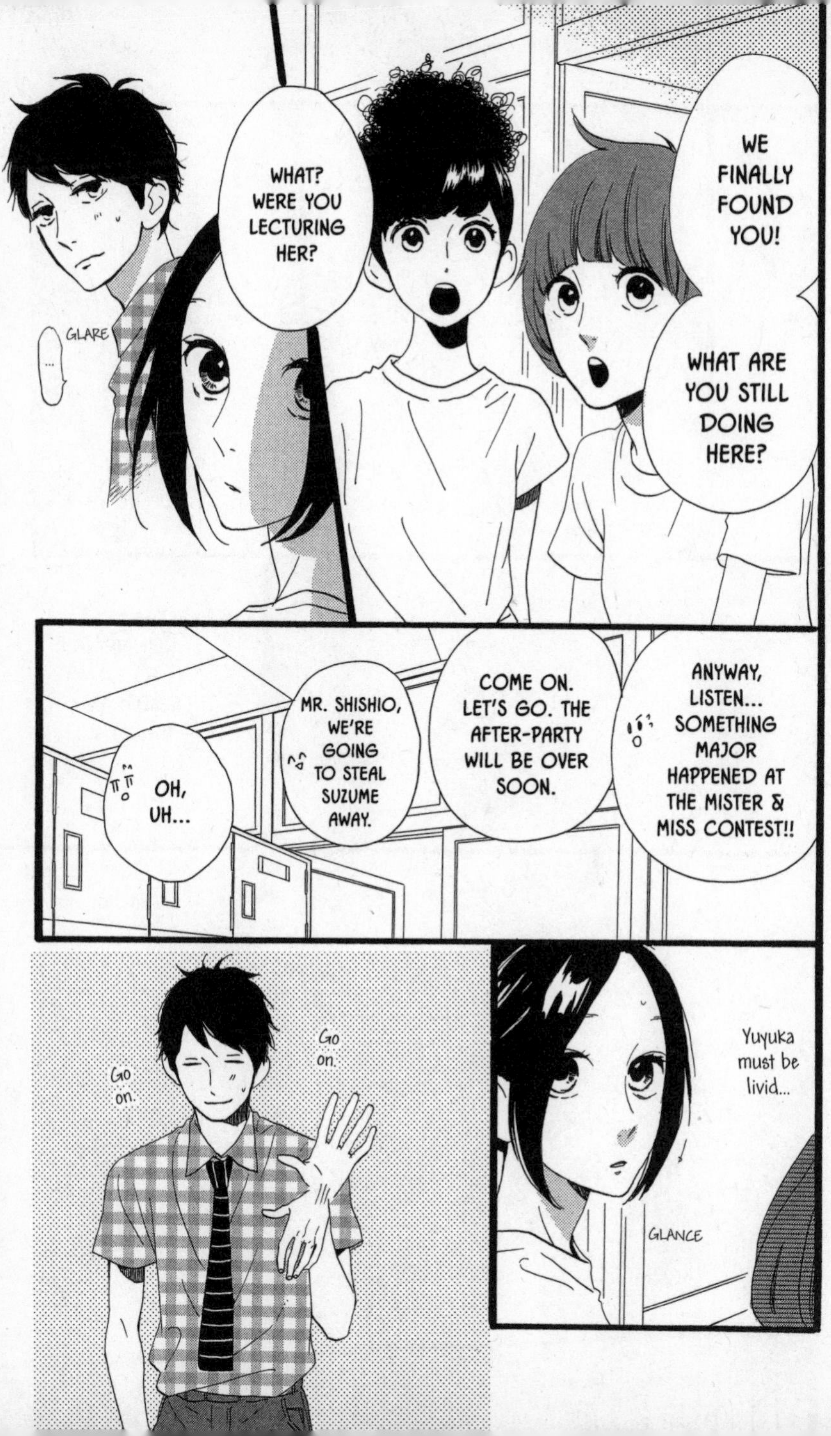
WE FINALLY FOUND YOU!
WHAT ARE YOU STILL DOING HERE?
WHAT? WERE YOU LECTURING HER?
GLARE
...
ANYWAY, LISTEN... SOMETHING MAJOR HAPPENED AT THE MISTER & MISS CONTEST!!
COME ON. LET'S GO. THE AFTER-PARTY WILL BE OVER SOON.
MR. SHISHIO, WE'RE GOING TO STEAL SUZUME AWAY.
OH, UH...
Yuyuka must be livid...
GLANCE
Go on.
Go on.

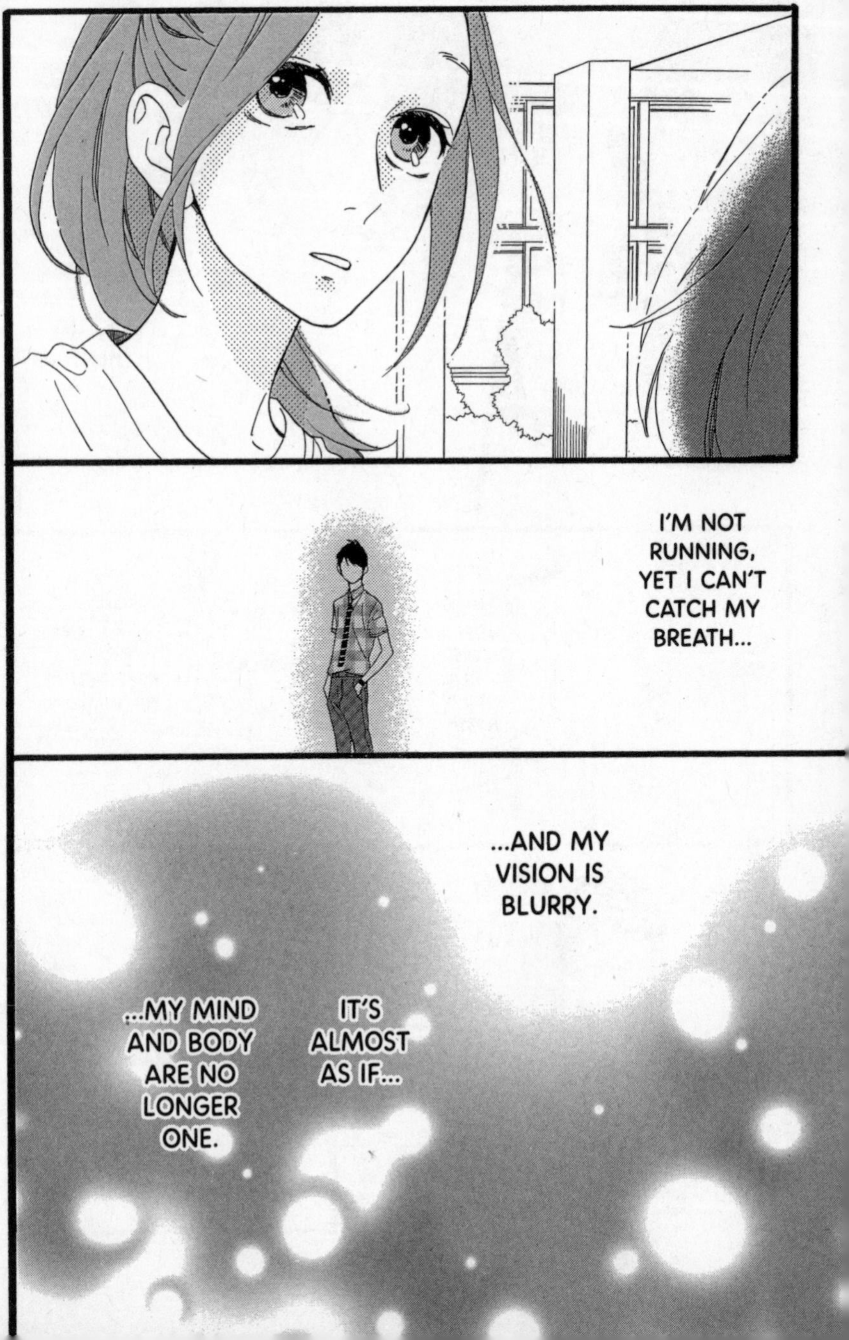
I'M NOT RUNNING, YET I CAN'T CATCH MY BREATH...
...AND MY VISION IS BLURRY.
IT'S ALMOST AS IF...
...MY MIND AND BODY ARE NO LONGER ONE.

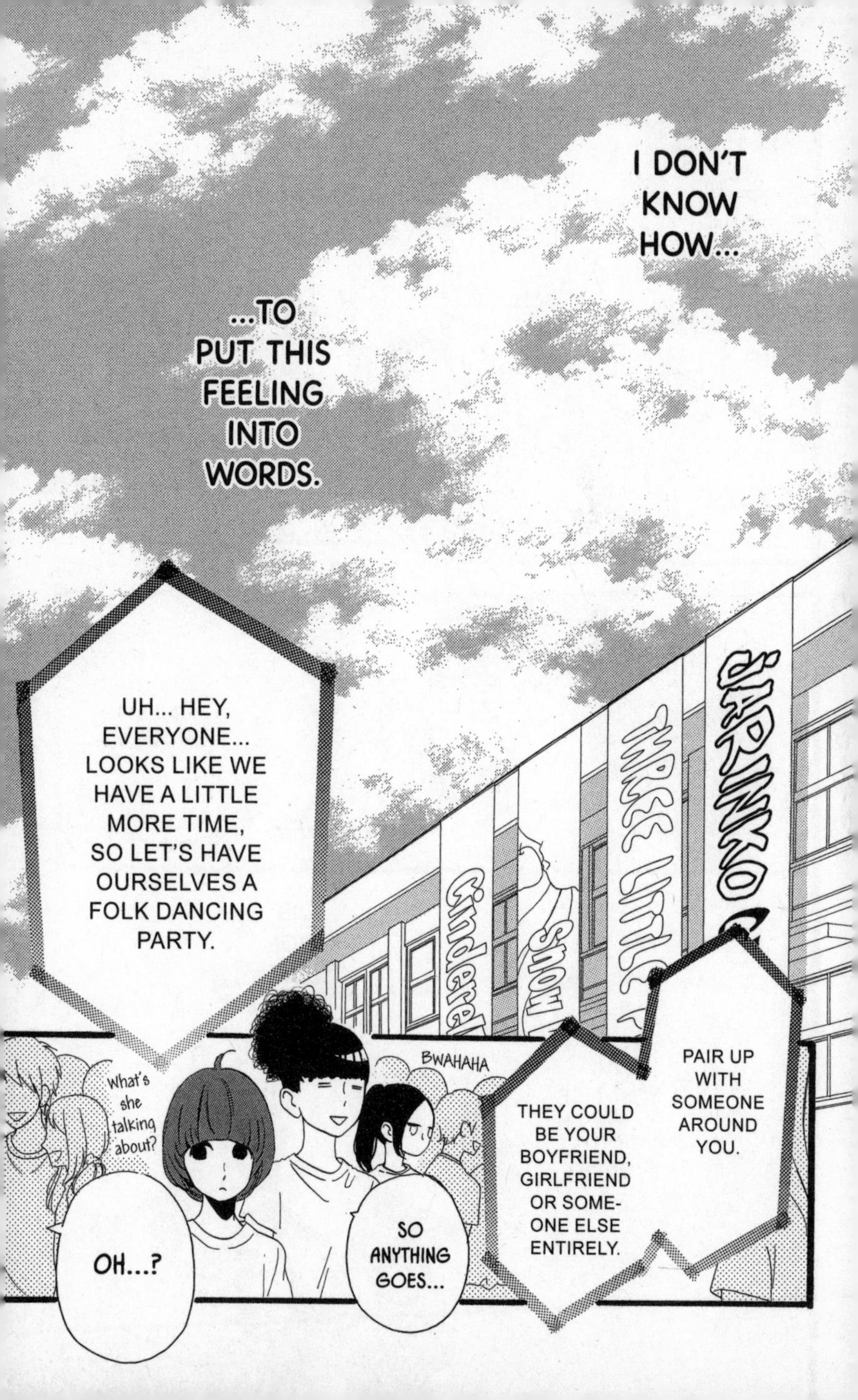
I DON'T KNOW HOW...
...TO PUT THIS FEELING INTO WORDS.
UH... HEY, EVERYONE... LOOKS LIKE WE HAVE A LITTLE MORE TIME, SO LET'S HAVE OURSELVES A FOLK DANCING PARTY.
PAIR UP WITH SOMEONE AROUND YOU.
THEY COULD BE YOUR BOYFRIEND, GIRLFRIEND OR SOME-ONE ELSE ENTIRELY.
SO ANYTHING GOES...
BWAHAHA
What's she talking about?
OH...?

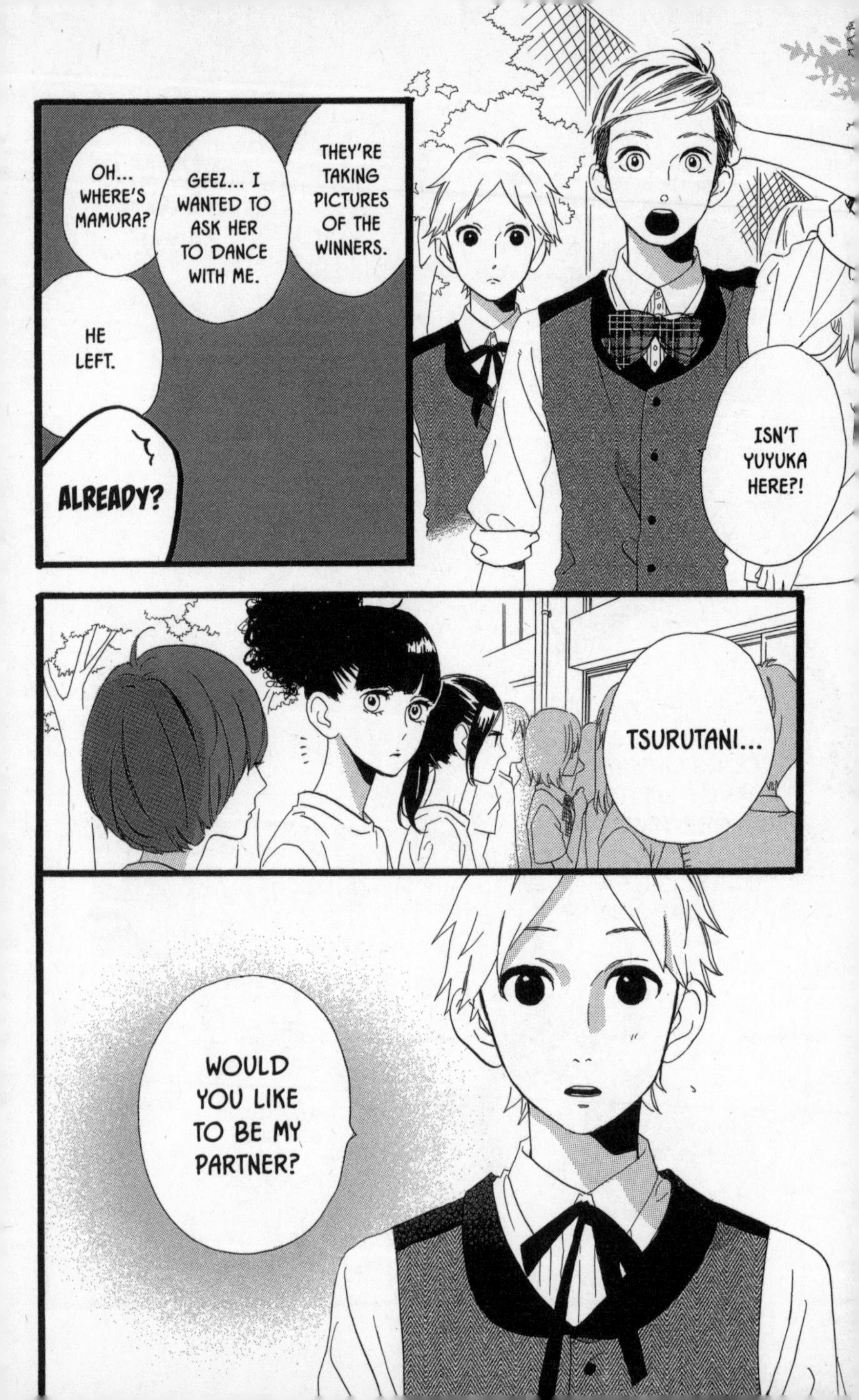
ISN'T YUYUKA HERE?!
THEY'RE TAKING PICTURES OF THE WINNERS.
GEEZ... I WANTED TO ASK HER TO DANCE WITH ME.
OH... WHERE'S MAMURA?
HE LEFT.
ALREADY?
TSURUTANI...
WOULD YOU LIKE TO BE MY PARTNER?

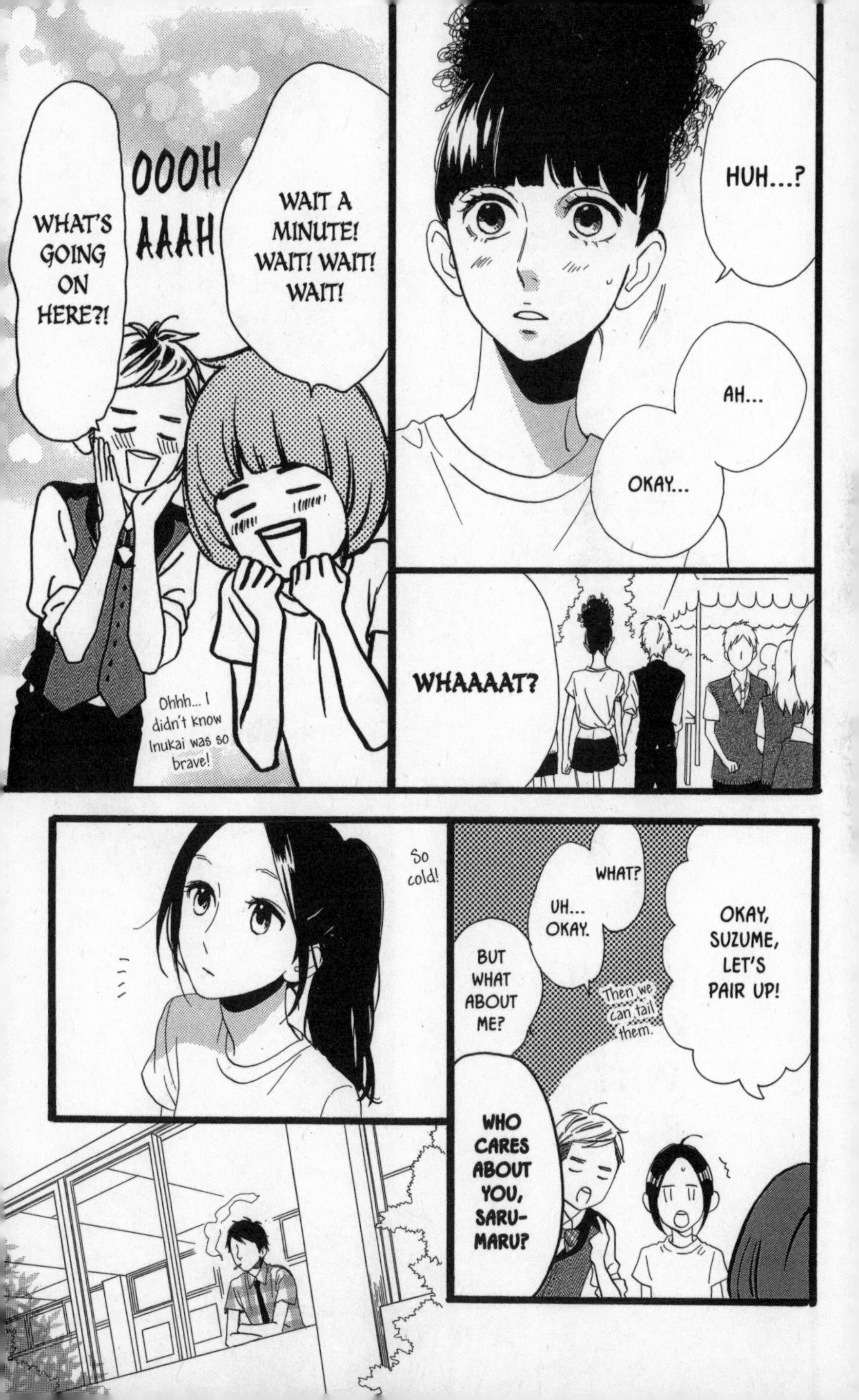
HUH...?
AH...
OKAY...
WHAAAAT?
WAIT A MINUTE! WAIT! WAIT! WAIT!
OOOH AAAH
WHAT'S GOING ON HERE?!
Ohhh... I didn't know Inukai was so brave!
OKAY, SUZUME, LET'S PAIR UP!
WHAT?
UH... OKAY.
Then we can tail them.
BUT WHAT ABOUT ME?
WHO CARES ABOUT YOU, SARU-MARU?
So cold!

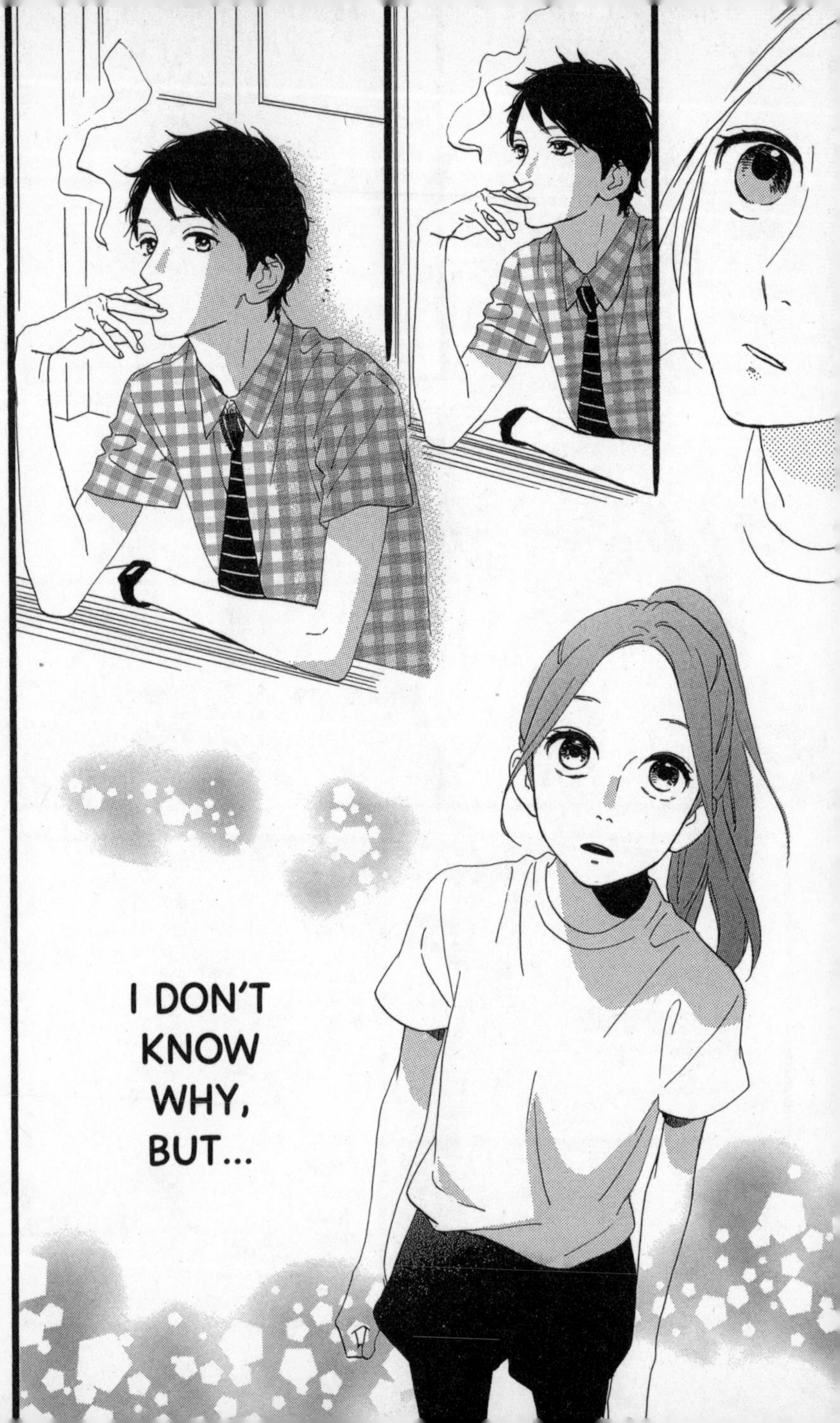
I DON'T KNOW WHY, BUT...

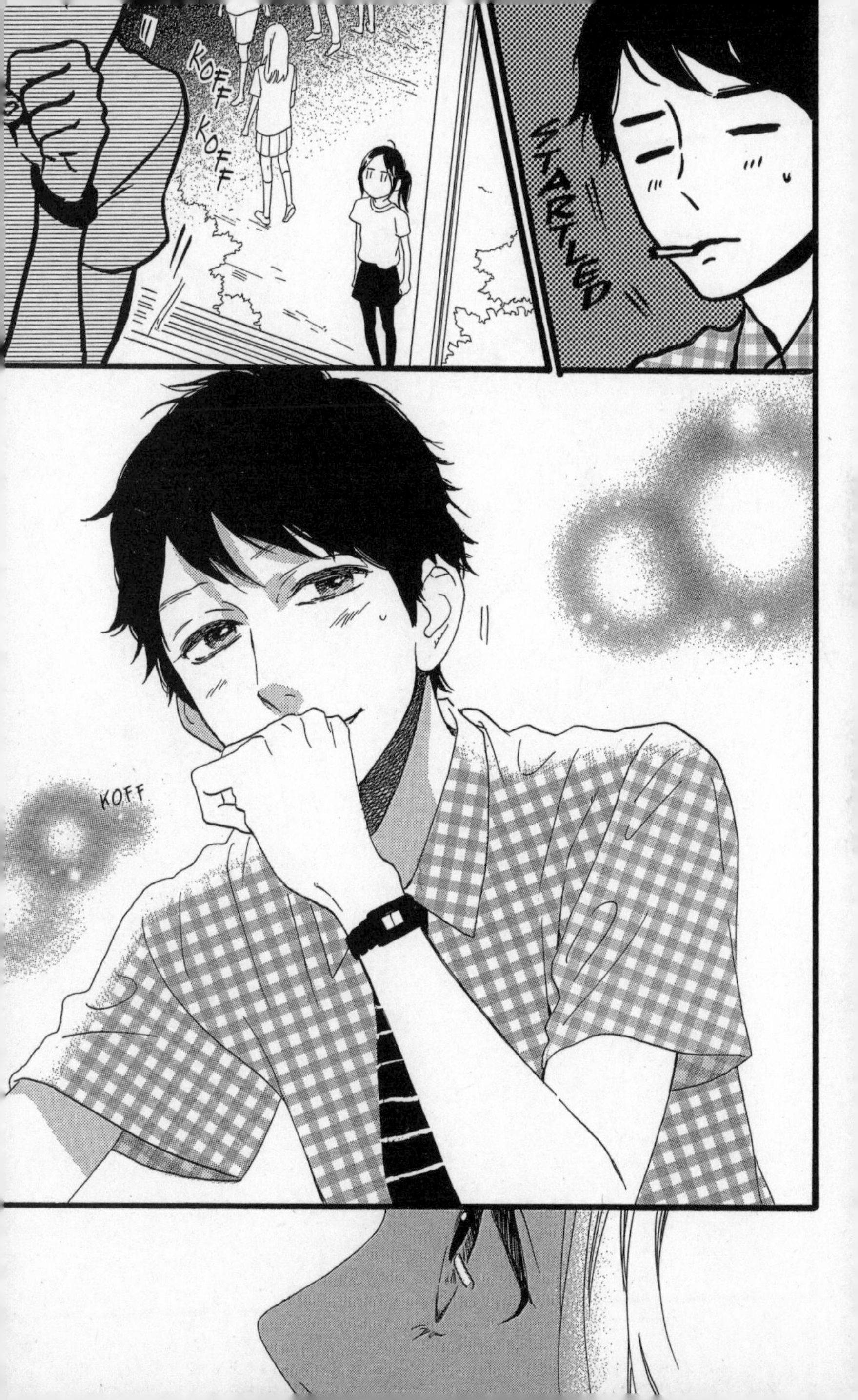
STARTLED
KOFF KOFF
KOFF

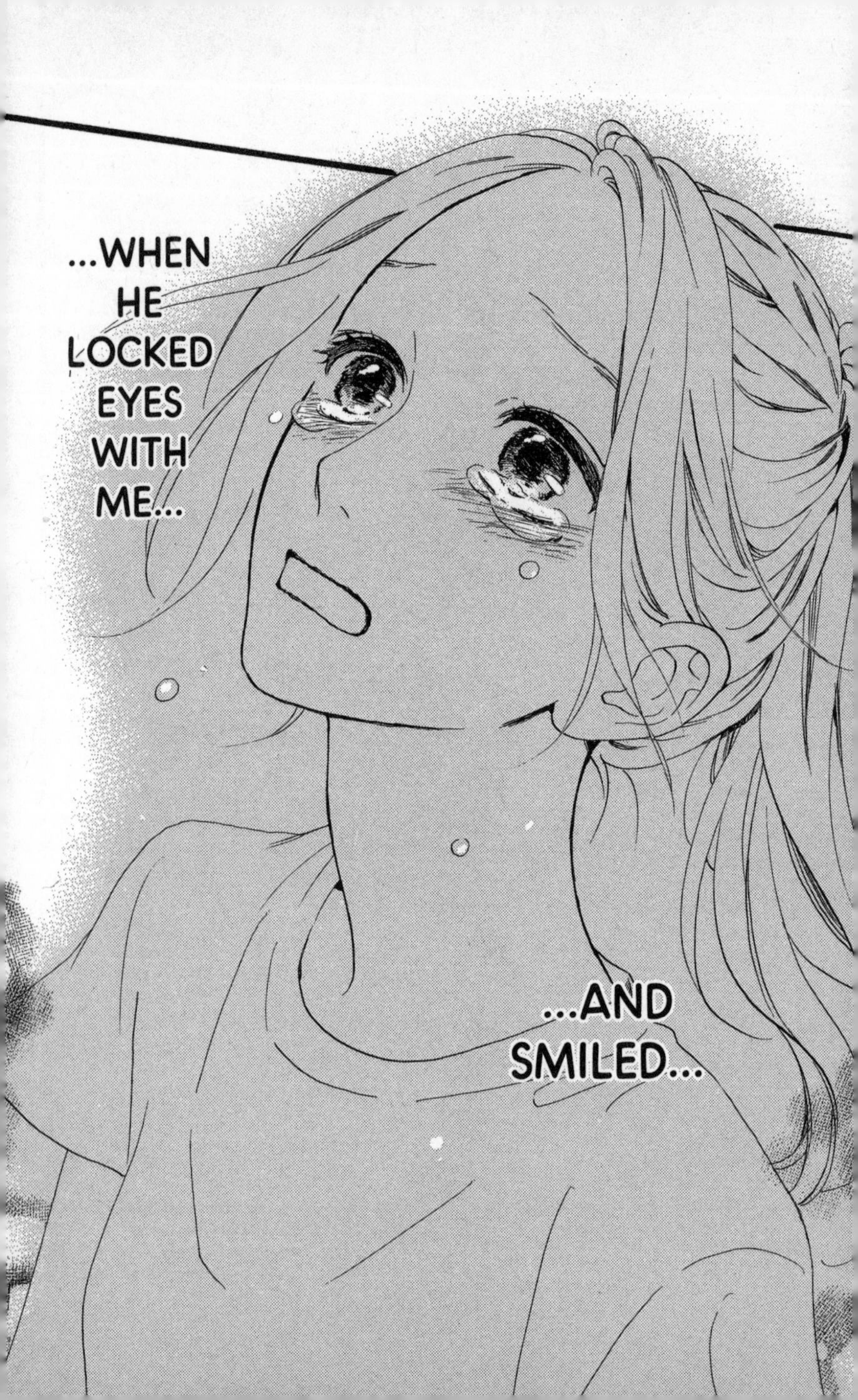
...WHEN HE LOCKED EYES WITH ME...
...AND SMILED...

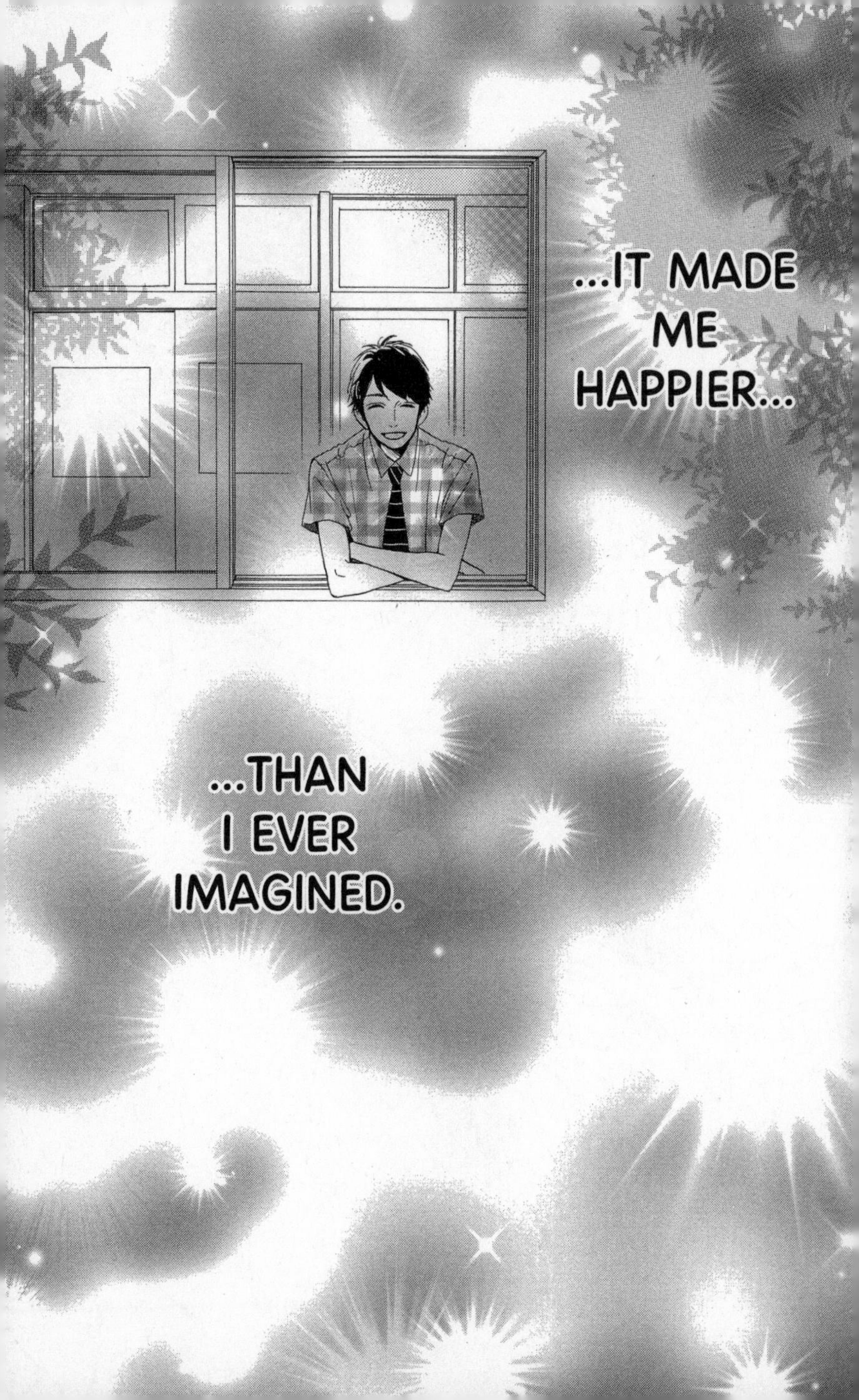
...IT MADE ME HAPPIER...
...THAN I EVER IMAGINED.

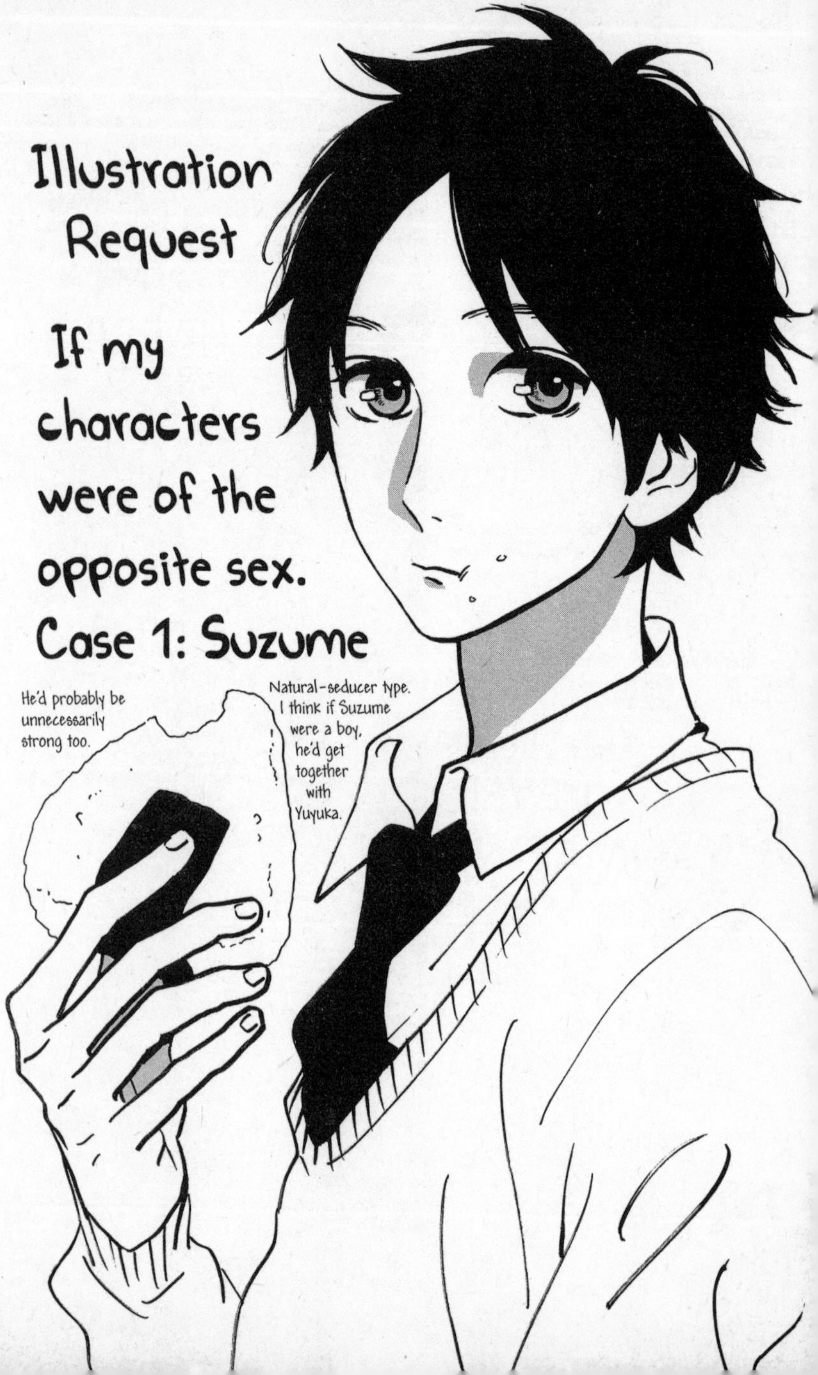
Illustration Request
If my characters were of the opposite sex.
Case 1: Suzume
He'd probably be unnecessarily strong too.
Natural-seducer type. I think if Suzume were a boy, he'd get together with Yuyuka.

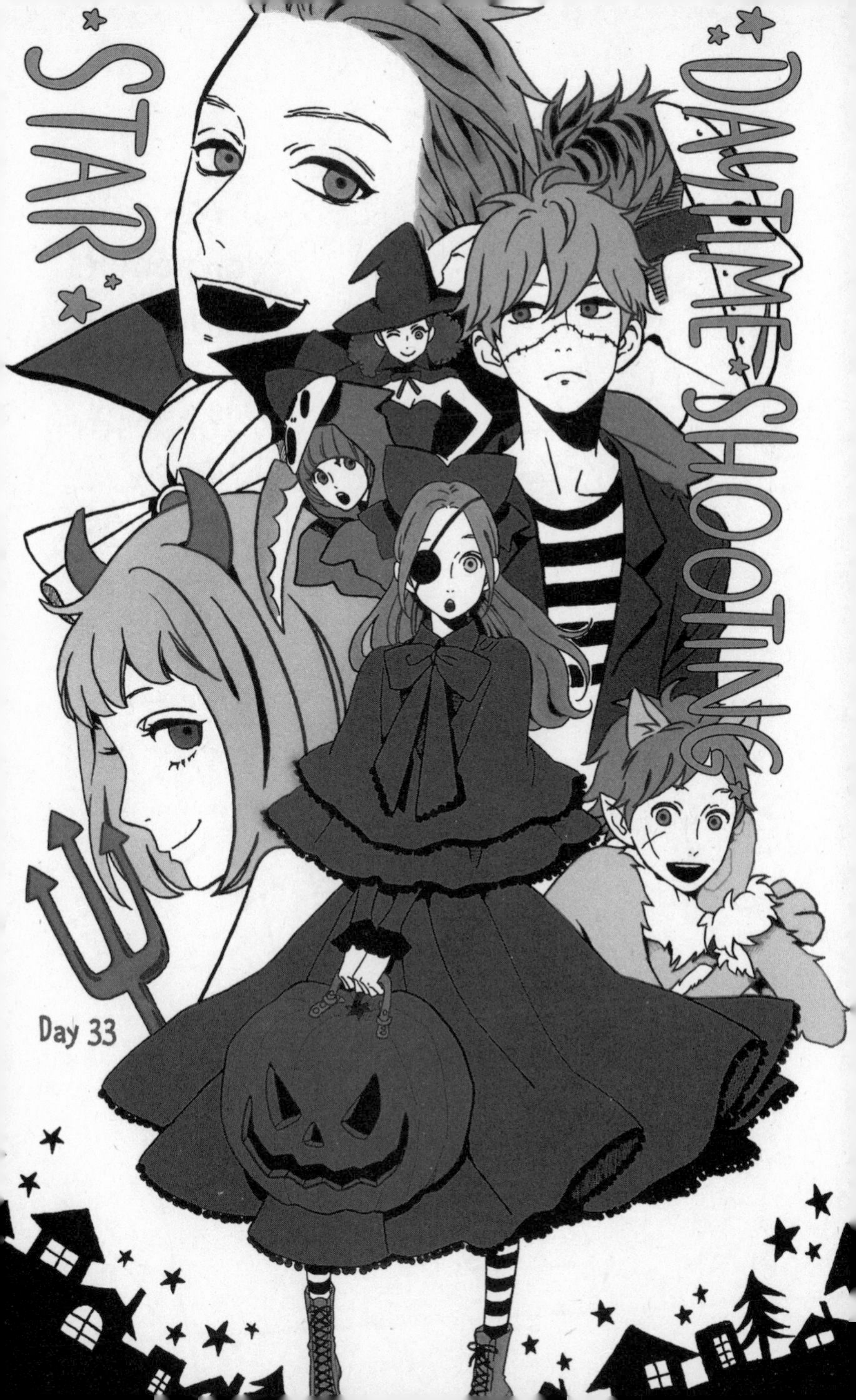
DAYTIME SHOOTING
STAR
Day 33

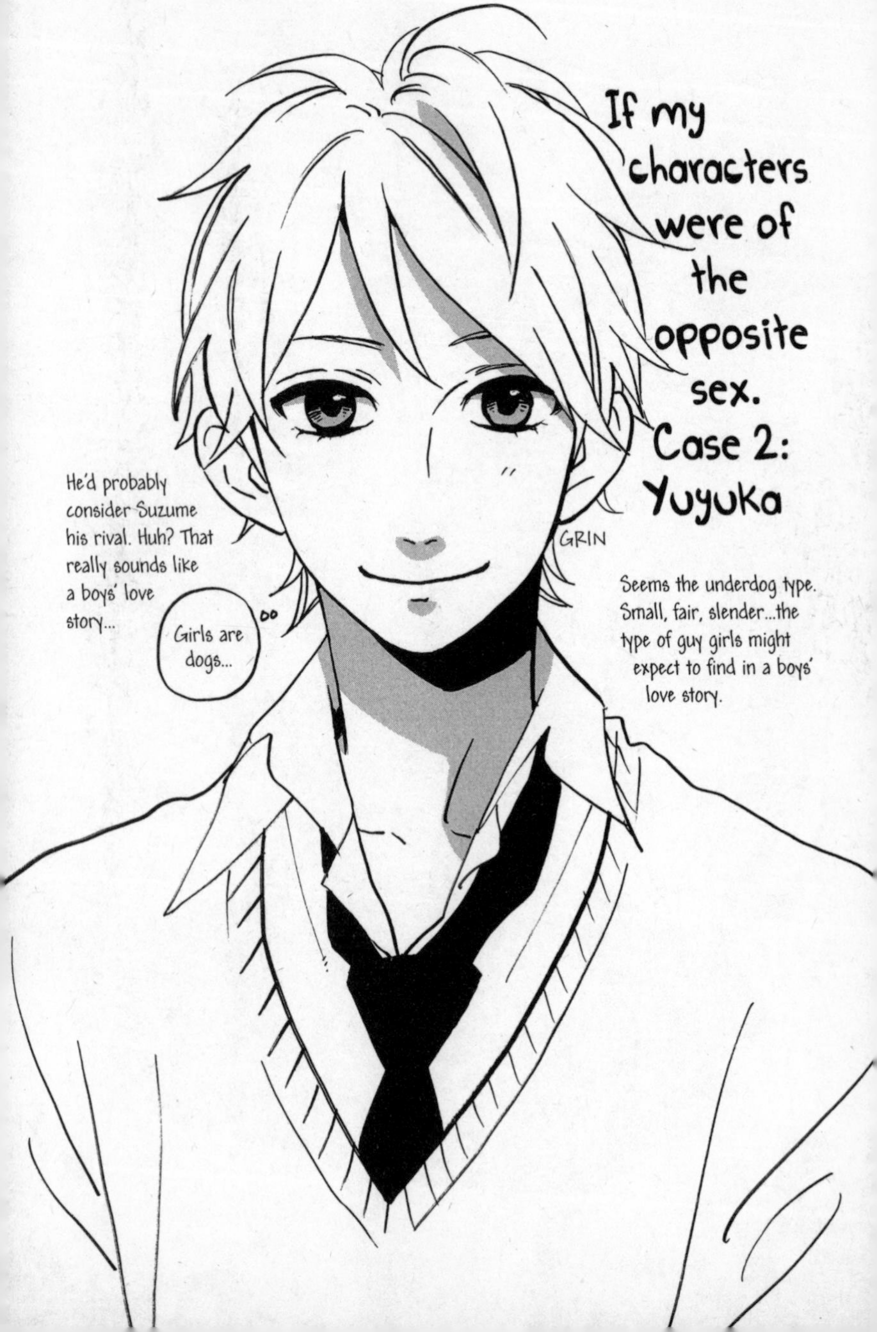
If my characters were of the opposite sex. Case 2: Yuyuka
GRIN
Seems the underdog type. Small, fair, slender...the type of guy girls might expect to find in a boys' love story.
He'd probably consider Suzume his rival. Huh? That really sounds like a boys' love story...
Girls are dogs...

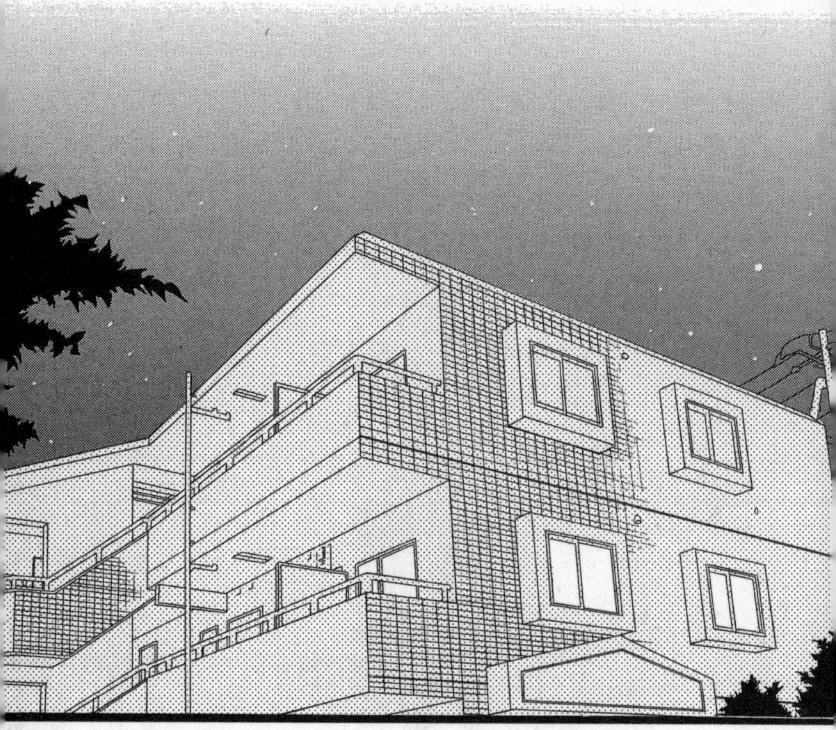

What's Yukichi's type?

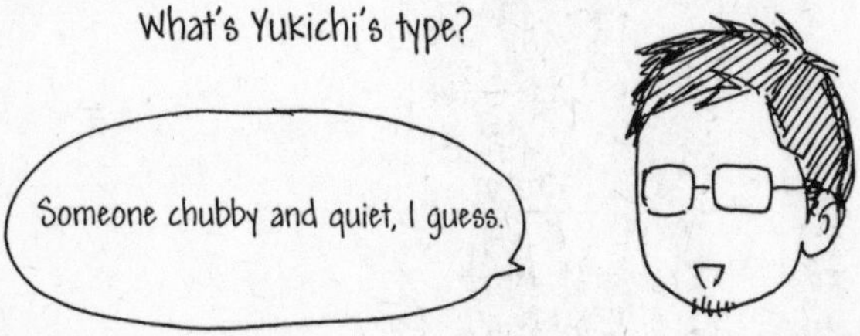
Someone chubby and quiet, I guess.

Good luck, Kame!

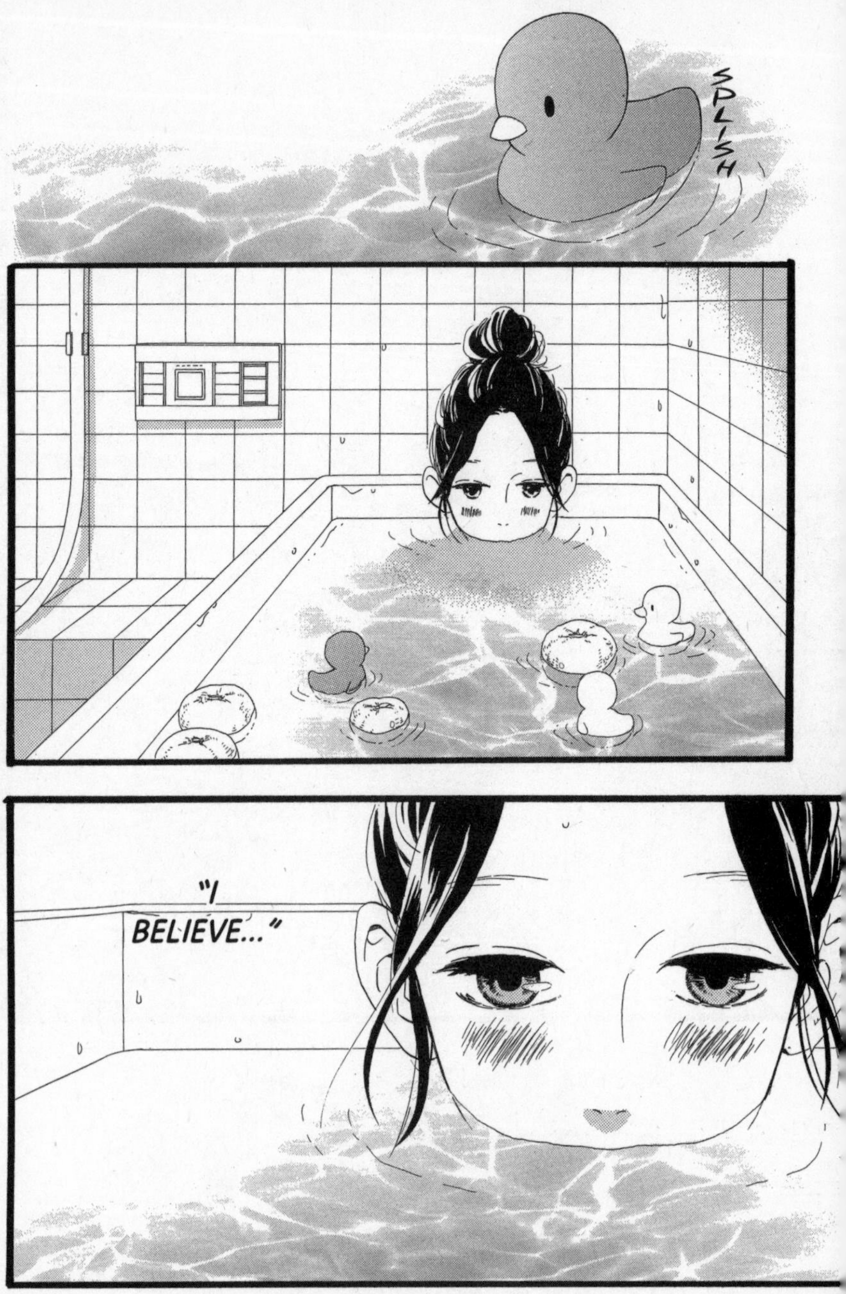
SPLISH
"I BELIEVE..."

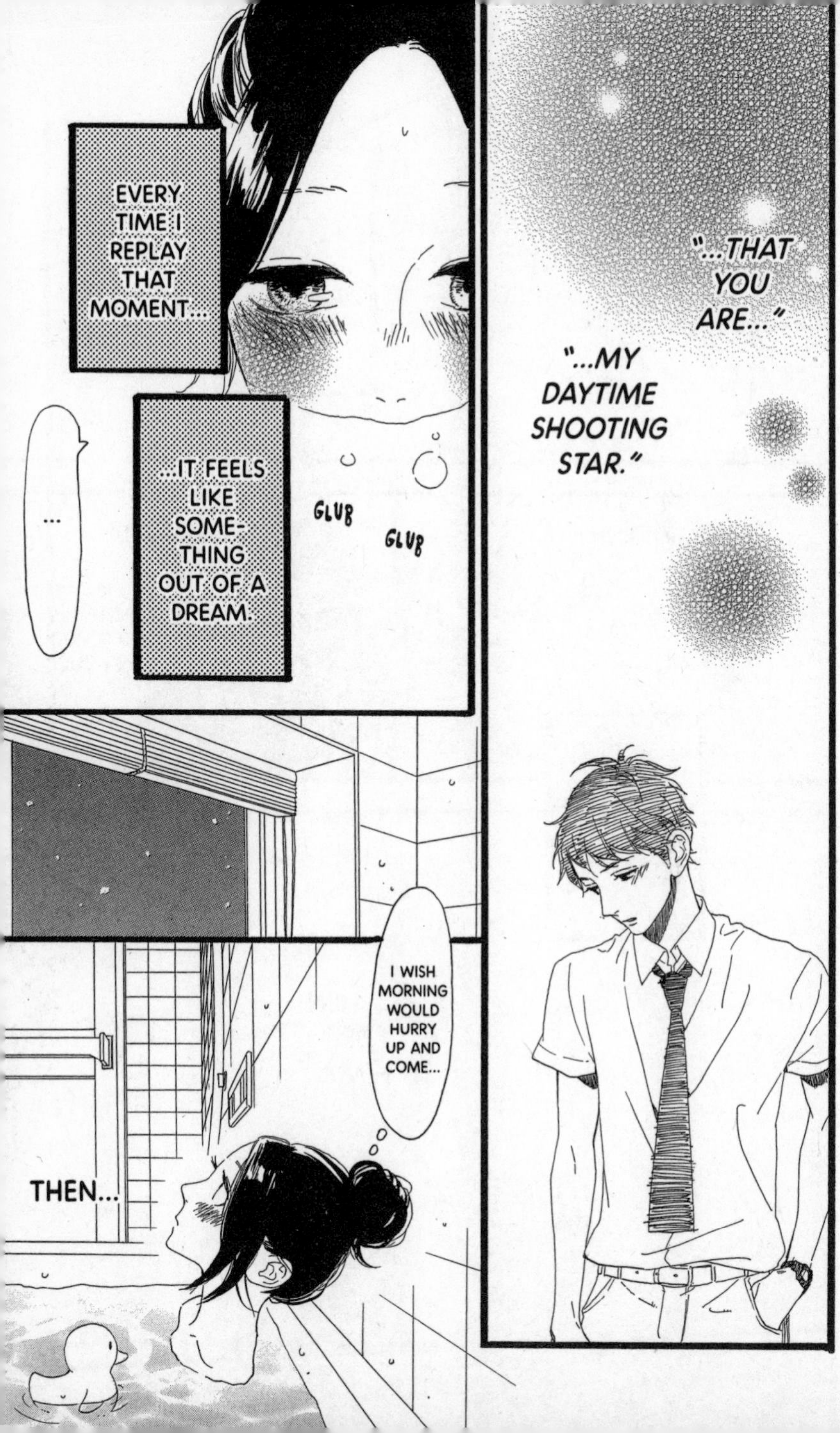
"...THAT YOU ARE..."
"...MY DAYTIME SHOOTING STAR."
EVERY TIME I REPLAY THAT MOMENT...
...IT FEELS LIKE SOME-THING OUT OF A DREAM.
GLUB
GLUB
...
I WISH MORNING WOULD HURRY UP AND COME...
THEN...

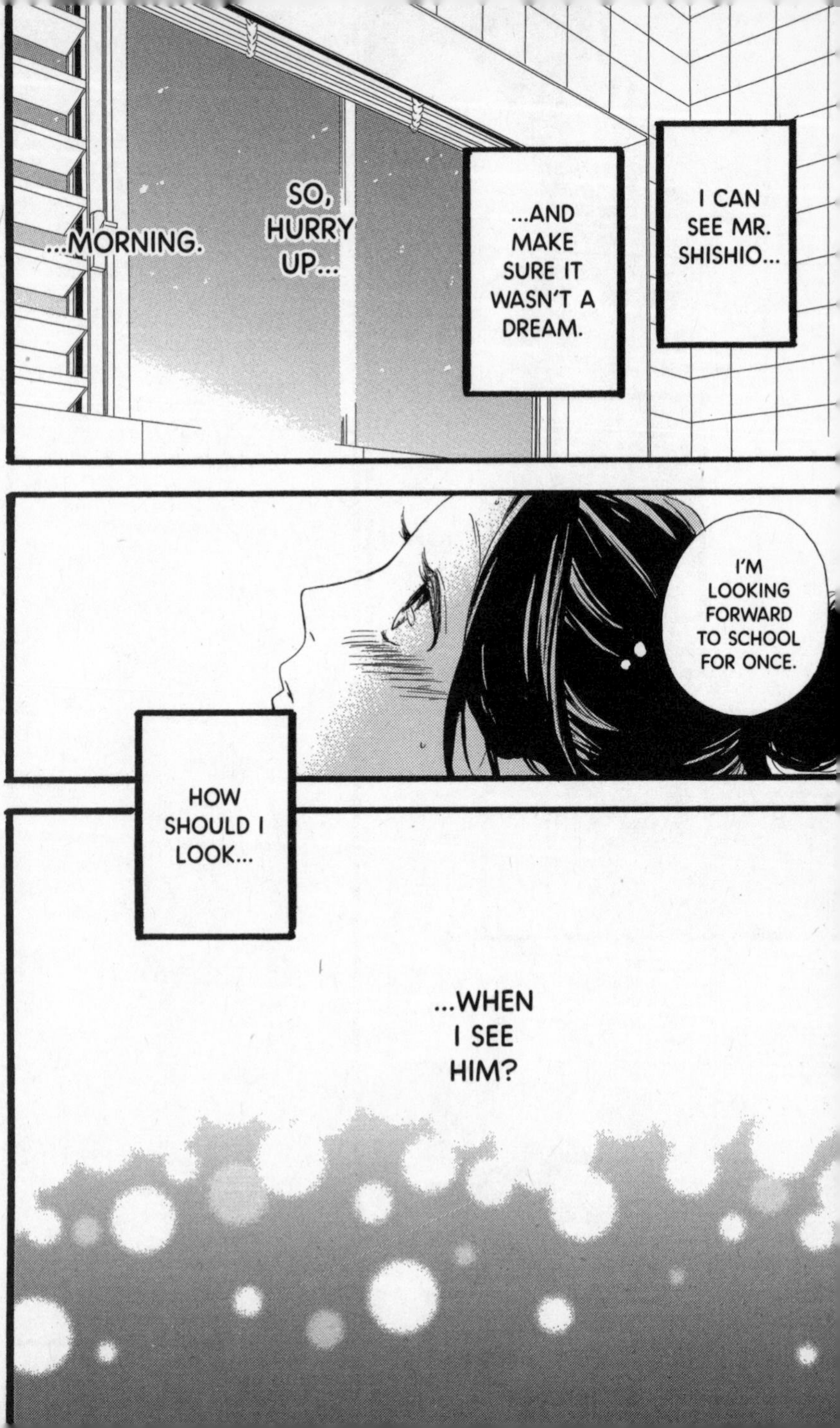
I CAN SEE MR. SHISHIO...
...AND MAKE SURE IT WASN'T A DREAM.
SO, HURRY UP...
...MORNING.
I'M LOOKING FORWARD TO SCHOOL FOR ONCE.
HOW SHOULD I LOOK...
...WHEN I SEE HIM?

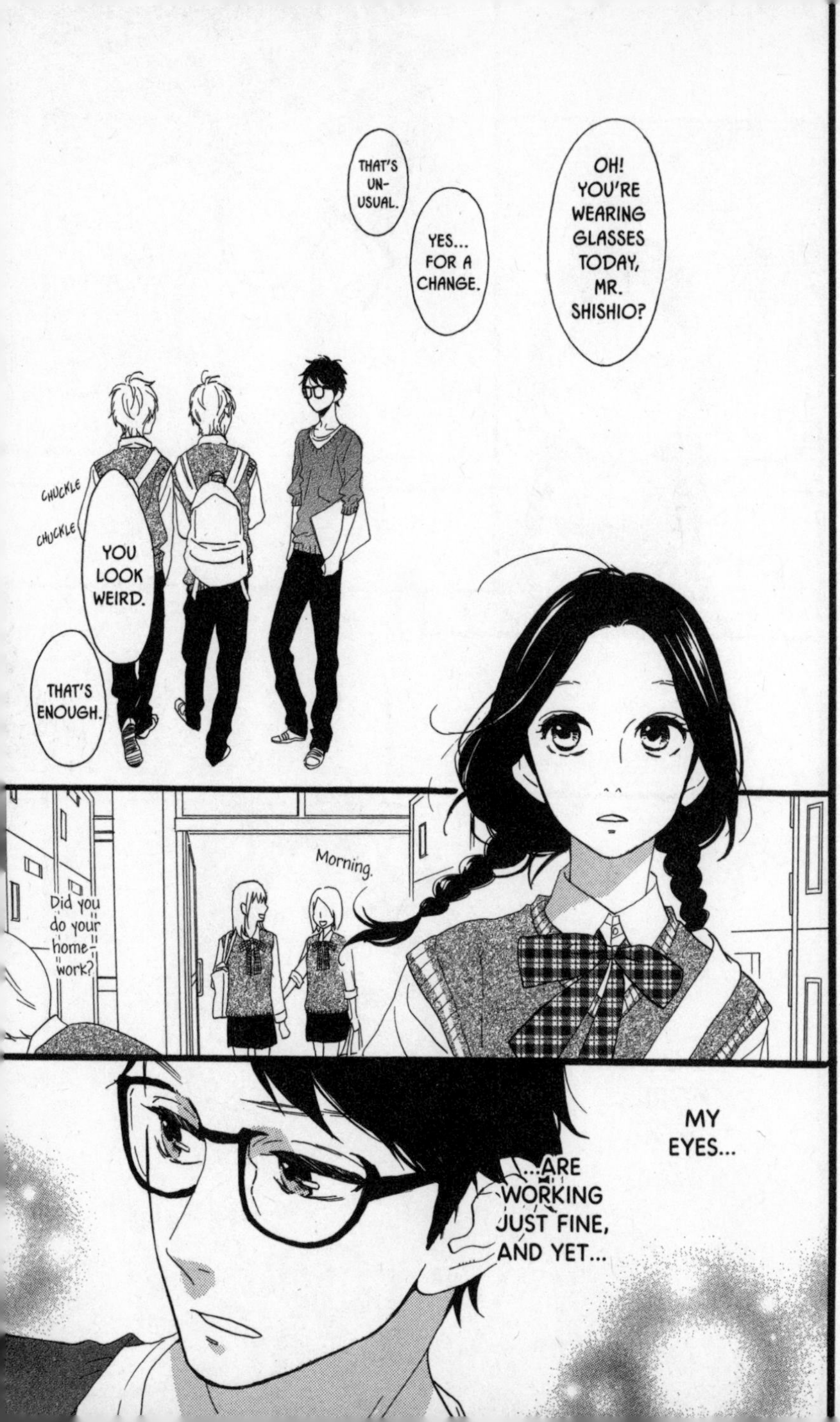
OH! YOU'RE WEARING GLASSES TODAY, MR. SHISHIO?
THAT'S UN-USUAL.
YES... FOR A CHANGE.
CHUCKLE
CHUCKLE
YOU LOOK WEIRD.
THAT'S ENOUGH.
Morning.
Did you do your home-work?
MY EYES...
...ARE WORKING JUST FINE, AND YET...

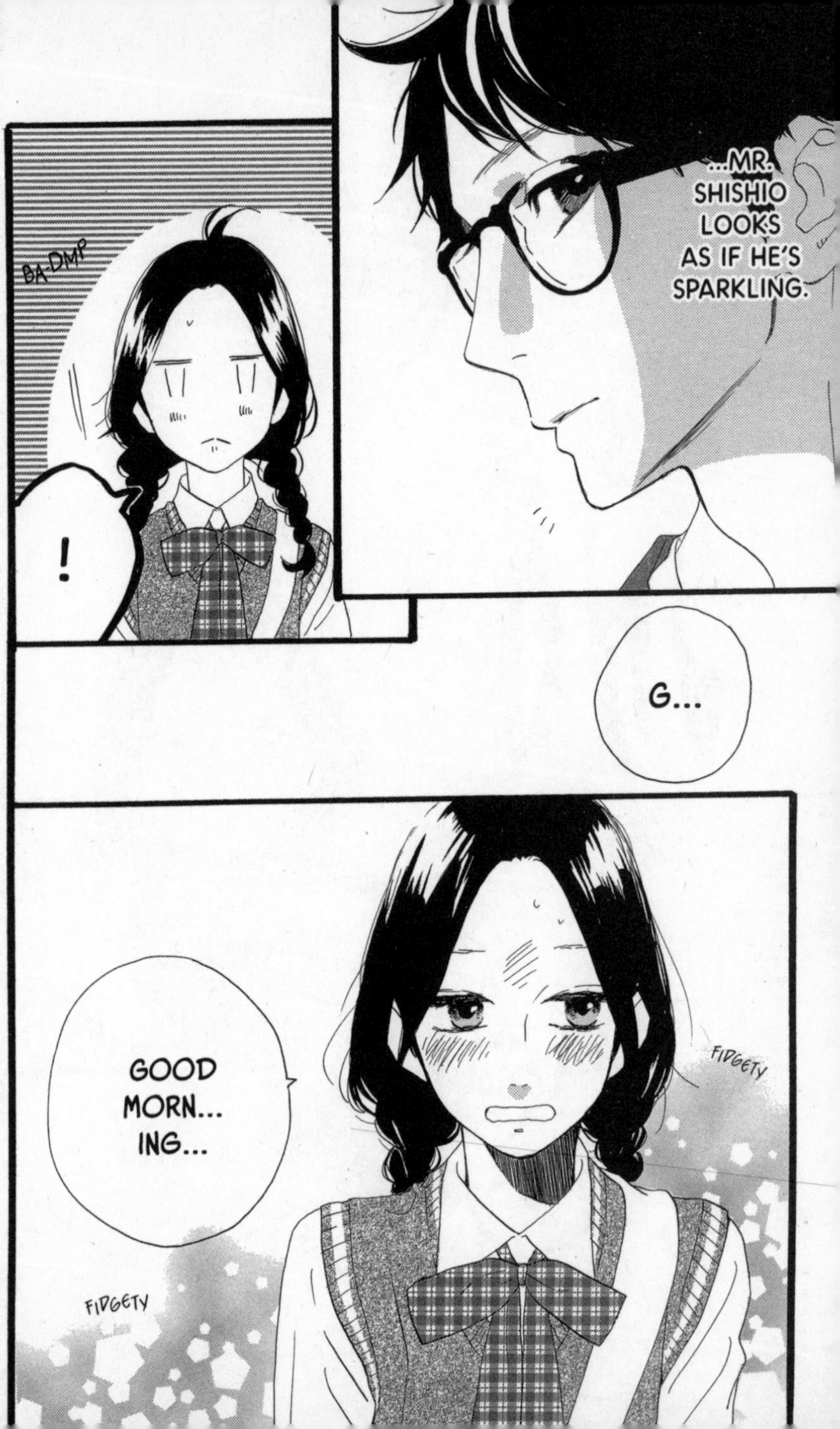
...MR. SHISHIO LOOKS AS IF HE'S SPARKLING.
BA-DMP
!
G...
FIDGETY
GOOD MORN... ING...
FIDGETY

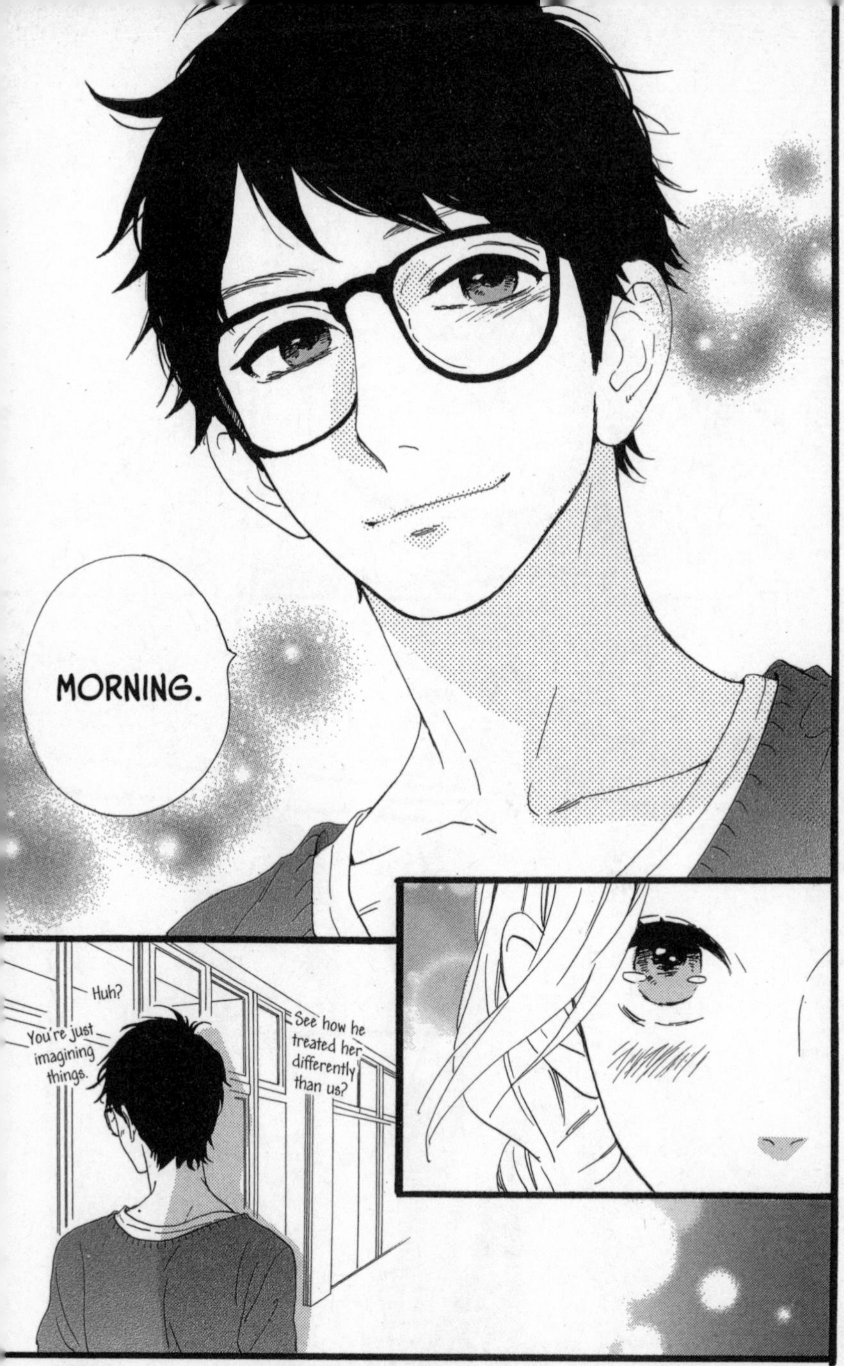
MORNING.
See how he treated her differently than us?
Huh?
You're just imagining things.

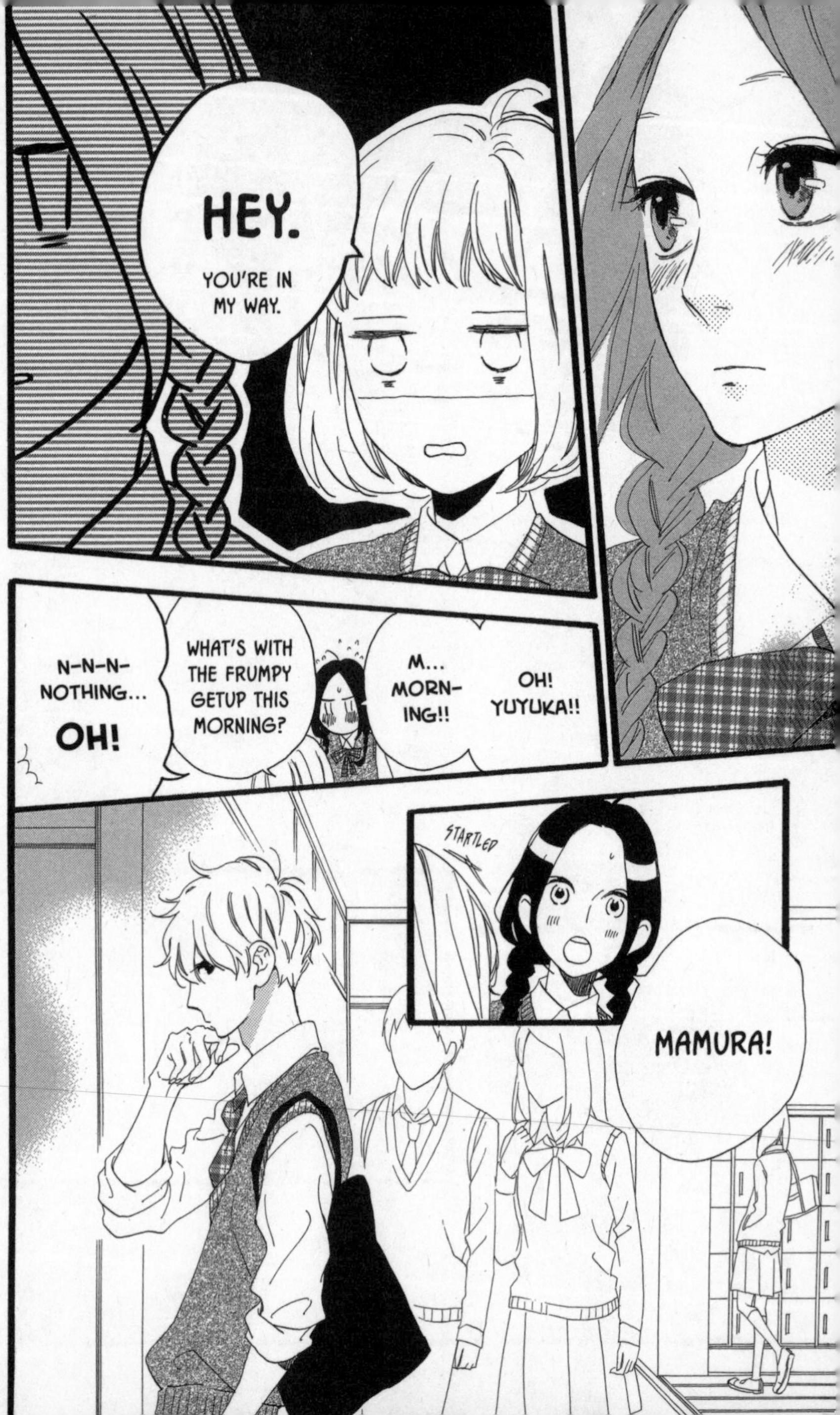
HEY.
YOU'RE IN MY WAY.
OH! YUYUKA!!
M... MORN-ING!!
WHAT'S WITH THE FRUMPY GETUP THIS MORNING?
N-N-N-NOTHING... OH!
STARTLED
MAMURA!

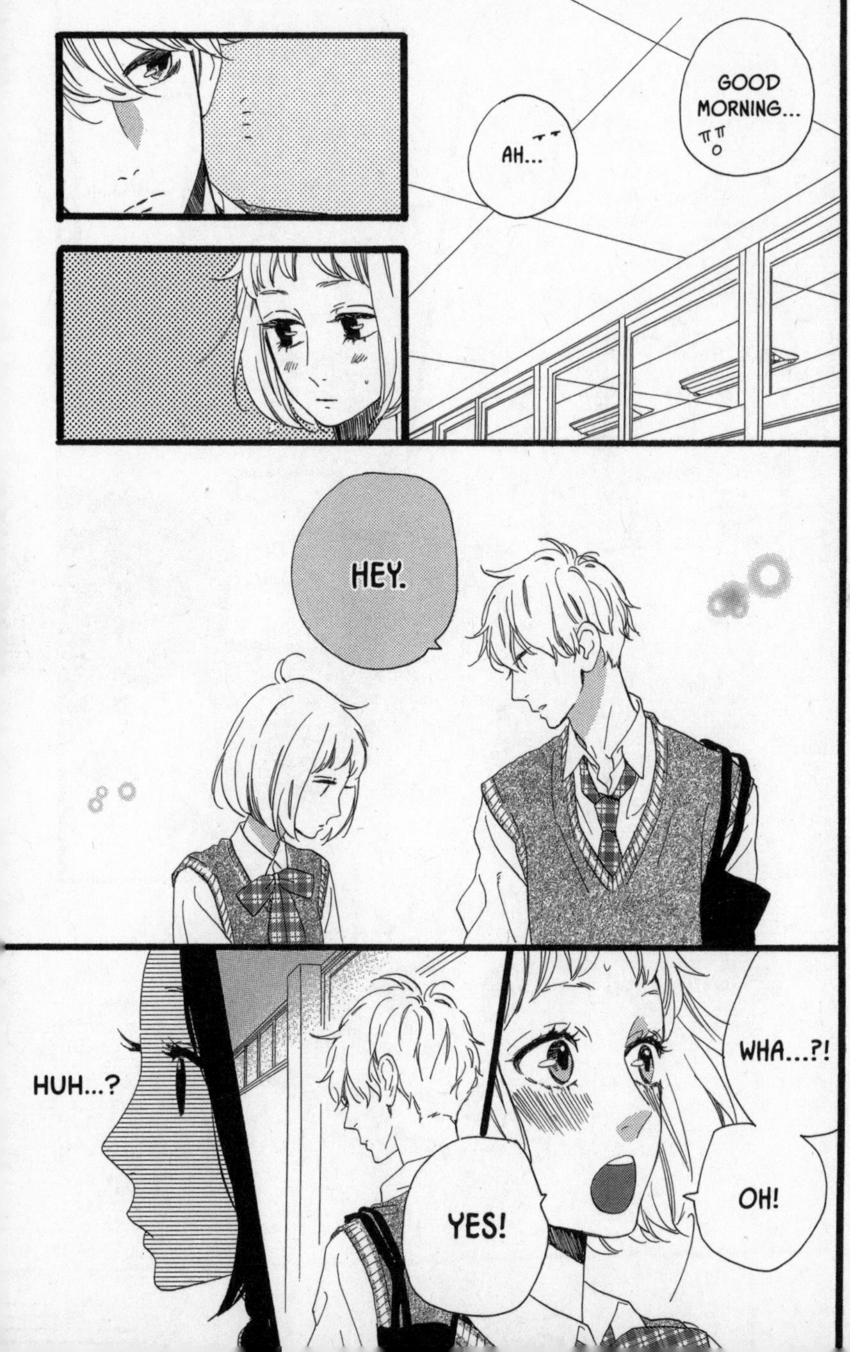
GOOD MORNING...
AH...
HEY.
WHA...?!
OH!
YES!
HUH...?

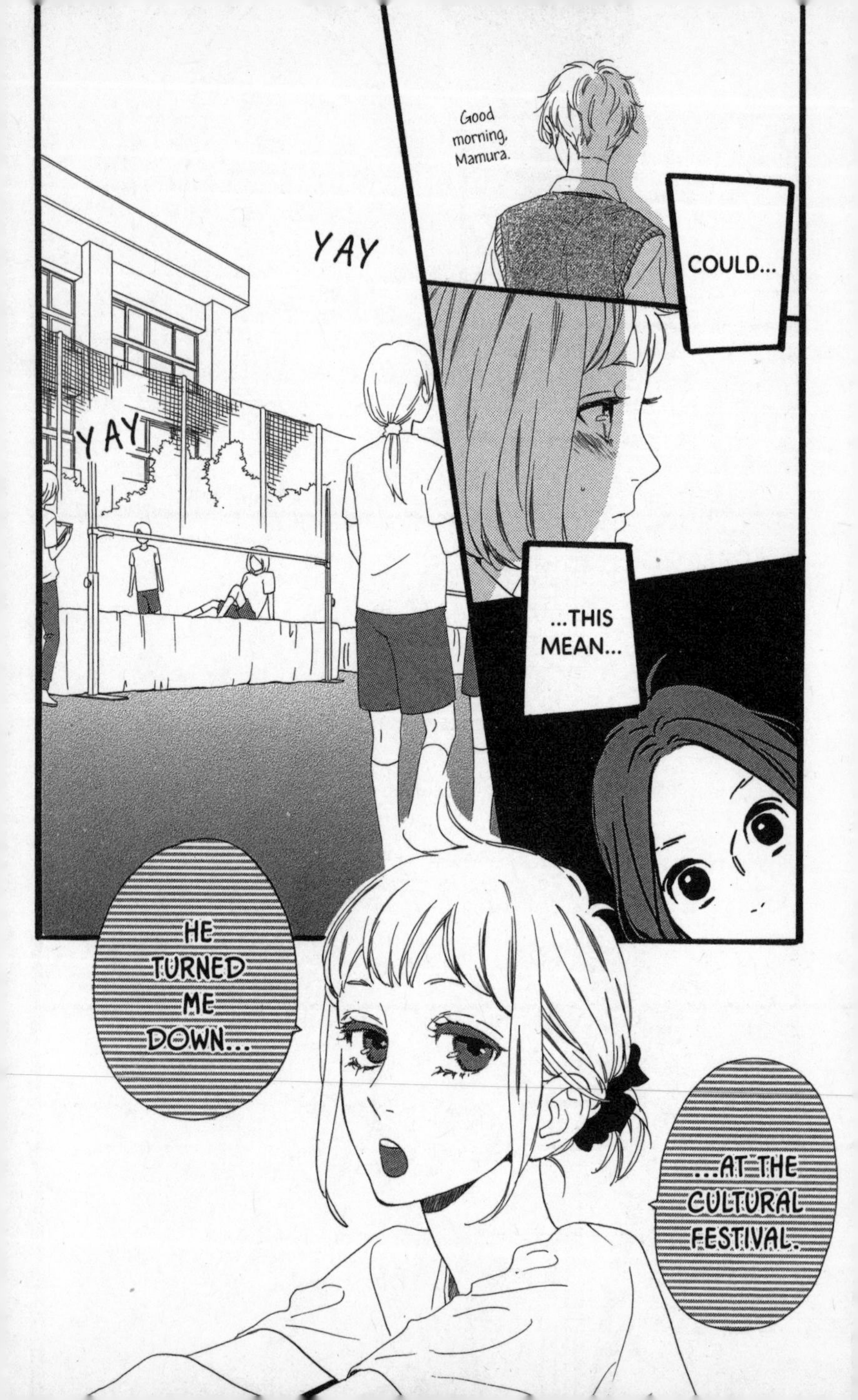
Good morning, Mamura.
COULD...
...THIS MEAN...
YAY
YAY
HE TURNED ME DOWN...
...AT THE CULTURAL FESTIVAL.

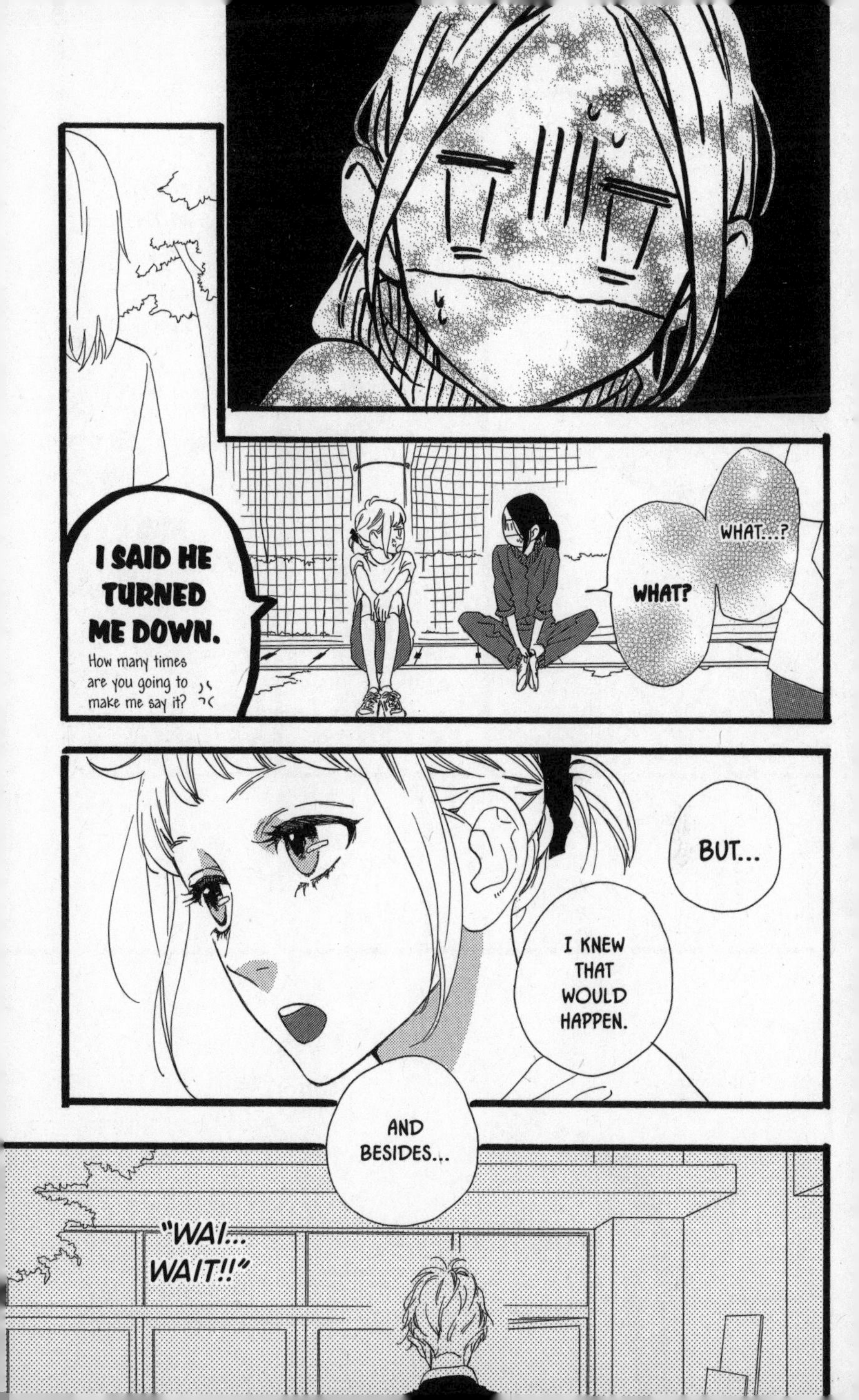
WHAT...?
WHAT?
I SAID HE TURNED ME DOWN.
How many times are you going to make me say it?
BUT...
I KNEW THAT WOULD HAPPEN.
AND BESIDES...
"WAI... WAIT!!"

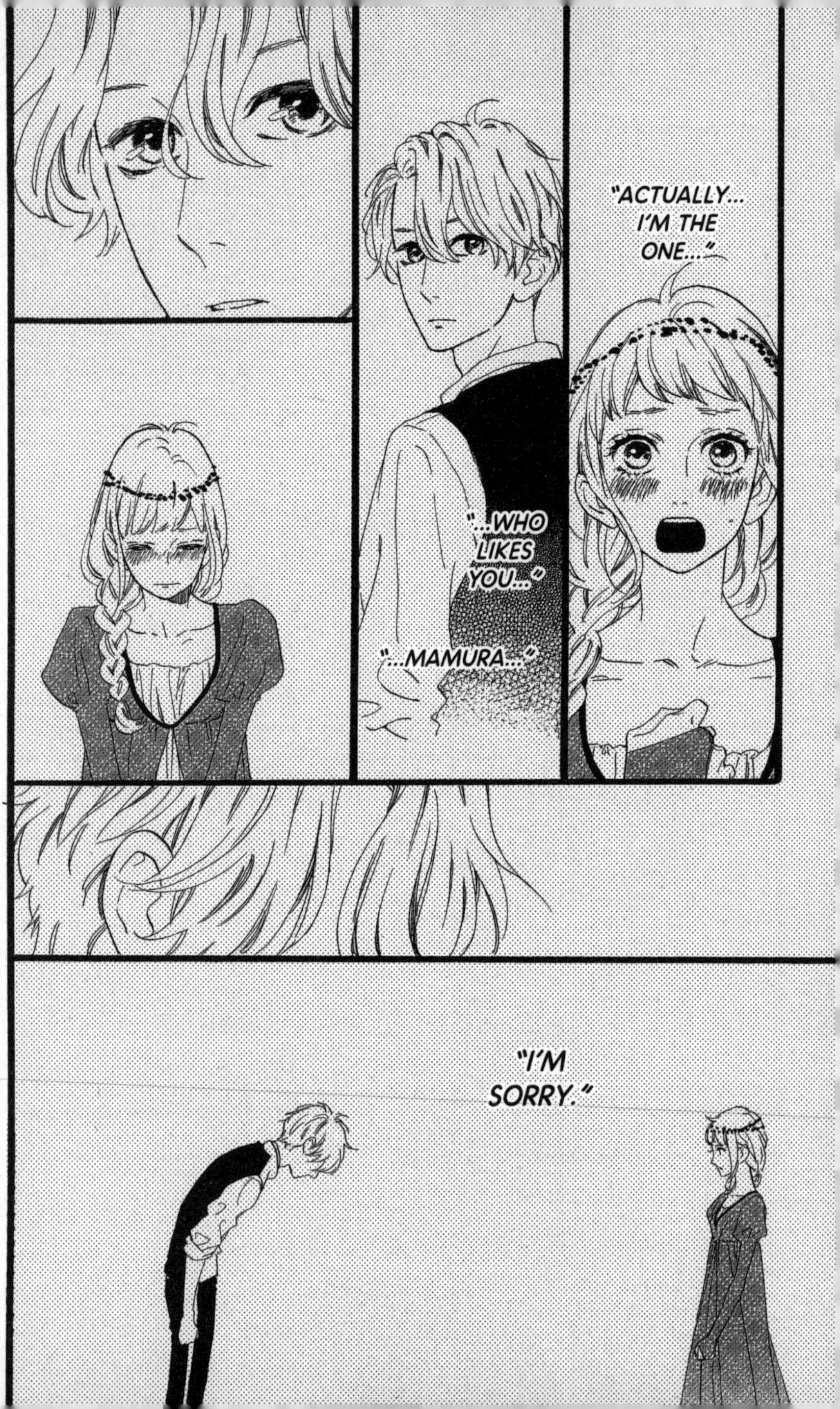
"ACTUALLY... I'M THE ONE..."
"...WHO LIKES YOU..."
"...MAMURA..."
"I'M SORRY."

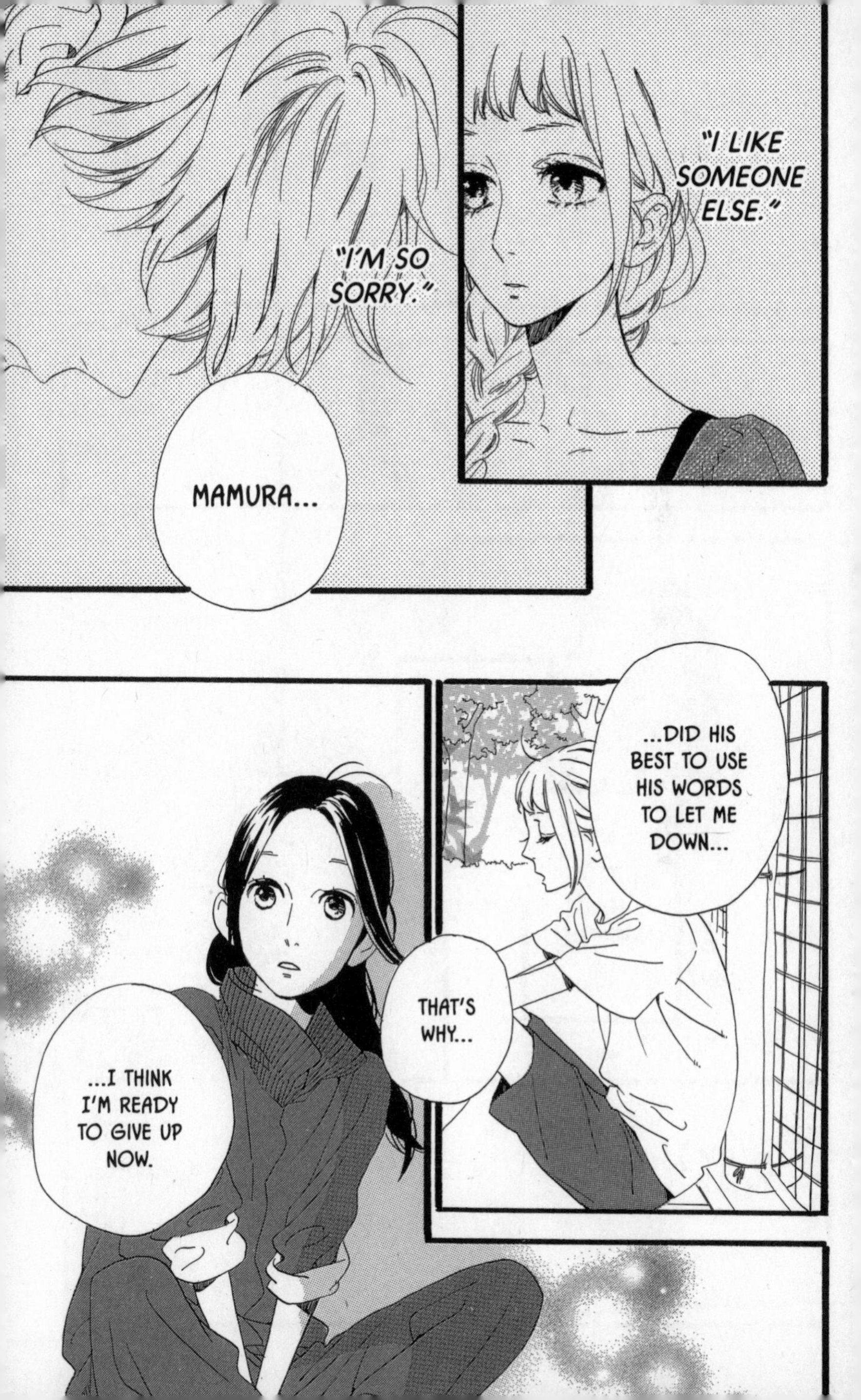
"I LIKE SOMEONE ELSE."
"I'M SO SORRY."
MAMURA...
...DID HIS BEST TO USE HIS WORDS TO LET ME DOWN...
THAT'S WHY...
...I THINK I'M READY TO GIVE UP NOW.

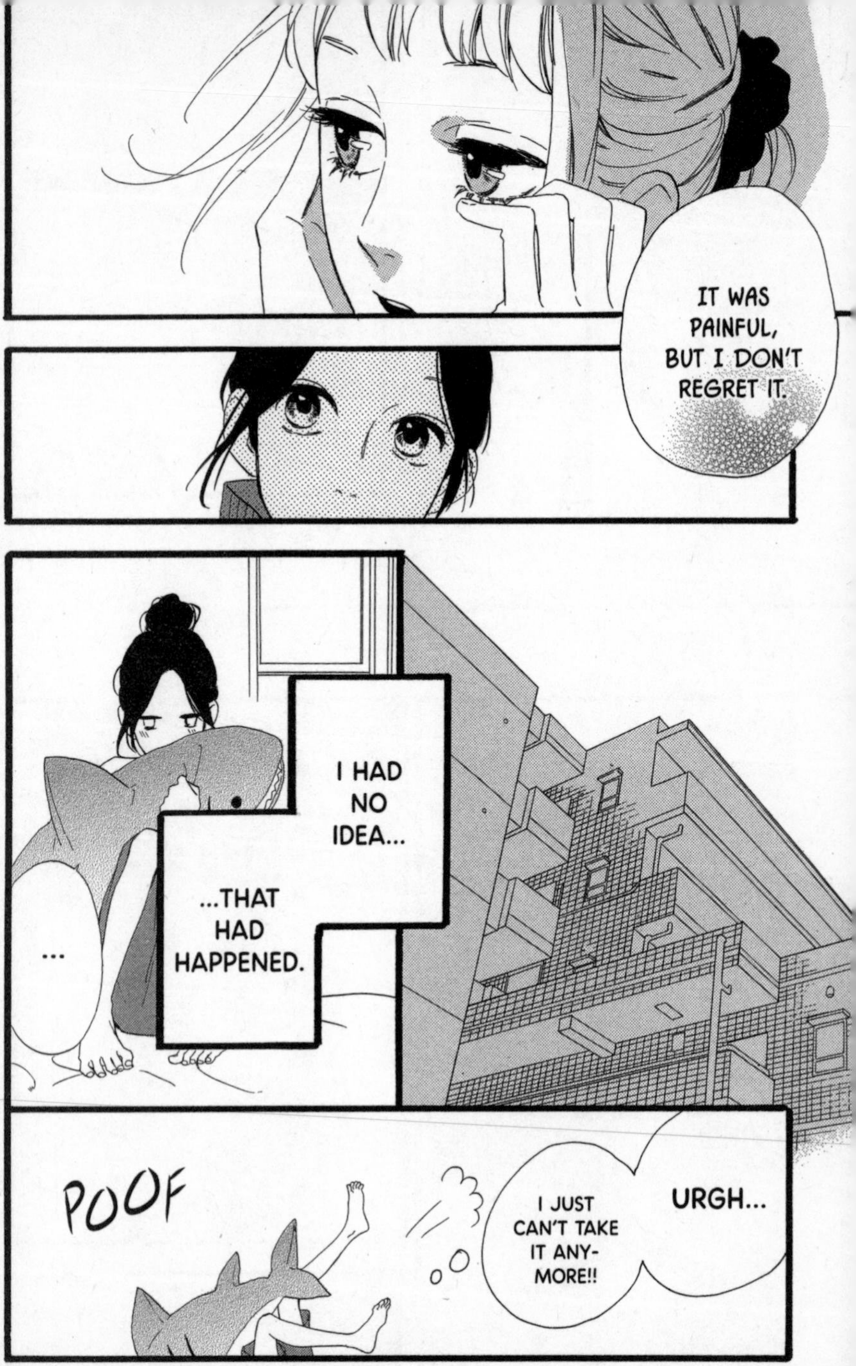
IT WAS PAINFUL, BUT I DON'T REGRET IT.
I HAD NO IDEA...
...THAT HAD HAPPENED.
...
URGH...
I JUST CAN'T TAKE IT ANY-MORE!!
POOF

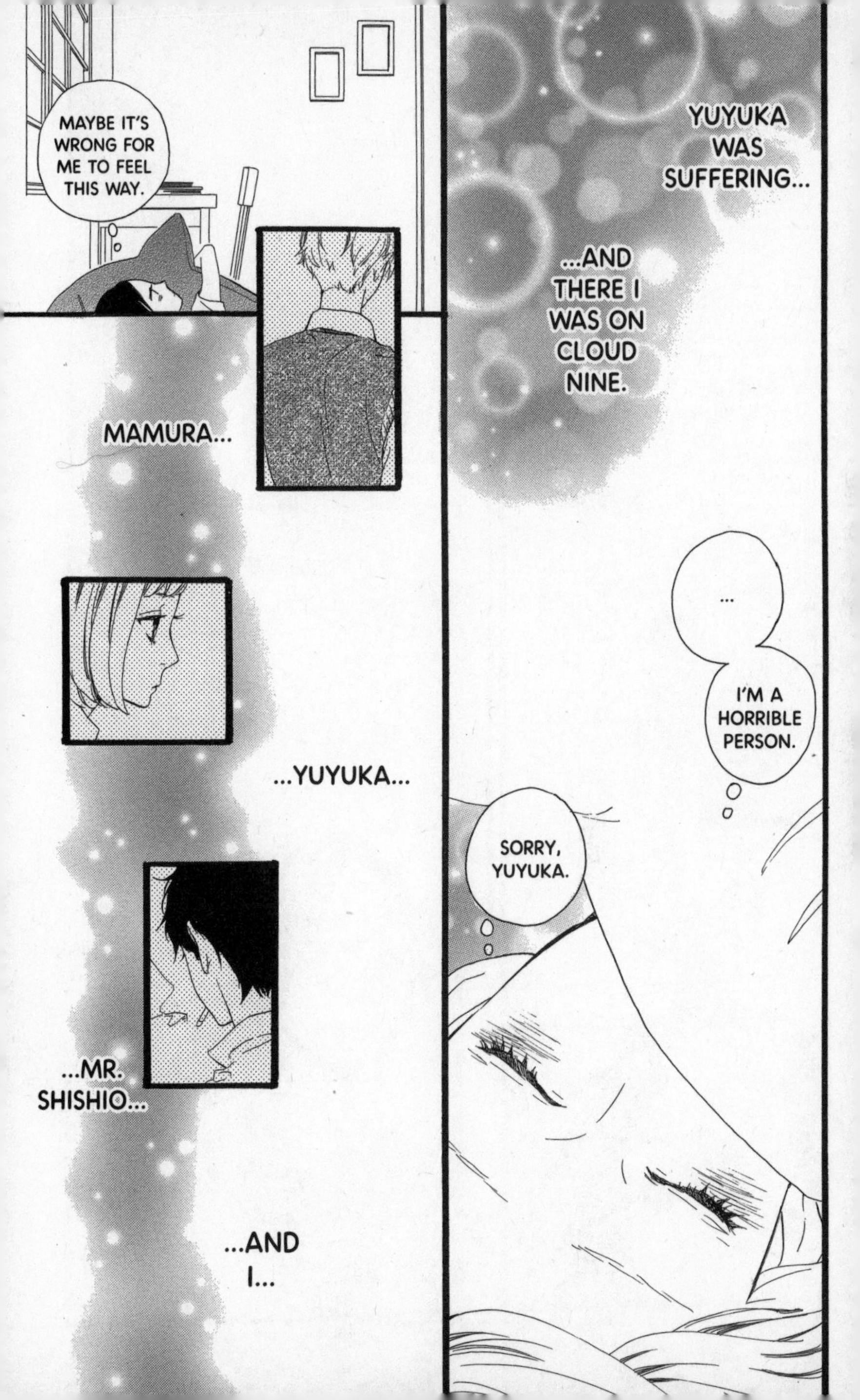
YUYUKA WAS SUFFERING...
...AND THERE I WAS ON CLOUD NINE.
...
I'M A HORRIBLE PERSON.
SORRY, YUYUKA.
MAYBE IT'S WRONG FOR ME TO FEEL THIS WAY.
MAMURA...
...YUYUKA...
...MR. SHISHIO...
...AND I...

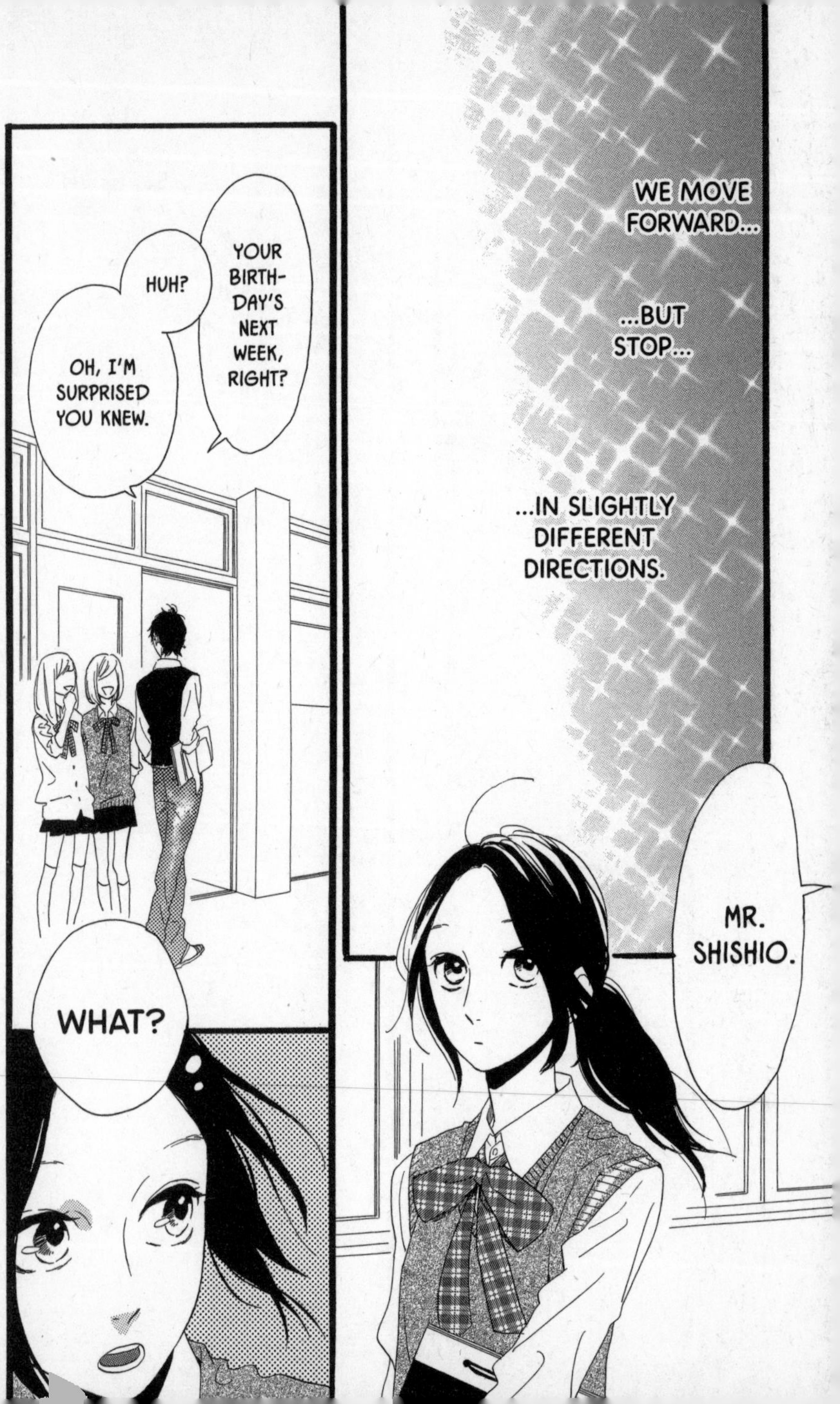
WE MOVE FORWARD...
...BUT STOP...
...IN SLIGHTLY DIFFERENT DIRECTIONS.
YOUR BIRTH-DAY'S NEXT WEEK, RIGHT?
HUH?
OH, I'M SURPRISED YOU KNEW.
MR. SHISHIO.
WHAT?

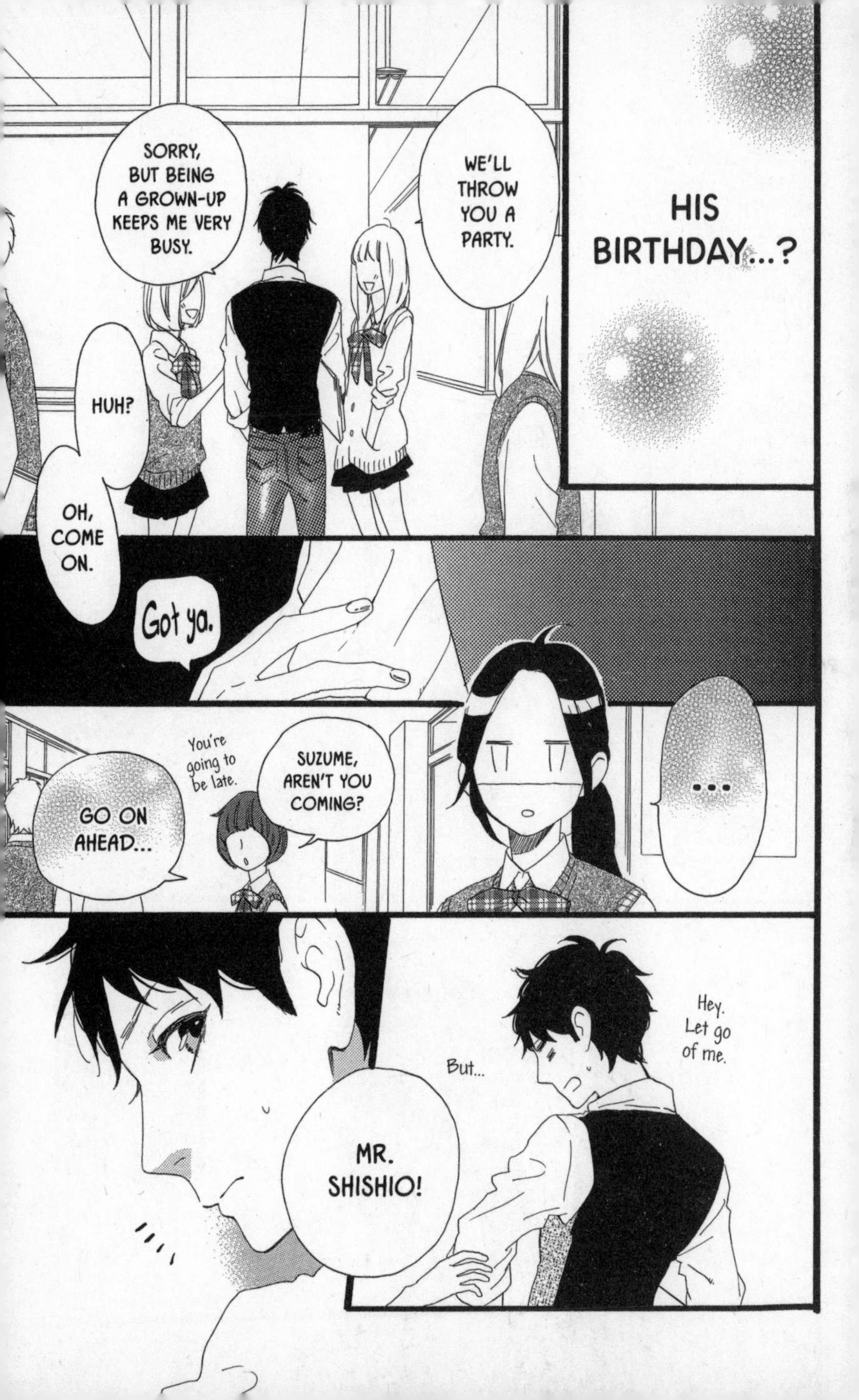
HIS BIRTHDAY...?
WE'LL THROW YOU A PARTY.
SORRY, BUT BEING A GROWN-UP KEEPS ME VERY BUSY.
HUH?
OH, COME ON.
Got ya.
...
SUZUME, AREN'T YOU COMING?
You're going to be late.
GO ON AHEAD...
Hey. Let go of me.
But...
MR. SHISHIO!

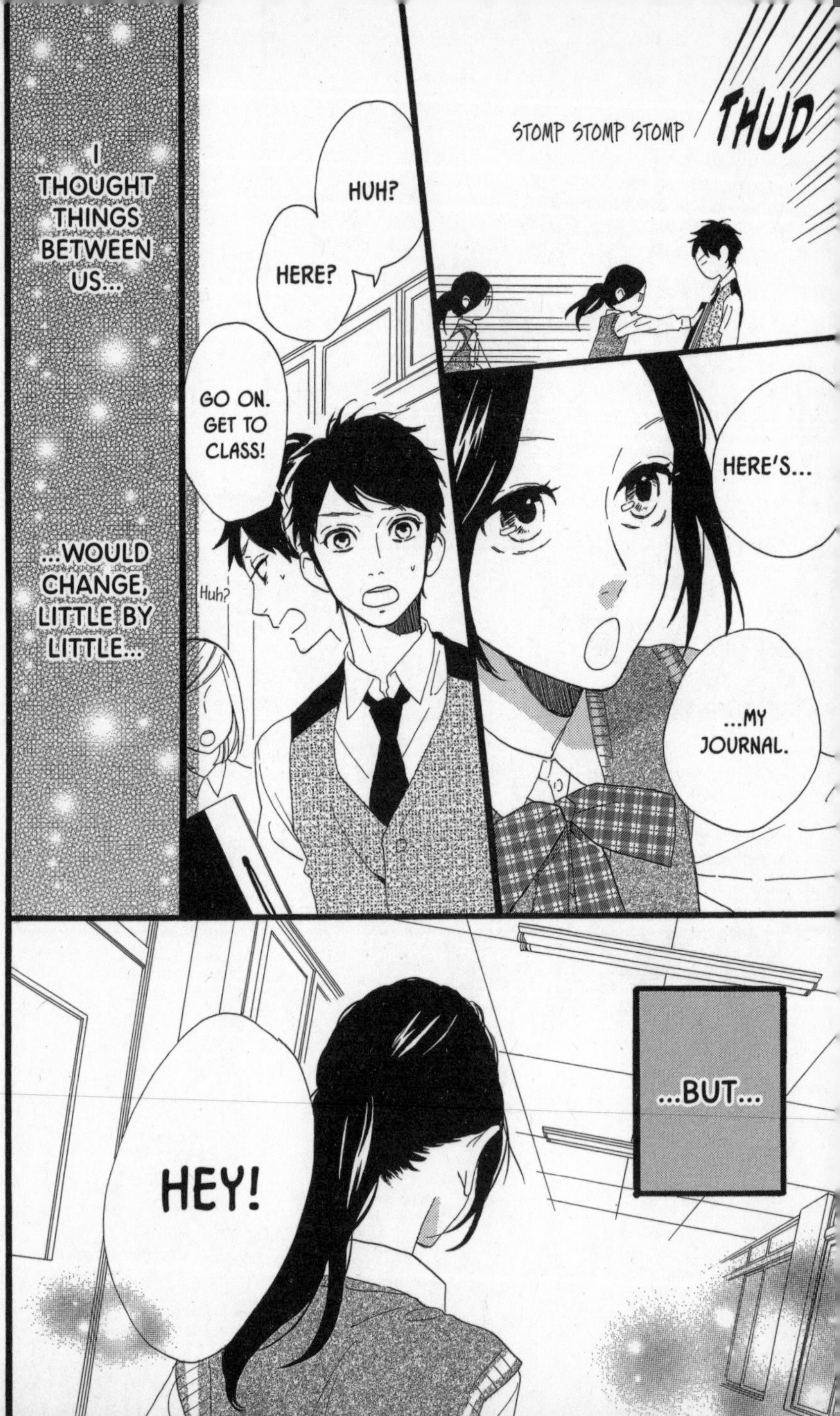
STOMP STOMP STOMP
THUD
HERE'S...
...MY JOURNAL.
HUH?
HERE?
GO ON. GET TO CLASS!
Huh?
I THOUGHT THINGS BETWEEN US...
...WOULD CHANGE, LITTLE BY LITTLE...
...BUT...
HEY!

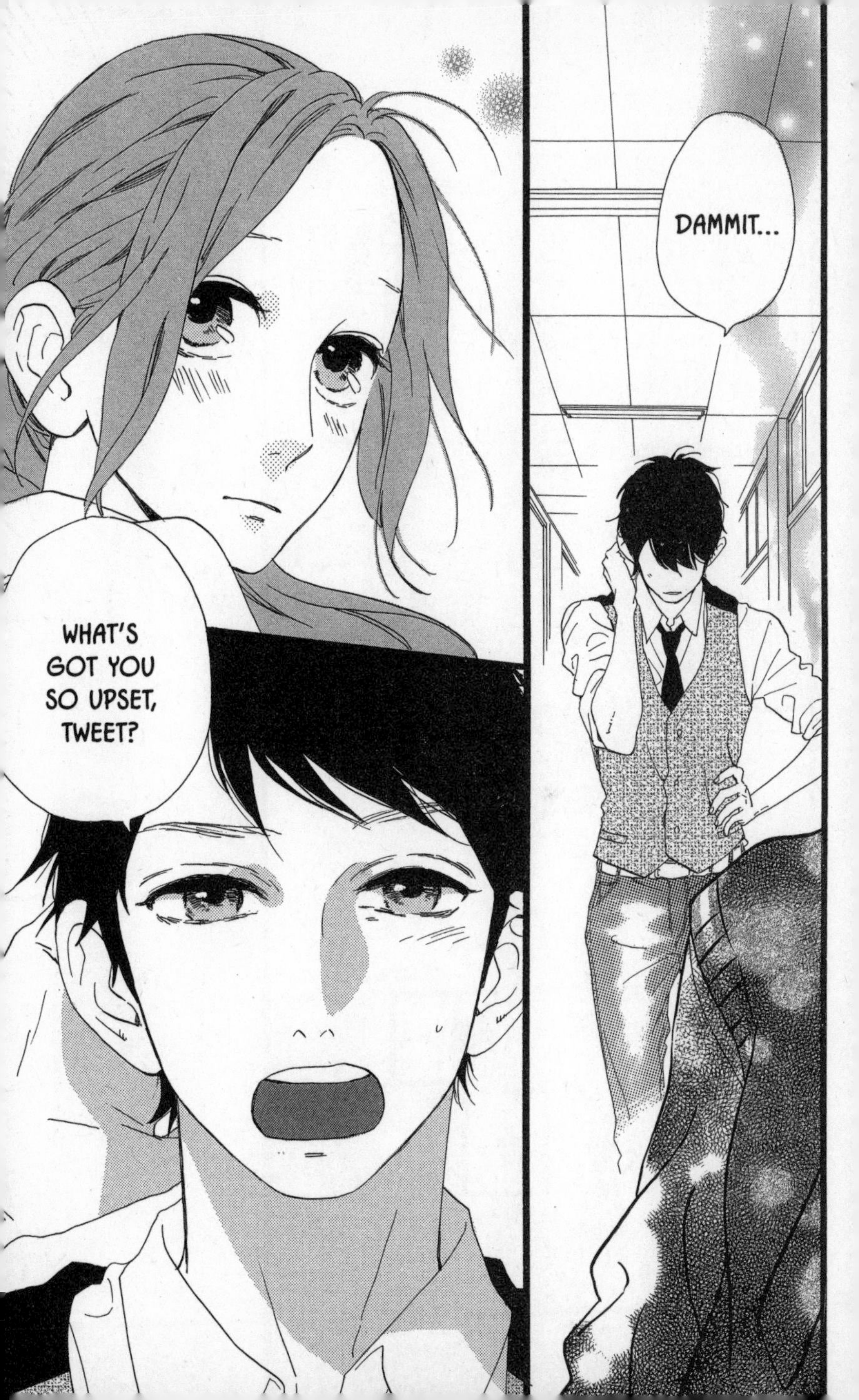
DAMMIT...
WHAT'S GOT YOU SO UPSET, TWEET?

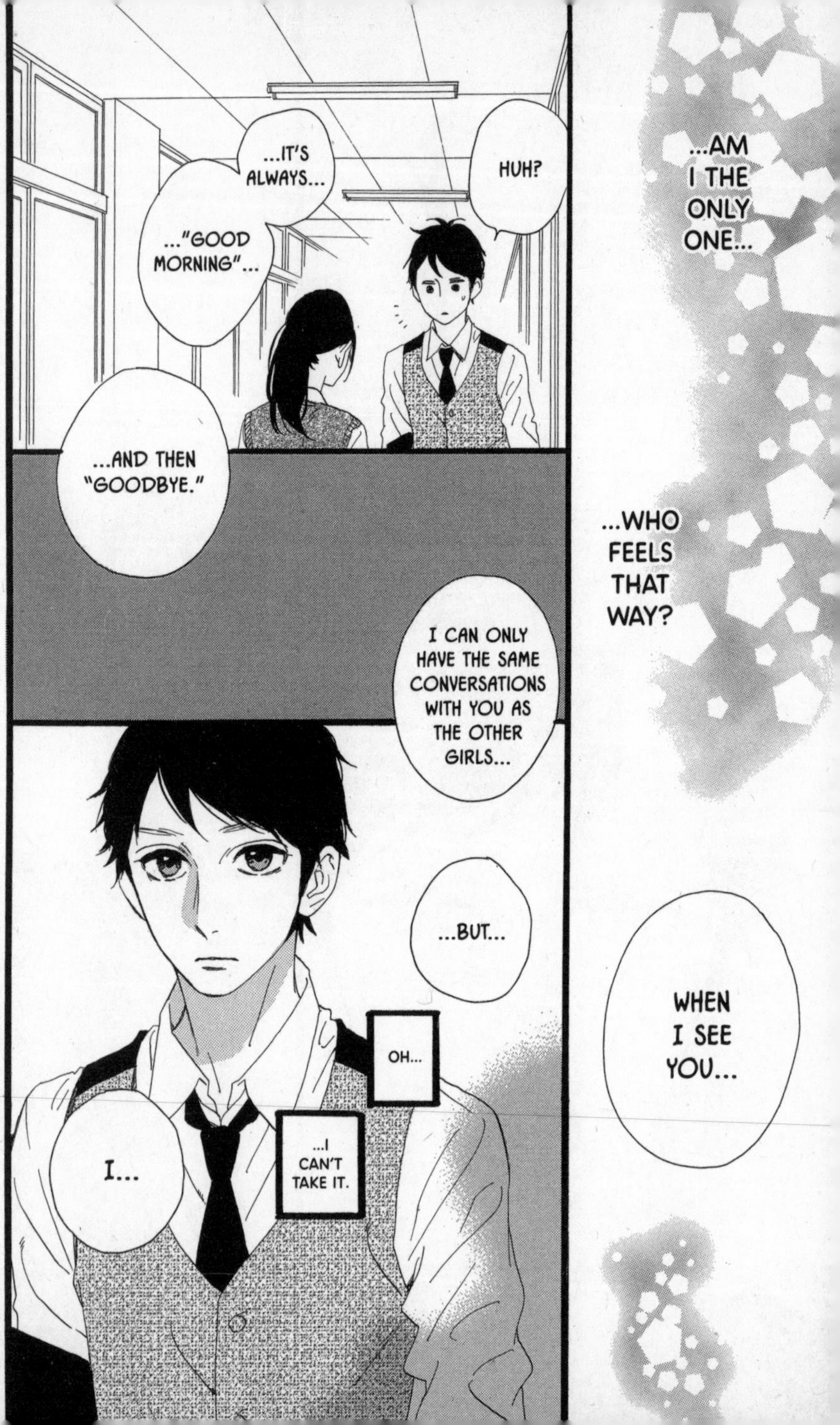
...AM I THE ONLY ONE...
...WHO FEELS THAT WAY?
WHEN I SEE YOU...
HUH?
...IT'S ALWAYS...
..."GOOD MORNING"...
...AND THEN "GOODBYE."
I CAN ONLY HAVE THE SAME CONVERSATIONS WITH YOU AS THE OTHER GIRLS...
...BUT...
OH...
...I CAN'T TAKE IT.
I...

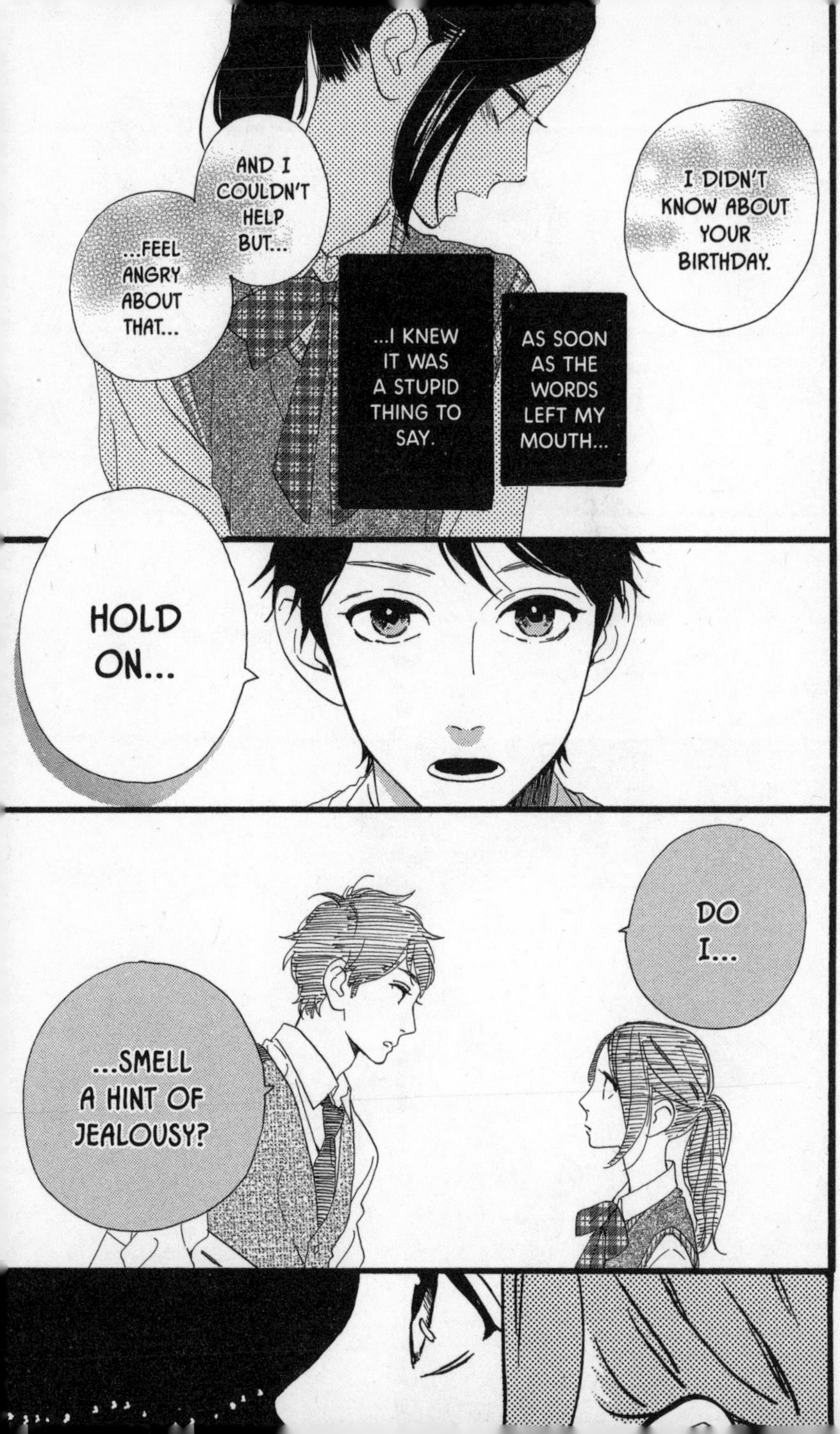
I DIDN'T KNOW ABOUT YOUR BIRTHDAY.
AS SOON AS THE WORDS LEFT MY MOUTH...
...I KNEW IT WAS A STUPID THING TO SAY.
AND I COULDN'T HELP BUT...
...FEEL ANGRY ABOUT THAT...
HOLD ON...
DO I...
...SMELL A HINT OF JEALOUSY?

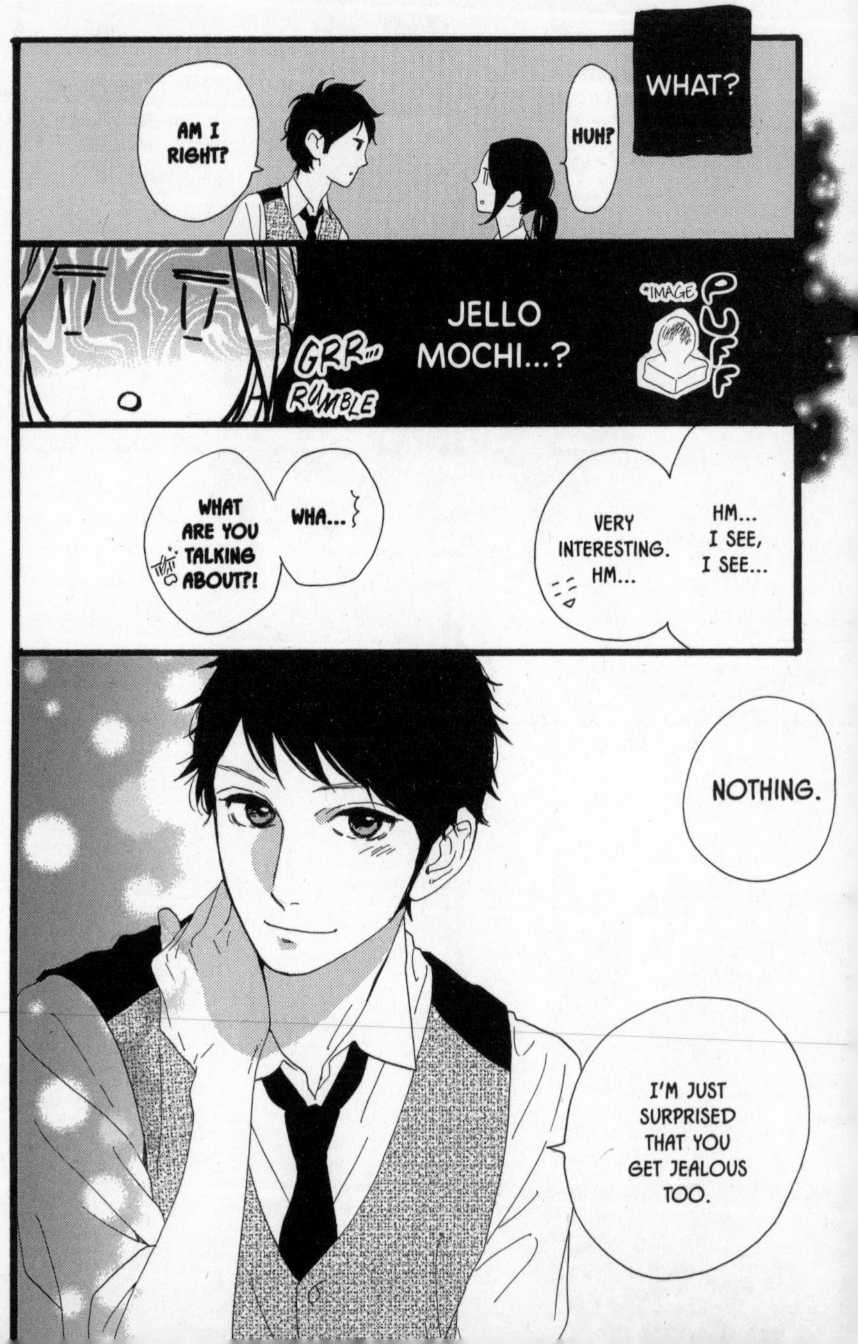
WHAT?
HUH?
AM I RIGHT?
*IMAGE
PUFF
JELLO MOCHI...?
GRR... RUMBLE
HM... I SEE, I SEE...
VERY INTERESTING. HM...
WHA...
WHAT ARE YOU TALKING ABOUT?!
NOTHING.
I'M JUST SURPRISED THAT YOU GET JEALOUS TOO.

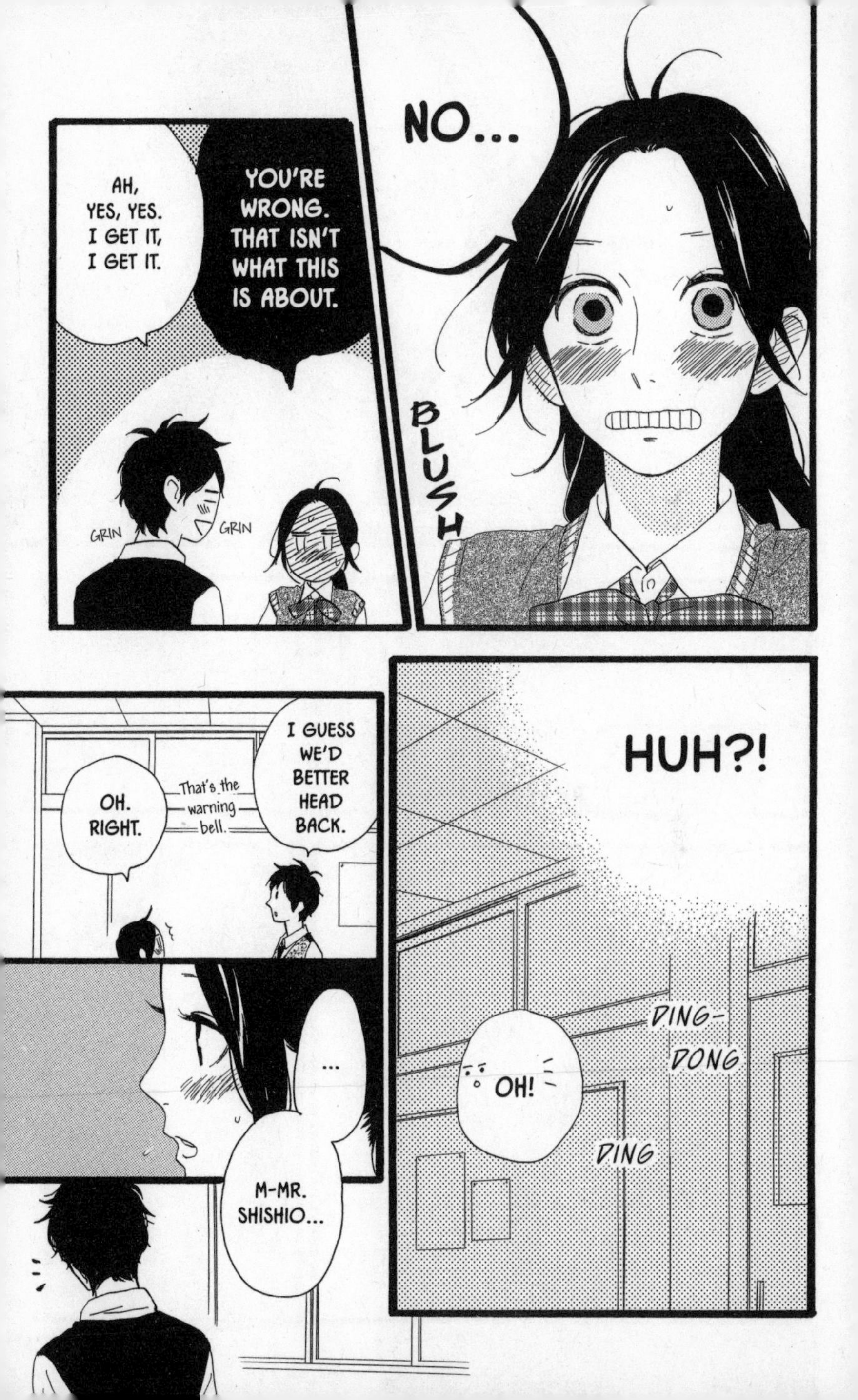

NO...
BLUSH
YOU'RE WRONG. THAT ISN'T WHAT THIS IS ABOUT.
AH, YES, YES. I GET IT, I GET IT.
GRIN
GRIN
HUH?!
DING-DONG
OH!
DING
I GUESS WE'D BETTER HEAD BACK.
That's the warning bell.
OH. RIGHT.
...
M-MR. SHISHIO...

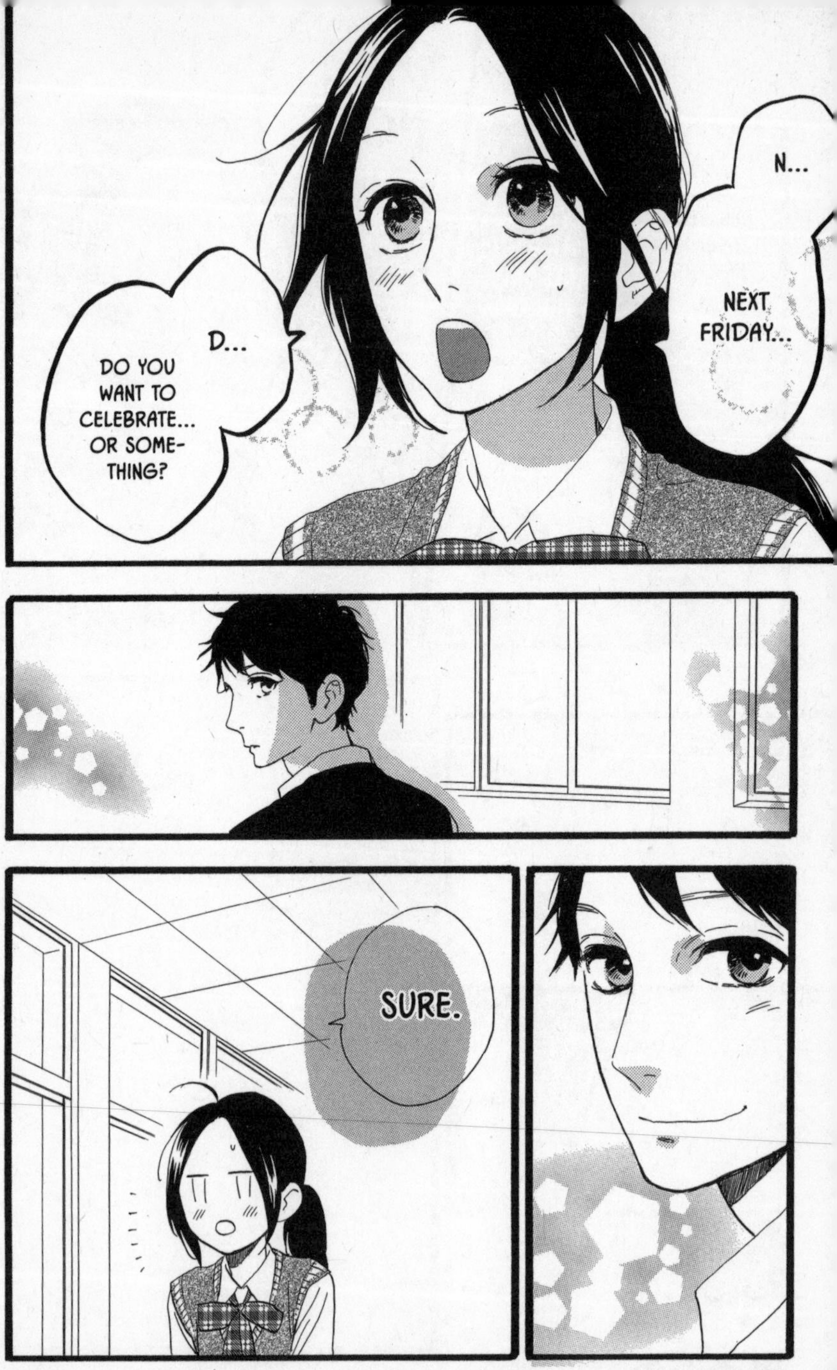
N...
NEXT FRIDAY...
D...
DO YOU WANT TO CELEBRATE... OR SOME-THING?
SURE.

I'LL BE LOOKING FORWARD TO IT.

TURNS OUT I HAD NOTHING TO WORRY ABOUT...

...AFTER ALL.

# And so... ②

The other day, I had a book signing in Ishikawa!! I was so nervous!!! They say when loners go out in public that **all their faults are exposed!!!** My mind went blank. I don't remember anything that I said!! I never thought I'd get so nervous. I really want to thank those of you who came all the way out to such a remote place!! It's not often that I get to meet my readers in person, so I was very moved!! It was the greatest experience of my life. I was so happy!! If I get another chance to do a book signing, I would like to look each person in the eye and thank them sincerely!! So, what do you think, *Margaret* Editorial Department? Maybe I could tag along with Momoko Koda...?

↑
She says to ask her directly.

I was so tense. These were my final words.

FIDGETY   FIDGETY

Be...

Be diligent!!

← And you should be!!
Ooh!!! wish I could bury myself!!

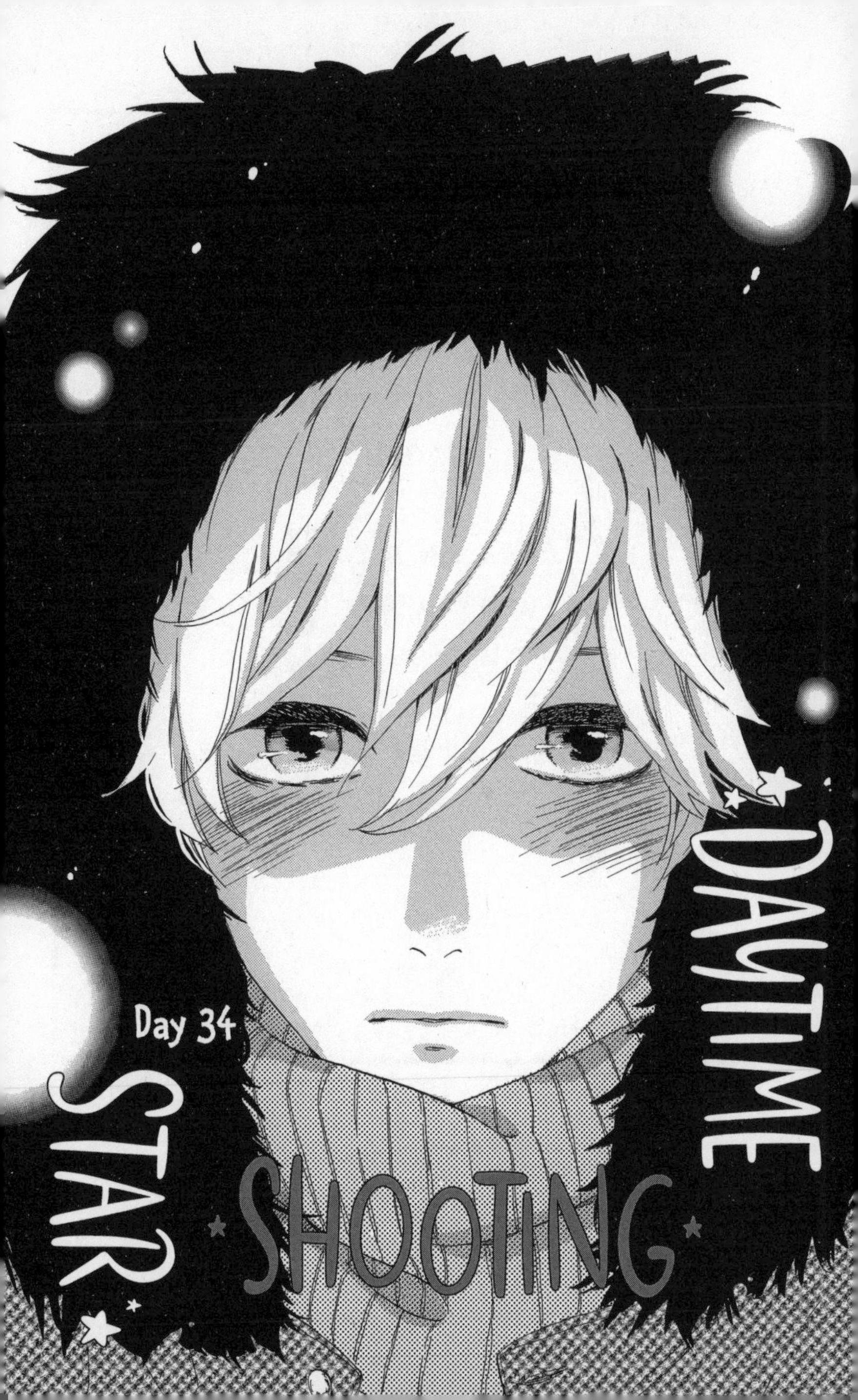

Day 34
DAYTIME
SHOOTING
STAR

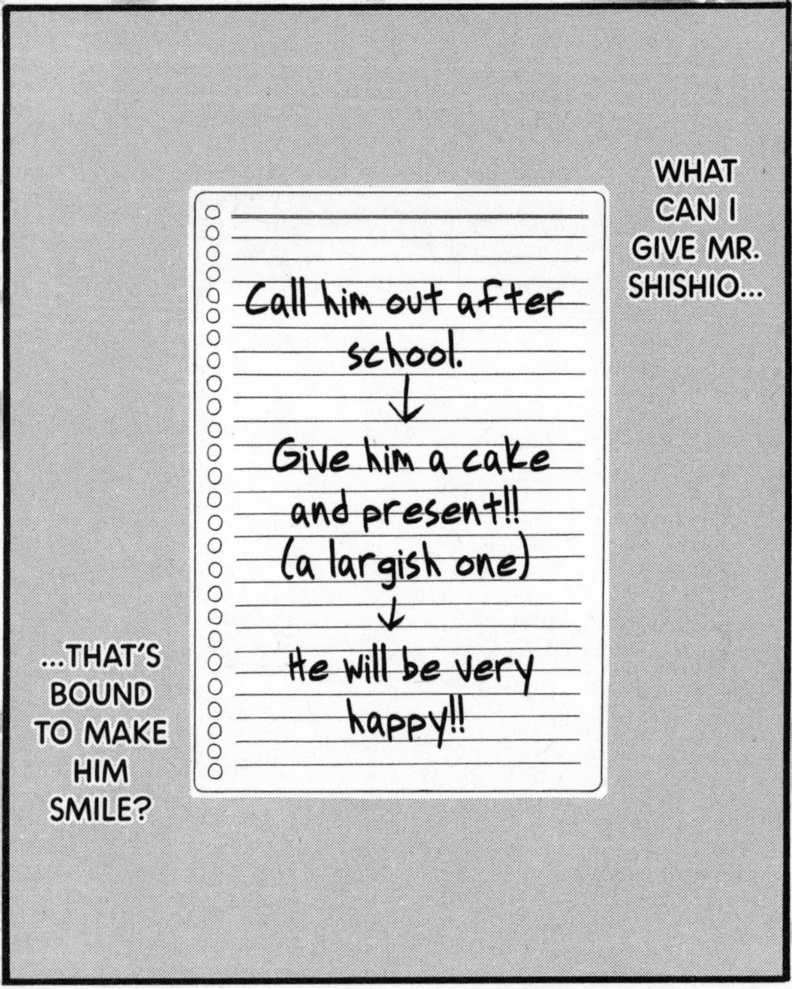
WHAT CAN I GIVE MR. SHISHIO...
Call him out after school.
↓
Give him a cake and present!! (a largish one)
↓
He will be very happy!!
...THAT'S BOUND TO MAKE HIM SMILE?

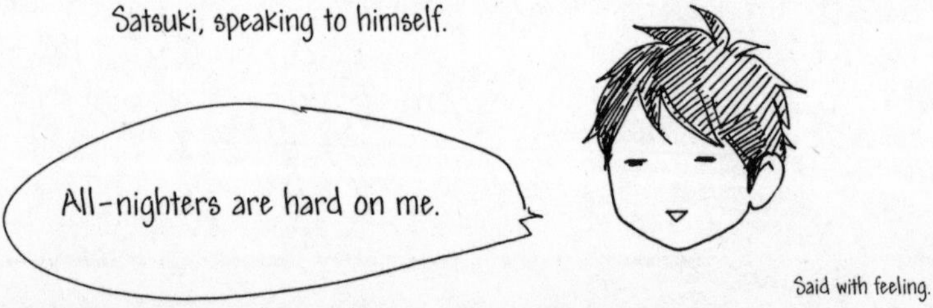
Satsuki, speaking to himself.
All-nighters are hard on me.
Said with feeling.

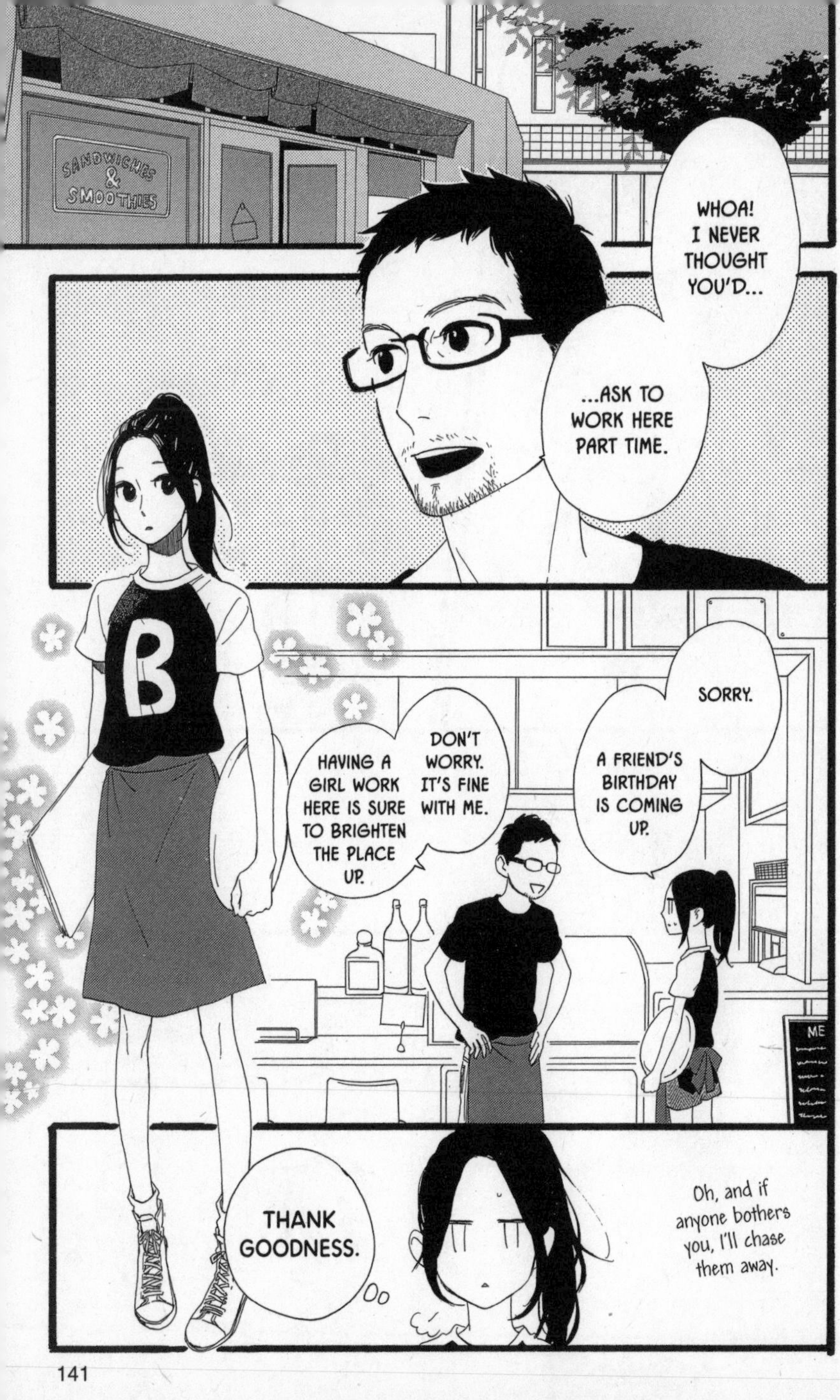
SANDWICHES & SMOOTHIES
WHOA! I NEVER THOUGHT YOU'D...
...ASK TO WORK HERE PART TIME.
SORRY.
A FRIEND'S BIRTHDAY IS COMING UP.
DON'T WORRY. IT'S FINE WITH ME.
HAVING A GIRL WORK HERE IS SURE TO BRIGHTEN THE PLACE UP.
Oh, and if anyone bothers you, I'll chase them away.
THANK GOODNESS.

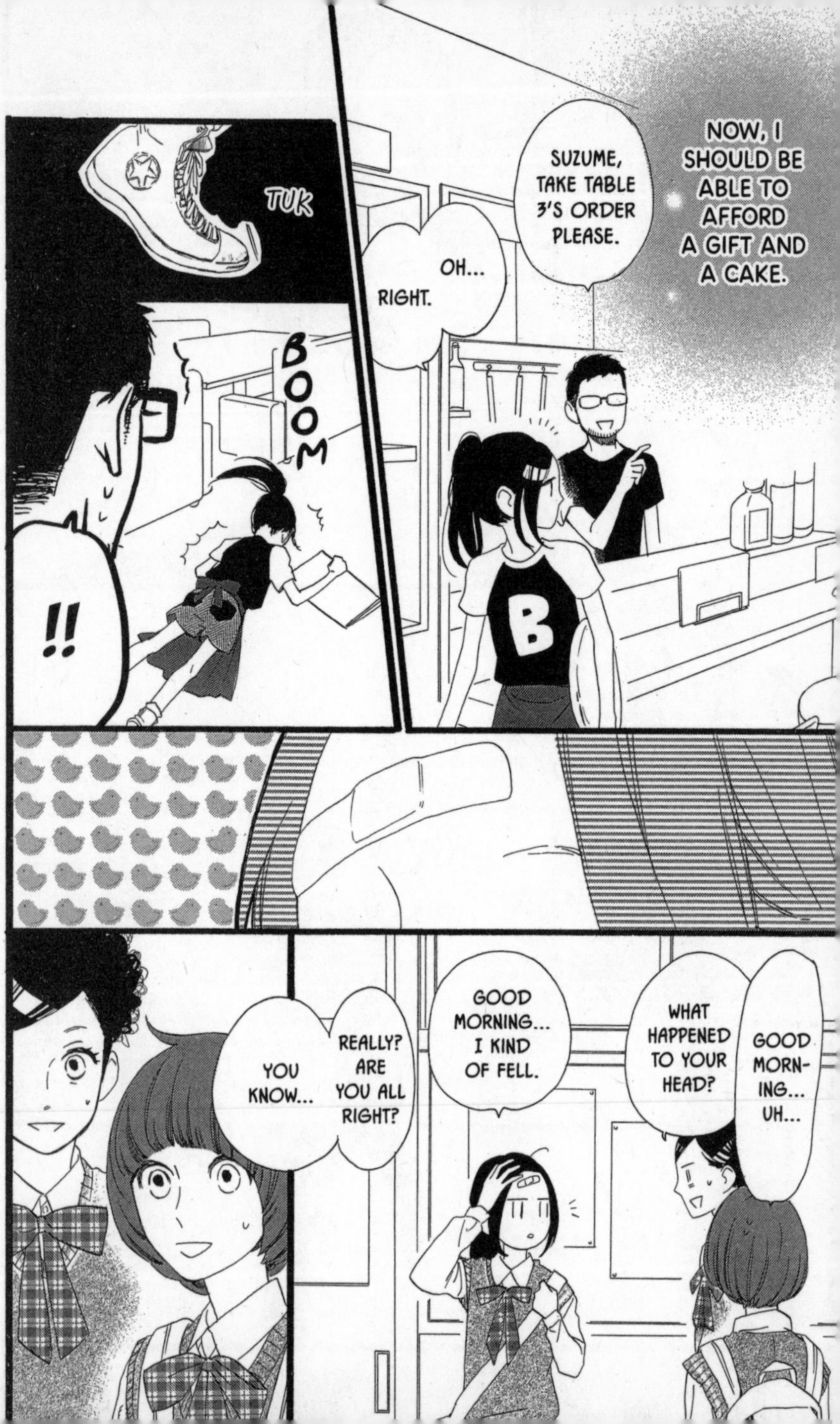
NOW, I SHOULD BE ABLE TO AFFORD A GIFT AND A CAKE.
SUZUME, TAKE TABLE 3'S ORDER PLEASE.
OH... RIGHT.
TUK
BOOM
!!
GOOD MORNING... UH...
WHAT HAPPENED TO YOUR HEAD?
GOOD MORNING... I KIND OF FELL.
REALLY? ARE YOU ALL RIGHT?
YOU KNOW...

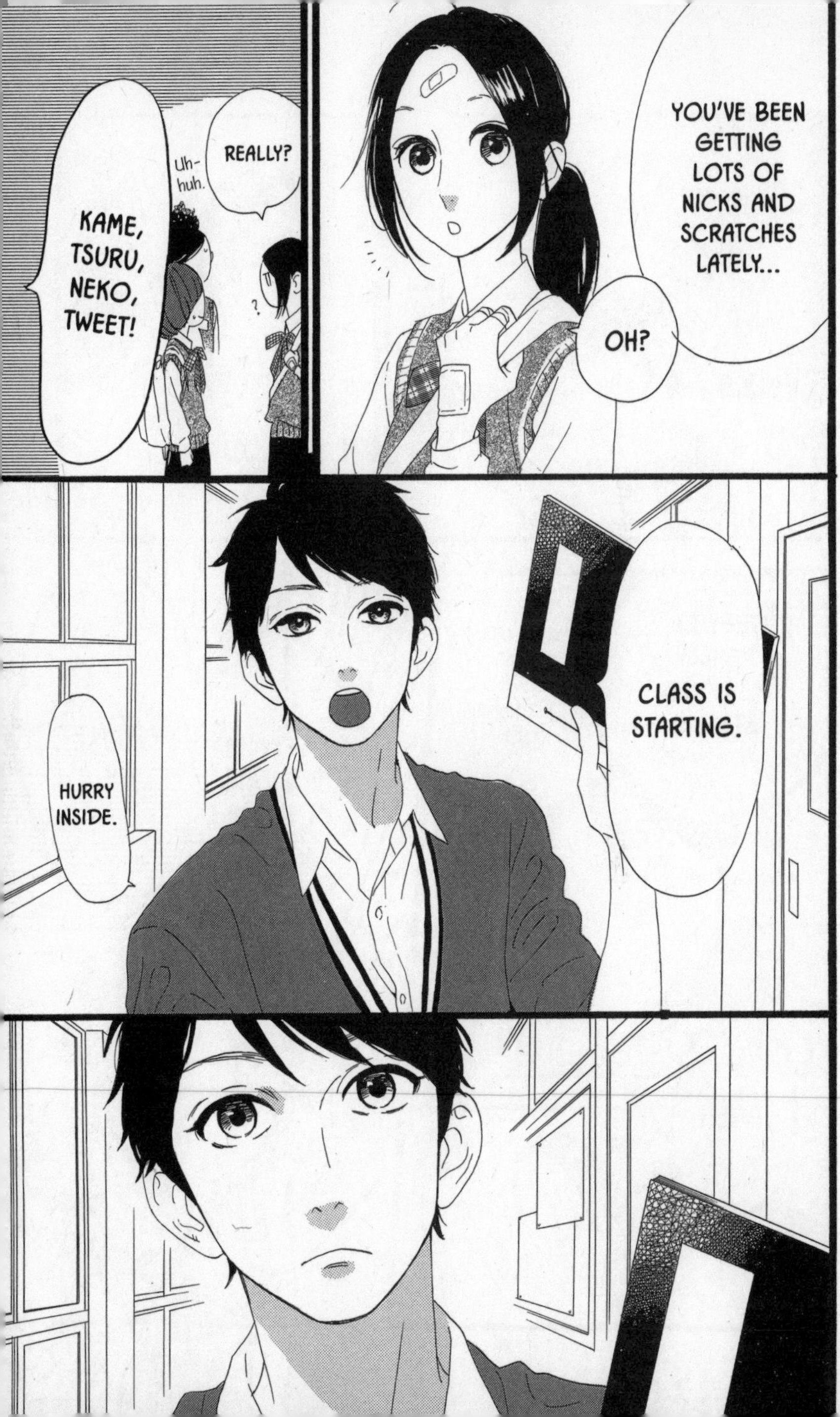
YOU'VE BEEN GETTING LOTS OF NICKS AND SCRATCHES LATELY...
OH?
REALLY?
Uh-huh.
KAME, TSURU, NEKO, TWEET!
CLASS IS STARTING.
HURRY INSIDE.

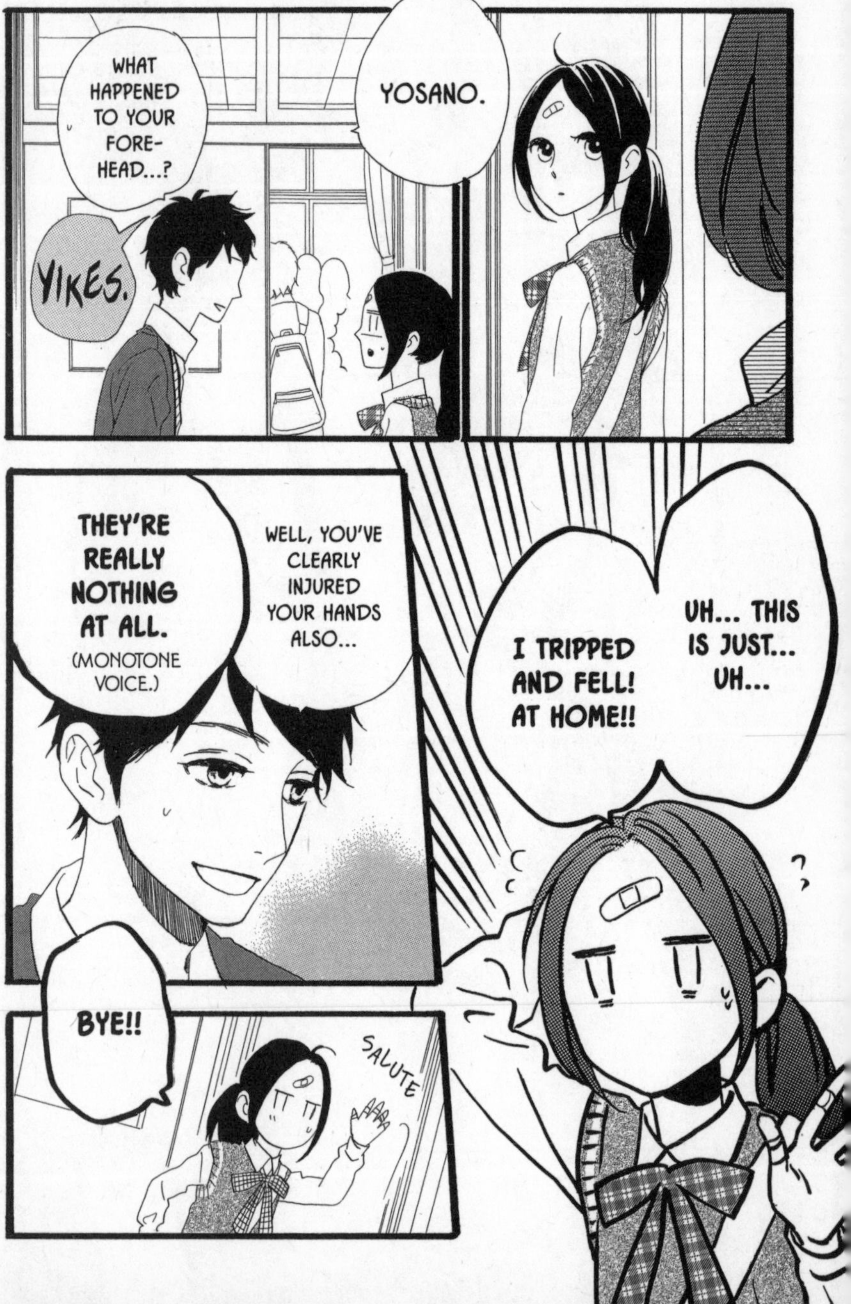
YOSANO.
WHAT HAPPENED TO YOUR FORE-HEAD...?
YIKES.
UH... THIS IS JUST... UH...
I TRIPPED AND FELL! AT HOME!!
WELL, YOU'VE CLEARLY INJURED YOUR HANDS ALSO...
THEY'RE REALLY NOTHING AT ALL.
(MONOTONE VOICE.)
BYE!!
SALUTE

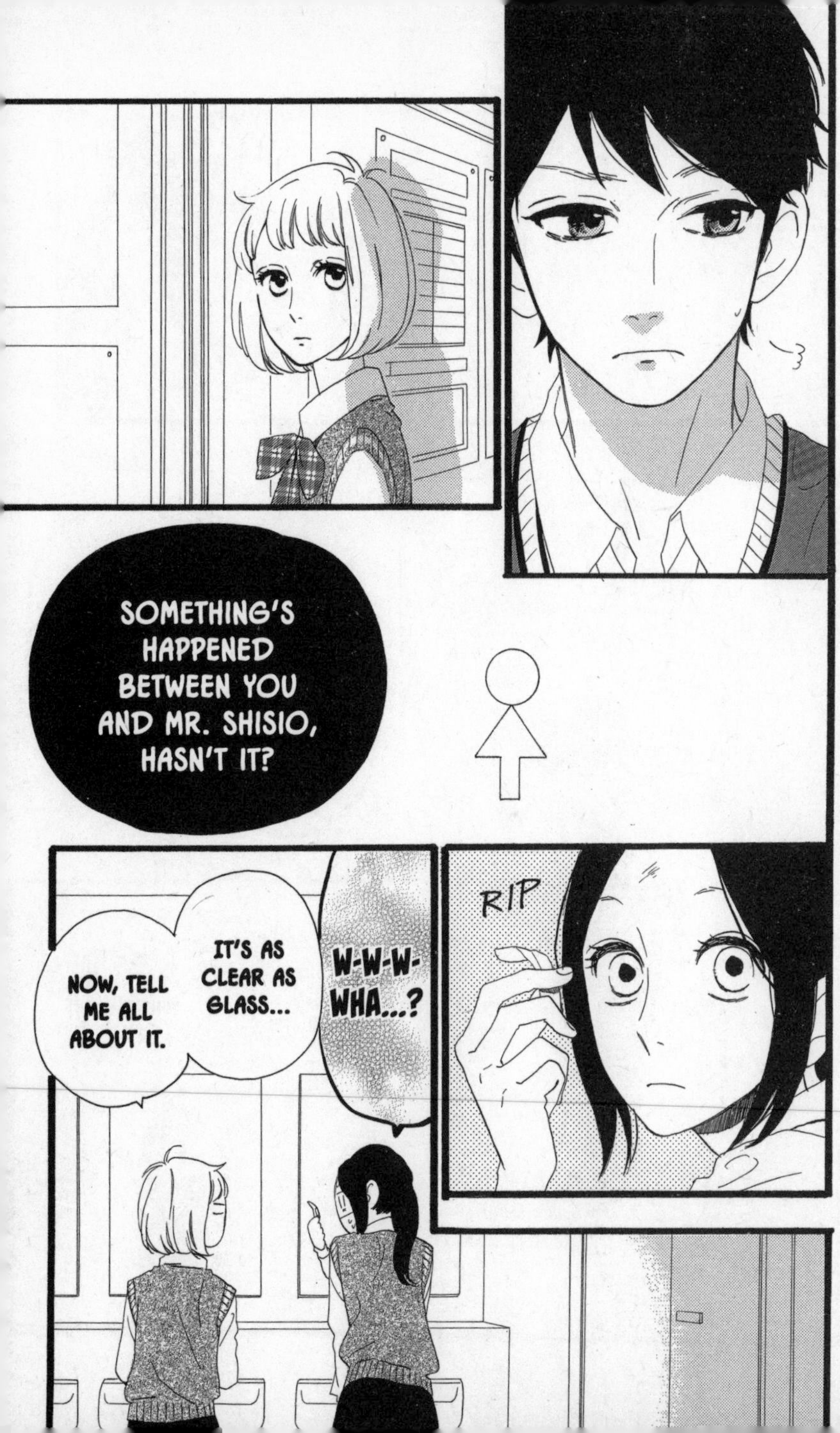
SOMETHING'S HAPPENED BETWEEN YOU AND MR. SHISIO, HASN'T IT?
RIP
W-W-W-WHA...?
IT'S AS CLEAR AS GLASS...
NOW, TELL ME ALL ABOUT IT.

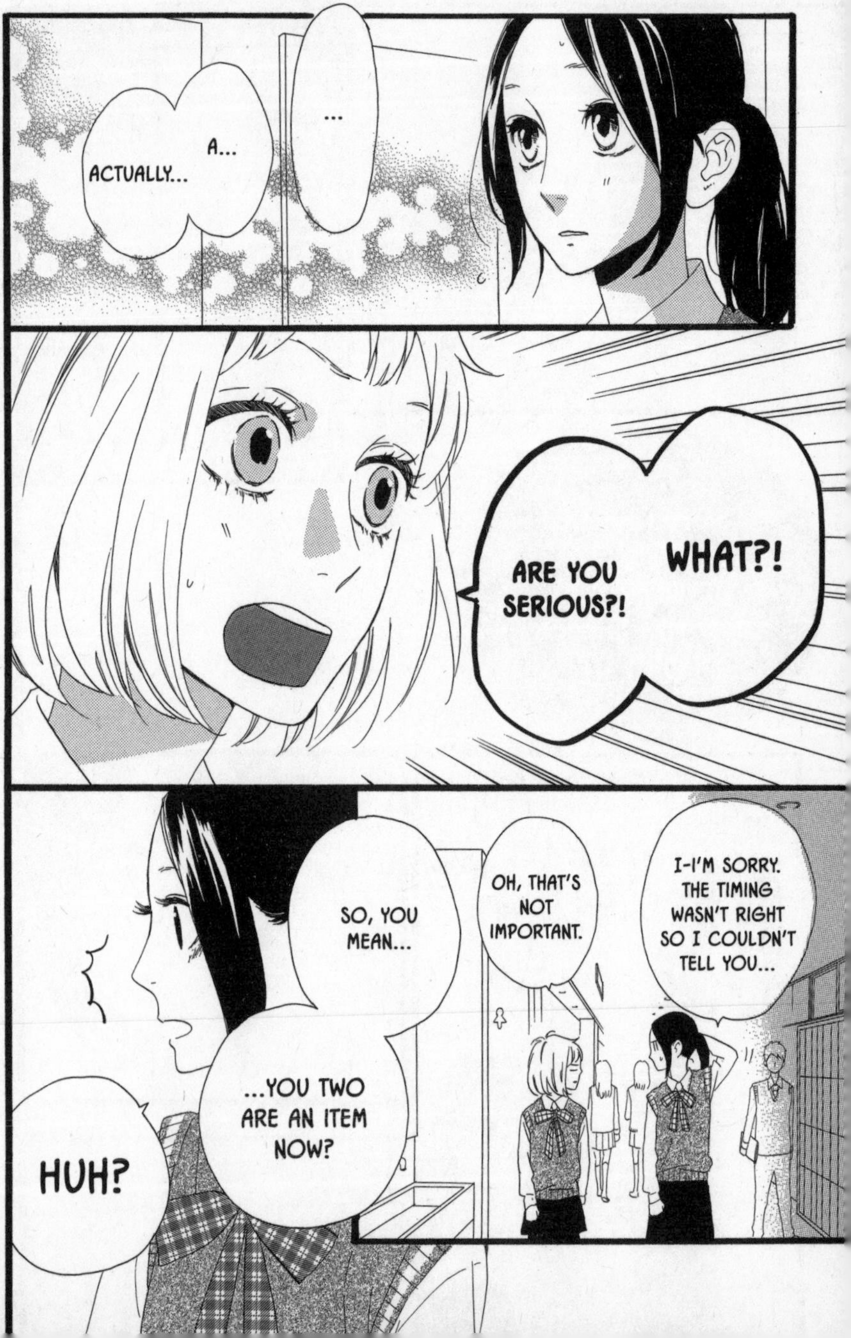
...
A... ACTUALLY...
WHAT?! ARE YOU SERIOUS?!
I-I'M SORRY. THE TIMING WASN'T RIGHT SO I COULDN'T TELL YOU...
OH, THAT'S NOT IMPORTANT.
SO, YOU MEAN...
...YOU TWO ARE AN ITEM NOW?
HUH?

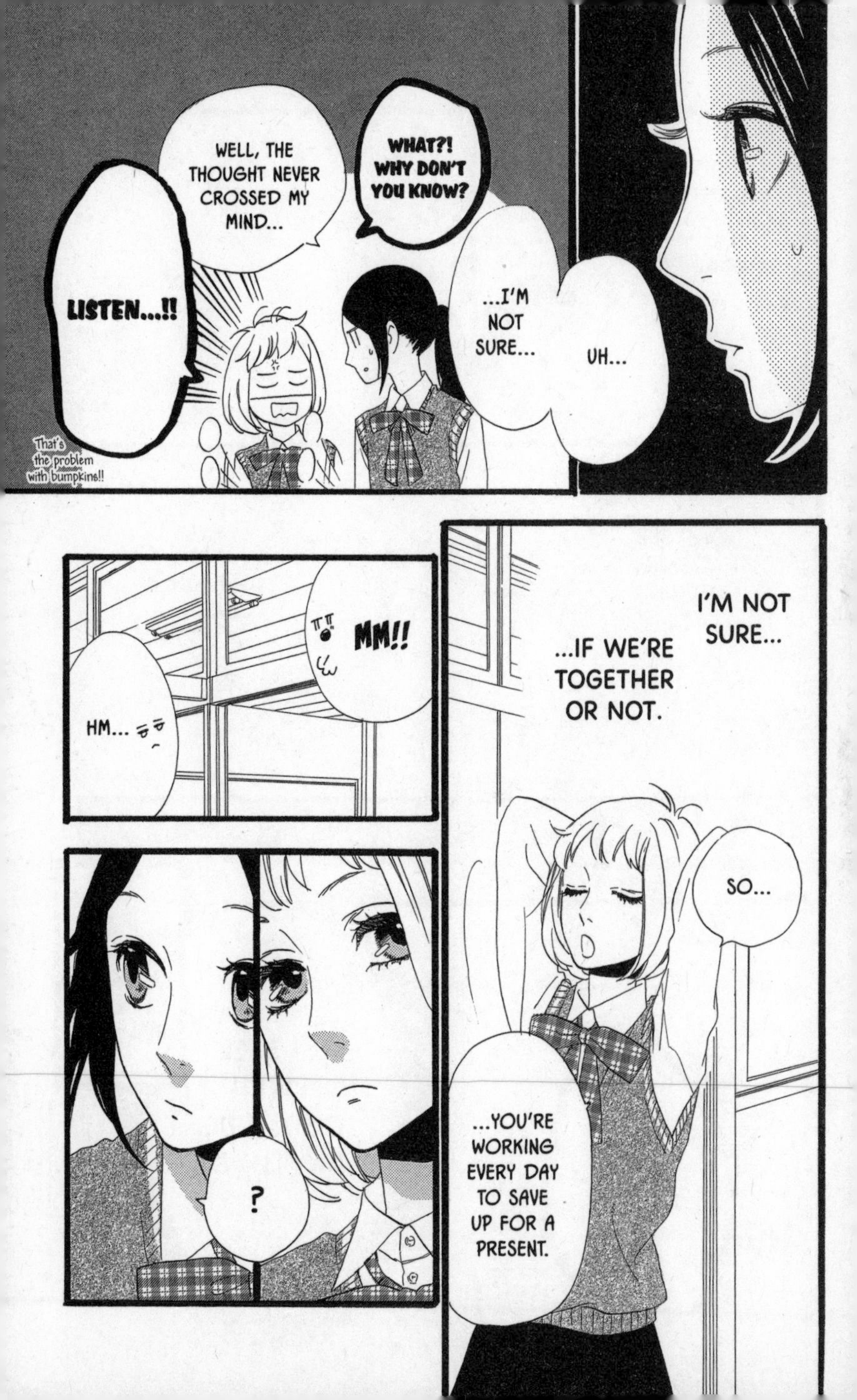
UH...
...I'M NOT SURE...
WHAT?! WHY DON'T YOU KNOW?
WELL, THE THOUGHT NEVER CROSSED MY MIND...
LISTEN...!!
That's the problem with bumpkins!!
I'M NOT SURE...
...IF WE'RE TOGETHER OR NOT.
SO...
...YOU'RE WORKING EVERY DAY TO SAVE UP FOR A PRESENT.
MM!!
HM...
?

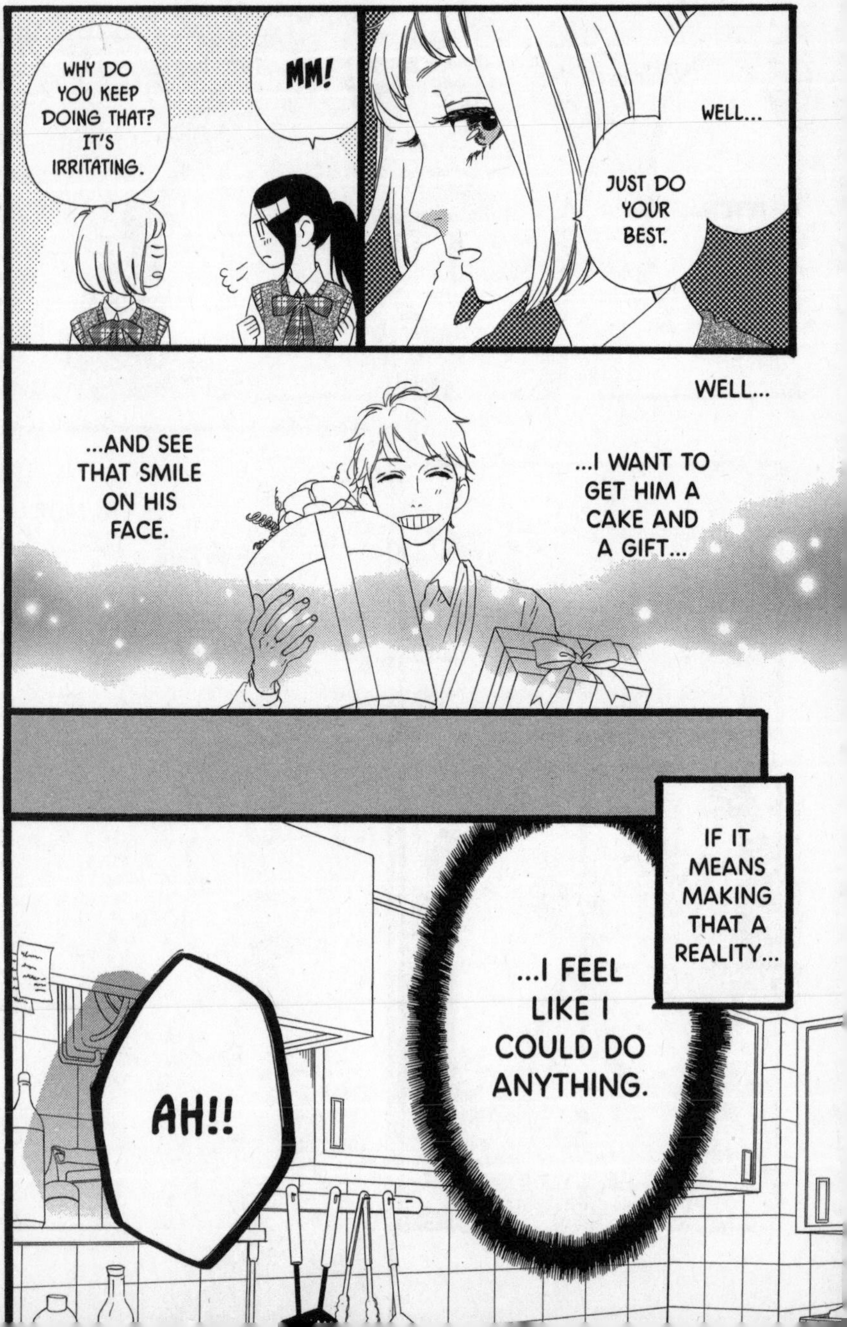
MM!
WHY DO YOU KEEP DOING THAT? IT'S IRRITATING.
WELL...
JUST DO YOUR BEST.
WELL...
...I WANT TO GET HIM A CAKE AND A GIFT...
...AND SEE THAT SMILE ON HIS FACE.
IF IT MEANS MAKING THAT A REALITY...
...I FEEL LIKE I COULD DO ANYTHING.
AH!!

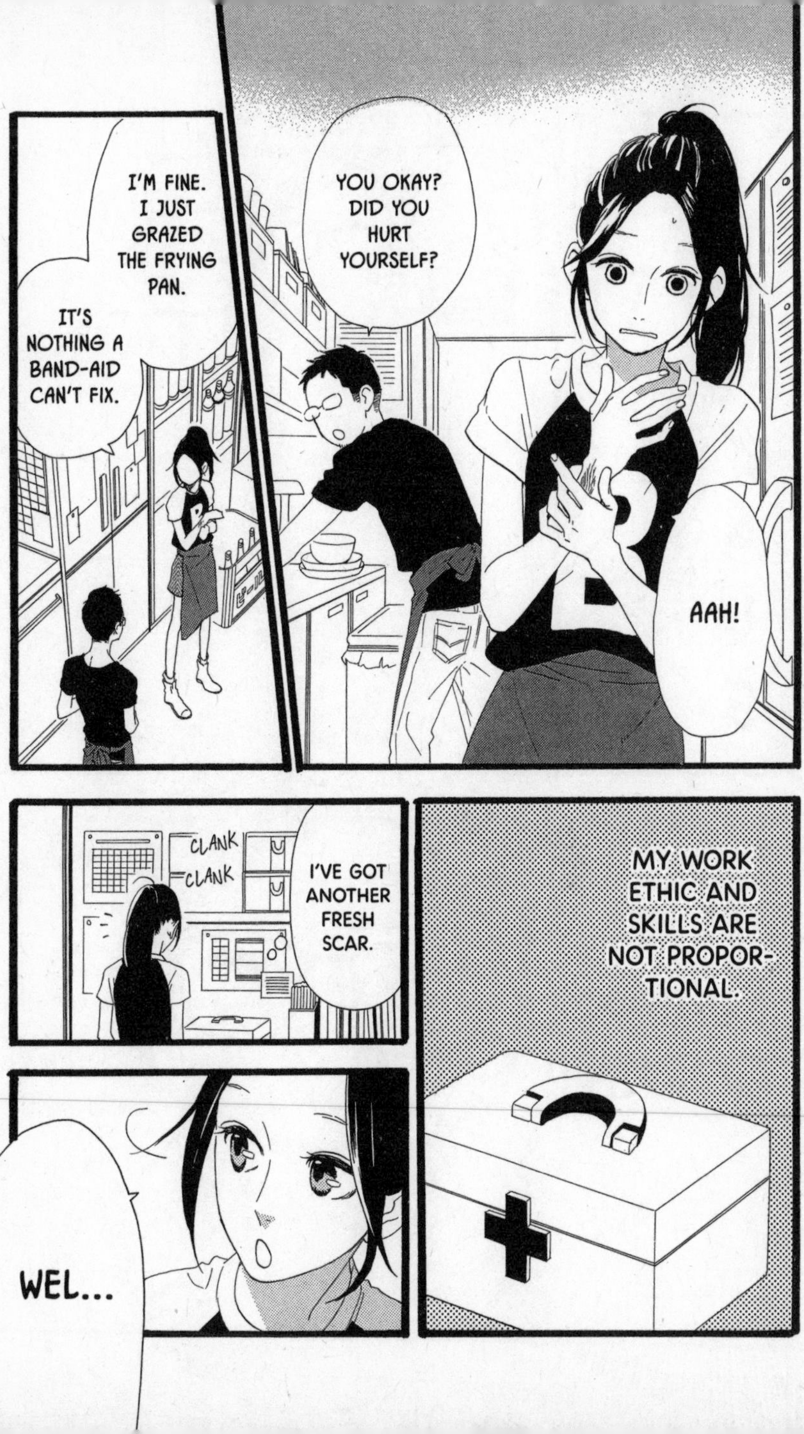
AAH!
YOU OKAY? DID YOU HURT YOURSELF?
I'M FINE. I JUST GRAZED THE FRYING PAN.
IT'S NOTHING A BAND-AID CAN'T FIX.
MY WORK ETHIC AND SKILLS ARE NOT PROPOR-TIONAL.
CLANK
CLANK
I'VE GOT ANOTHER FRESH SCAR.
WEL...

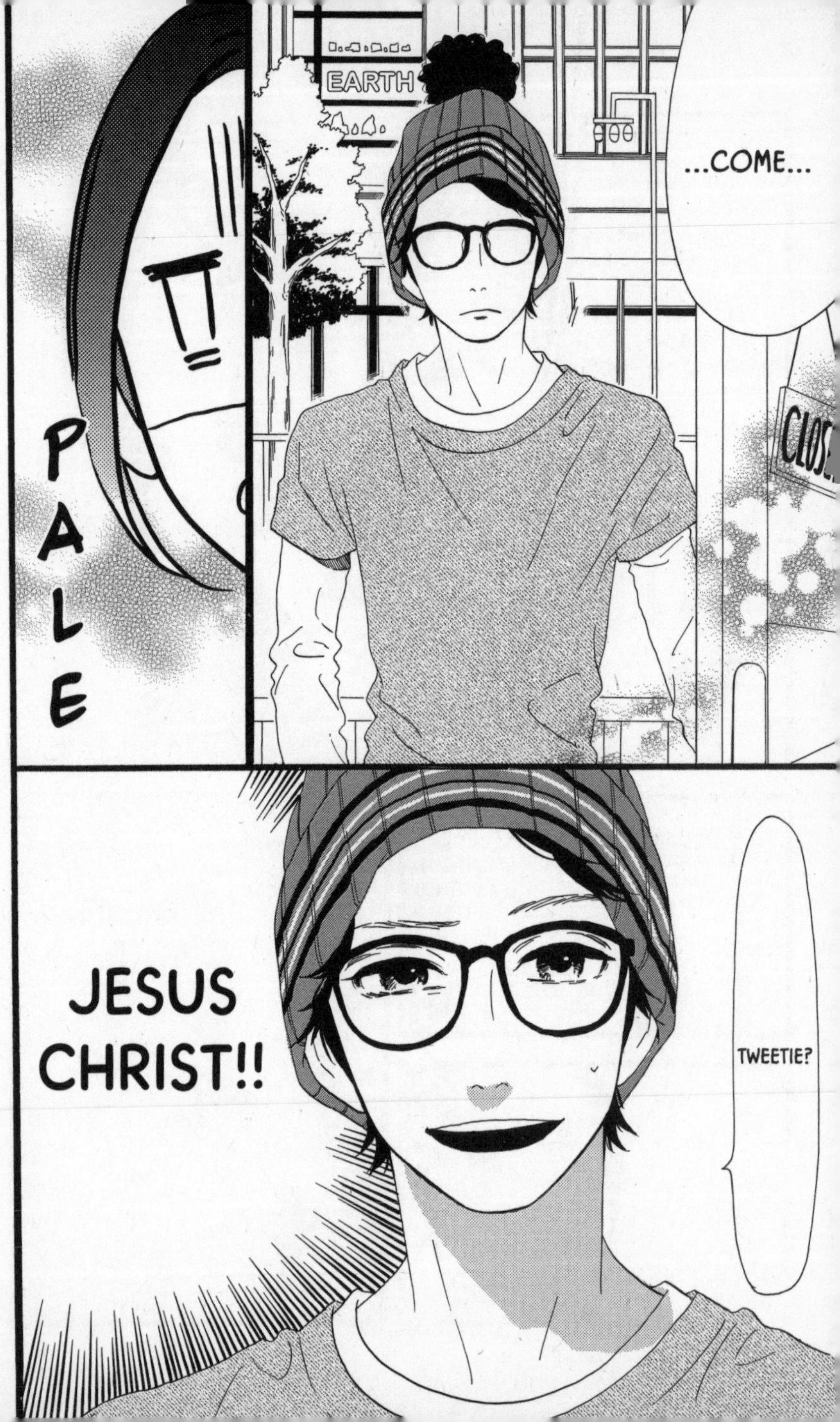
EARTH
...COME...
PALE
TWEETIE?
JESUS CHRIST!!

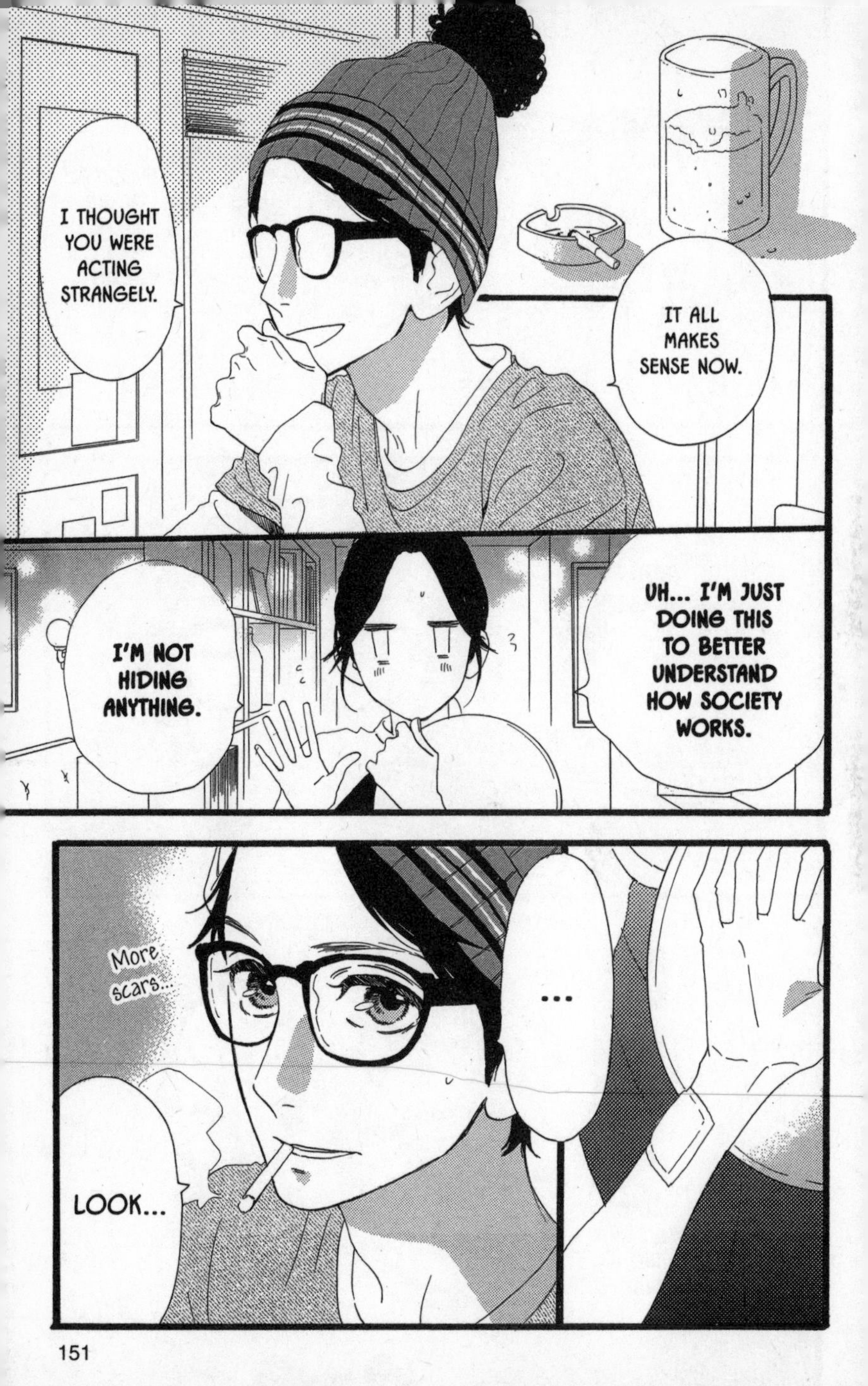
IT ALL MAKES SENSE NOW.
I THOUGHT YOU WERE ACTING STRANGELY.
UH... I'M JUST DOING THIS TO BETTER UNDERSTAND HOW SOCIETY WORKS.
I'M NOT HIDING ANYTHING.
...
More scars...
LOOK...

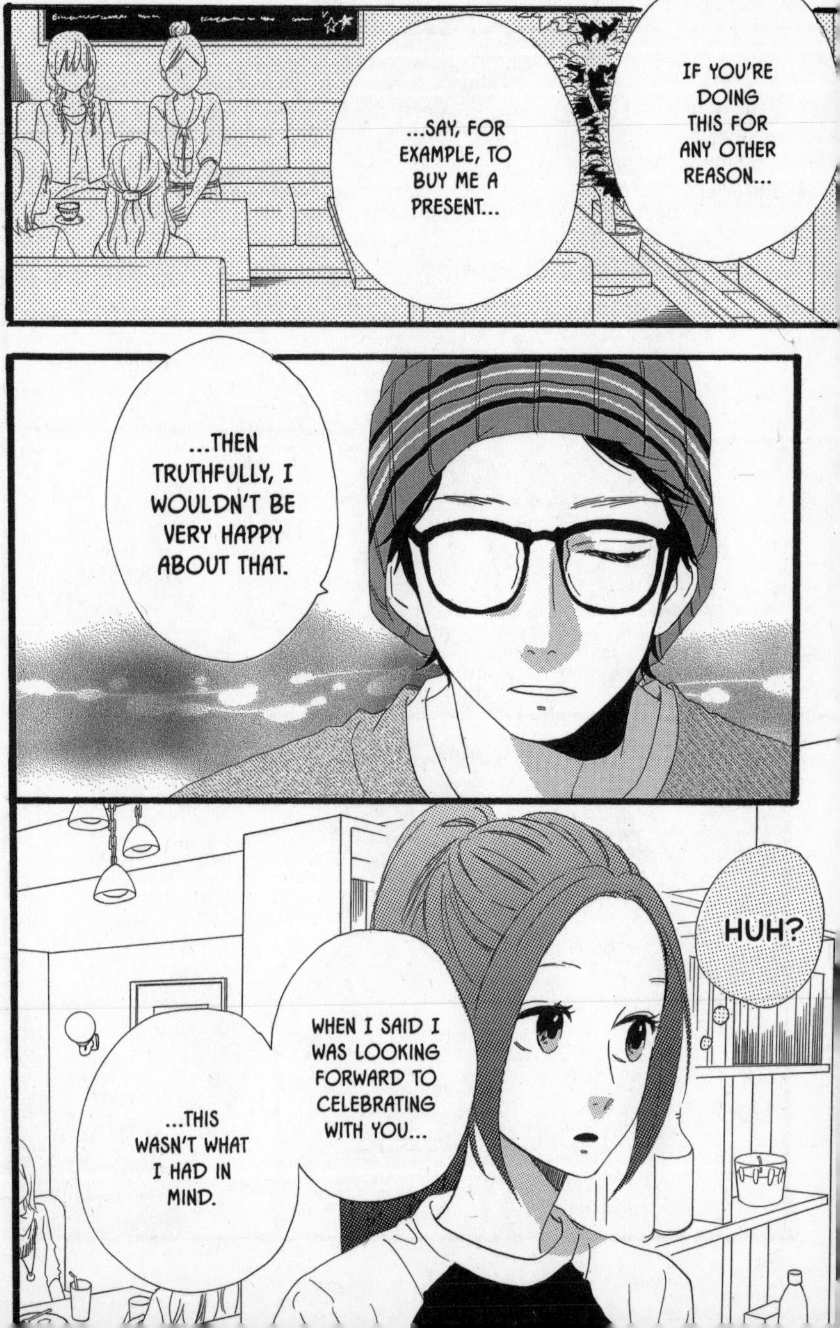
IF YOU'RE DOING THIS FOR ANY OTHER REASON...
...SAY, FOR EXAMPLE, TO BUY ME A PRESENT...
...THEN TRUTHFULLY, I WOULDN'T BE VERY HAPPY ABOUT THAT.
HUH?
WHEN I SAID I WAS LOOKING FORWARD TO CELEBRATING WITH YOU...
...THIS WASN'T WHAT I HAD IN MIND.

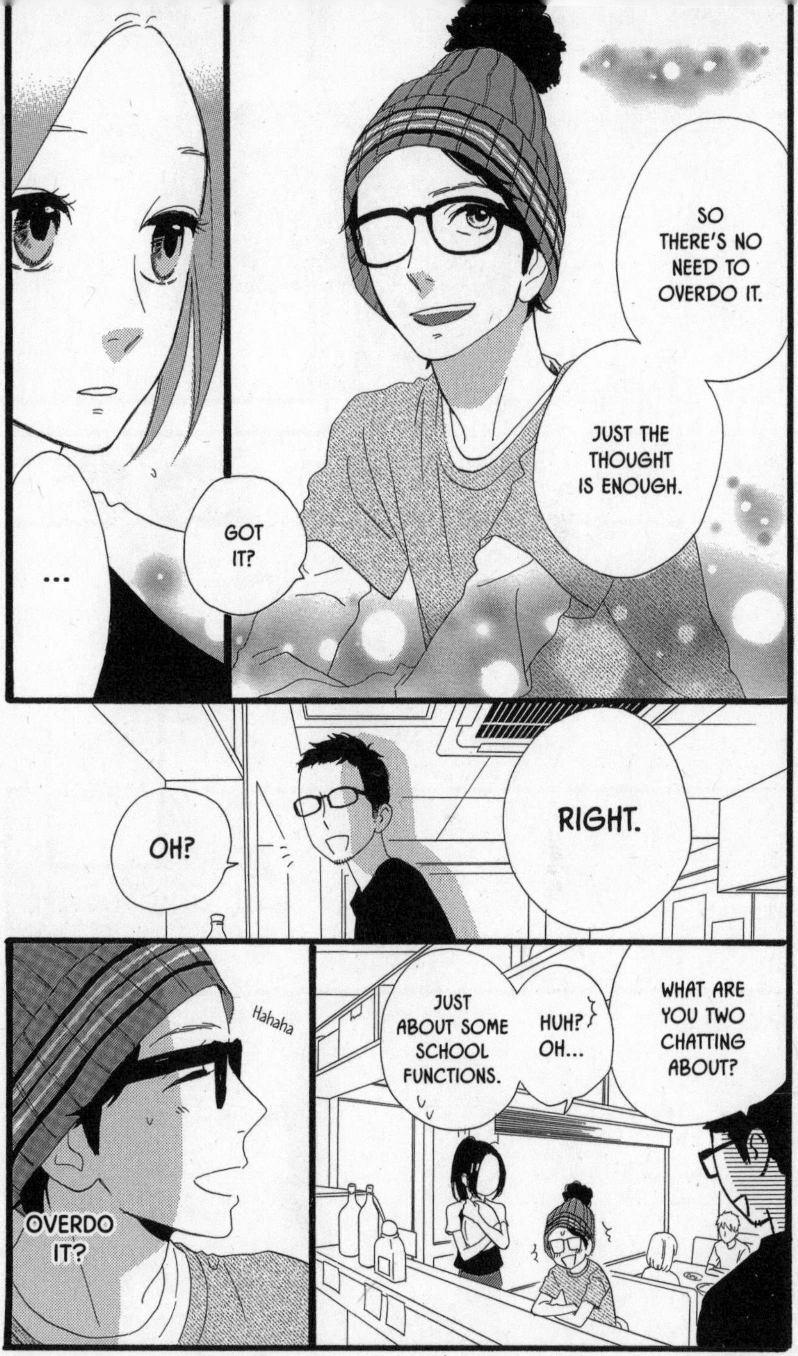
SO THERE'S NO NEED TO OVERDO IT.
JUST THE THOUGHT IS ENOUGH.
GOT IT?
...
RIGHT.
OH?
WHAT ARE YOU TWO CHATTING ABOUT?
HUH? OH...
JUST ABOUT SOME SCHOOL FUNCTIONS.
Hahaha
OVERDO IT?

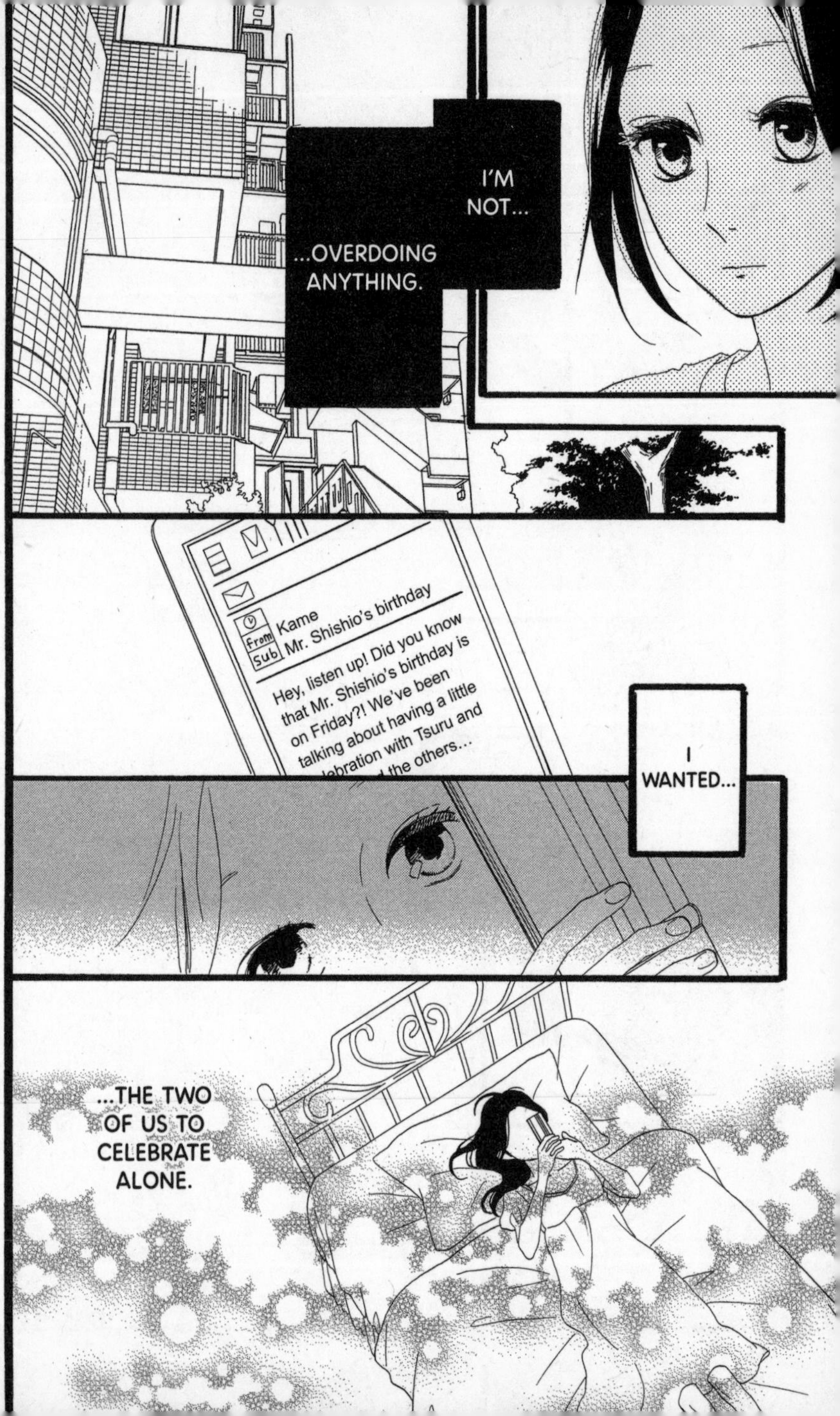
I'M NOT...
...OVERDOING ANYTHING.
From Kame
Sub Mr. Shishio's birthday
Hey, listen up! Did you know that Mr. Shishio's birthday is on Friday?! We've been talking about having a little
I WANTED...
...THE TWO OF US TO CELEBRATE ALONE.

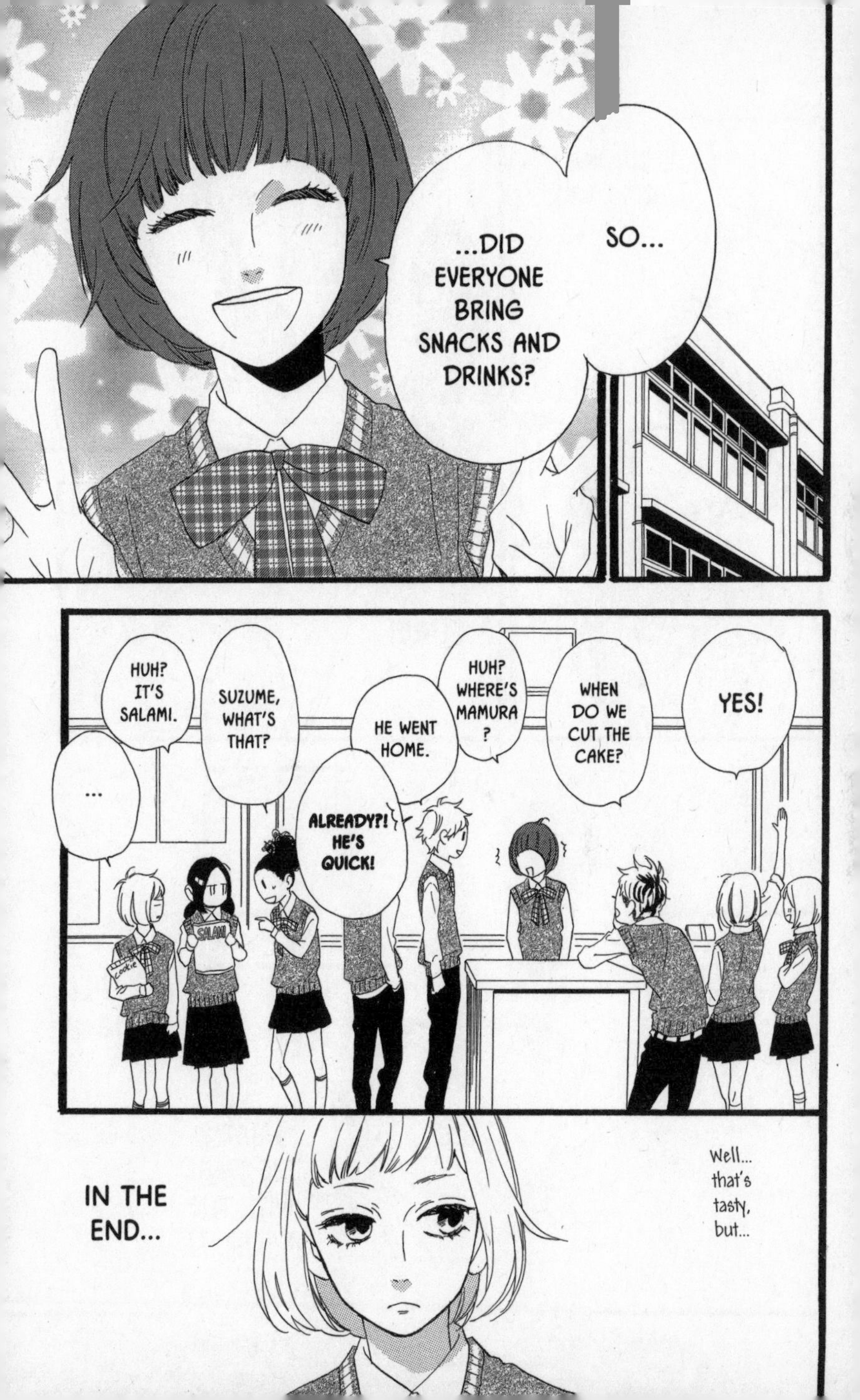
SO...
...DID EVERYONE BRING SNACKS AND DRINKS?
YES!
WHEN DO WE CUT THE CAKE?
HUH? WHERE'S MAMURA?
HE WENT HOME.
ALREADY?! HE'S QUICK!
SUZUME, WHAT'S THAT?
HUH? IT'S SALAMI.
...
SALAMI
cookie
Well... that's tasty, but...
IN THE END...

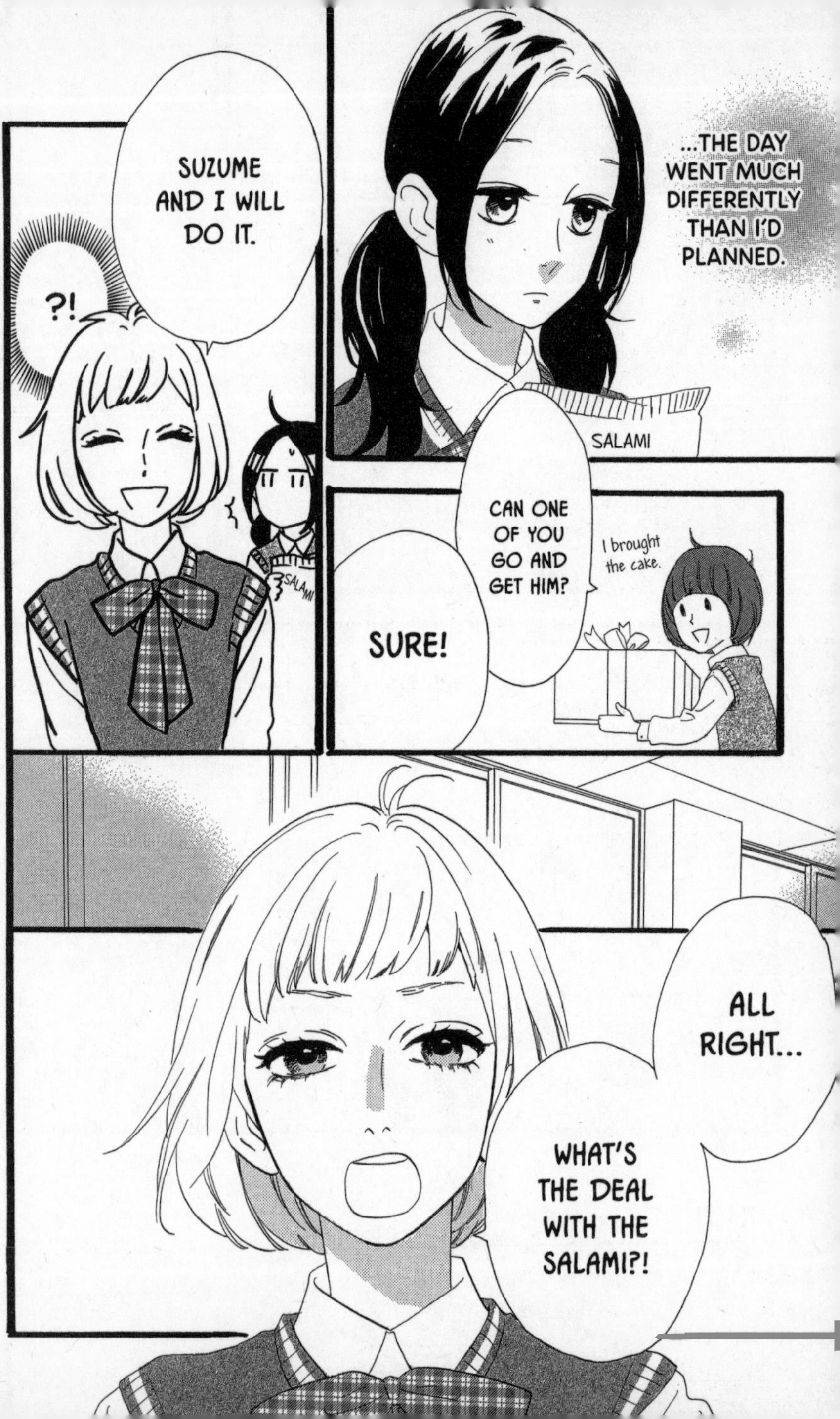
...THE DAY WENT MUCH DIFFERENTLY THAN I'D PLANNED.
SALAMI
I brought the cake.
CAN ONE OF YOU GO AND GET HIM?
SURE!
SUZUME AND I WILL DO IT.
?!
SALAMI
ALL RIGHT...
WHAT'S THE DEAL WITH THE SALAMI?!

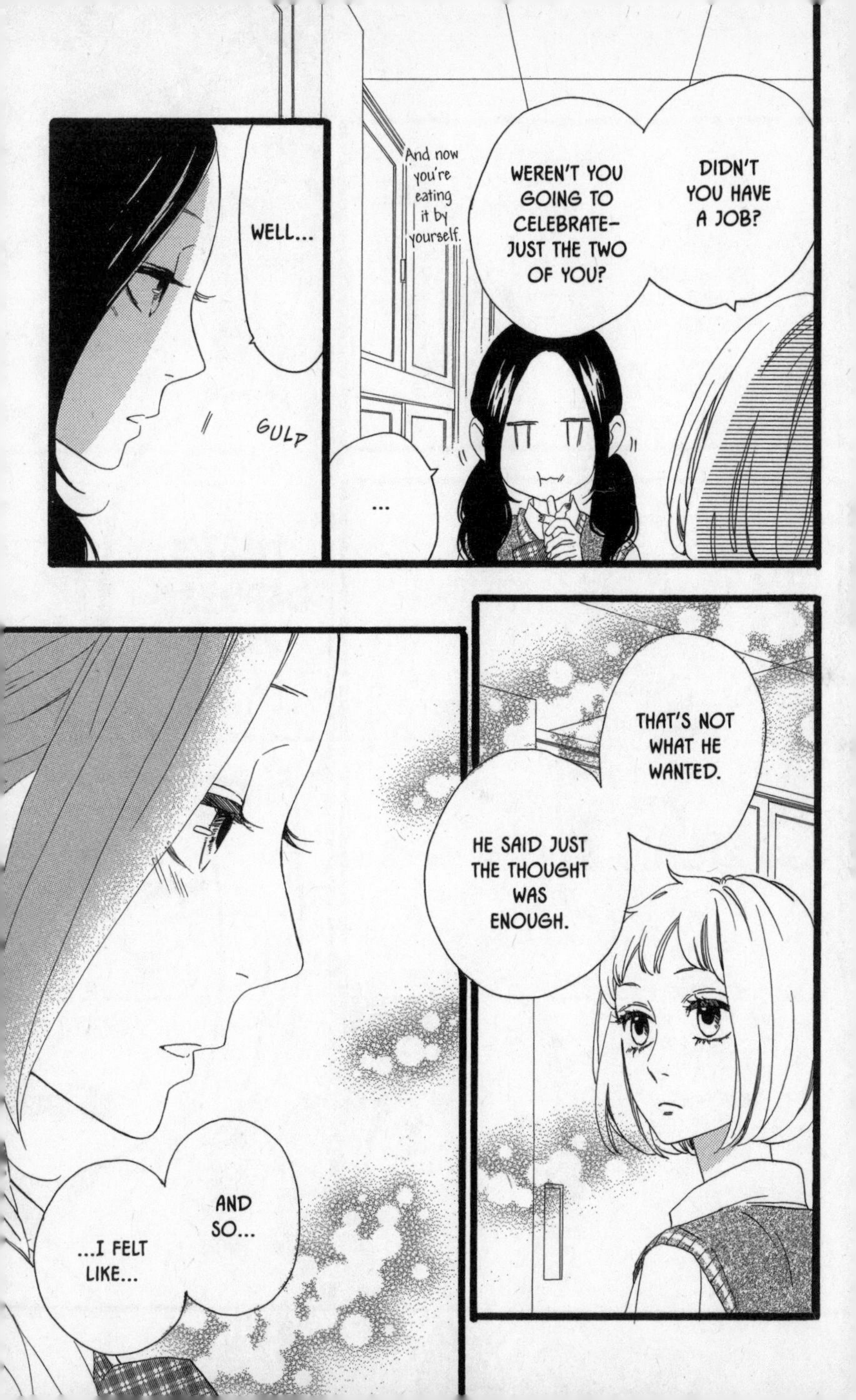
DIDN'T YOU HAVE A JOB?
WEREN'T YOU GOING TO CELEBRATE– JUST THE TWO OF YOU?
And now you're eating it by yourself.
...
WELL...
GULP
THAT'S NOT WHAT HE WANTED.
HE SAID JUST THE THOUGHT WAS ENOUGH.
AND SO...
...I FELT LIKE...

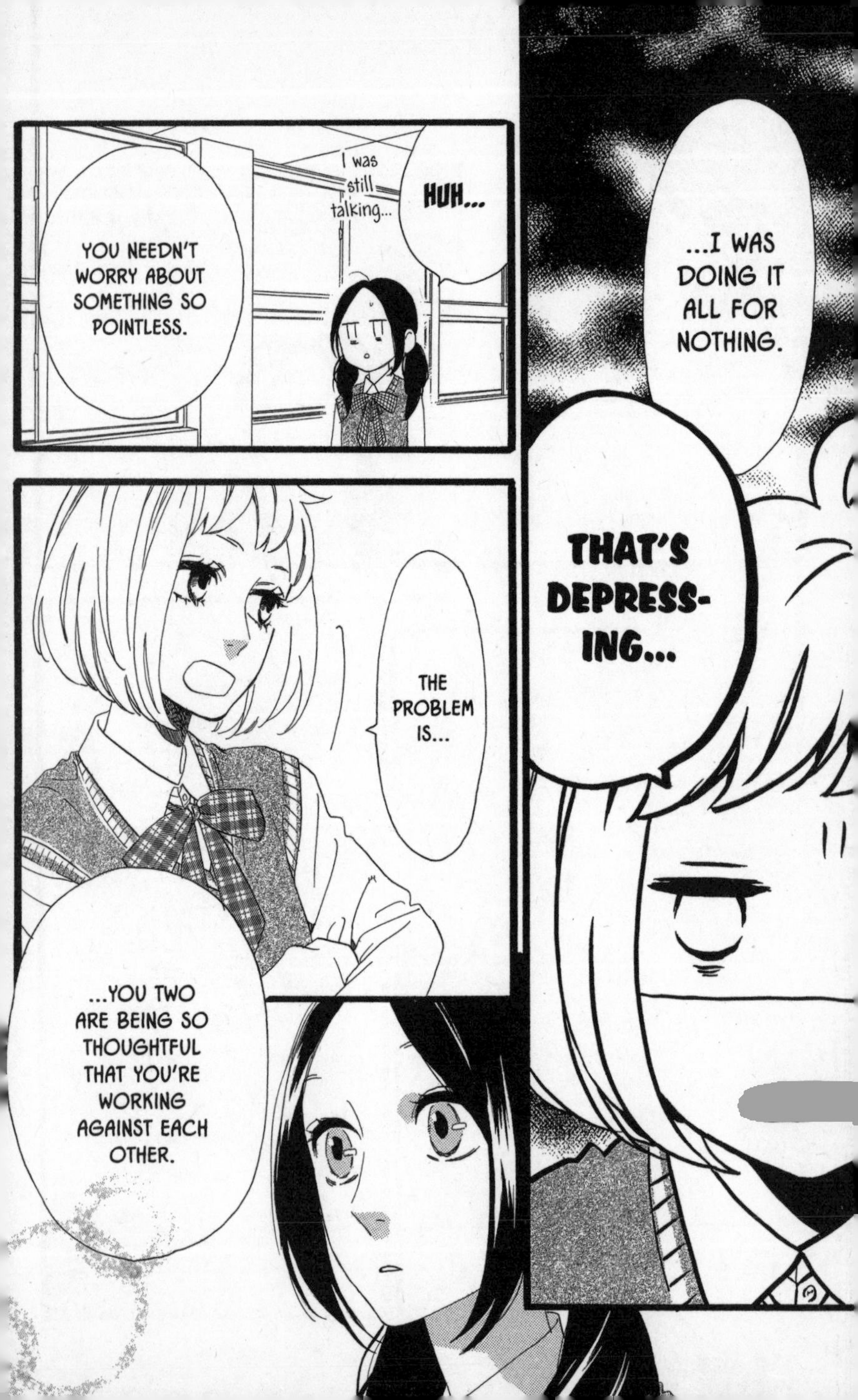

...I WAS DOING IT ALL FOR NOTHING.
THAT'S DEPRESS-ING...
HUH...
I was still talking...
YOU NEEDN'T WORRY ABOUT SOMETHING SO POINTLESS.
THE PROBLEM IS...
...YOU TWO ARE BEING SO THOUGHTFUL THAT YOU'RE WORKING AGAINST EACH OTHER.

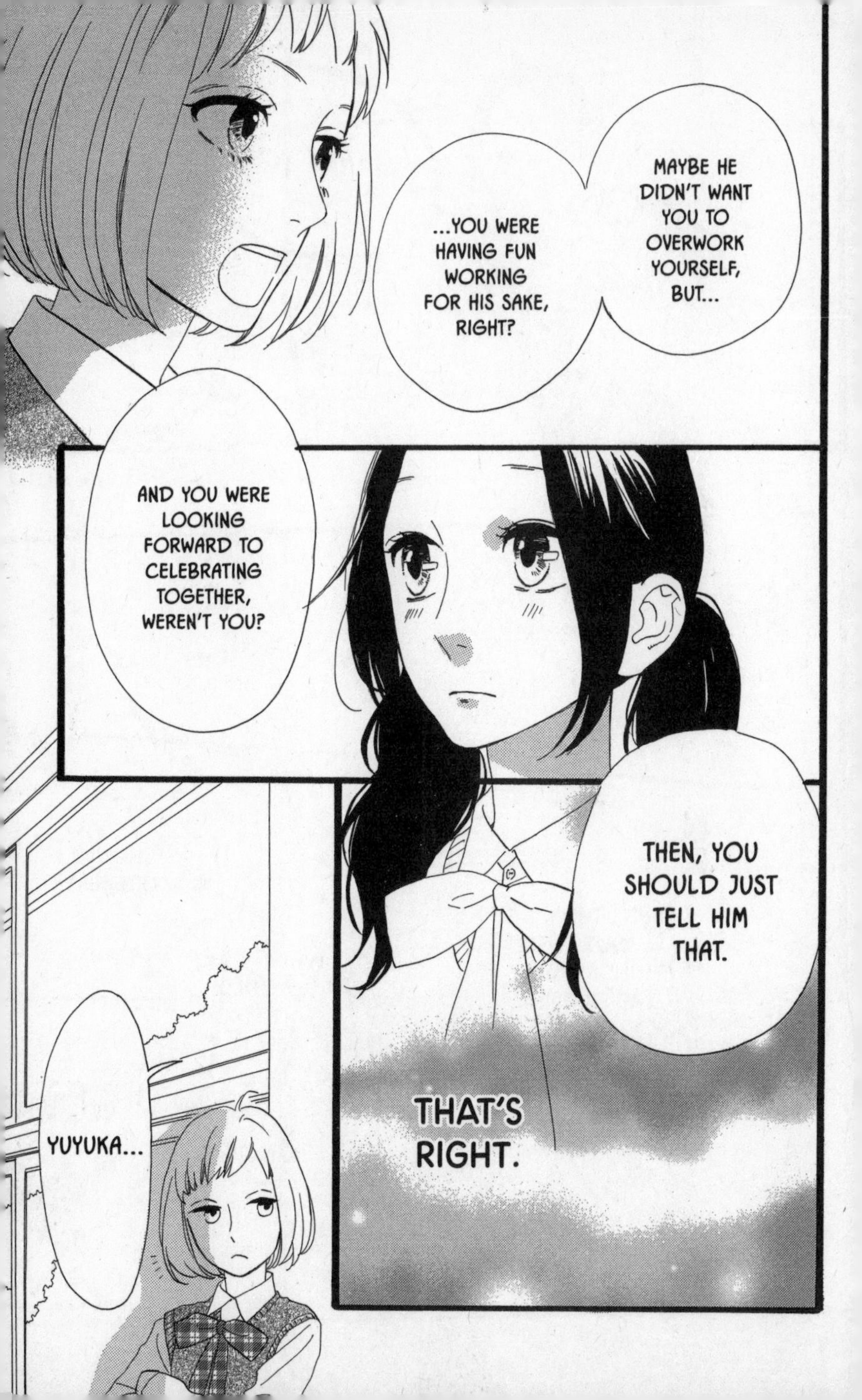
MAYBE HE DIDN'T WANT YOU TO OVERWORK YOURSELF, BUT...
...YOU WERE HAVING FUN WORKING FOR HIS SAKE, RIGHT?
AND YOU WERE LOOKING FORWARD TO CELEBRATING TOGETHER, WEREN'T YOU?
THEN, YOU SHOULD JUST TELL HIM THAT.
THAT'S RIGHT.
YUYUKA...

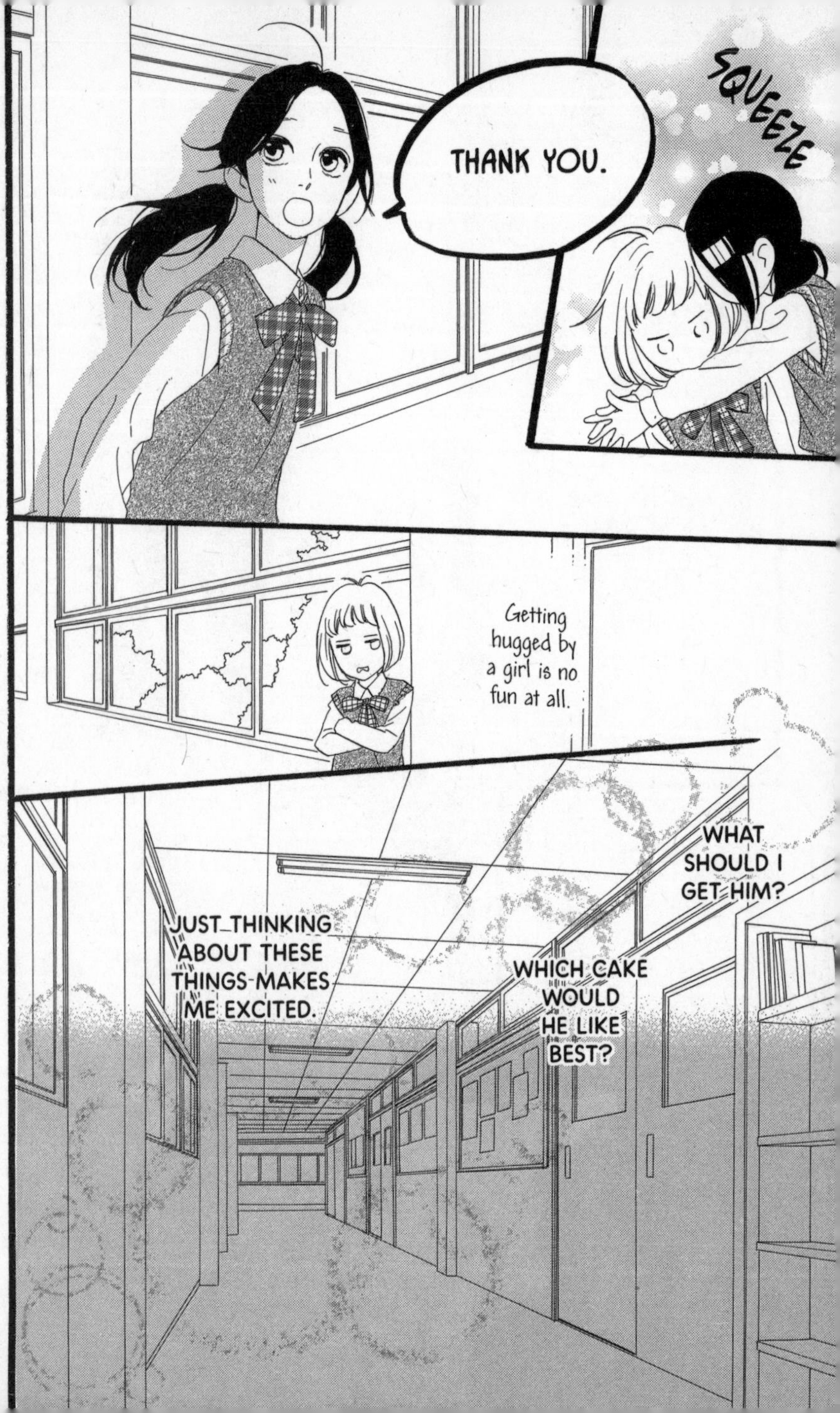
SQUEEZE
THANK YOU.
Getting hugged by a girl is no fun at all.
WHAT SHOULD I GET HIM?
WHICH CAKE WOULD HE LIKE BEST?
JUST THINKING ABOUT THESE THINGS MAKES ME EXCITED.

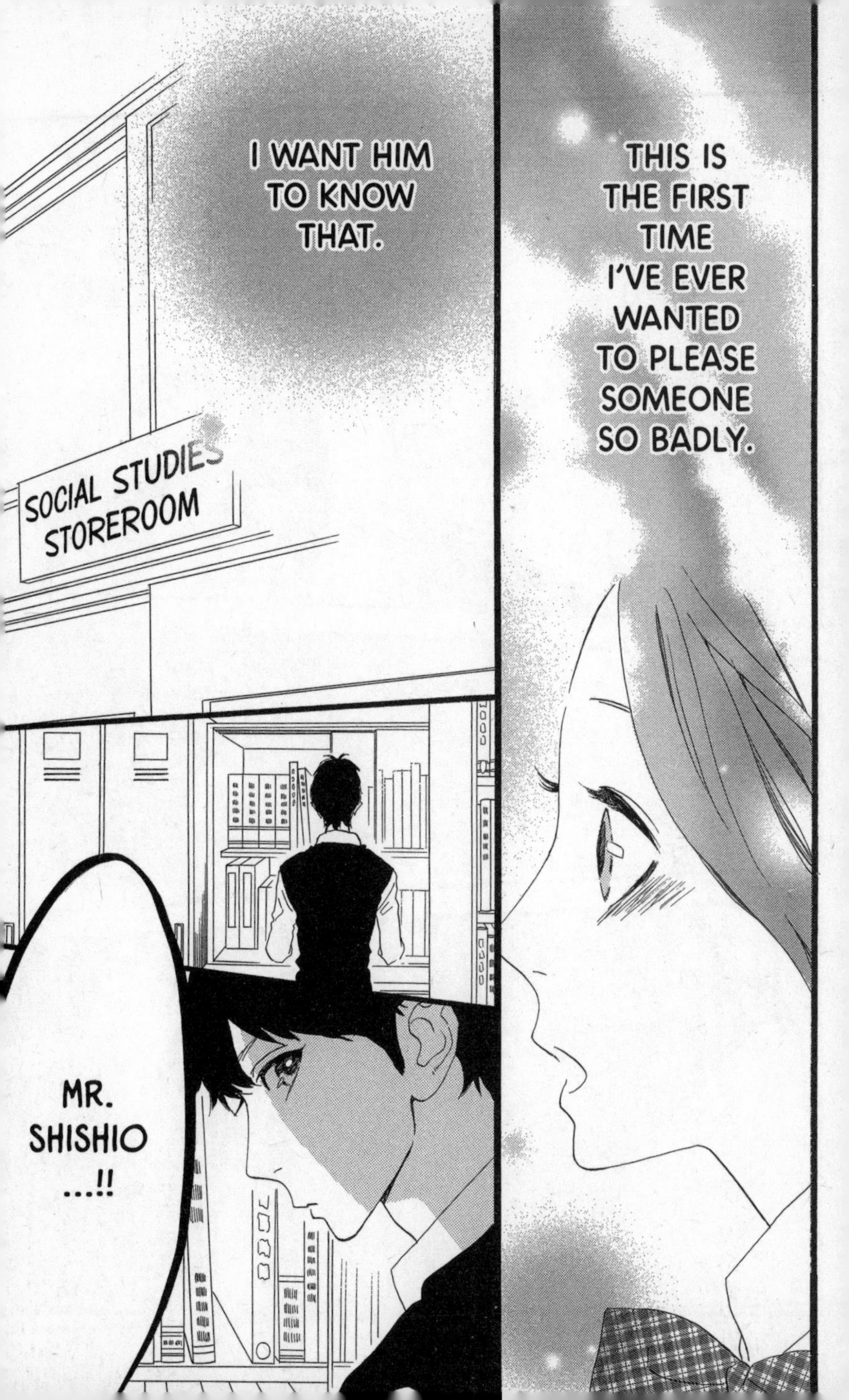
THIS IS THE FIRST TIME I'VE EVER WANTED TO PLEASE SOMEONE SO BADLY.
I WANT HIM TO KNOW THAT.
SOCIAL STUDIES STOREROOM
MR. SHISHIO ...!!

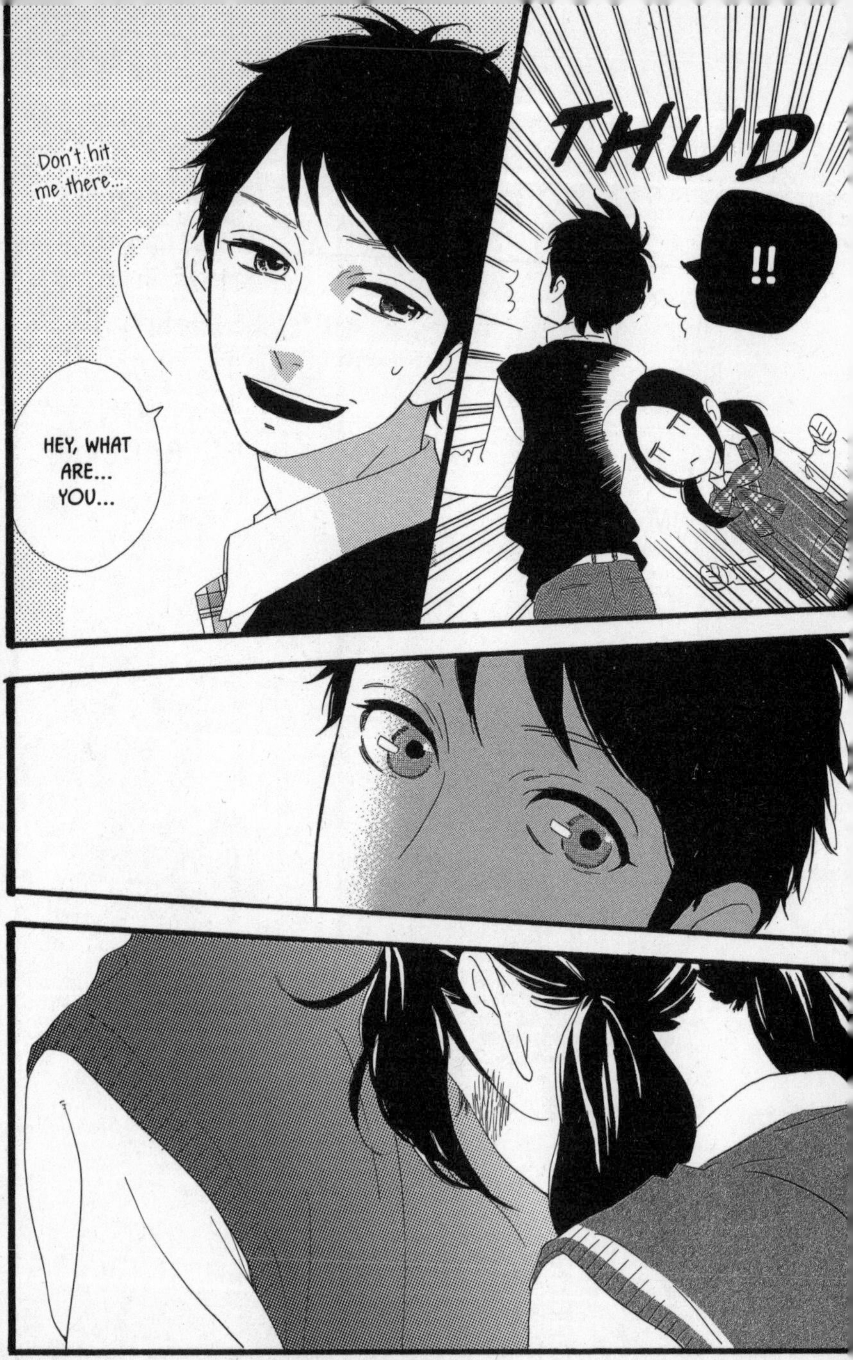
THUD
!!
Don't hit me there...
HEY, WHAT ARE... YOU...

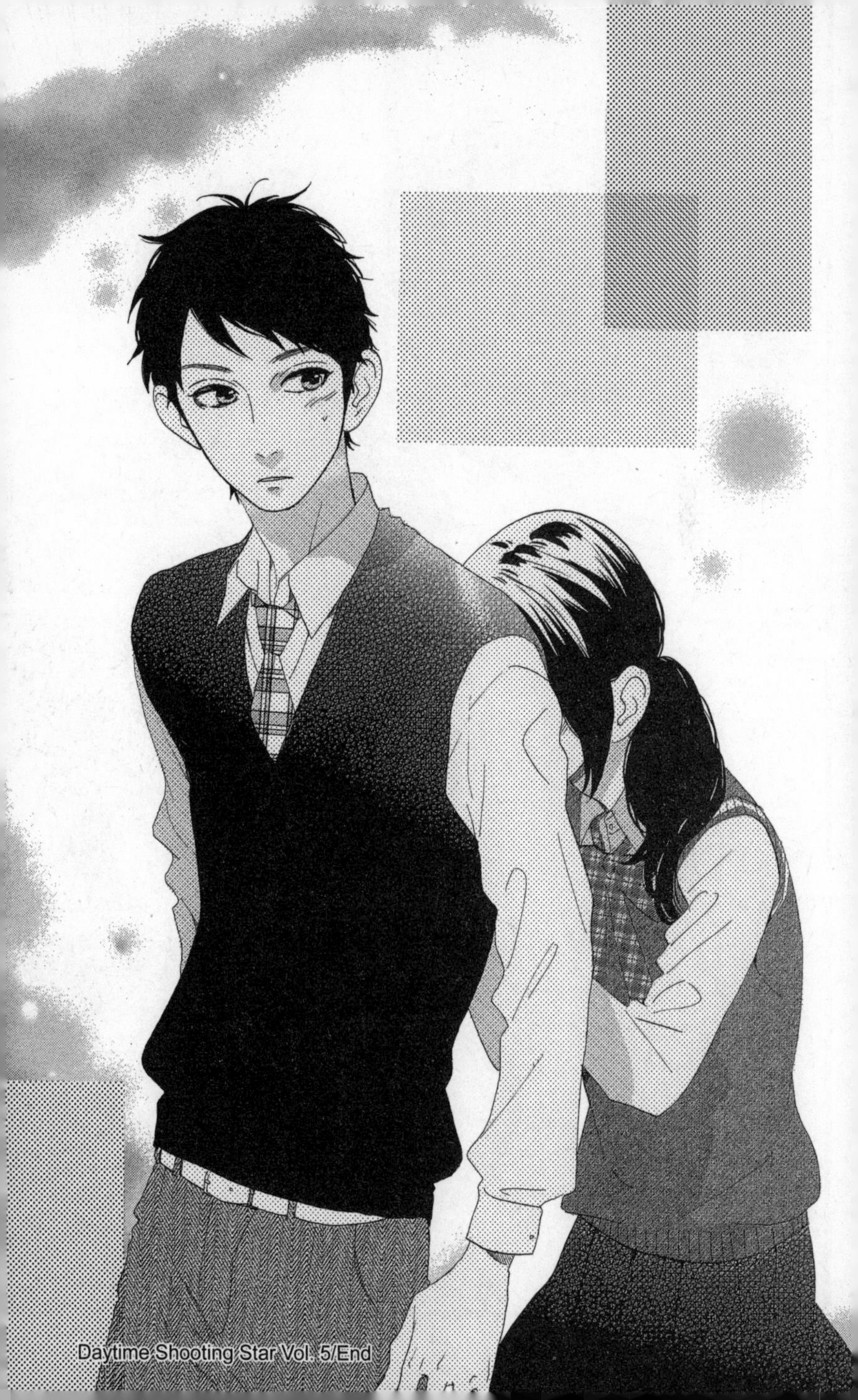
Daytime Shooting Star Vol. 5/End

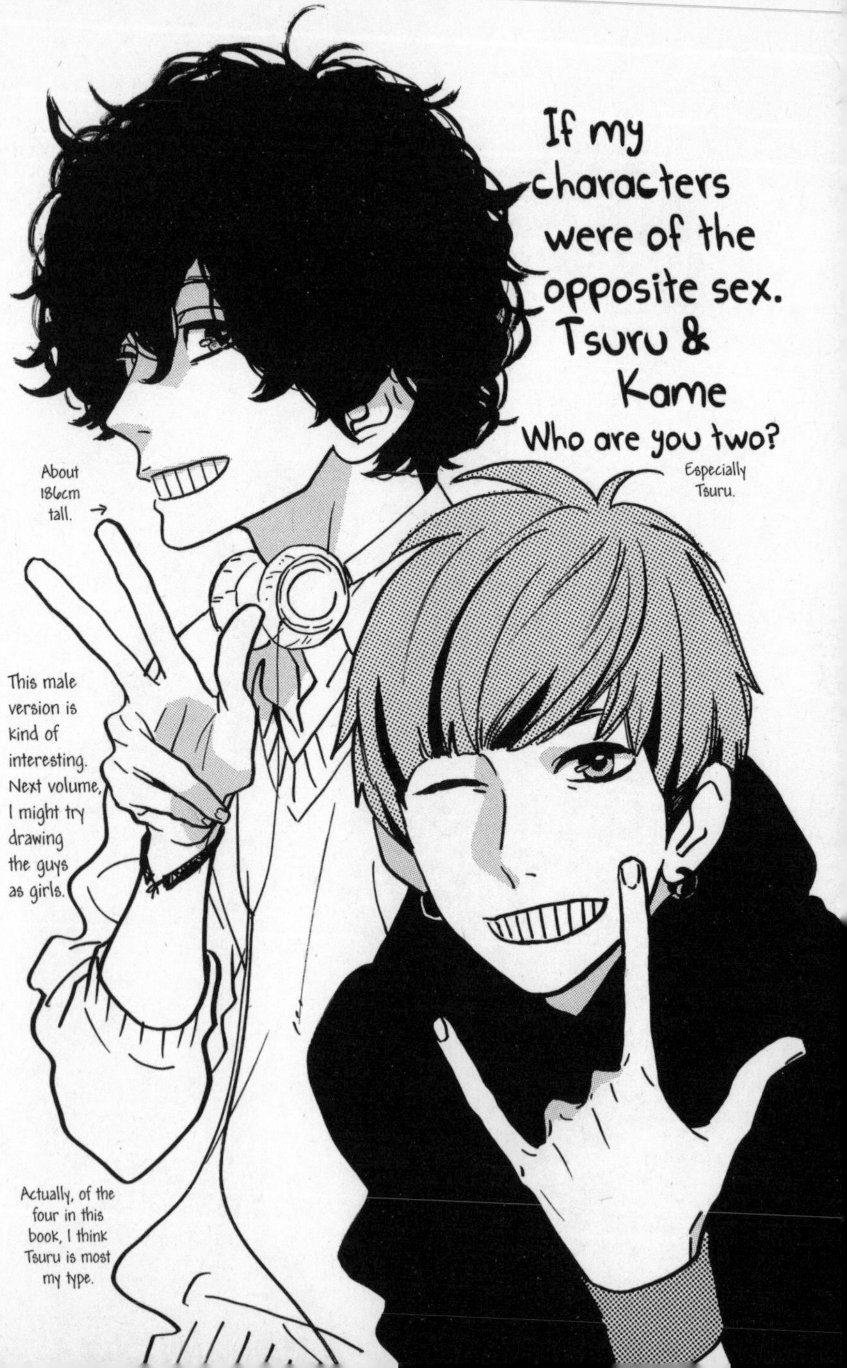
If my characters were of the opposite sex. Tsuru & Kame
Who are you two?
Especially Tsuru.
About 186cm tall.
This male version is kind of interesting. Next volume, I might try drawing the guys as girls.
Actually, of the four in this book, I think Tsuru is most my type.

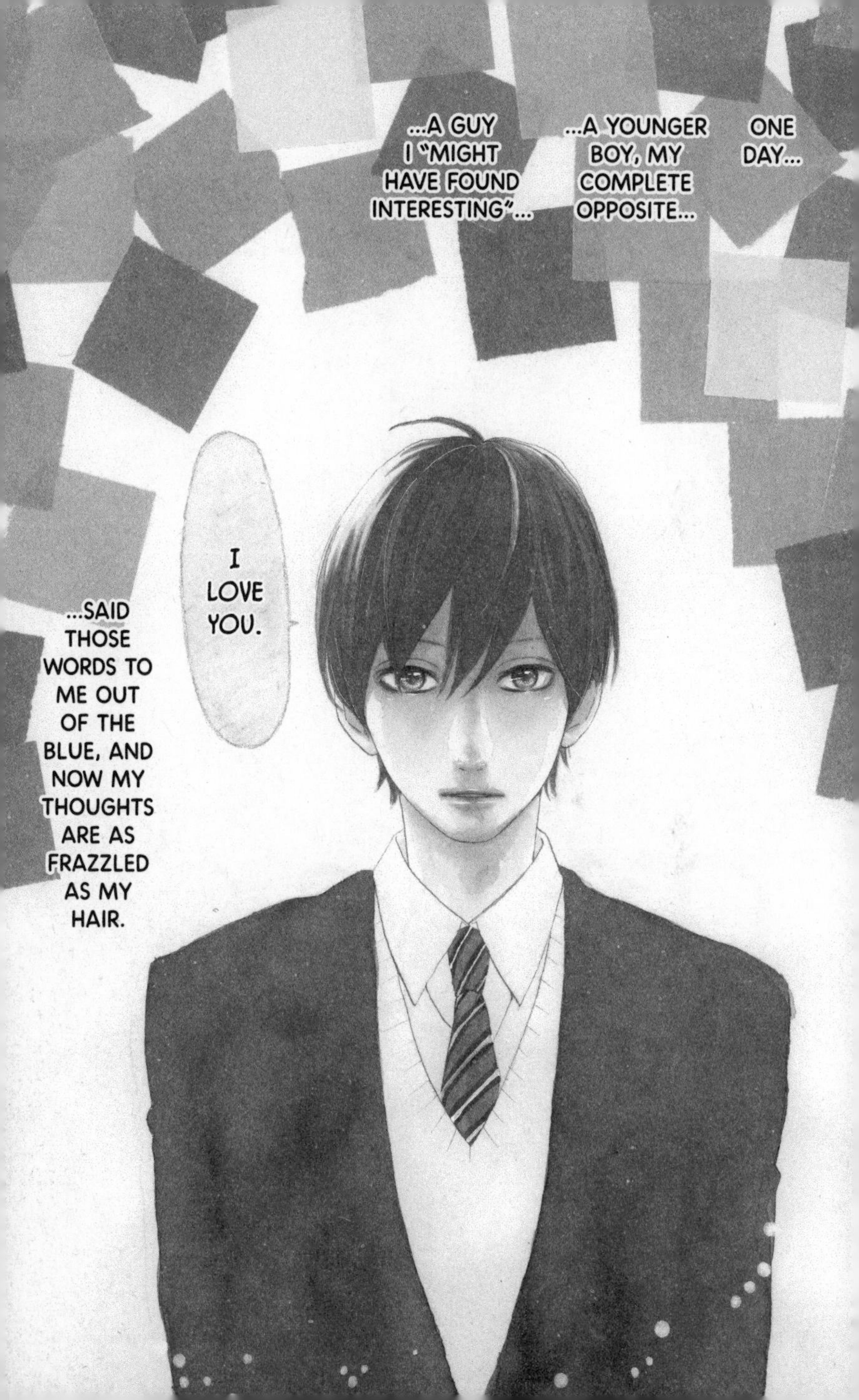
ONE DAY...
...A YOUNGER BOY, MY COMPLETE OPPOSITE...
...A GUY I "MIGHT HAVE FOUND INTERESTING"...
I LOVE YOU.
...SAID THOSE WORDS TO ME OUT OF THE BLUE, AND NOW MY THOUGHTS ARE AS FRAZZLED AS MY HAIR.

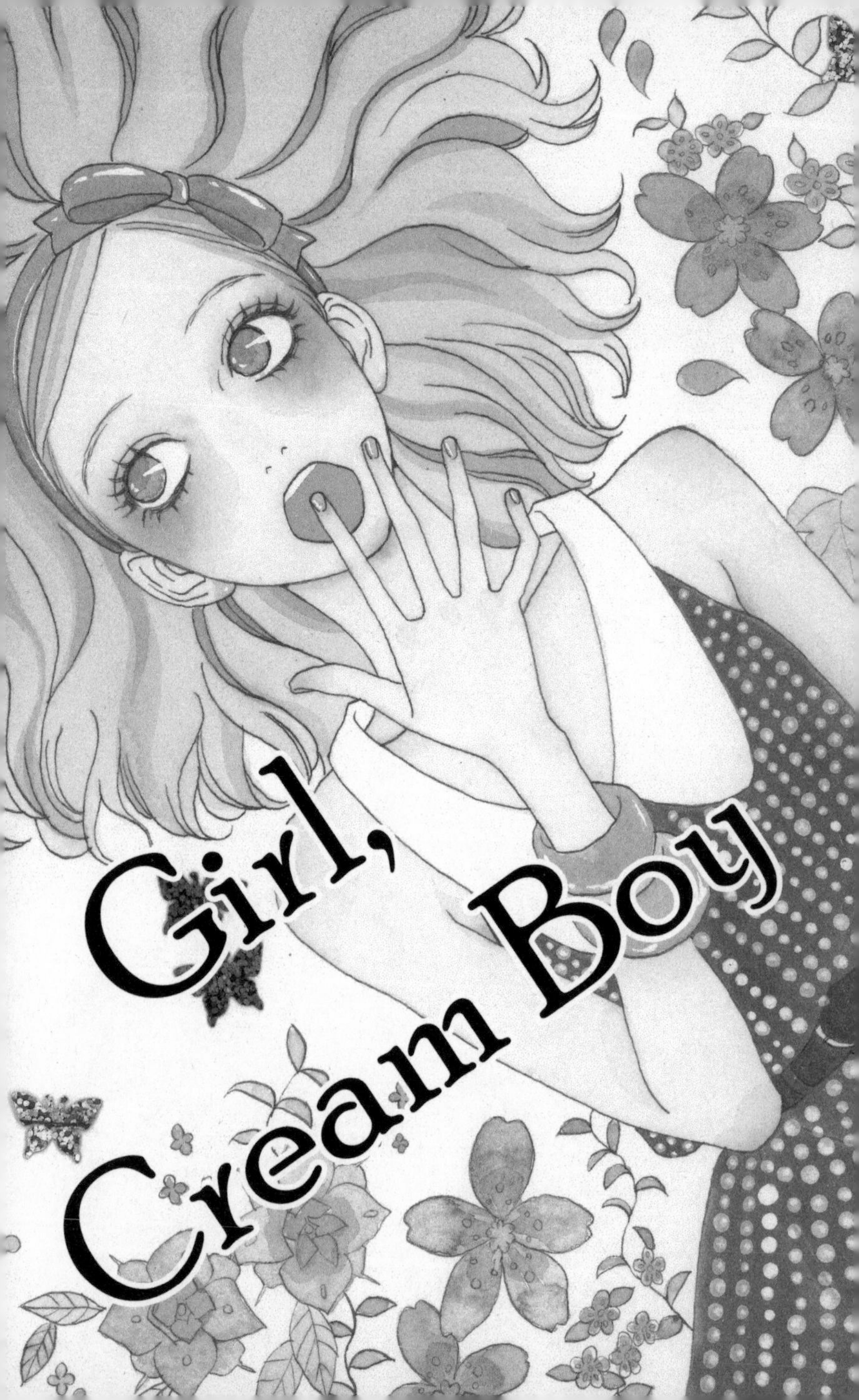
Girl, Cream Boy

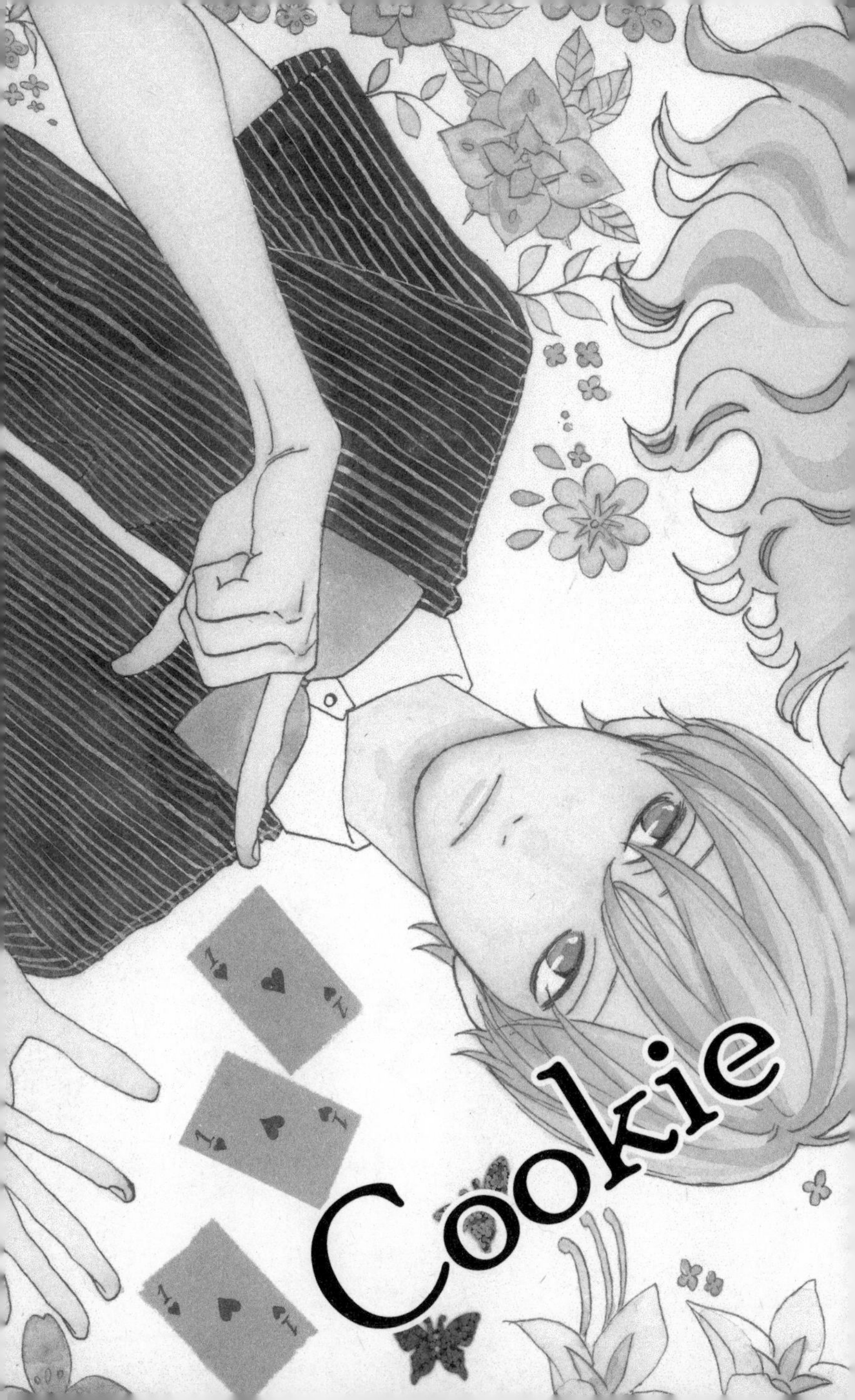
Cookie

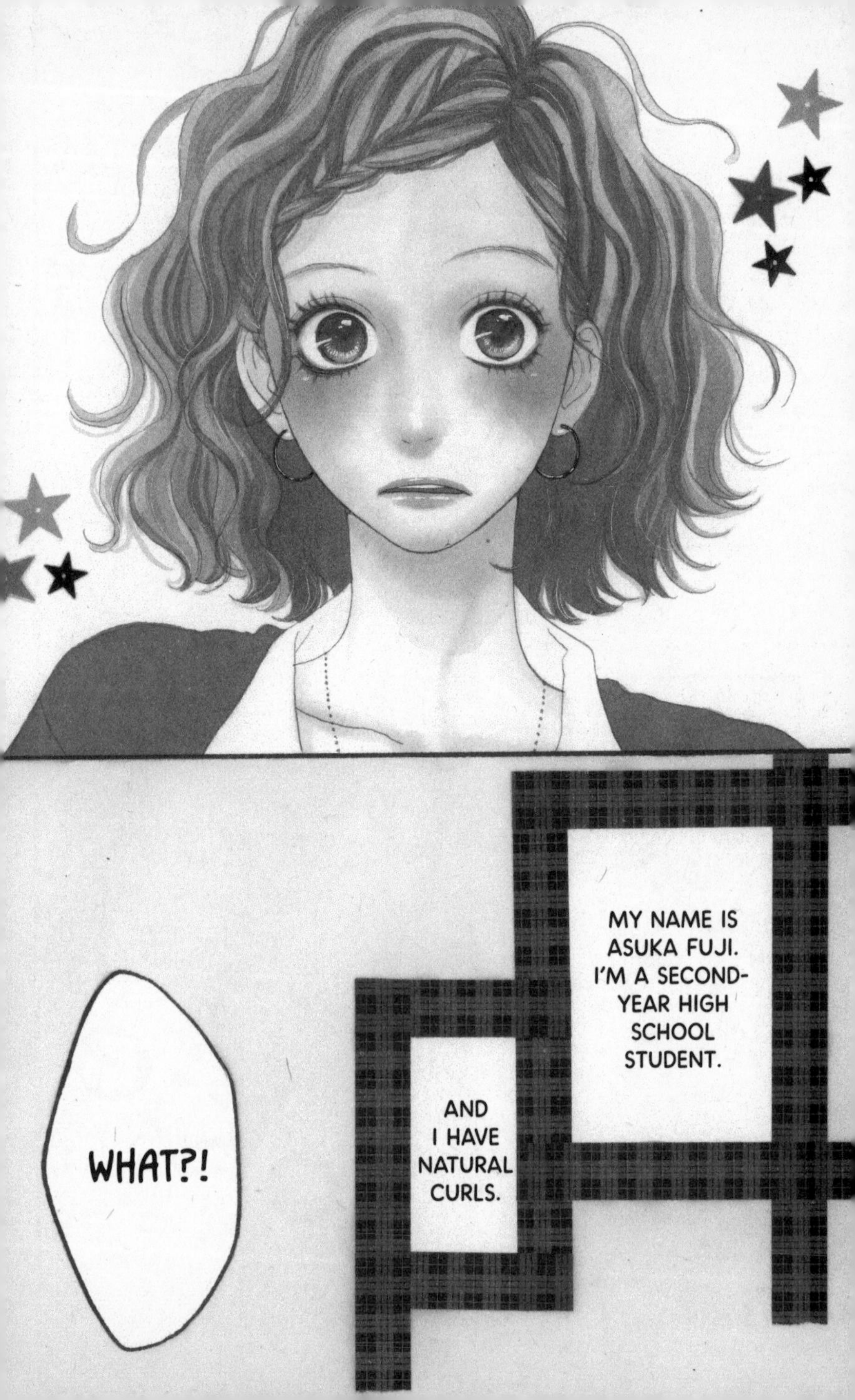
MY NAME IS ASUKA FUJI. I'M A SECOND-YEAR HIGH SCHOOL STUDENT.
AND I HAVE NATURAL CURLS.
WHAT?!

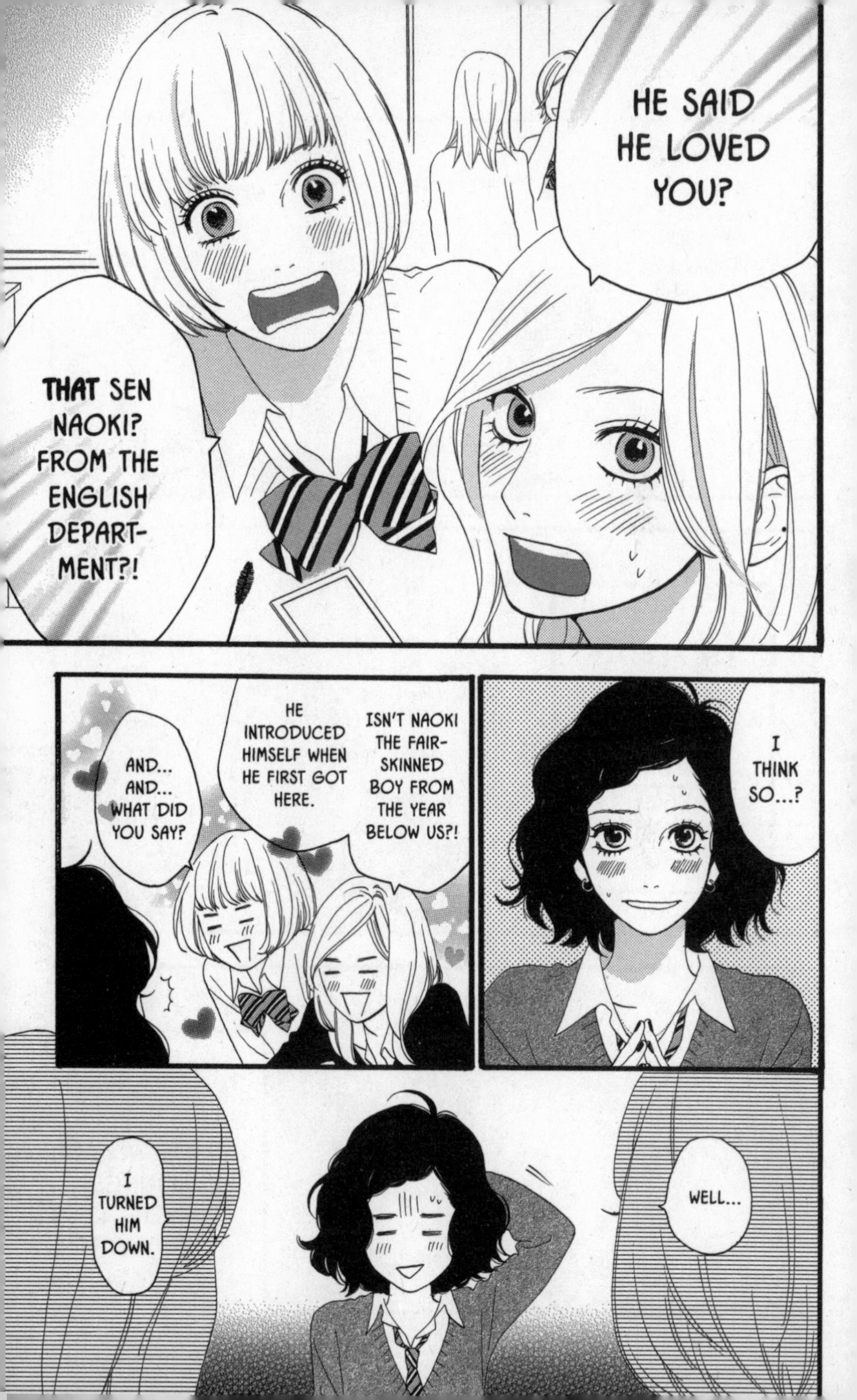
HE SAID HE LOVED YOU?
THAT SEN NAOKI? FROM THE ENGLISH DEPARTMENT?!
I THINK SO...?
ISN'T NAOKI THE FAIR-SKINNED BOY FROM THE YEAR BELOW US?!
HE INTRODUCED HIMSELF WHEN HE FIRST GOT HERE.
AND... AND... WHAT DID YOU SAY?
WELL...
I TURNED HIM DOWN.

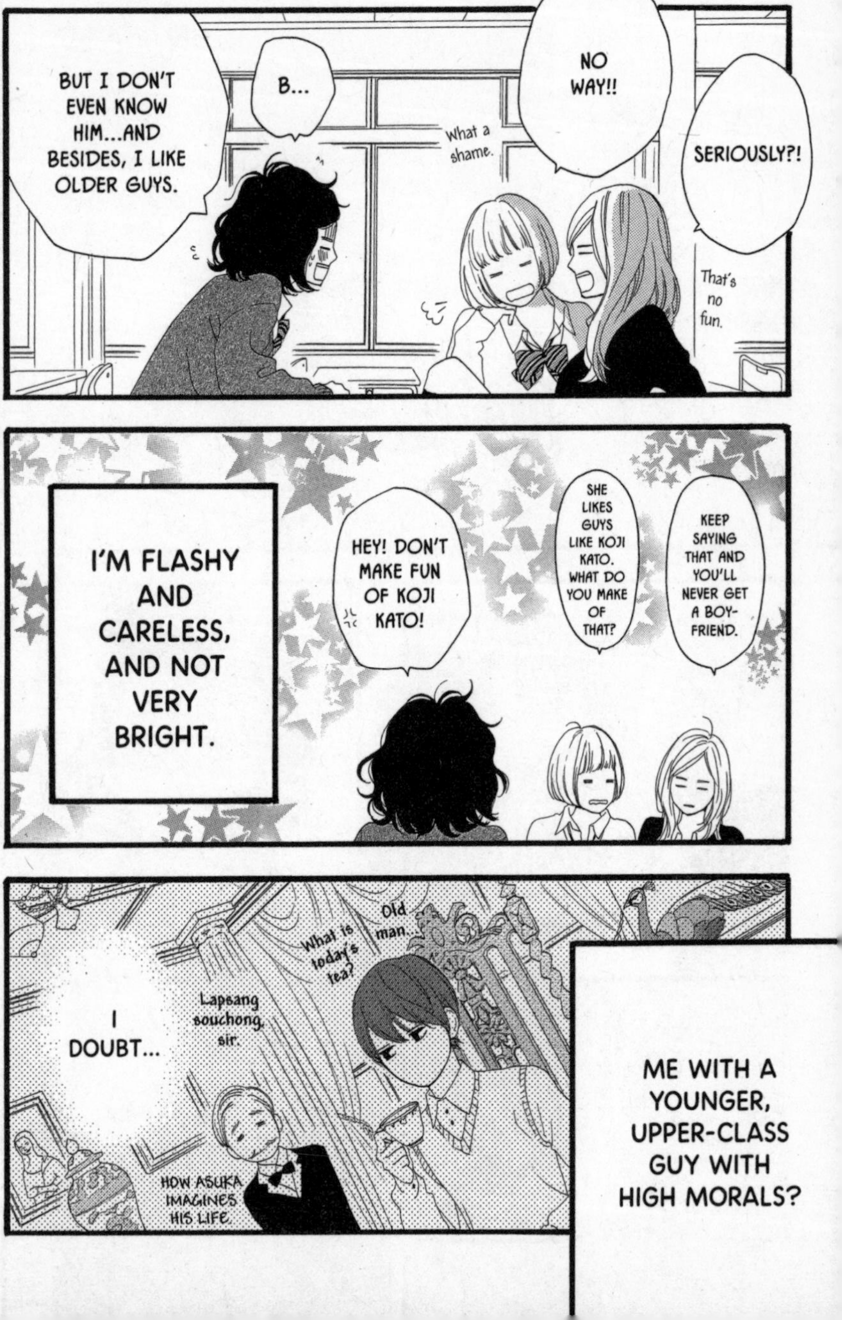
SERIOUSLY?!
That's no fun.
NO WAY!!
What a shame.
B...
BUT I DON'T EVEN KNOW HIM...AND BESIDES, I LIKE OLDER GUYS.
KEEP SAYING THAT AND YOU'LL NEVER GET A BOY-FRIEND.
SHE LIKES GUYS LIKE KOJI KATO. WHAT DO YOU MAKE OF THAT?
HEY! DON'T MAKE FUN OF KOJI KATO!
I'M FLASHY AND CARELESS, AND NOT VERY BRIGHT.
Old man...
What is today's tea?
Lapsang souchong, sir.
HOW ASUKA IMAGINES HIS LIFE
I DOUBT...
ME WITH A YOUNGER, UPPER-CLASS GUY WITH HIGH MORALS?

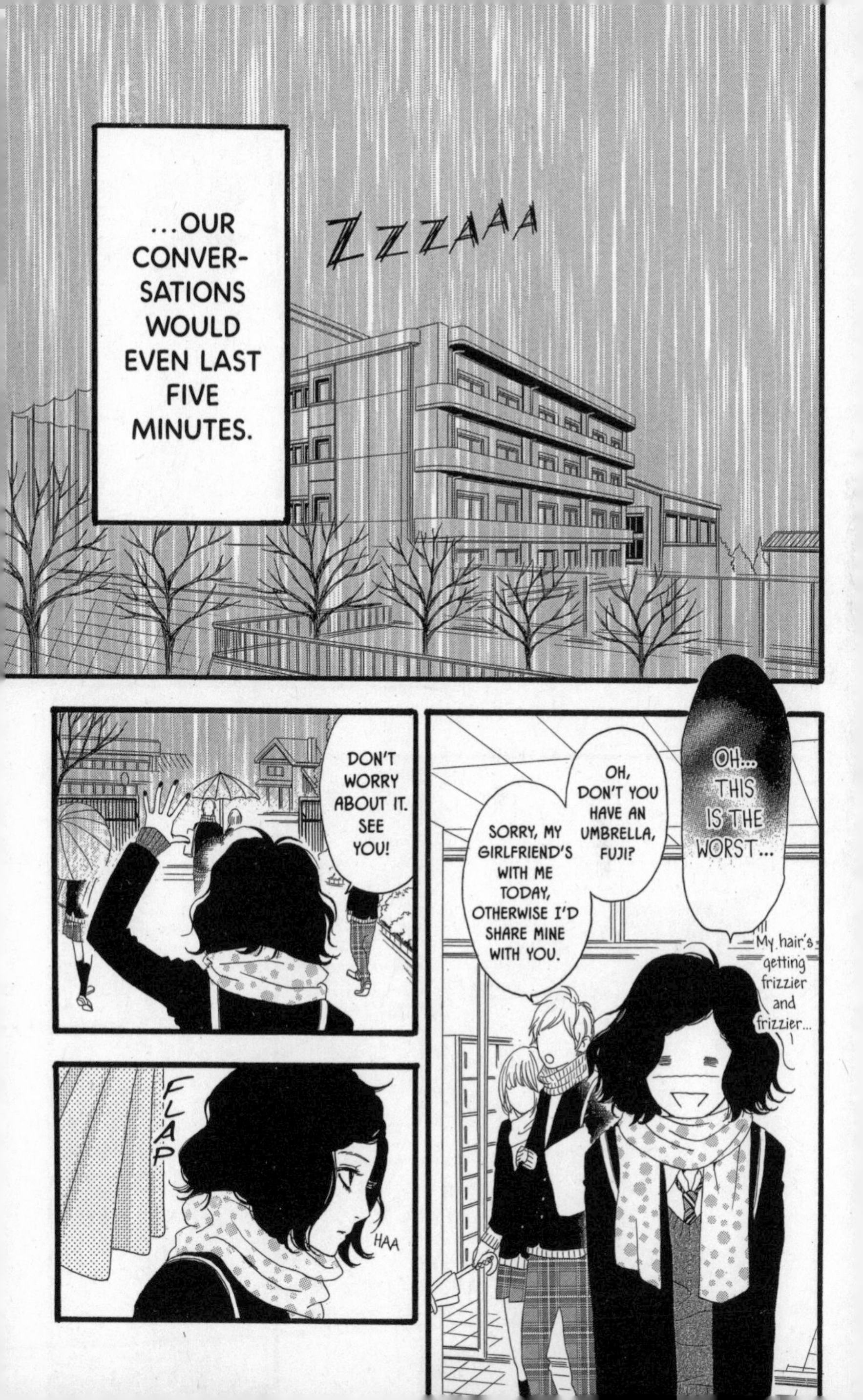
...OUR CONVERSATIONS WOULD EVEN LAST FIVE MINUTES.
ZZZAAA
OH... THIS IS THE WORST...
OH, DON'T YOU HAVE AN UMBRELLA, FUJI?
SORRY, MY GIRLFRIEND'S WITH ME TODAY, OTHERWISE I'D SHARE MINE WITH YOU.
My hair's getting frizzier and frizzier...
DON'T WORRY ABOUT IT. SEE YOU!
FLAP
HAA

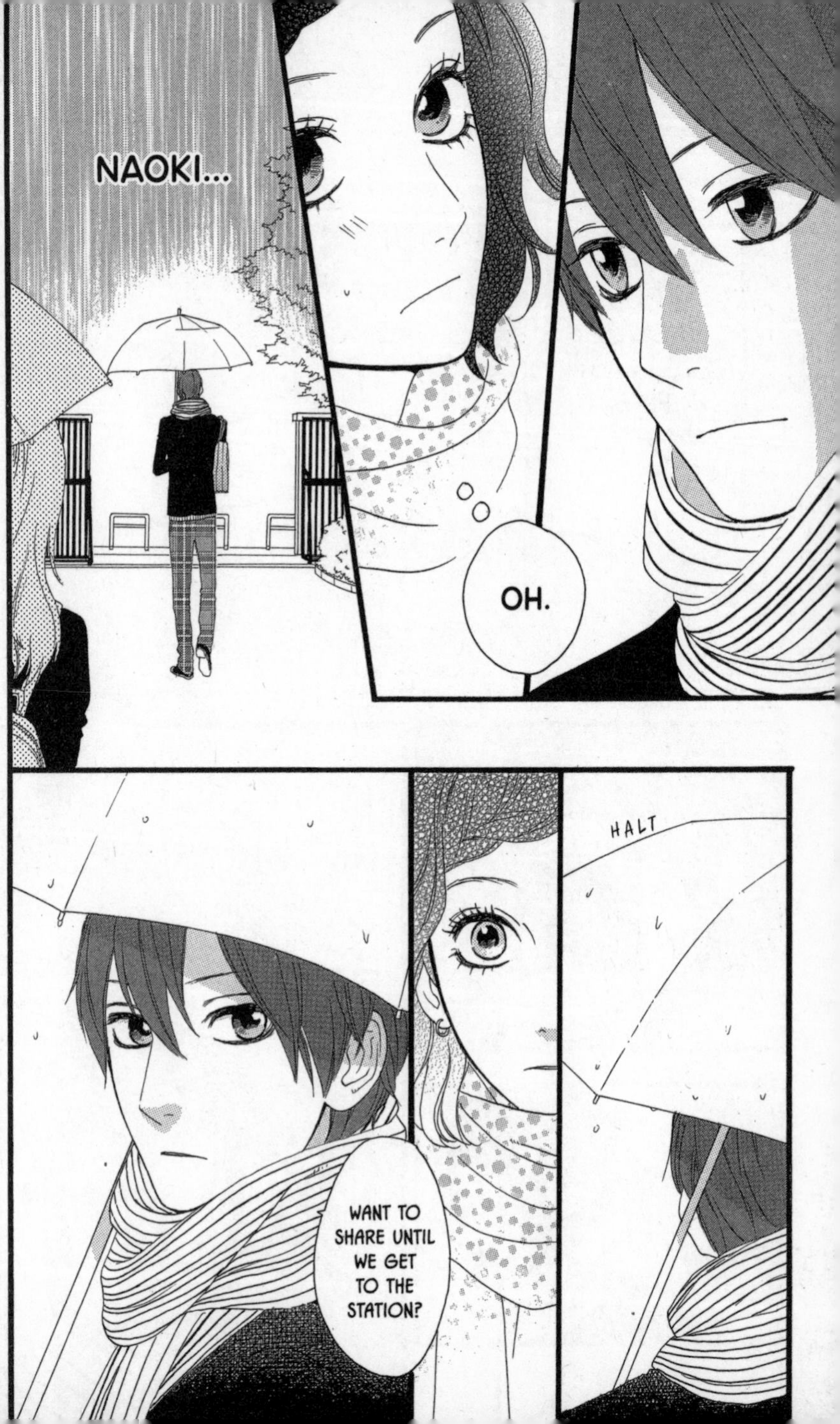
OH.
NAOKI...
HALT
WANT TO SHARE UNTIL WE GET TO THE STATION?

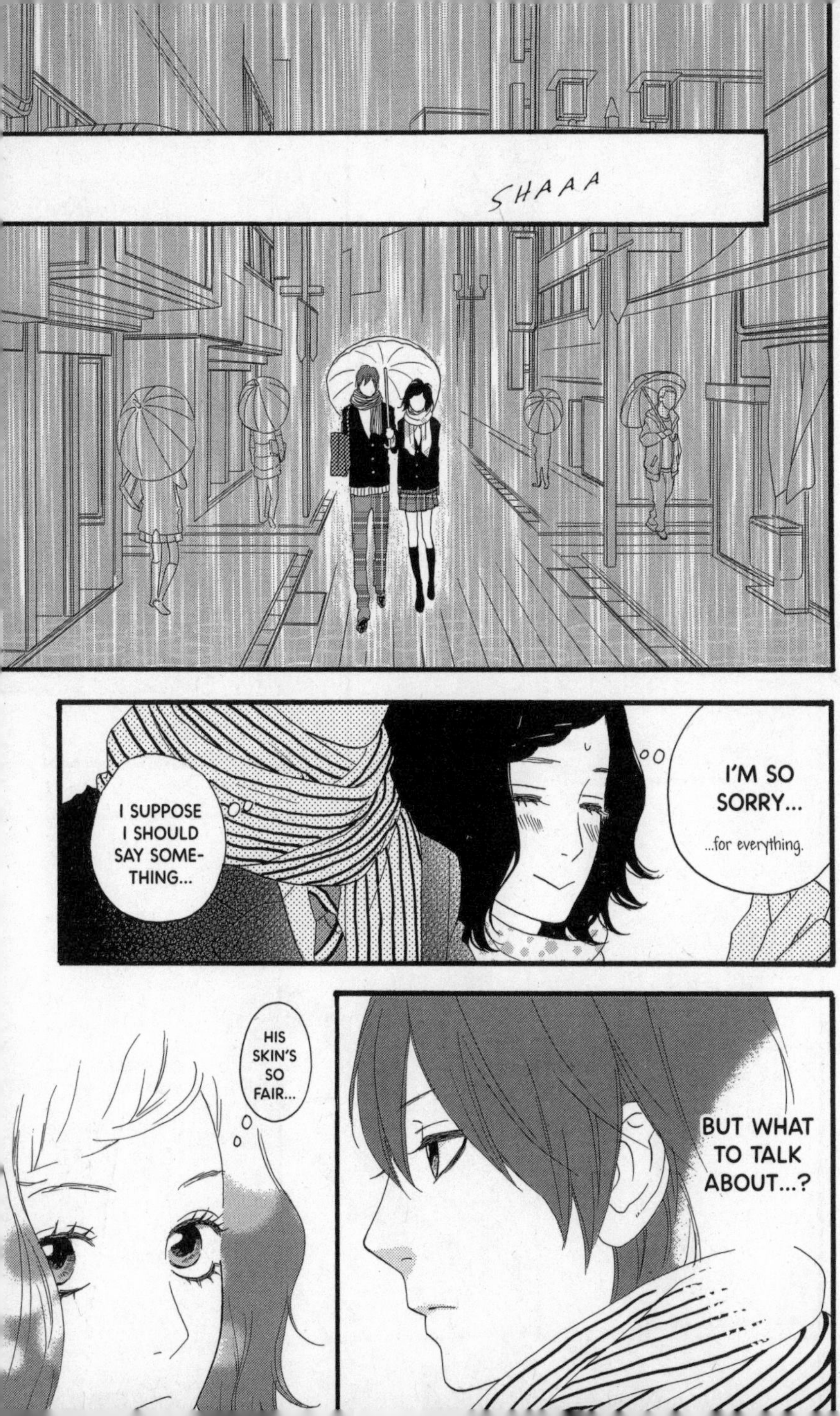
SHAAA
I'M SO SORRY...
...for everything.
I SUPPOSE I SHOULD SAY SOME-THING...
BUT WHAT TO TALK ABOUT...?
HIS SKIN'S SO FAIR...

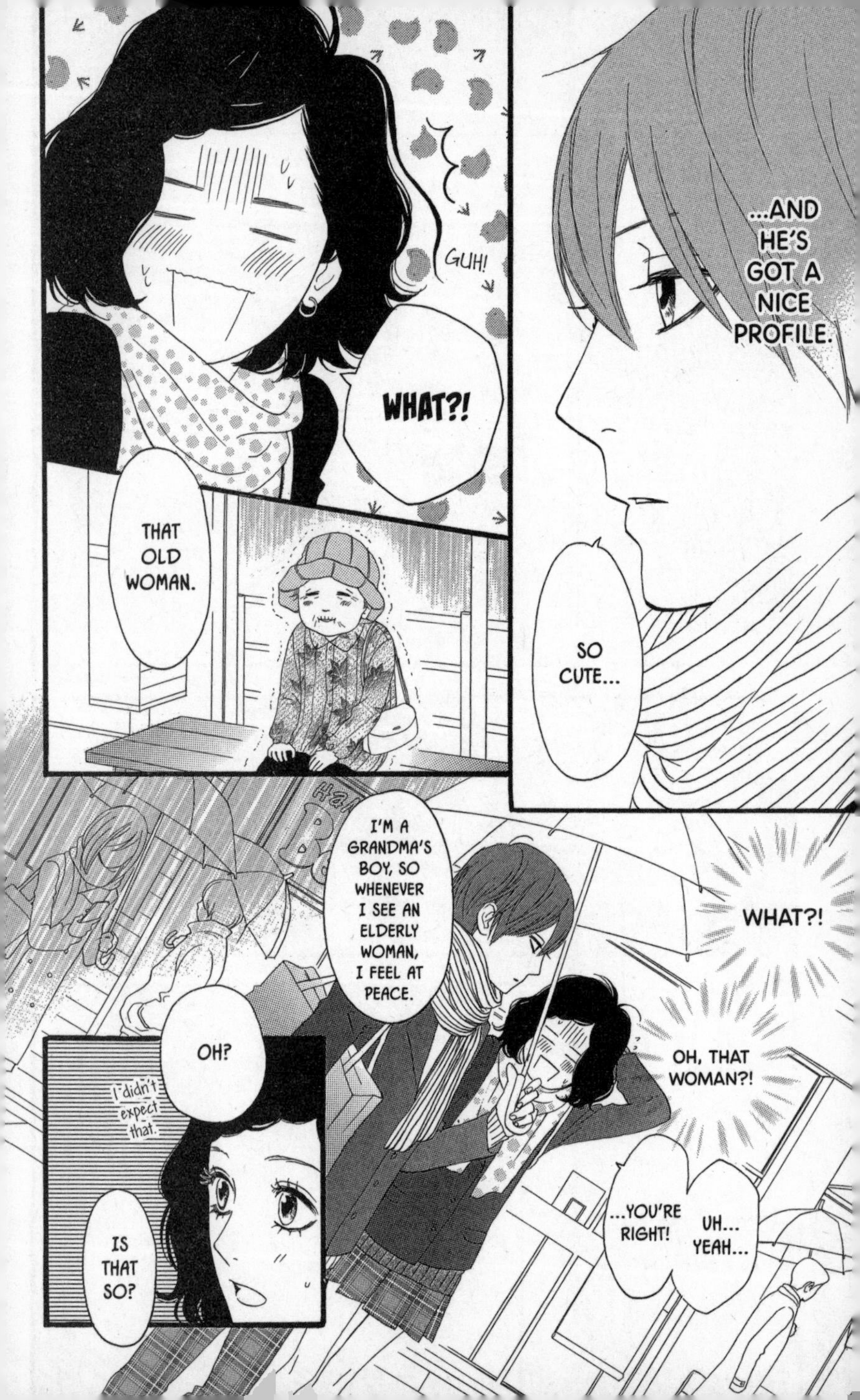

...AND HE'S GOT A NICE PROFILE.
SO CUTE...
GUH!
WHAT?!
THAT OLD WOMAN.
WHAT?!
I'M A GRANDMA'S BOY, SO WHENEVER I SEE AN ELDERLY WOMAN, I FEEL AT PEACE.
OH, THAT WOMAN?!
UH... YEAH...
...YOU'RE RIGHT!
OH?
I didn't expect that.
IS THAT SO?

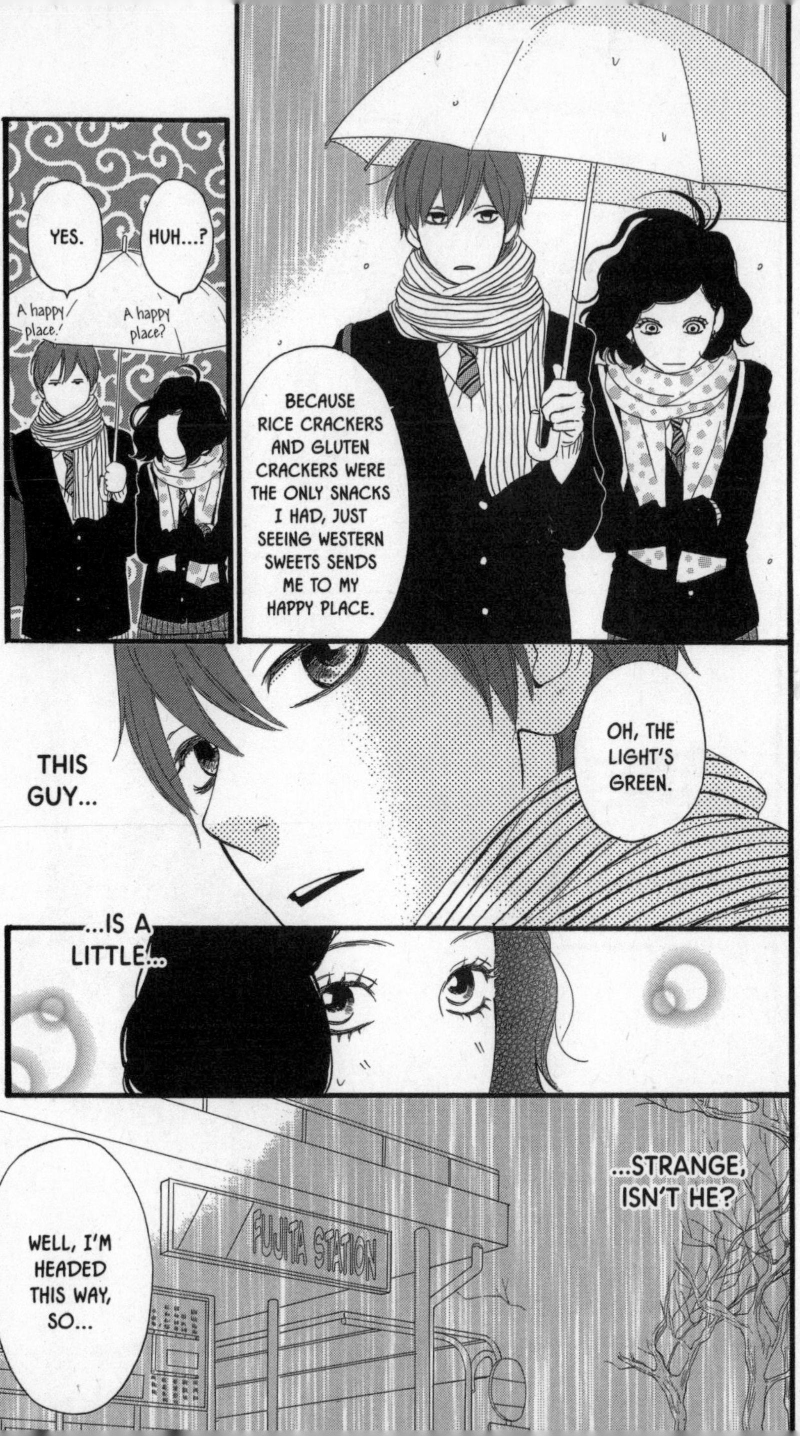
BECAUSE RICE CRACKERS AND GLUTEN CRACKERS WERE THE ONLY SNACKS I HAD, JUST SEEING WESTERN SWEETS SENDS ME TO MY HAPPY PLACE.
HUH...?
YES.
A happy place?
A happy place.
OH, THE LIGHT'S GREEN.
THIS GUY...
...IS A LITTLE...
...STRANGE, ISN'T HE?
FUJITA STATION
WELL, I'M HEADED THIS WAY, SO...

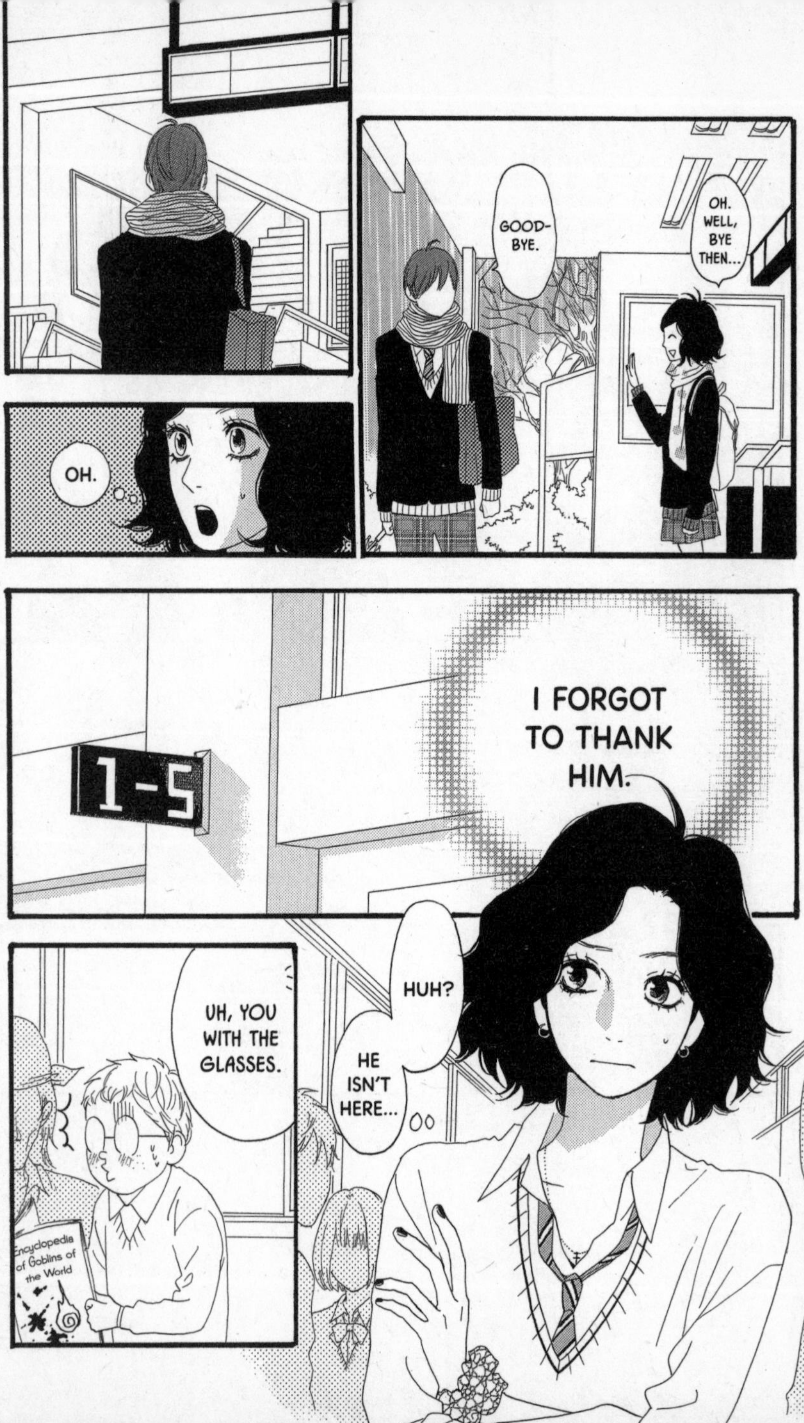
OH. WELL, BYE THEN...
GOOD-BYE.
OH.
I FORGOT TO THANK HIM.
HUH?
HE ISN'T HERE...
UH, YOU WITH THE GLASSES.
Encyclopedia of Goblins of the World

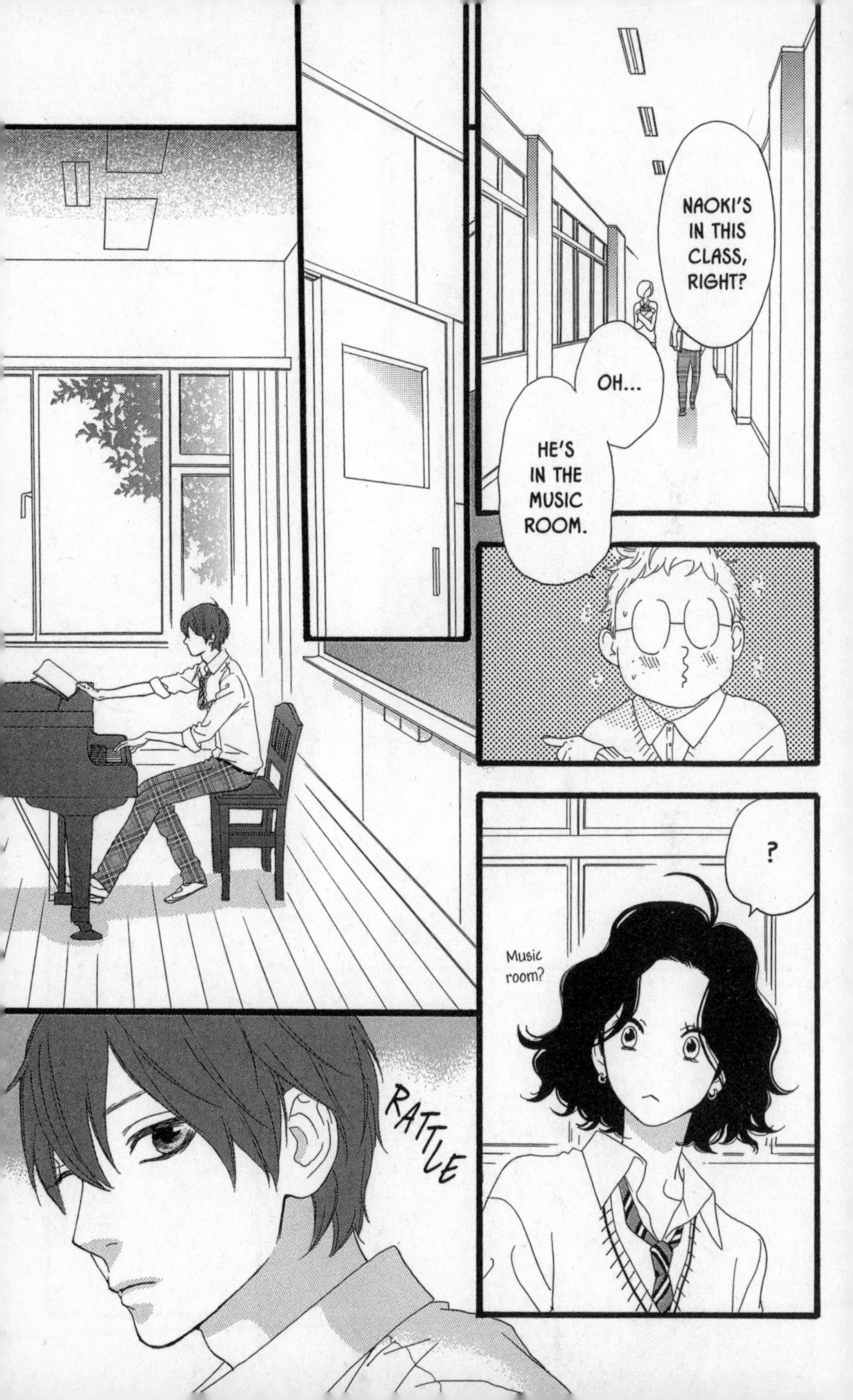
NAOKI'S IN THIS CLASS, RIGHT?
OH...
HE'S IN THE MUSIC ROOM.
?
Music room?
RATTLE

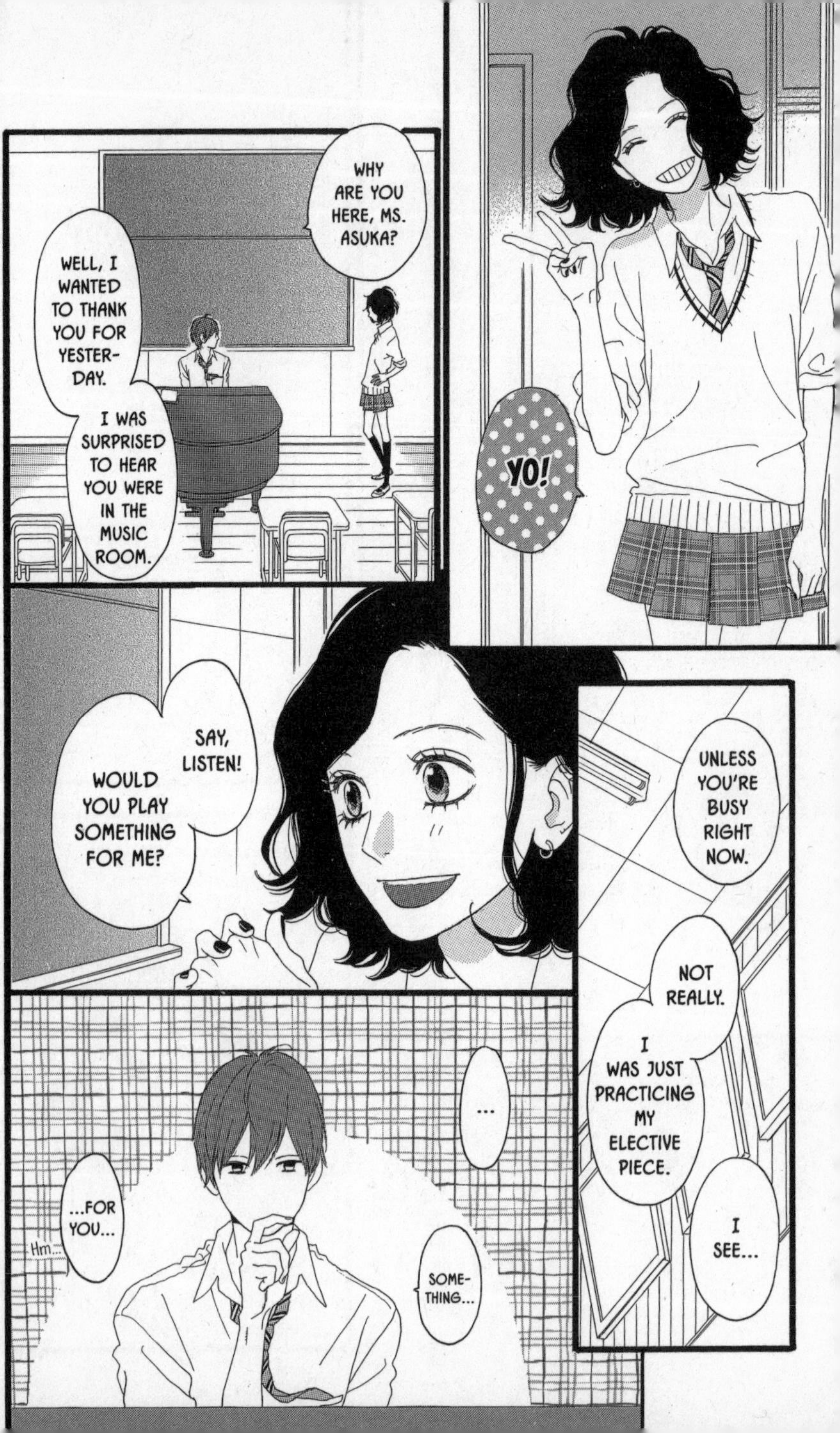
YO!
WHY ARE YOU HERE, MS. ASUKA?
WELL, I WANTED TO THANK YOU FOR YESTER-DAY.
I WAS SURPRISED TO HEAR YOU WERE IN THE MUSIC ROOM.
SAY, LISTEN!
WOULD YOU PLAY SOMETHING FOR ME?
UNLESS YOU'RE BUSY RIGHT NOW.
NOT REALLY.
I WAS JUST PRACTICING MY ELECTIVE PIECE.
I SEE...
...
SOME-THING...
...FOR YOU...
Hm...

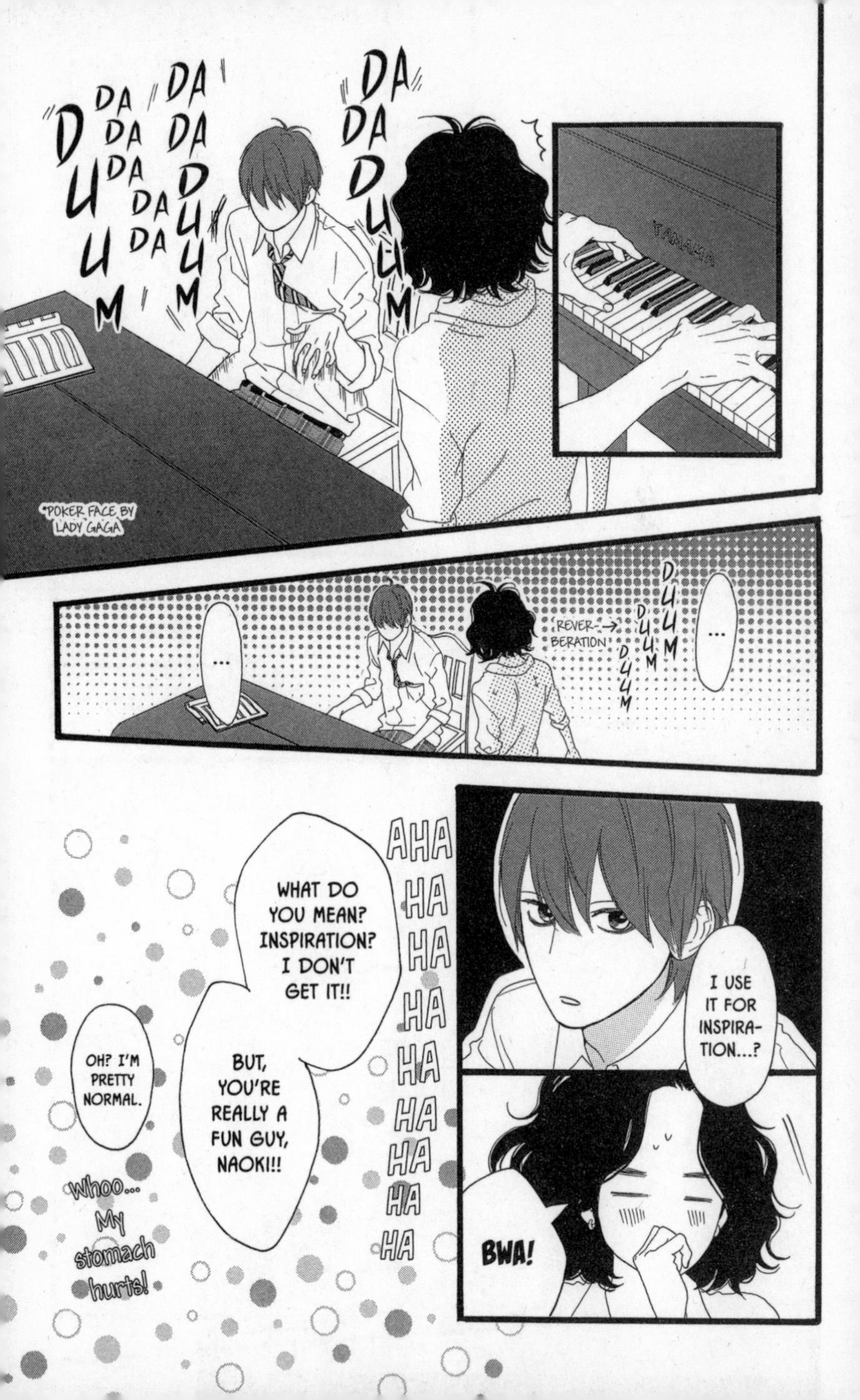
DA DA DUUM
DA DA DUUM
DUUM DA DA DA DA DA
*POKER FACE BY LADY GAGA
...
REVER-BERATION → DUUM DUUM DUUM
...
I USE IT FOR INSPIRA-TION...?
BWA!
AHA HA HA HA HA HA HA HA HA HA
WHAT DO YOU MEAN? INSPIRATION? I DON'T GET IT!!
BUT, YOU'RE REALLY A FUN GUY, NAOKI!!
OH? I'M PRETTY NORMAL.
Whoo... My stomach hurts!

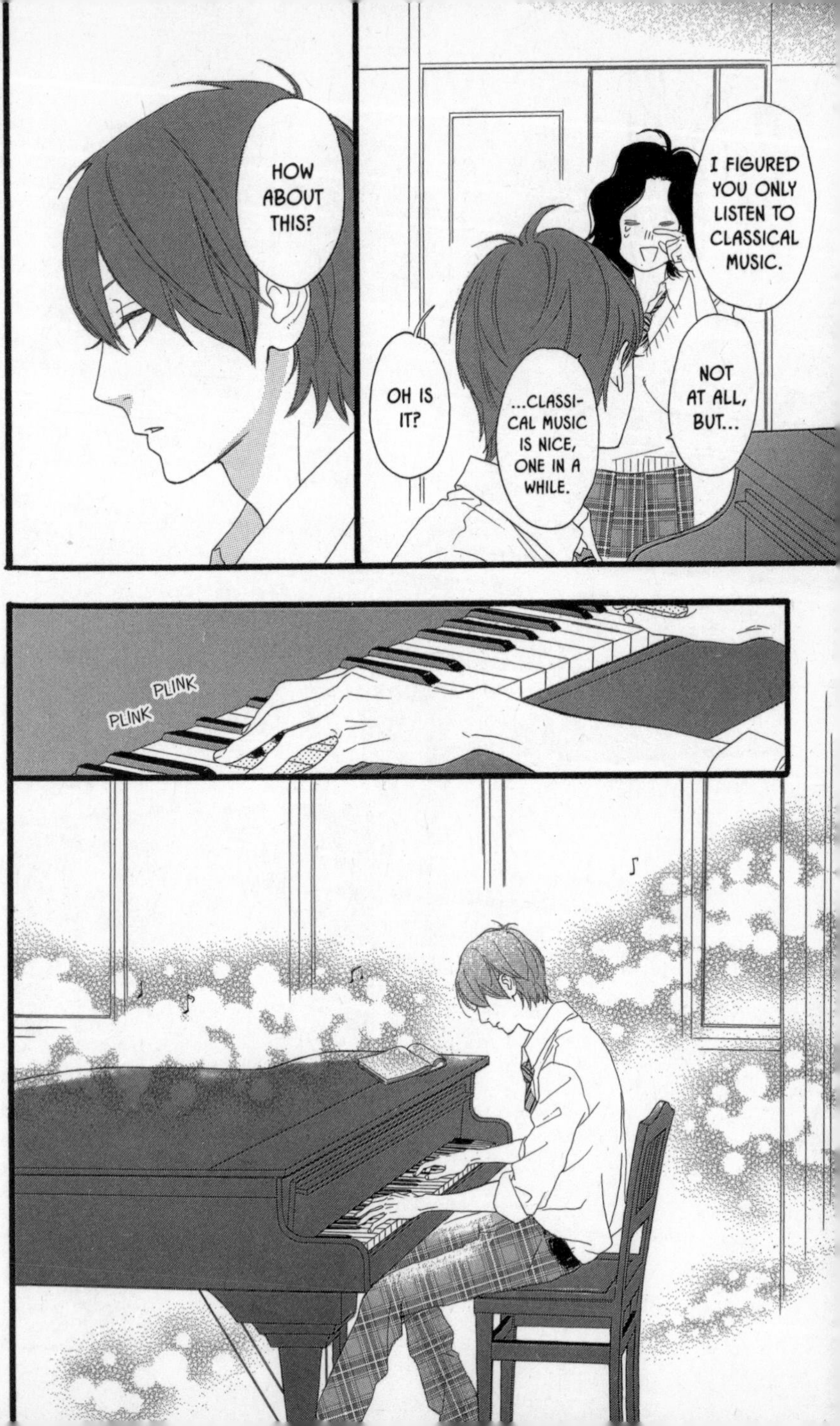
I FIGURED YOU ONLY LISTEN TO CLASSICAL MUSIC.
NOT AT ALL, BUT...
...CLASSICAL MUSIC IS NICE, ONE IN A WHILE.
OH IS IT?
HOW ABOUT THIS?
PLINK
PLINK

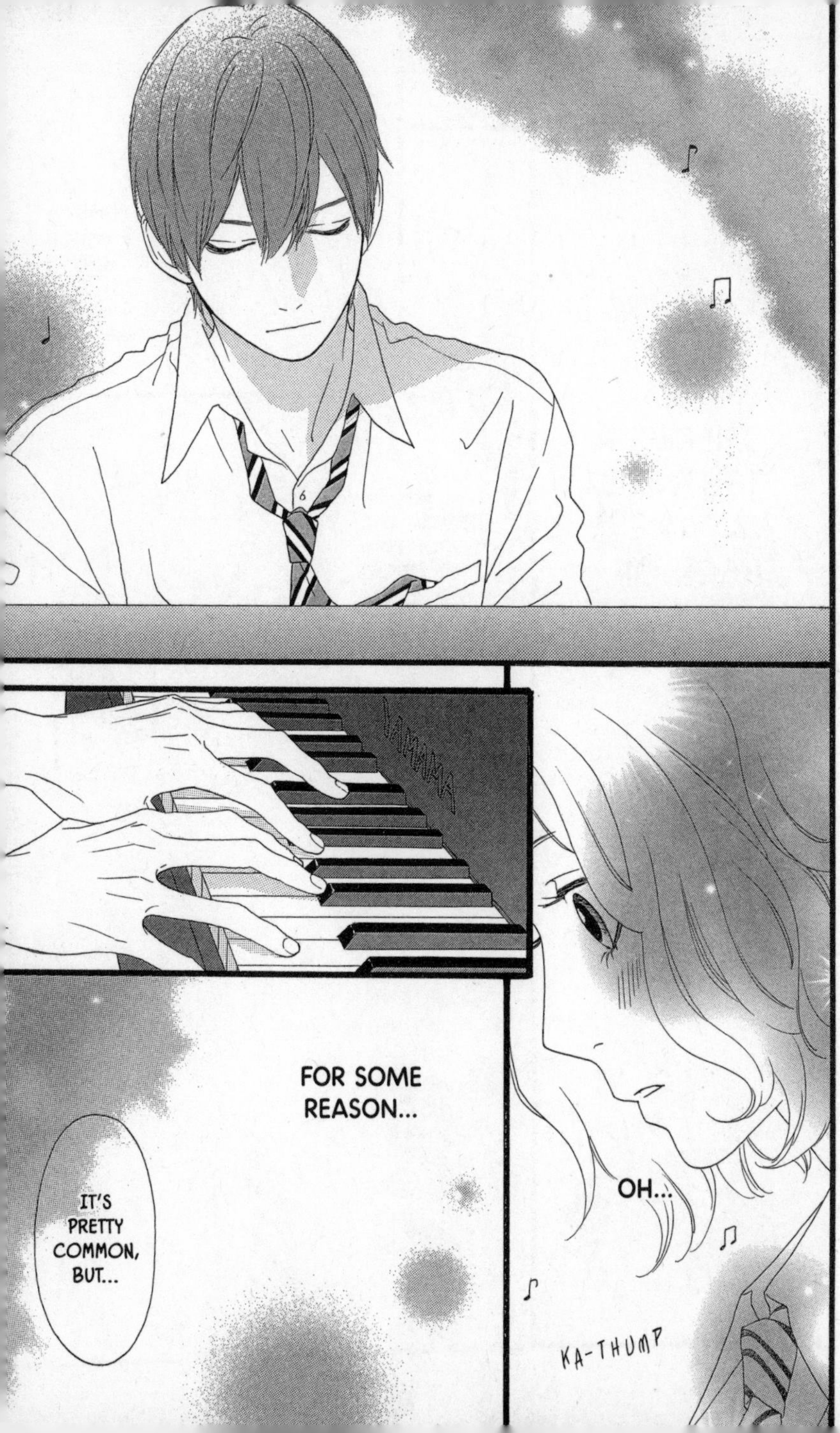
OH...
KA-THUMP
FOR SOME REASON...
IT'S PRETTY COMMON, BUT...

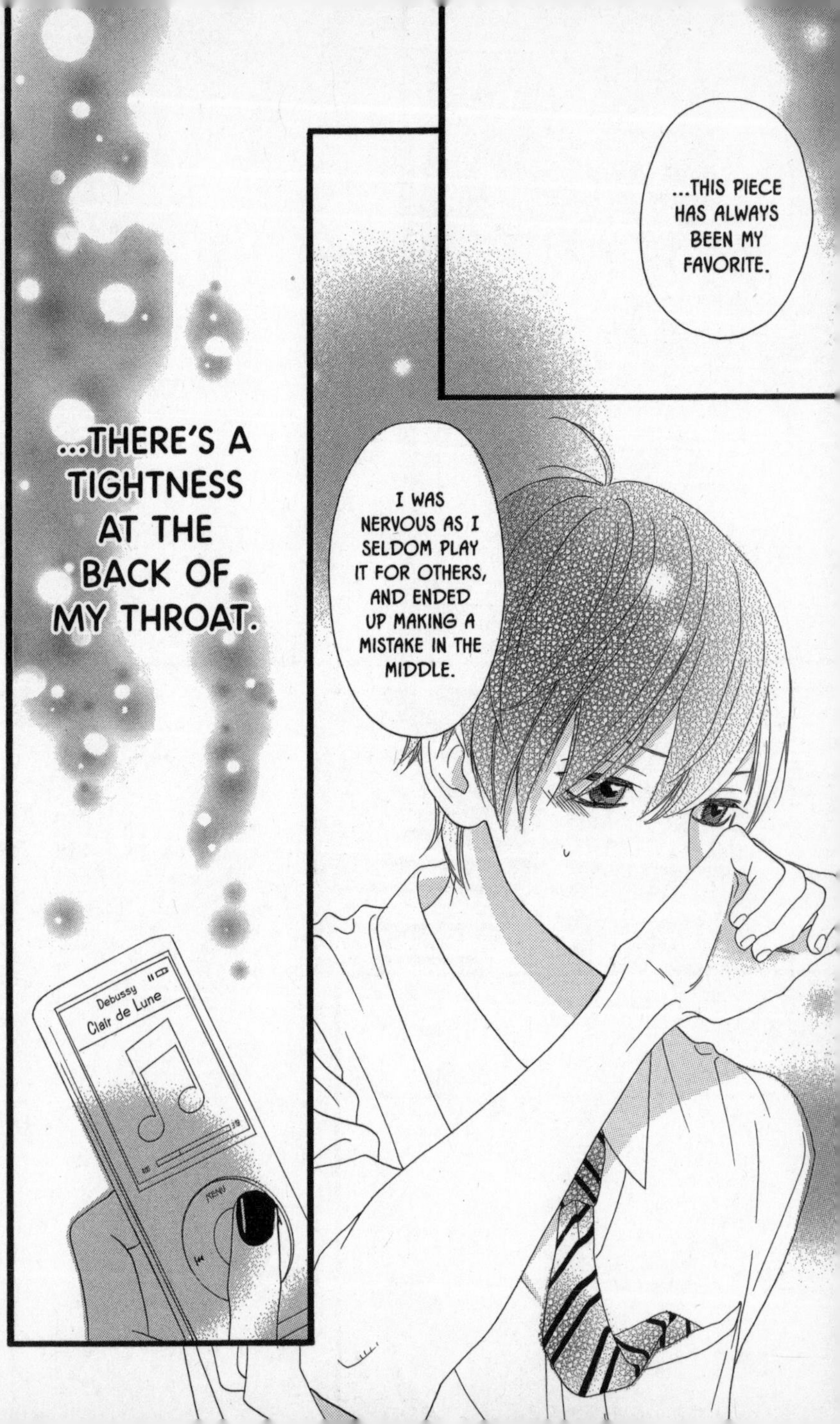
...THIS PIECE HAS ALWAYS BEEN MY FAVORITE.
I WAS NERVOUS AS I SELDOM PLAY IT FOR OTHERS, AND ENDED UP MAKING A MISTAKE IN THE MIDDLE.
...THERE'S A TIGHTNESS AT THE BACK OF MY THROAT.
Debussy
Clair de Lune

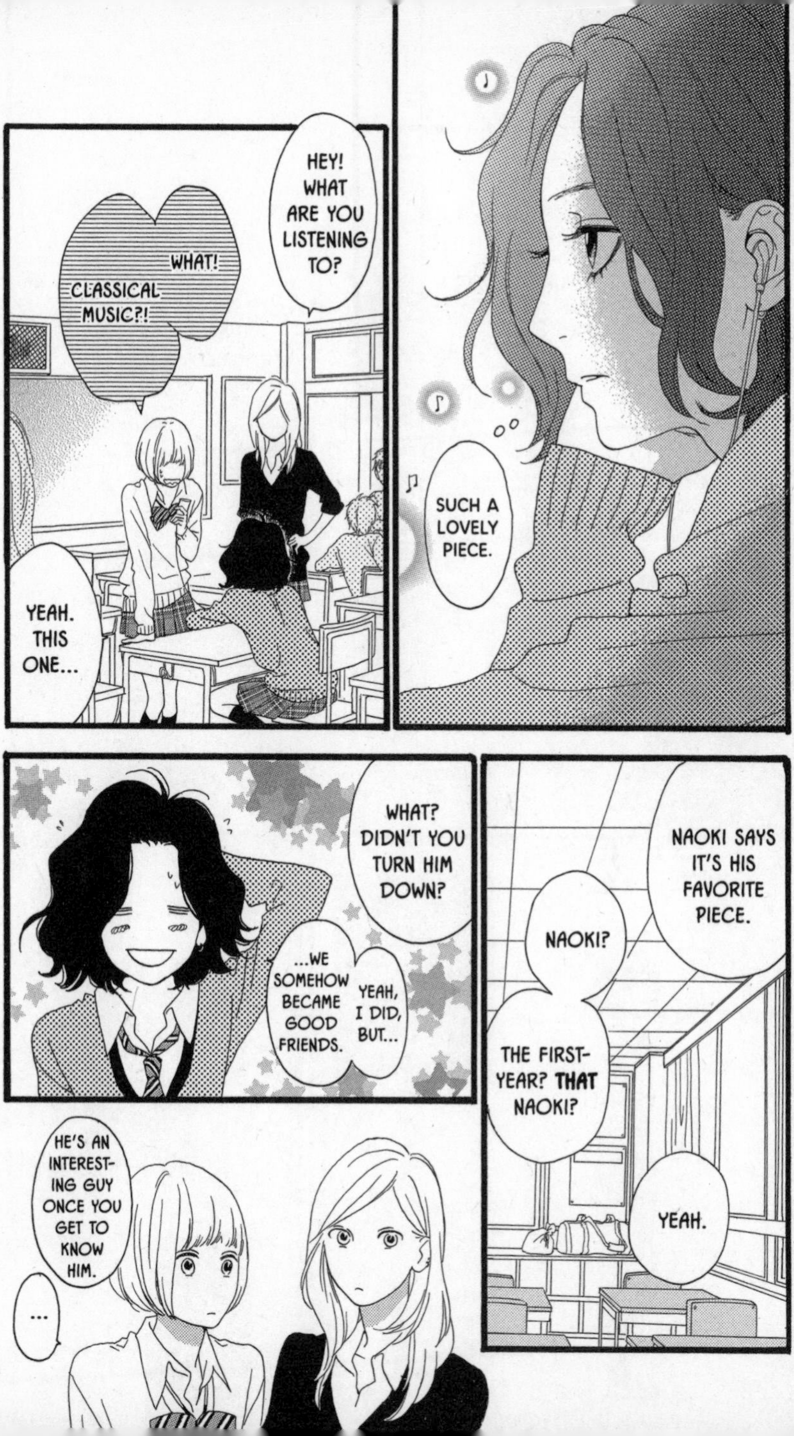
SUCH A LOVELY PIECE.
HEY! WHAT ARE YOU LISTENING TO?
WHAT! CLASSICAL MUSIC?!
YEAH. THIS ONE...
NAOKI SAYS IT'S HIS FAVORITE PIECE.
NAOKI?
THE FIRST-YEAR? **THAT** NAOKI?
YEAH.
WHAT? DIDN'T YOU TURN HIM DOWN?
YEAH, I DID, BUT...
...WE SOMEHOW BECAME GOOD FRIENDS.
HE'S AN INTERESTING GUY ONCE YOU GET TO KNOW HIM.
...

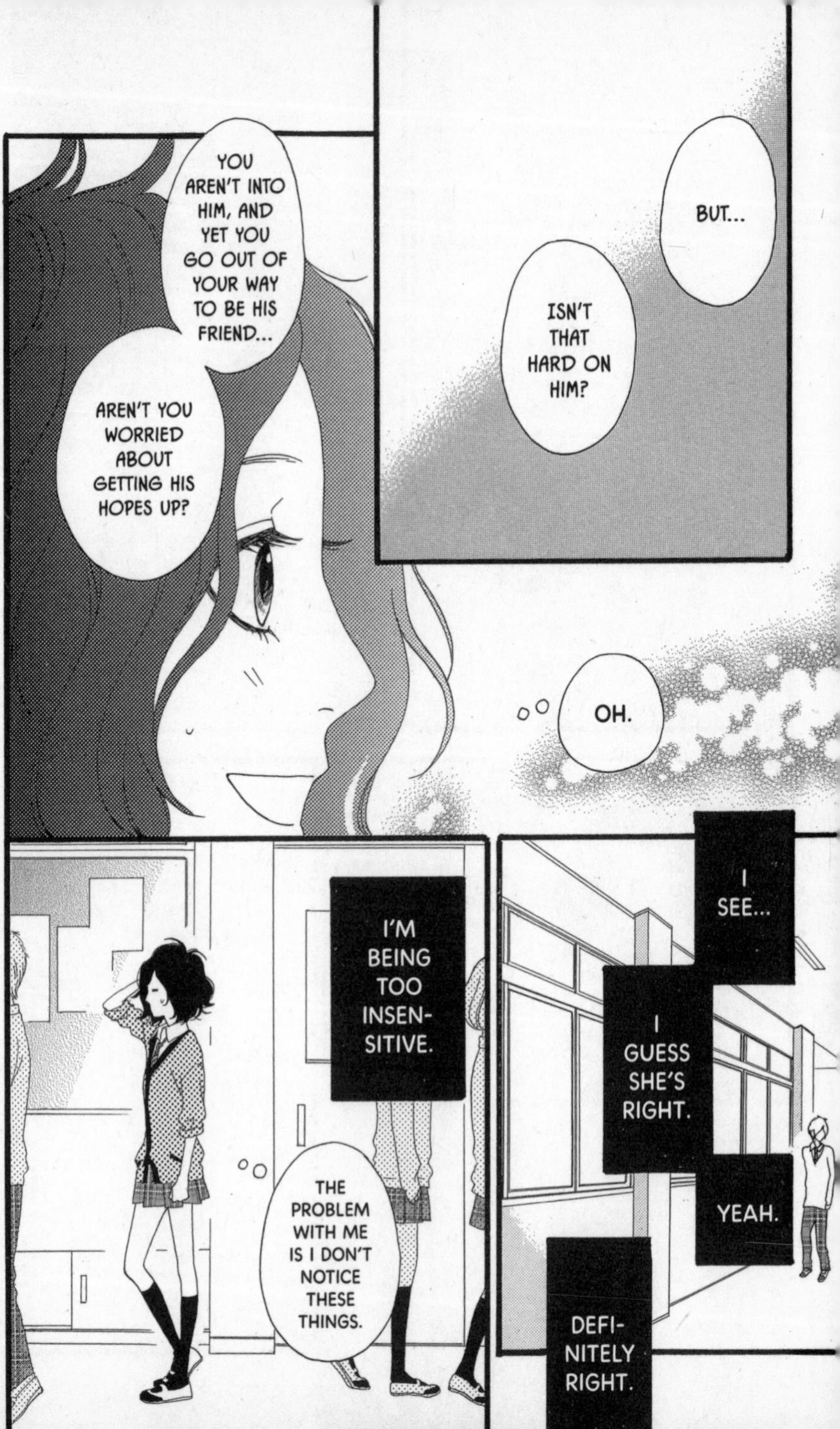
BUT...
ISN'T THAT HARD ON HIM?
YOU AREN'T INTO HIM, AND YET YOU GO OUT OF YOUR WAY TO BE HIS FRIEND...
AREN'T YOU WORRIED ABOUT GETTING HIS HOPES UP?
OH.
I SEE...
I GUESS SHE'S RIGHT.
YEAH.
DEFI-NITELY RIGHT.
I'M BEING TOO INSEN-SITIVE.
THE PROBLEM WITH ME IS I DON'T NOTICE THESE THINGS.

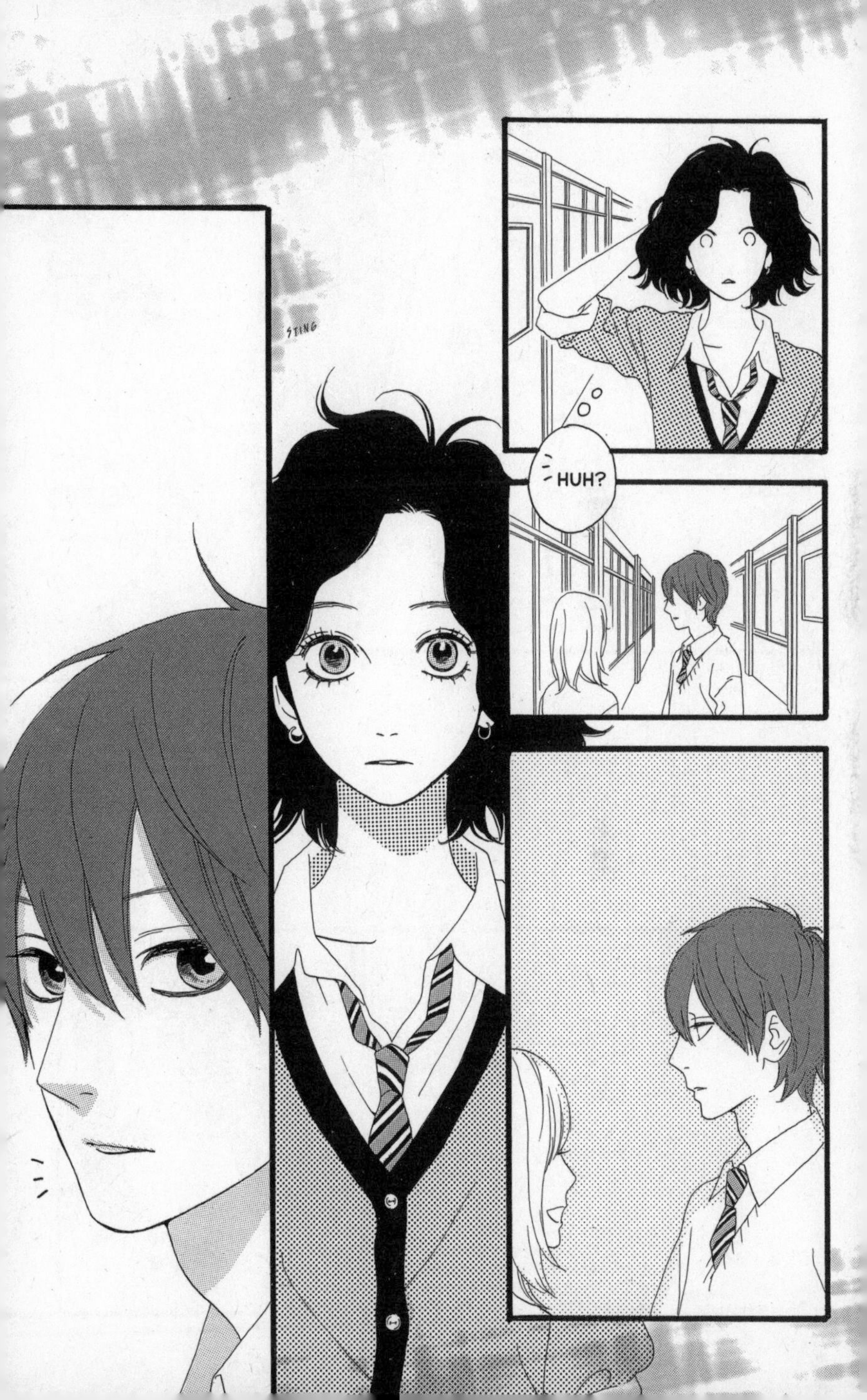
HUH?
STING

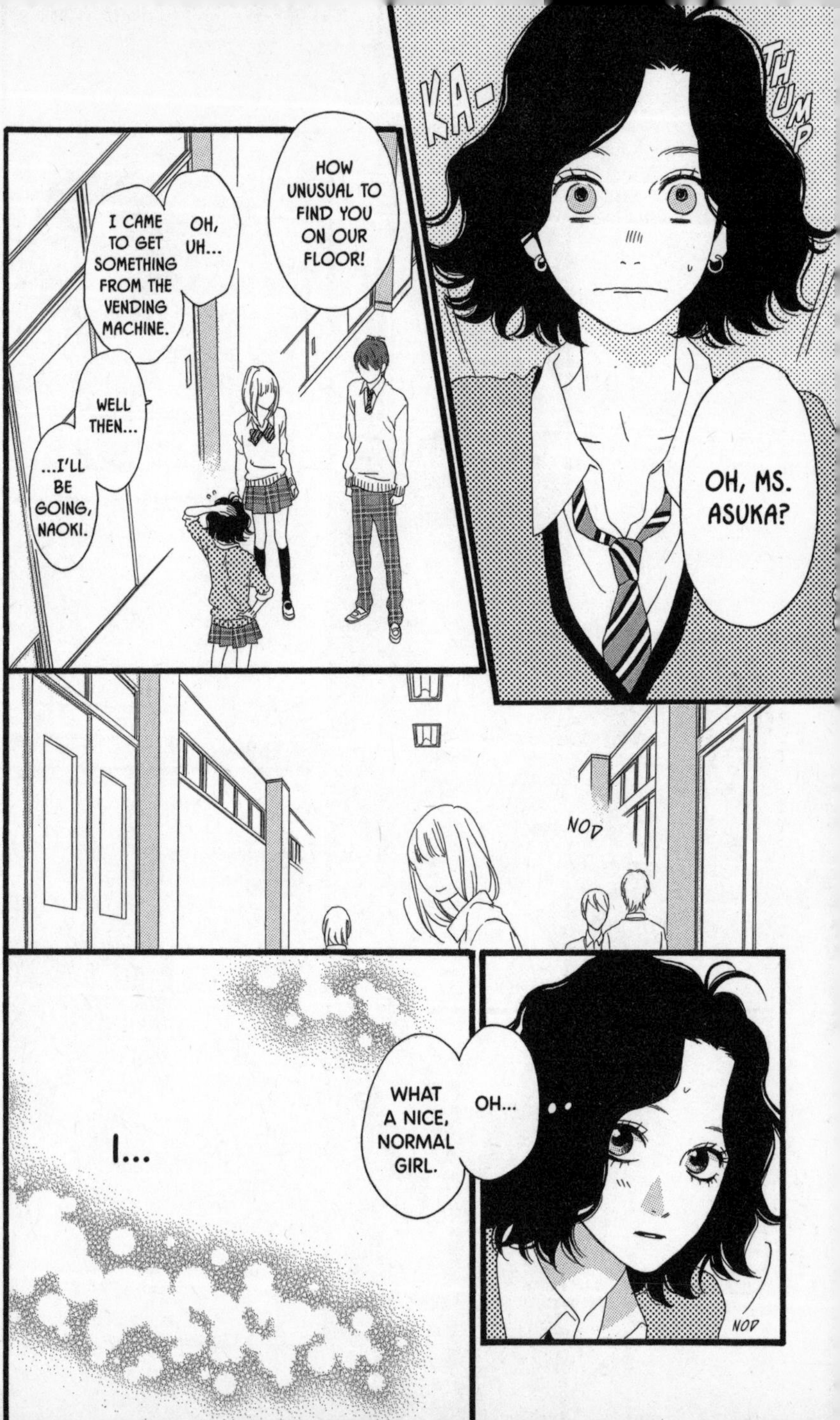
KA-THUMP
OH, MS. ASUKA?
HOW UNUSUAL TO FIND YOU ON OUR FLOOR!
OH, UH...
I CAME TO GET SOMETHING FROM THE VENDING MACHINE.
WELL THEN...
...I'LL BE GOING, NAOKI.
NOD
OH...
WHAT A NICE, NORMAL GIRL.
NOD
I...

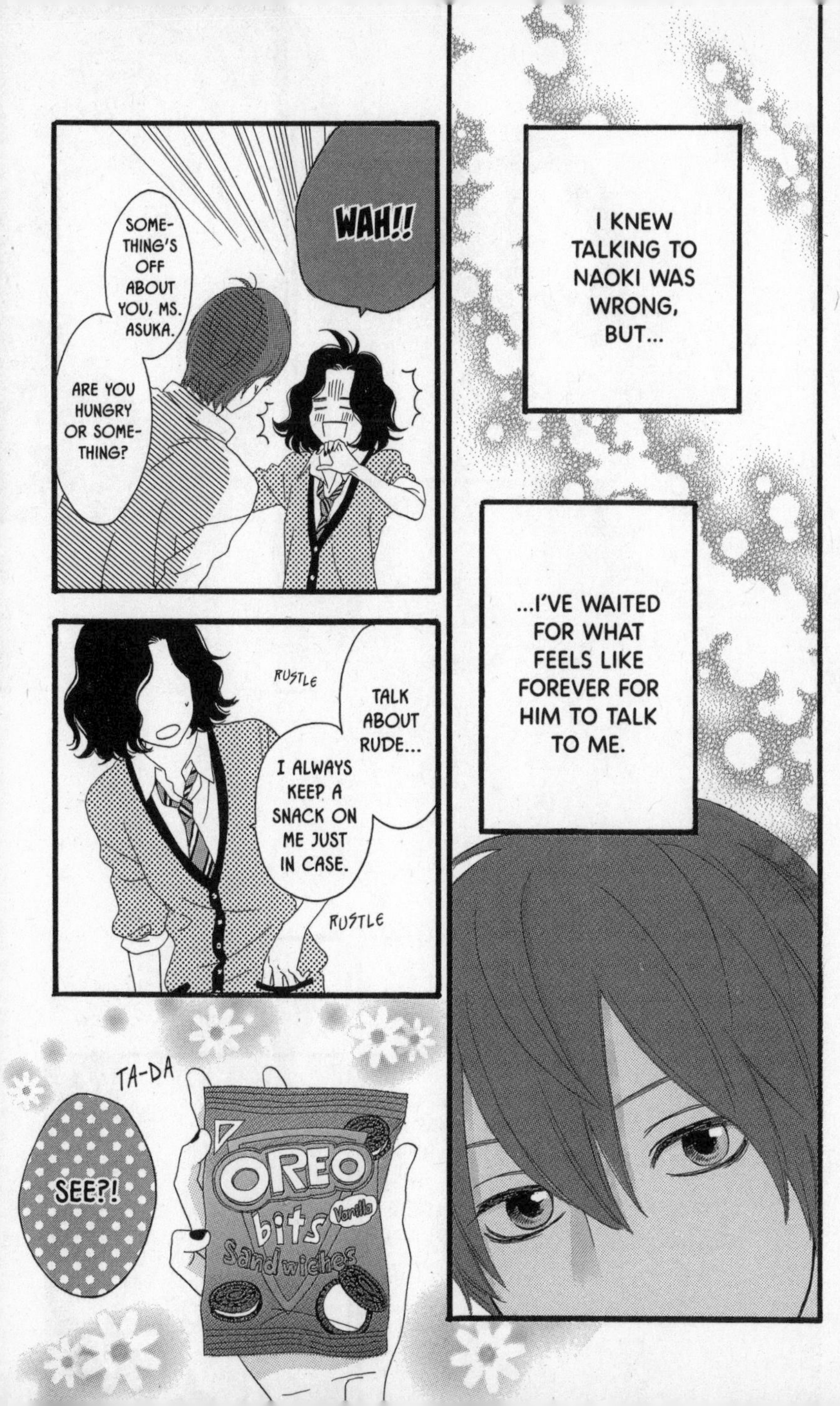
I KNEW TALKING TO NAOKI WAS WRONG, BUT...
...I'VE WAITED FOR WHAT FEELS LIKE FOREVER FOR HIM TO TALK TO ME.
WAH!!
SOME-THING'S OFF ABOUT YOU, MS. ASUKA.
ARE YOU HUNGRY OR SOME-THING?
TALK ABOUT RUDE...
RUSTLE
I ALWAYS KEEP A SNACK ON ME JUST IN CASE.
RUSTLE
TA-DA
OREO bits Vanilla Sandwiches
SEE?!

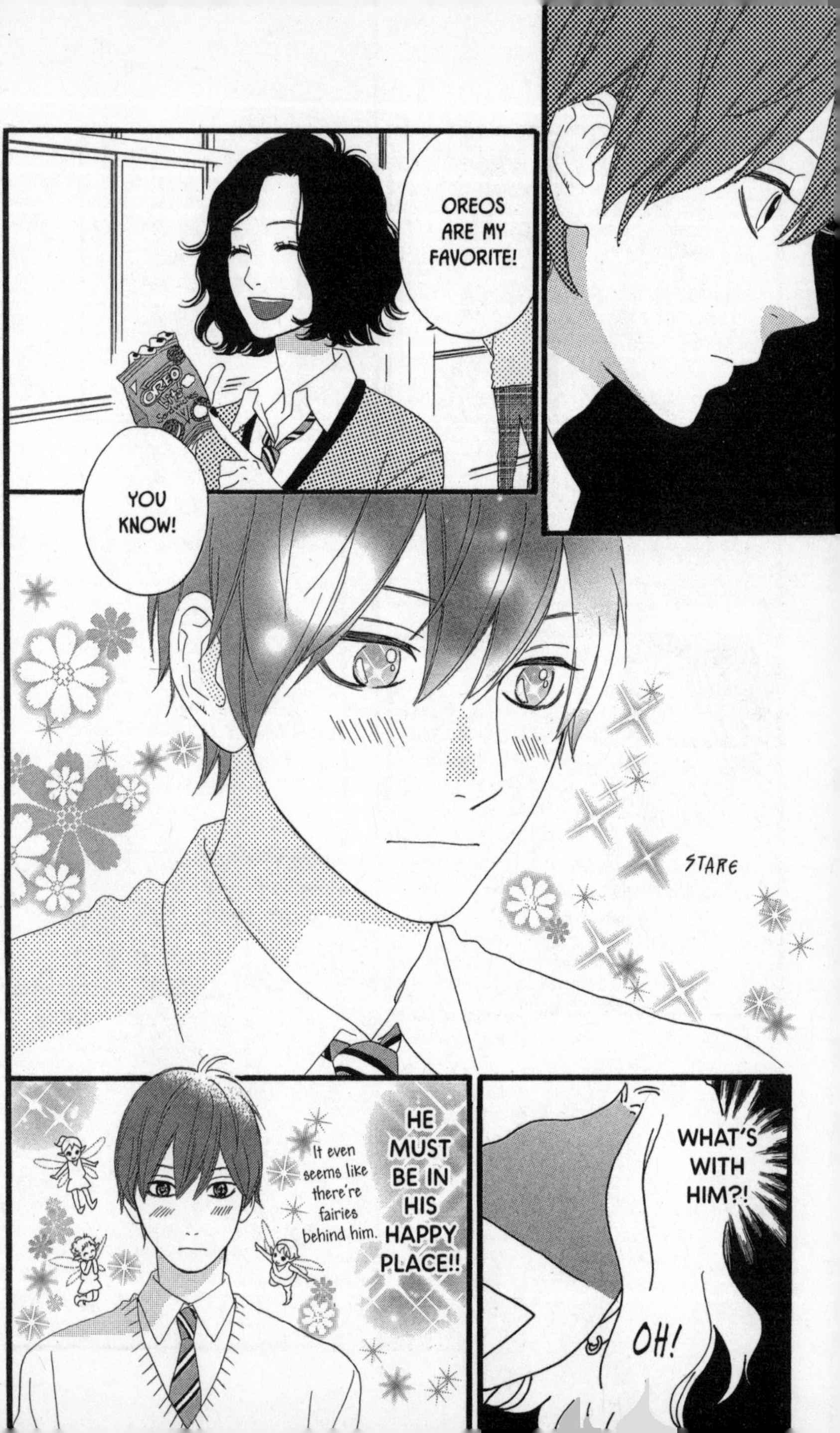
OREOS ARE MY FAVORITE!
YOU KNOW!
OREO
STARE
WHAT'S WITH HIM?!
OH!
HE MUST BE IN HIS HAPPY PLACE!!
It even seems like there're fairies behind him.

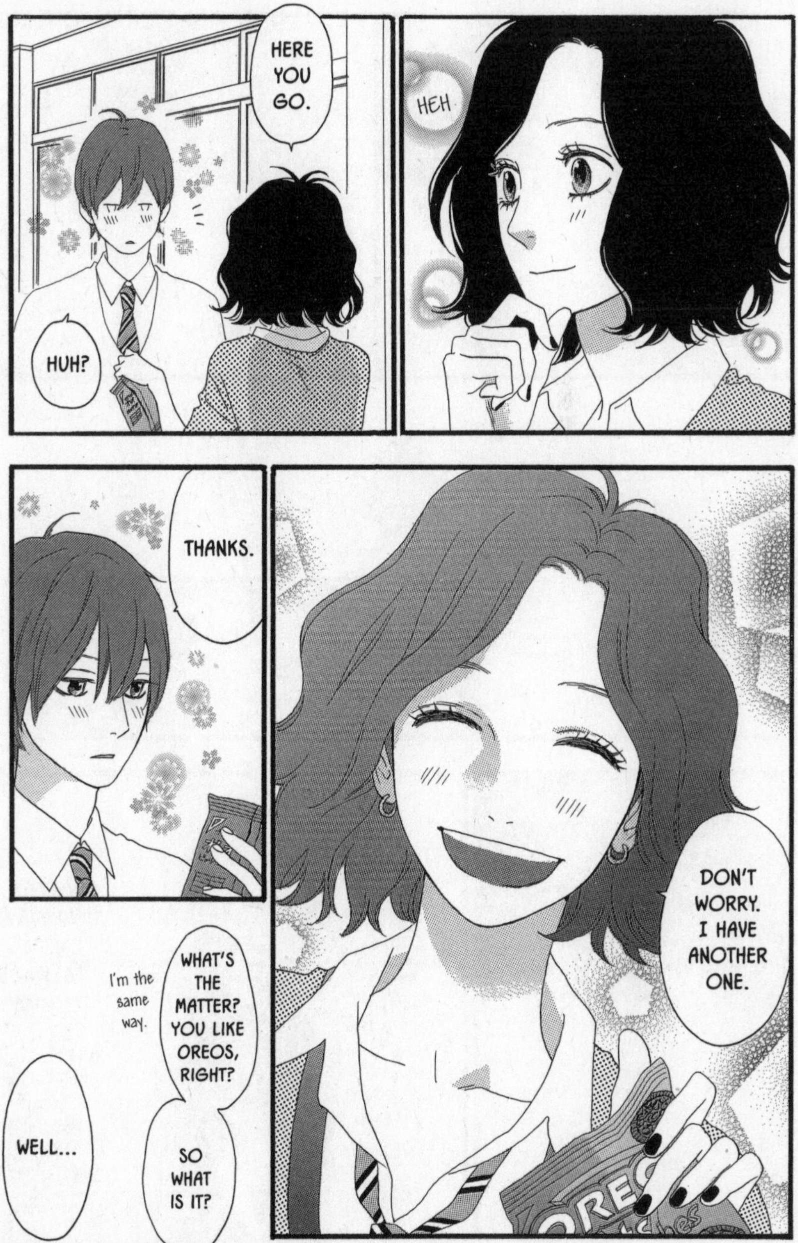
HEH
HERE YOU GO.
HUH?
DON'T WORRY. I HAVE ANOTHER ONE.
THANKS.
WHAT'S THE MATTER? YOU LIKE OREOS, RIGHT?
I'm the same way.
SO WHAT IS IT?
WELL...
OREOS

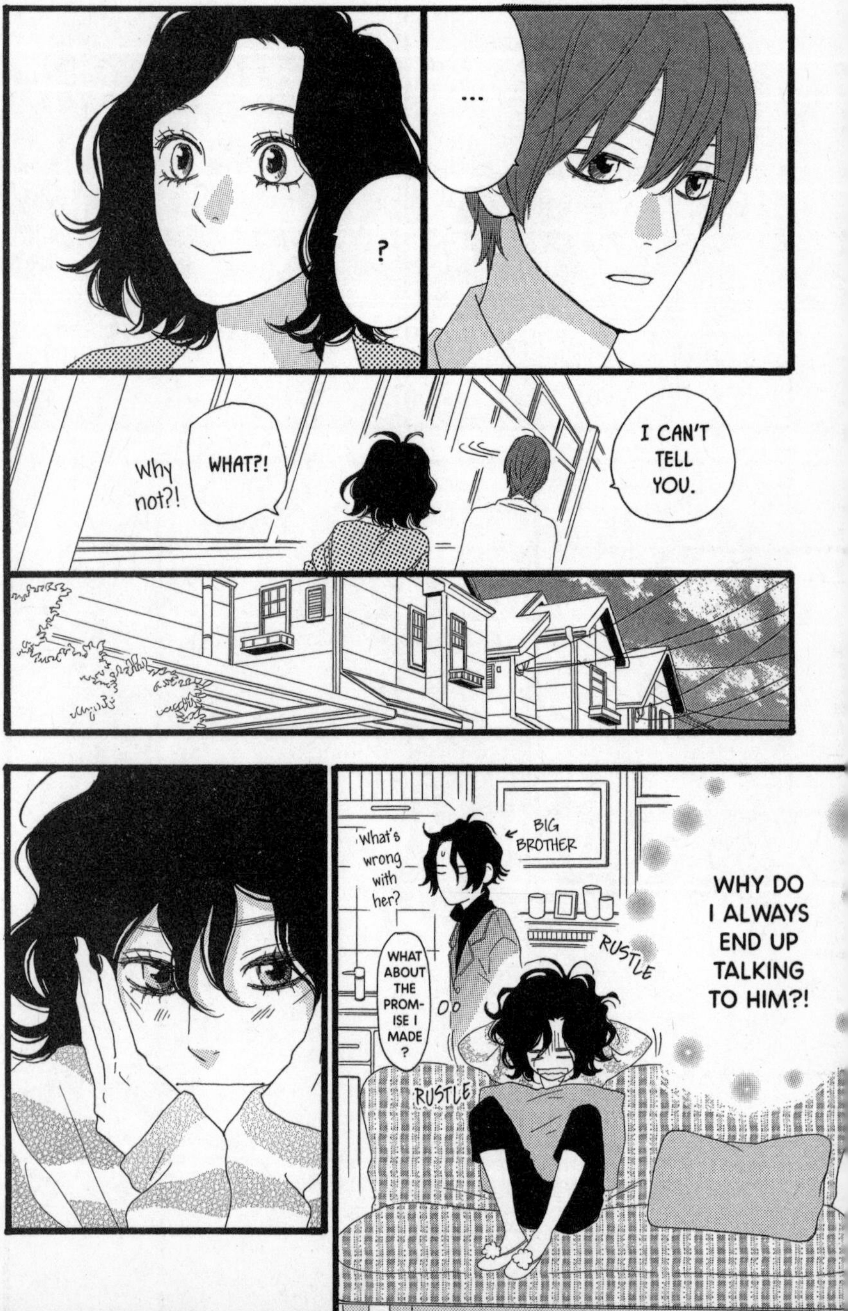
...
?
I CAN'T TELL YOU.
WHAT?!
Why not?!
WHY DO I ALWAYS END UP TALKING TO HIM?!
BIG BROTHER
What's wrong with her?
RUSTLE
WHAT ABOUT THE PROM-ISE I MADE?
RUSTLE

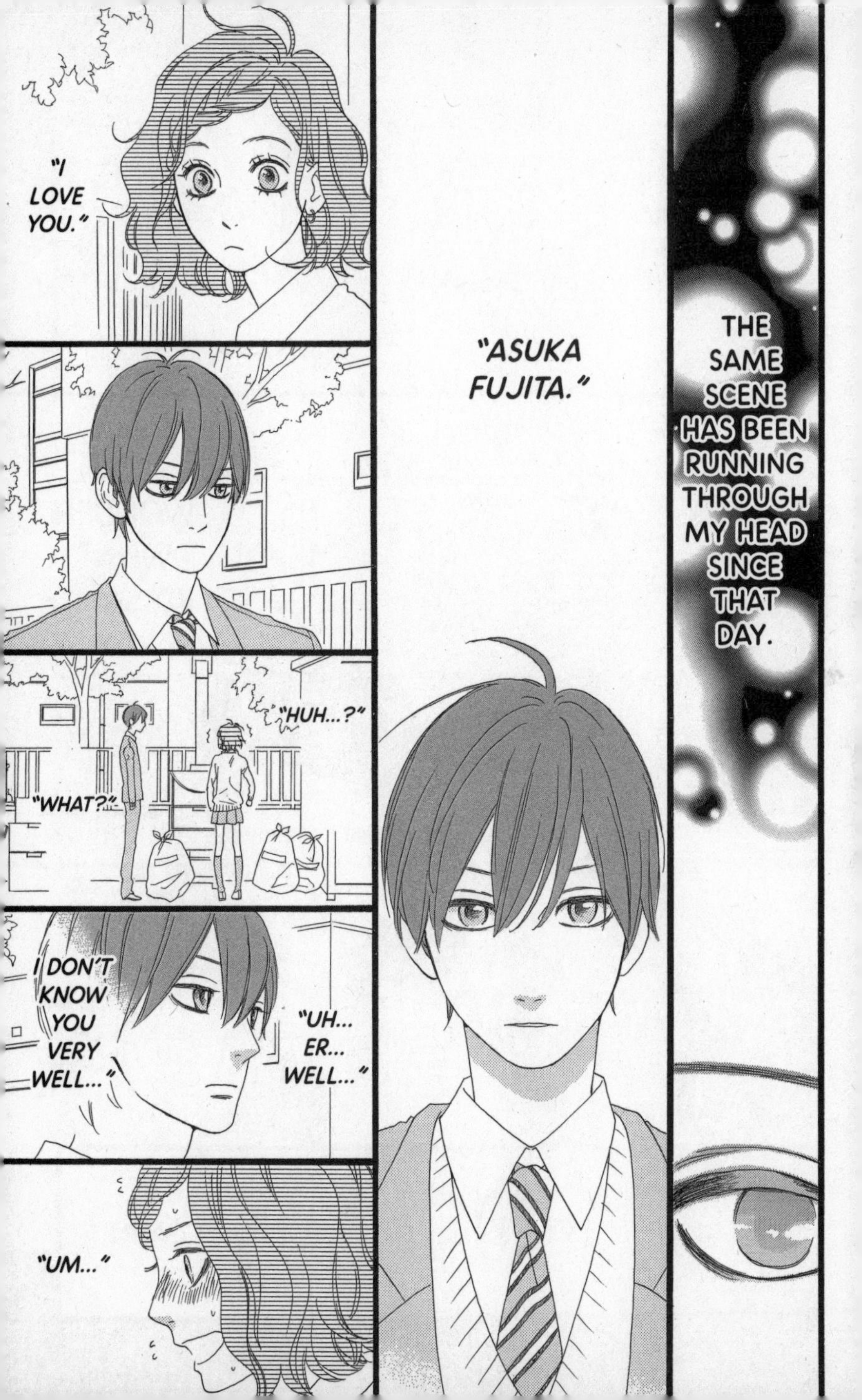
THE SAME SCENE HAS BEEN RUNNING THROUGH MY HEAD SINCE THAT DAY.
"ASUKA FUJITA."
"I LOVE YOU."
"HUH...?"
"WHAT?"
"UH... ER... WELL..."
I DON'T KNOW YOU VERY WELL..."
"UM..."

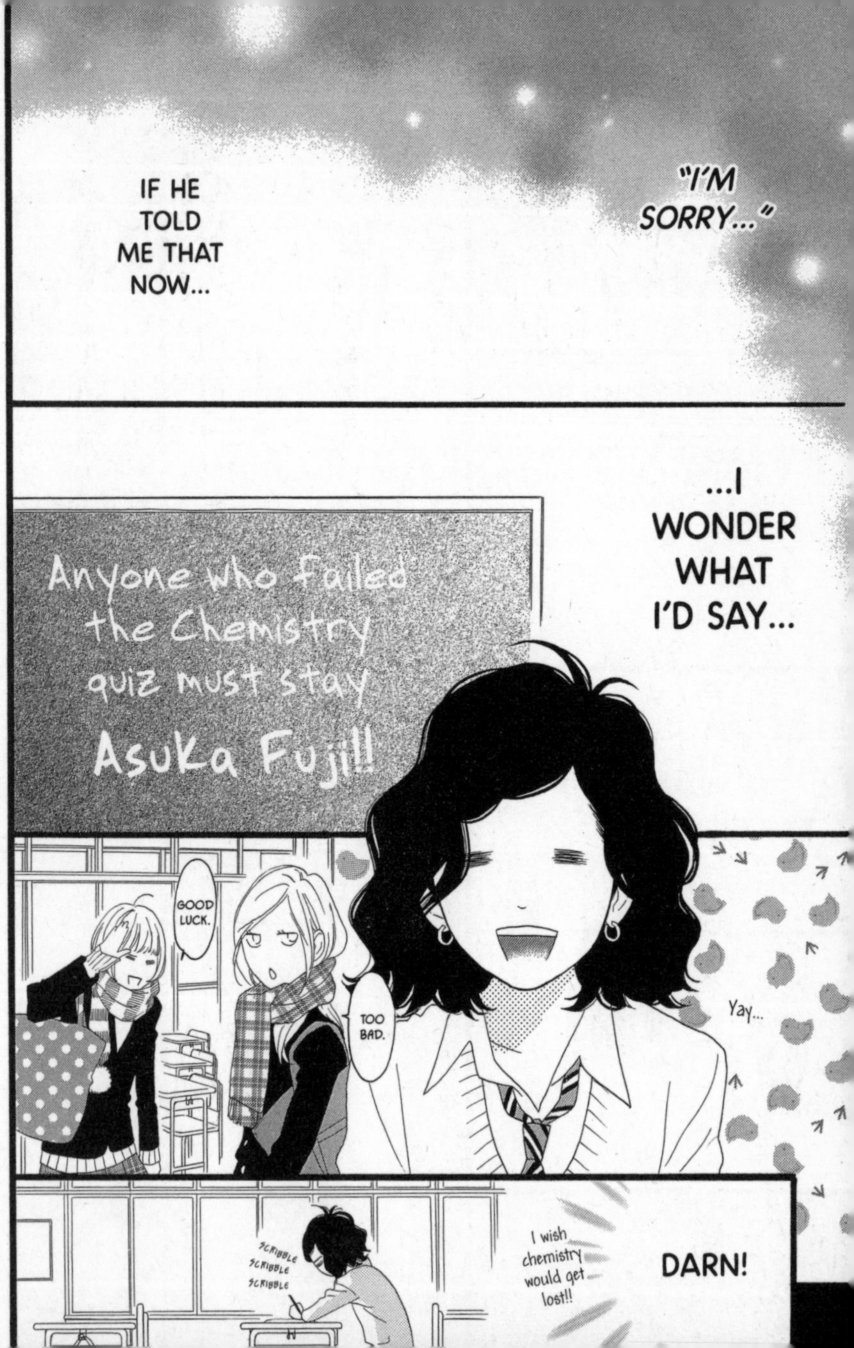
"I'M SORRY..."
IF HE TOLD ME THAT NOW...
...I WONDER WHAT I'D SAY...
Anyone who failed the Chemistry quiz must stay
Asuka Fuji!!
Yay...
GOOD LUCK.
TOO BAD.
DARN!
I wish chemistry would get lost!!
SCRIBBLE SCRIBBLE SCRIBBLE

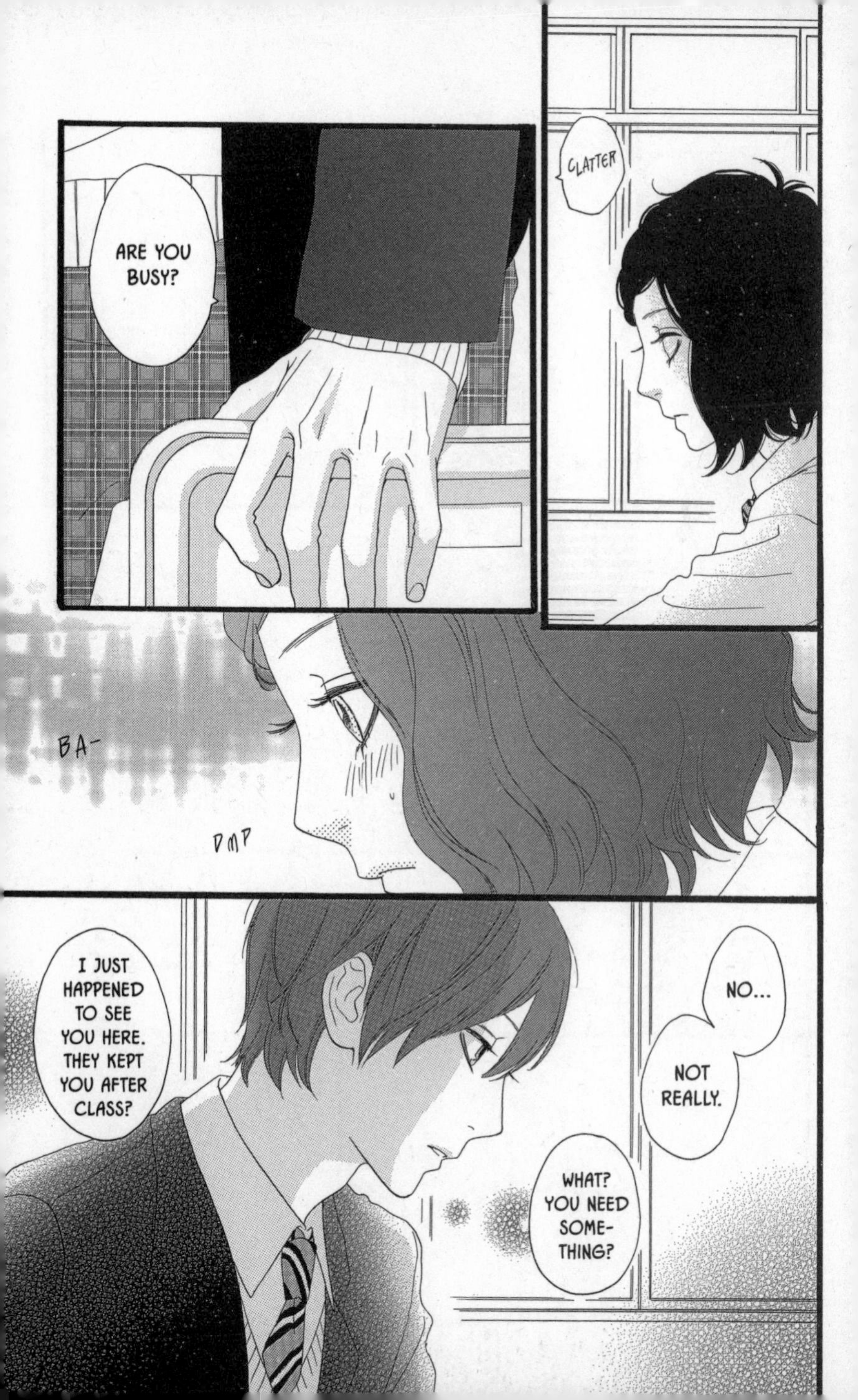
CLATTER
ARE YOU BUSY?
BA-
DMP
NO...
NOT REALLY.
I JUST HAPPENED TO SEE YOU HERE. THEY KEPT YOU AFTER CLASS?
WHAT? YOU NEED SOMETHING?

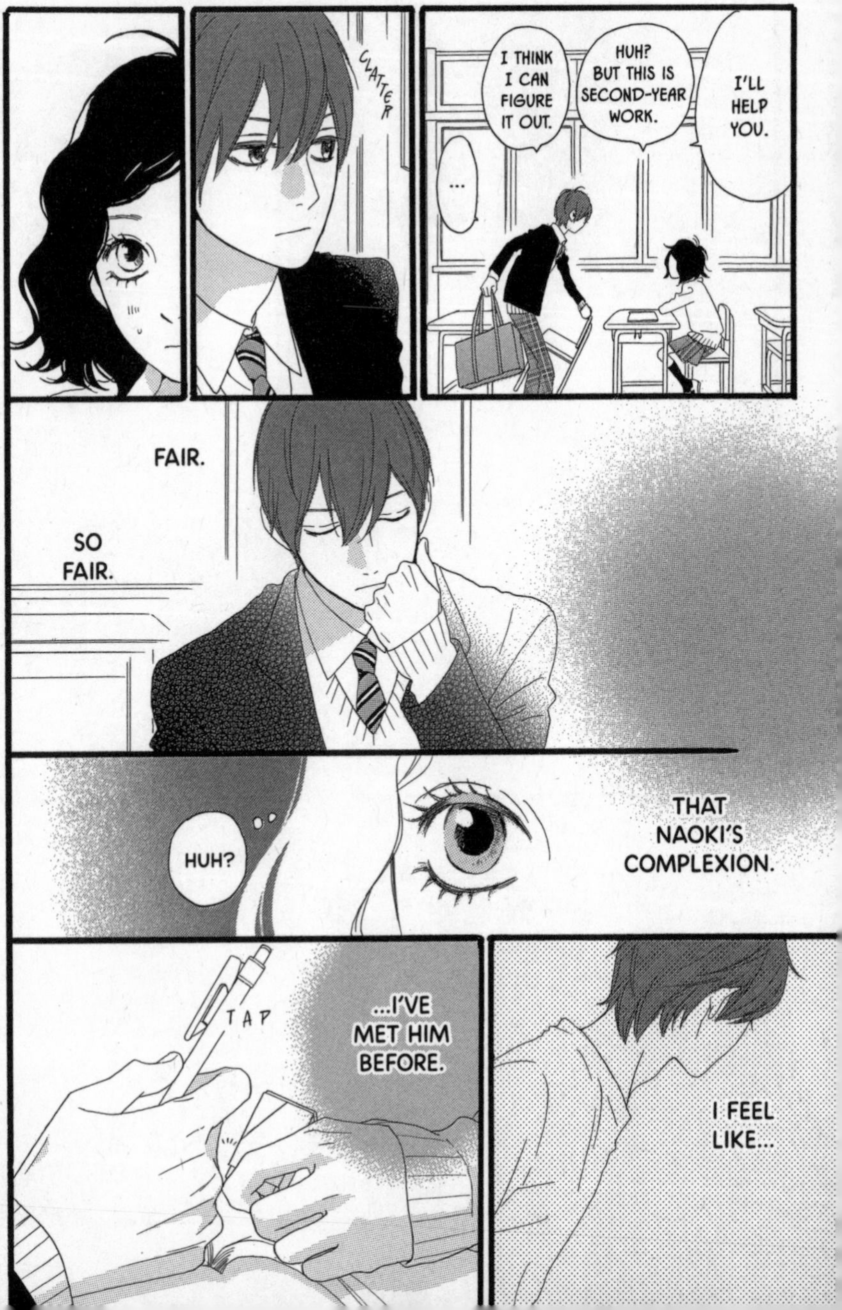
I'LL HELP YOU.
HUH? BUT THIS IS SECOND-YEAR WORK.
I THINK I CAN FIGURE IT OUT.
...
CLATTER
FAIR.
SO FAIR.
THAT NAOKI'S COMPLEXION.
HUH?
I FEEL LIKE...
...I'VE MET HIM BEFORE.
TAP

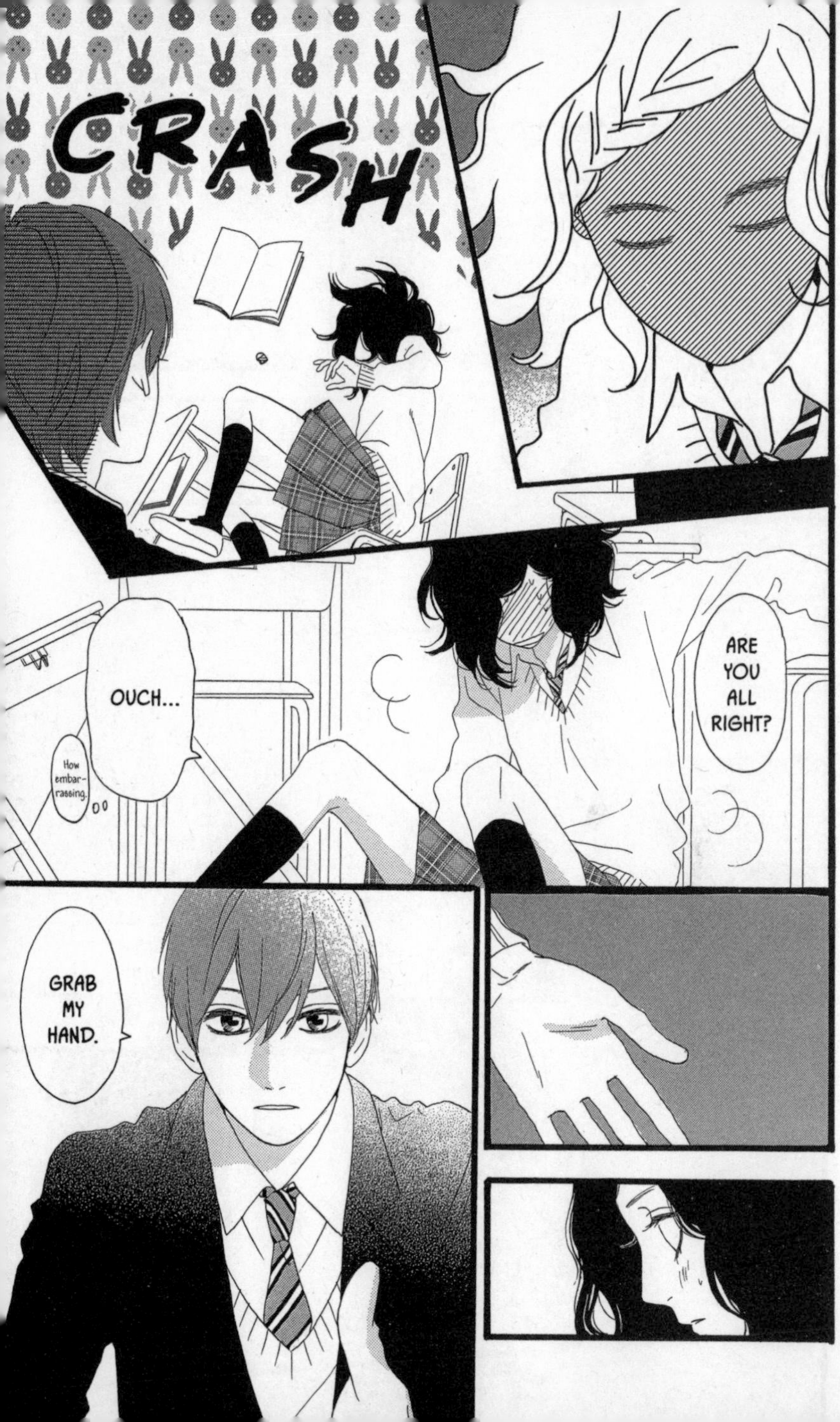
CRASH
ARE YOU ALL RIGHT?
OUCH...
How embarrassing.
GRAB MY HAND.

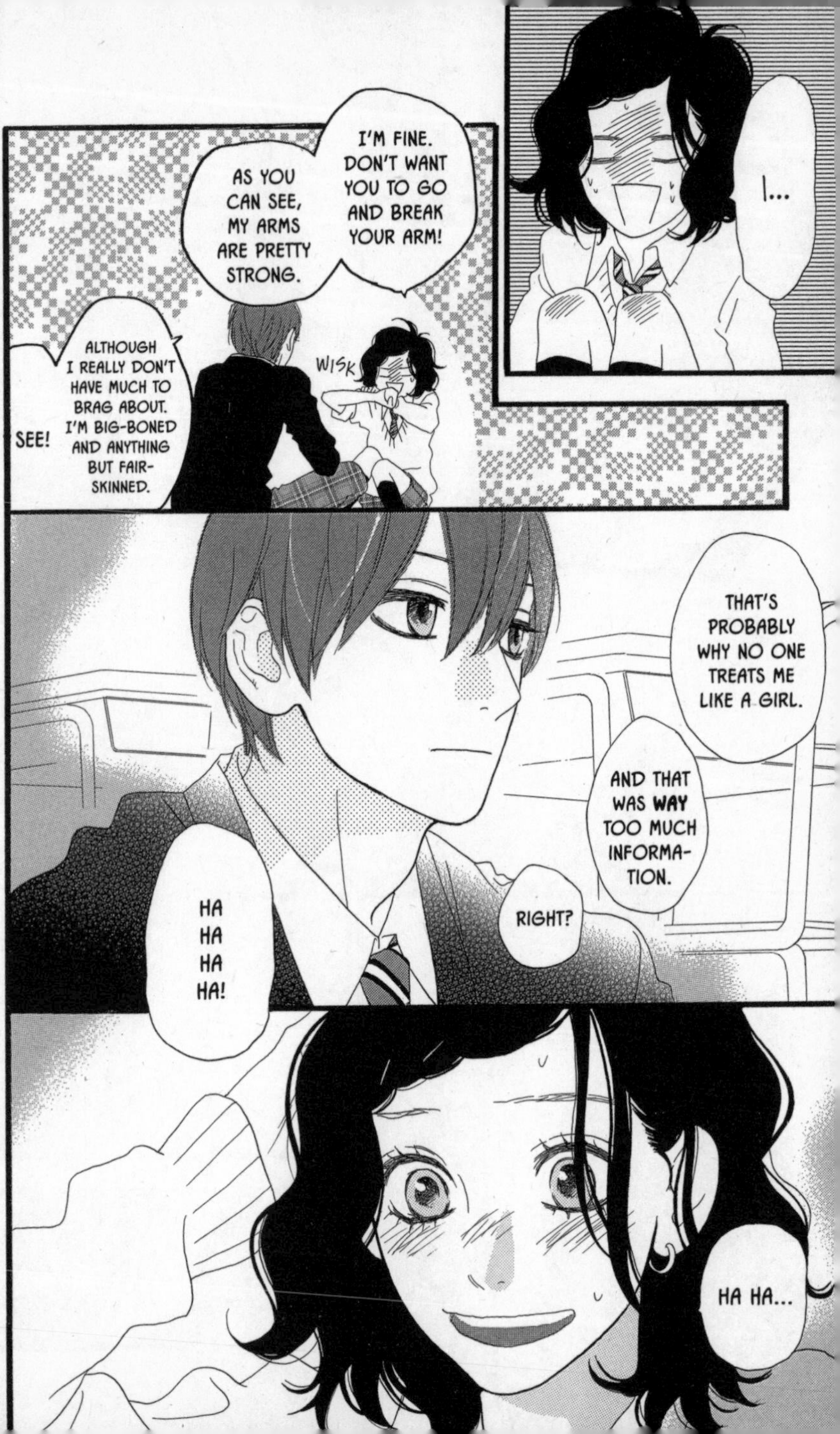
I...
I'M FINE. DON'T WANT YOU TO GO AND BREAK YOUR ARM!
AS YOU CAN SEE, MY ARMS ARE PRETTY STRONG.
WISK
ALTHOUGH I REALLY DON'T HAVE MUCH TO BRAG ABOUT. I'M BIG-BONED AND ANYTHING BUT FAIR-SKINNED.
SEE!
THAT'S PROBABLY WHY NO ONE TREATS ME LIKE A GIRL.
AND THAT WAS **WAY** TOO MUCH INFORMATION.
RIGHT?
HA HA HA HA!
HA HA...

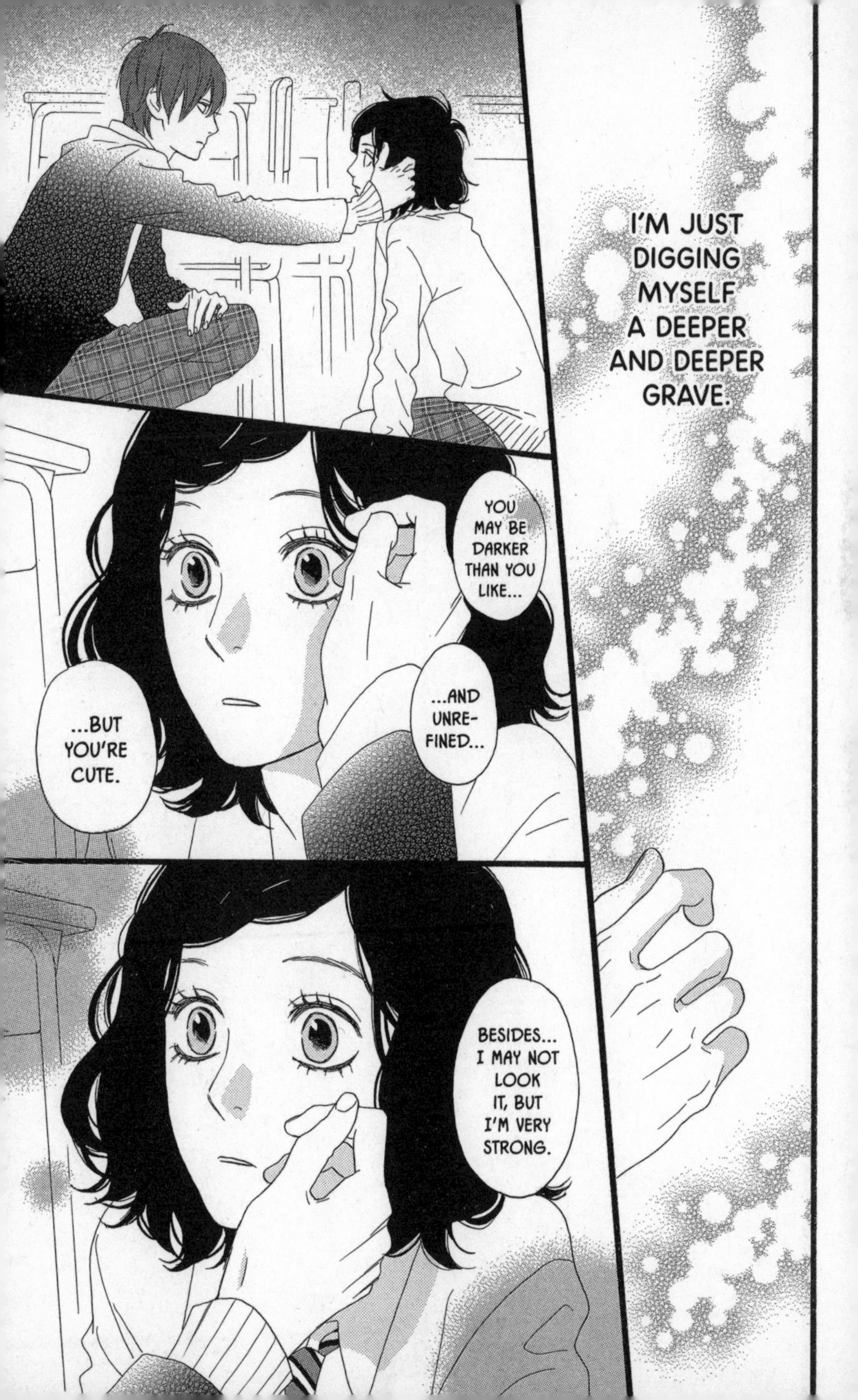
I'M JUST DIGGING MYSELF A DEEPER AND DEEPER GRAVE.
YOU MAY BE DARKER THAN YOU LIKE...
...AND UNRE-FINED...
...BUT YOU'RE CUTE.
BESIDES... I MAY NOT LOOK IT, BUT I'M VERY STRONG.

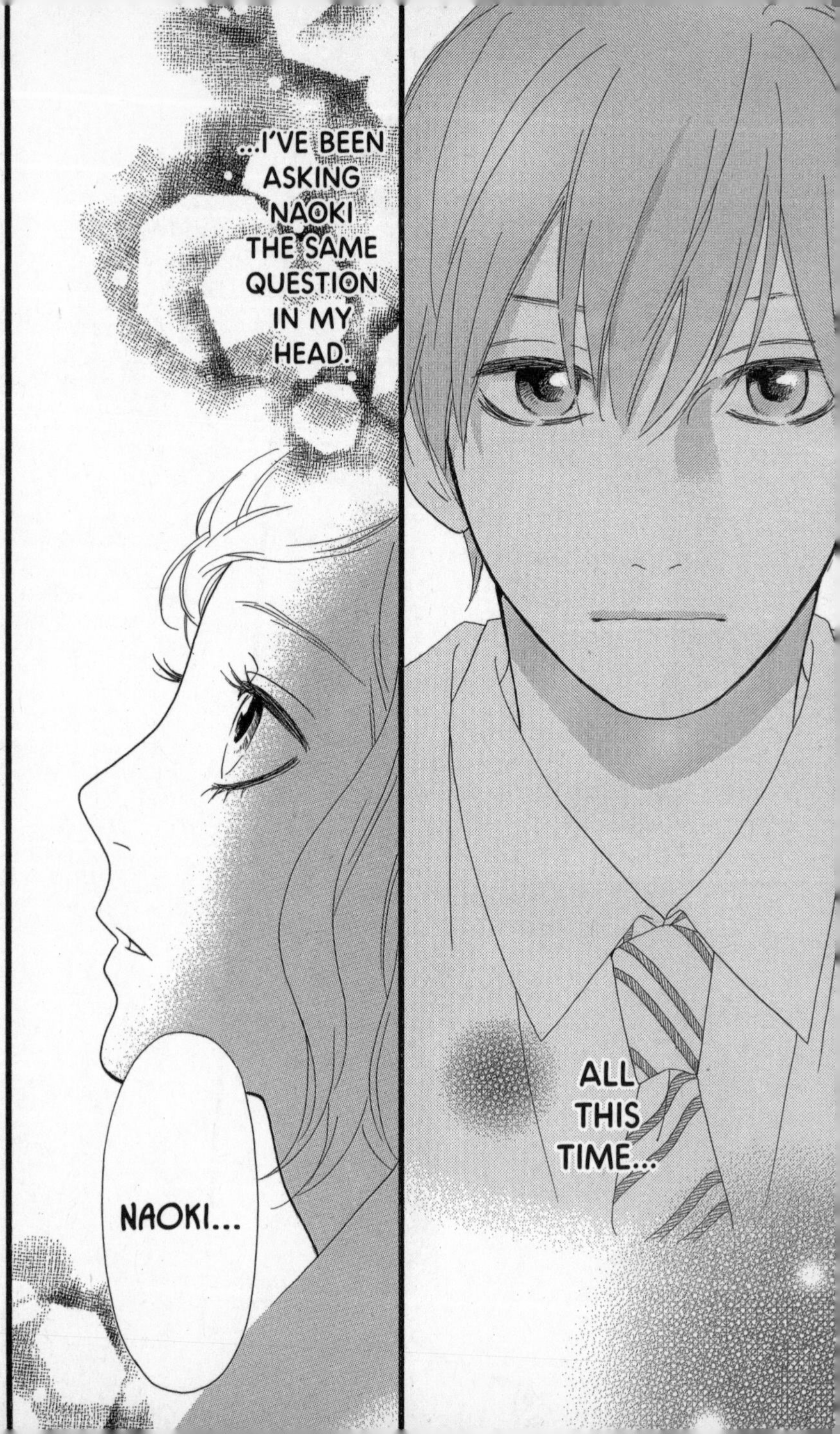
ALL THIS TIME...
...I'VE BEEN ASKING NAOKI THE SAME QUESTION IN MY HEAD.
NAOKI...

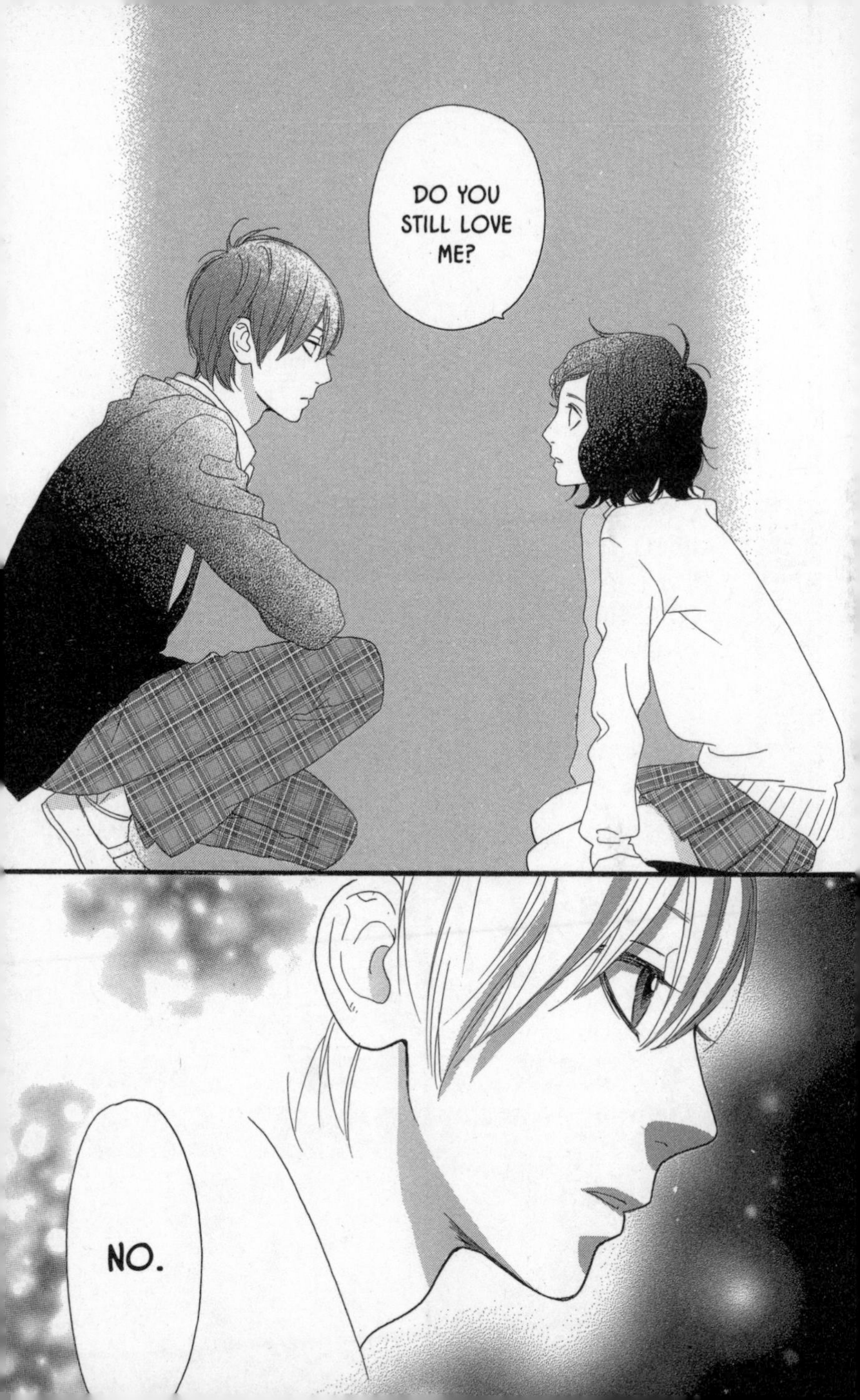
DO YOU STILL LOVE ME?
NO.

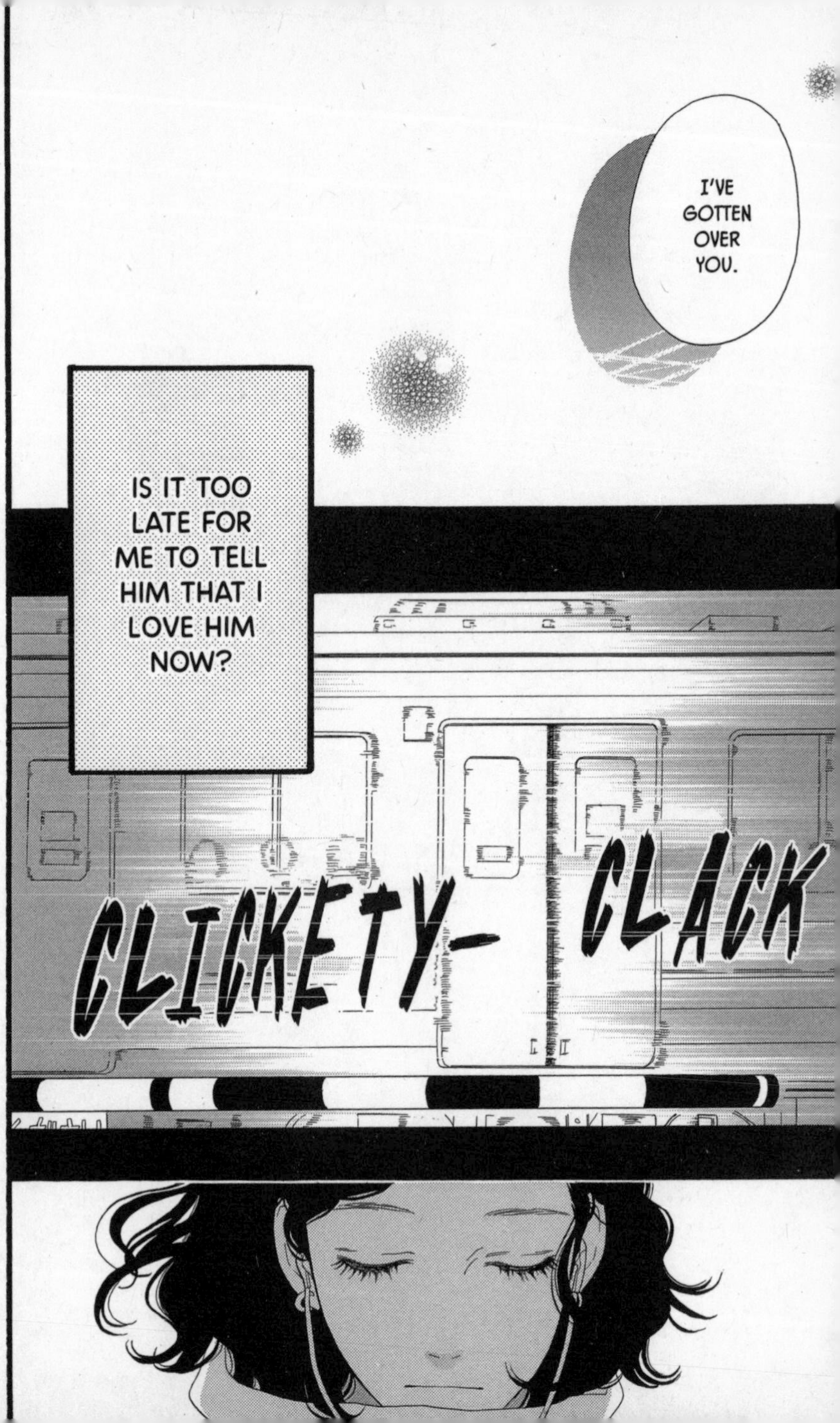
I'VE GOTTEN OVER YOU.
IS IT TOO LATE FOR ME TO TELL HIM THAT I LOVE HIM NOW?
CLICKETY-CLACK

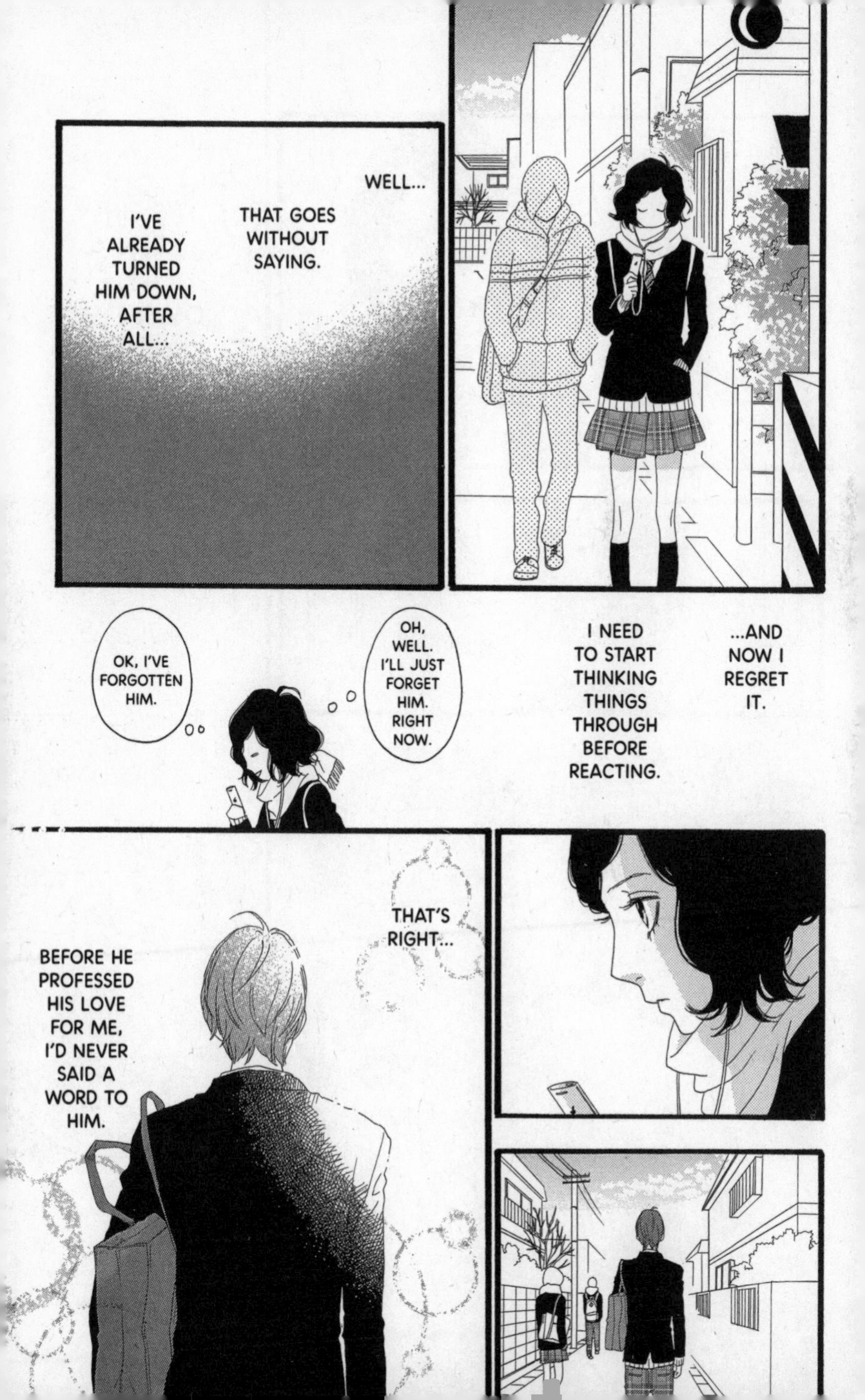
WELL...
THAT GOES WITHOUT SAYING.
I'VE ALREADY TURNED HIM DOWN, AFTER ALL...
...AND NOW I REGRET IT.
I NEED TO START THINKING THINGS THROUGH BEFORE REACTING.
OH, WELL. I'LL JUST FORGET HIM. RIGHT NOW.
OK, I'VE FORGOTTEN HIM.
THAT'S RIGHT...
BEFORE HE PROFESSED HIS LOVE FOR ME, I'D NEVER SAID A WORD TO HIM.

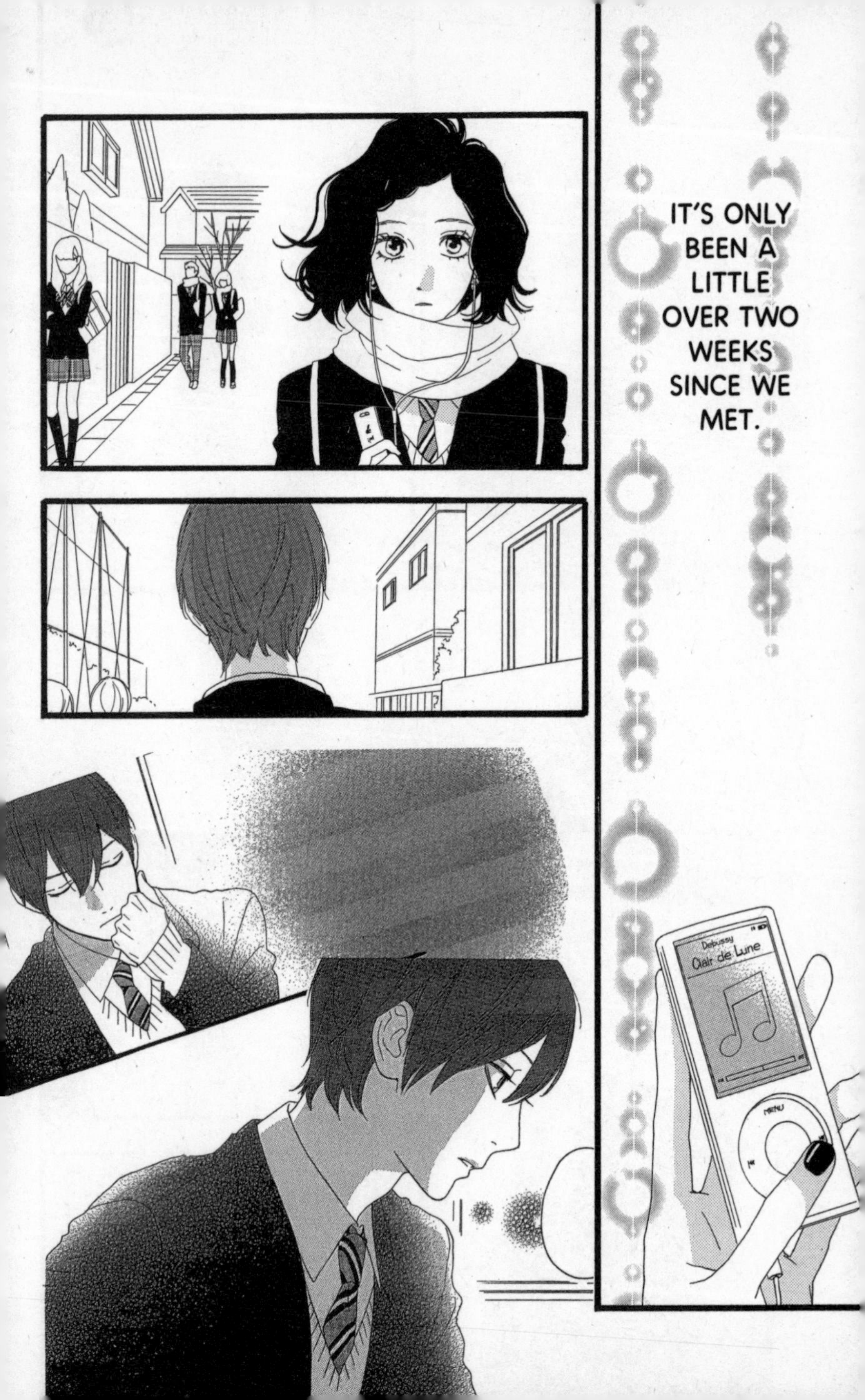
IT'S ONLY BEEN A LITTLE OVER TWO WEEKS SINCE WE MET.
Debussy
Clair de Lune
MENU

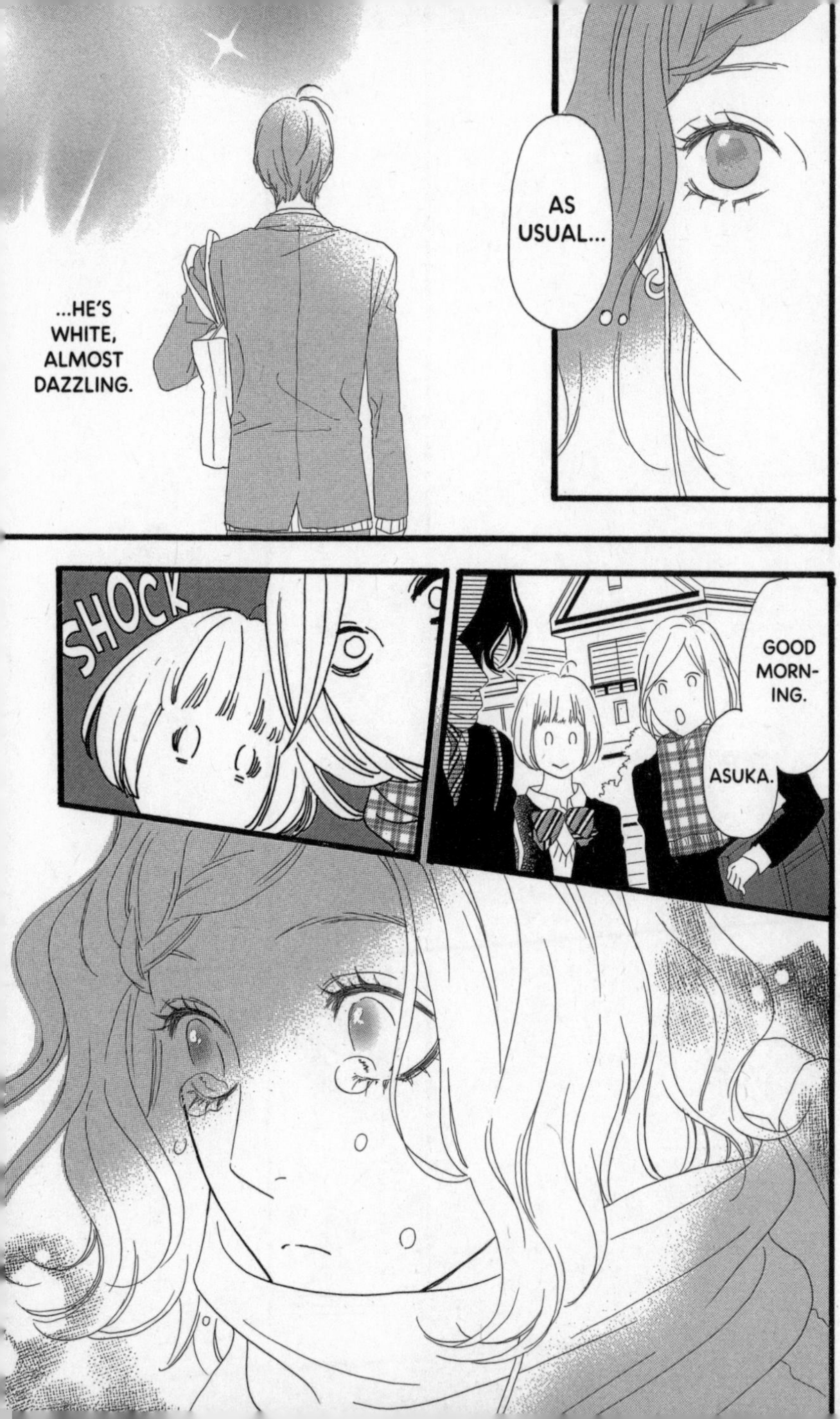
AS USUAL...
...HE'S WHITE, ALMOST DAZZLING.
GOOD MORNING.
ASUKA.
SHOCK

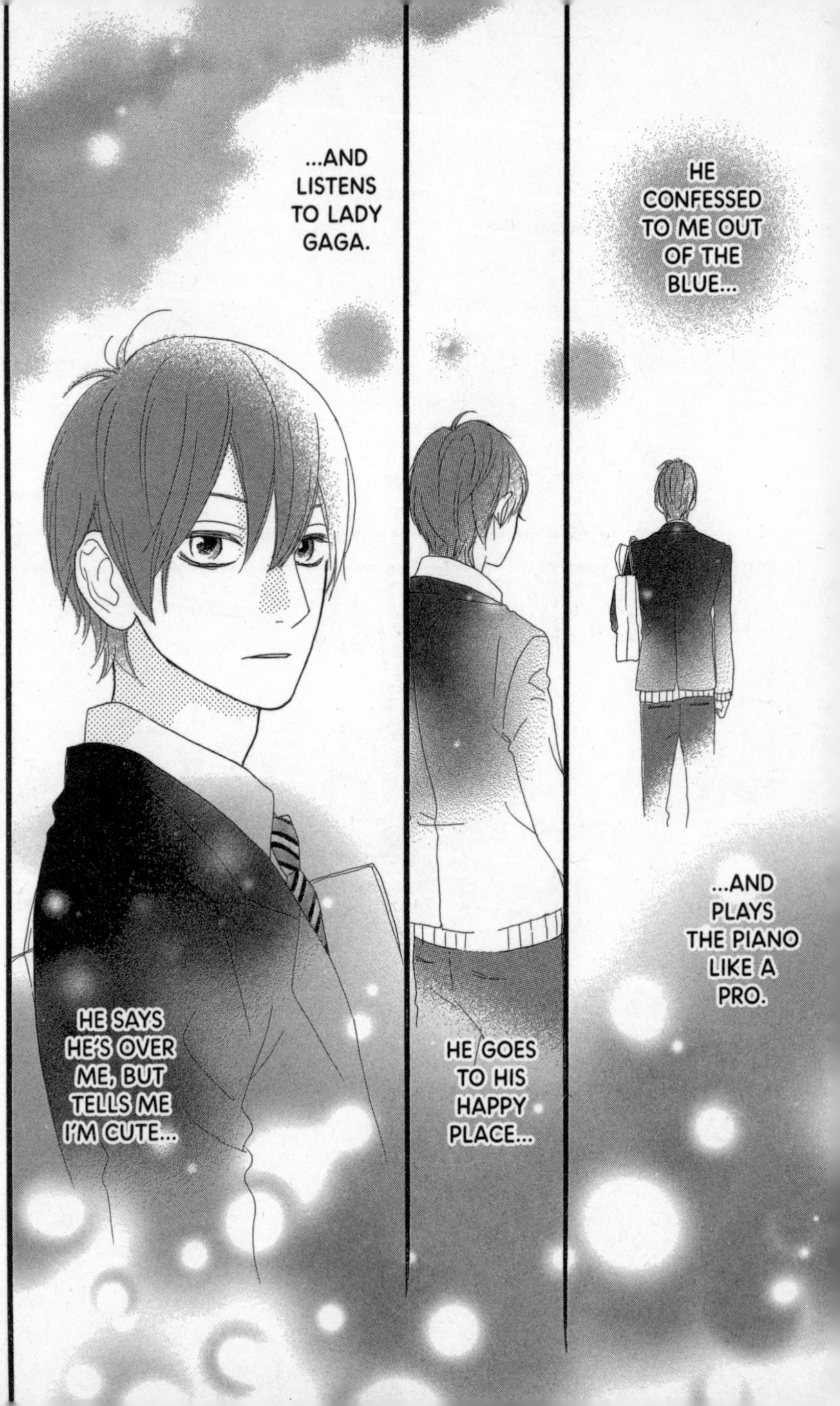
HE CONFESSED TO ME OUT OF THE BLUE...
...AND PLAYS THE PIANO LIKE A PRO.
HE GOES TO HIS HAPPY PLACE...
...AND LISTENS TO LADY GAGA.
HE SAYS HE'S OVER ME, BUT TELLS ME I'M CUTE...

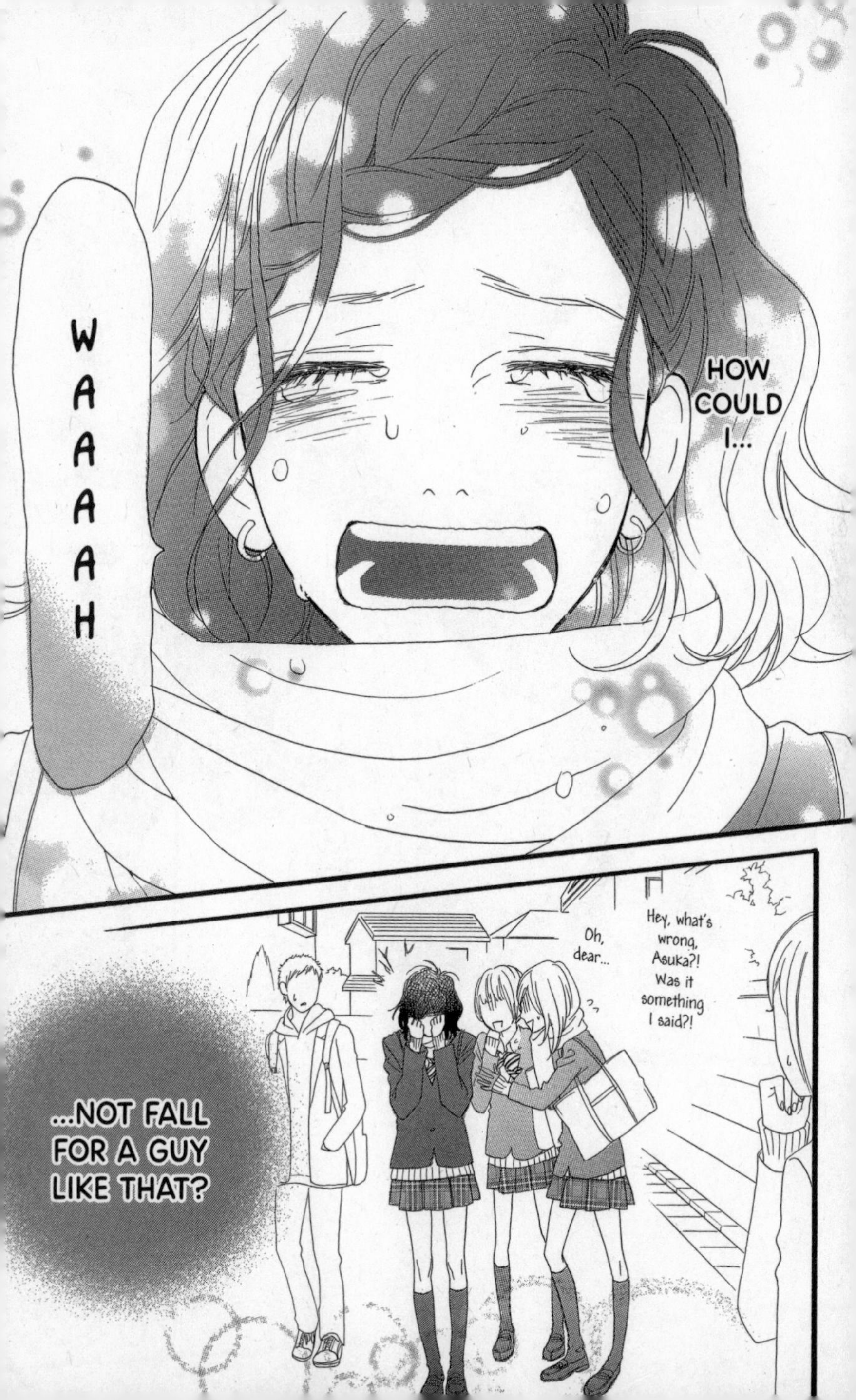
HOW COULD I...
WAAAAAH
...NOT FALL FOR A GUY LIKE THAT?
Hey, what's wrong, Asuka?! Was it something I said?!
Oh, dear...

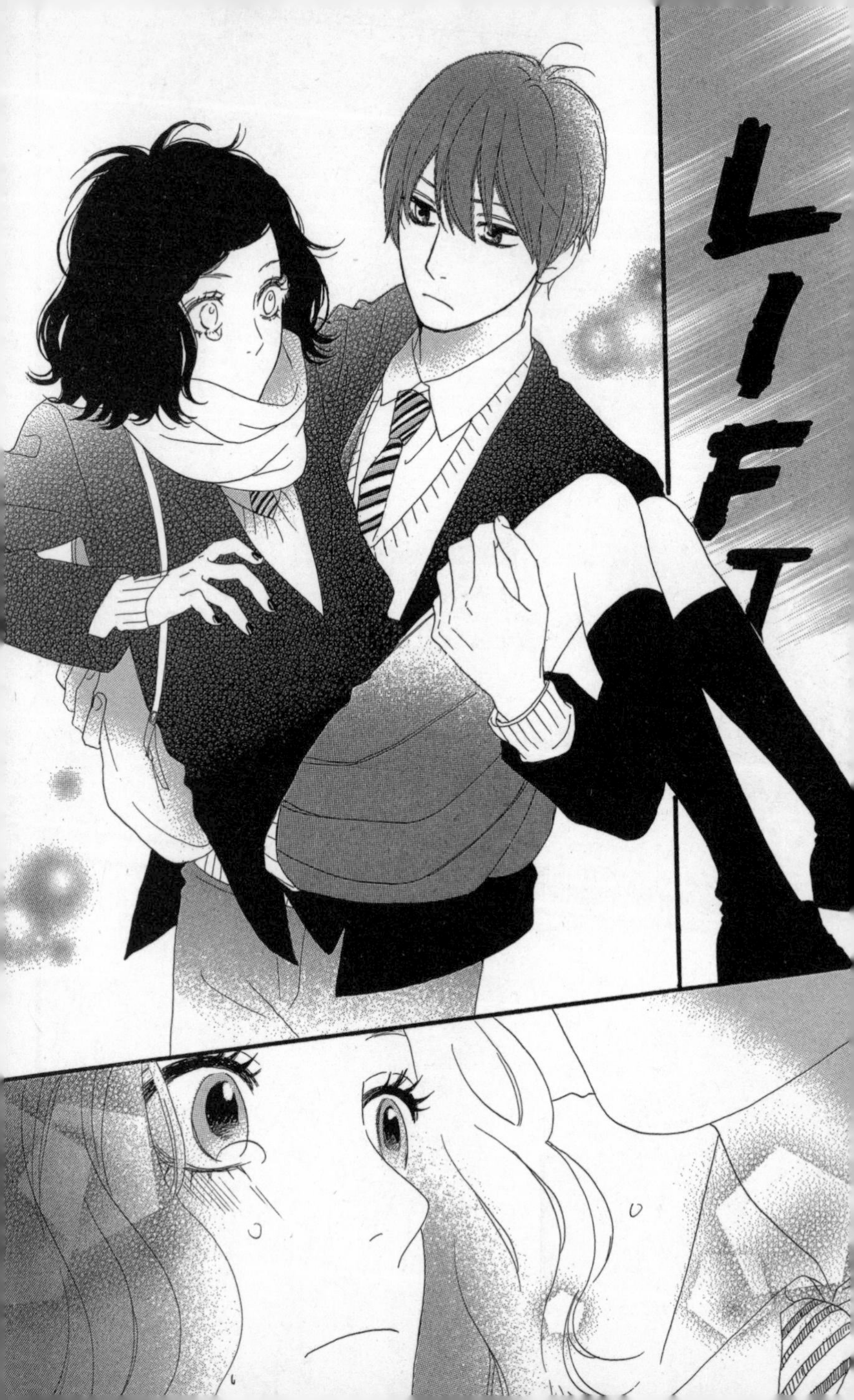
LIFT

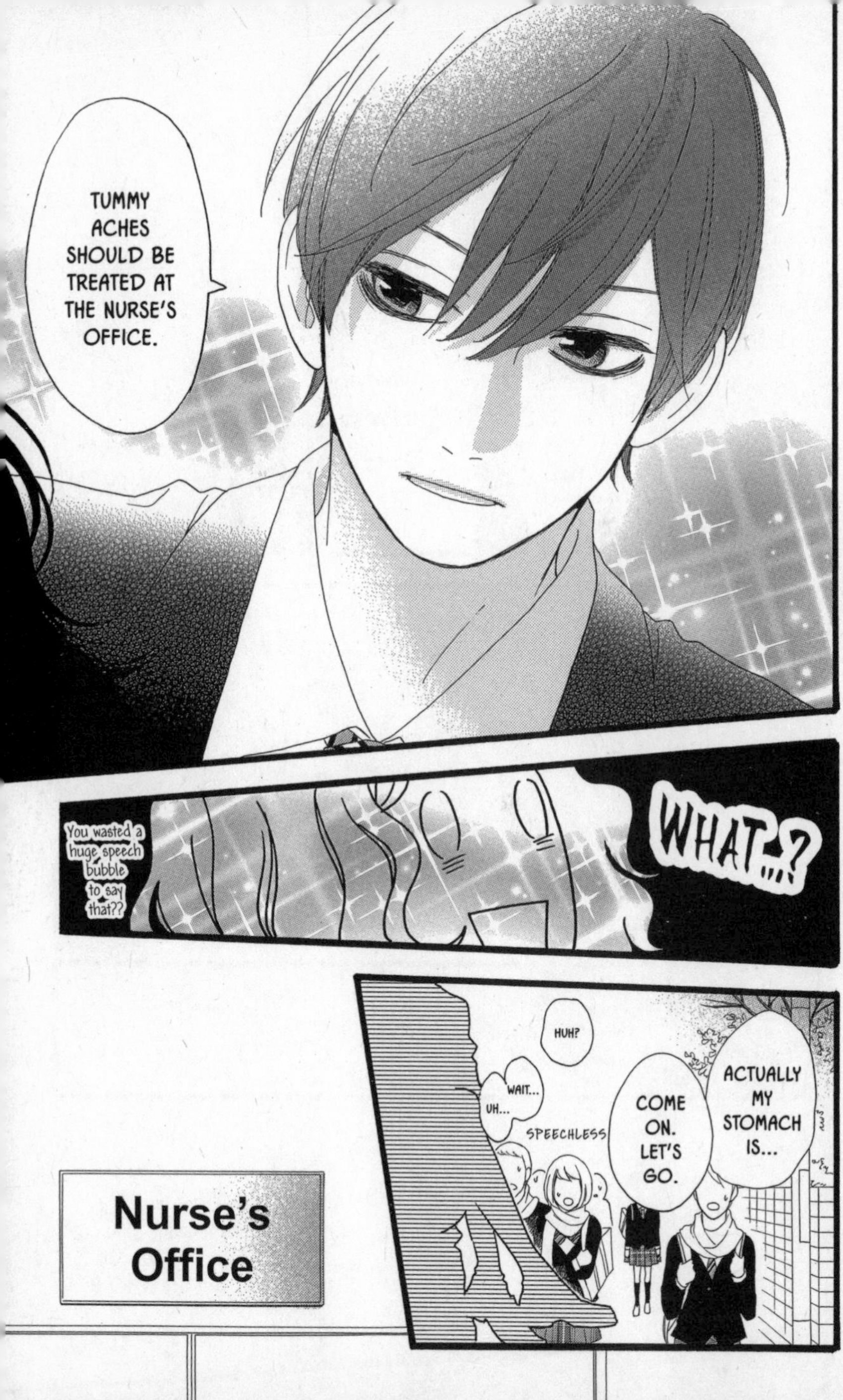
TUMMY ACHES SHOULD BE TREATED AT THE NURSE'S OFFICE.
WHAT...?
You wasted a huge speech bubble to say that??
ACTUALLY MY STOMACH IS...
COME ON. LET'S GO.
HUH?
WAIT... UH...
SPEECHLESS
Nurse's Office

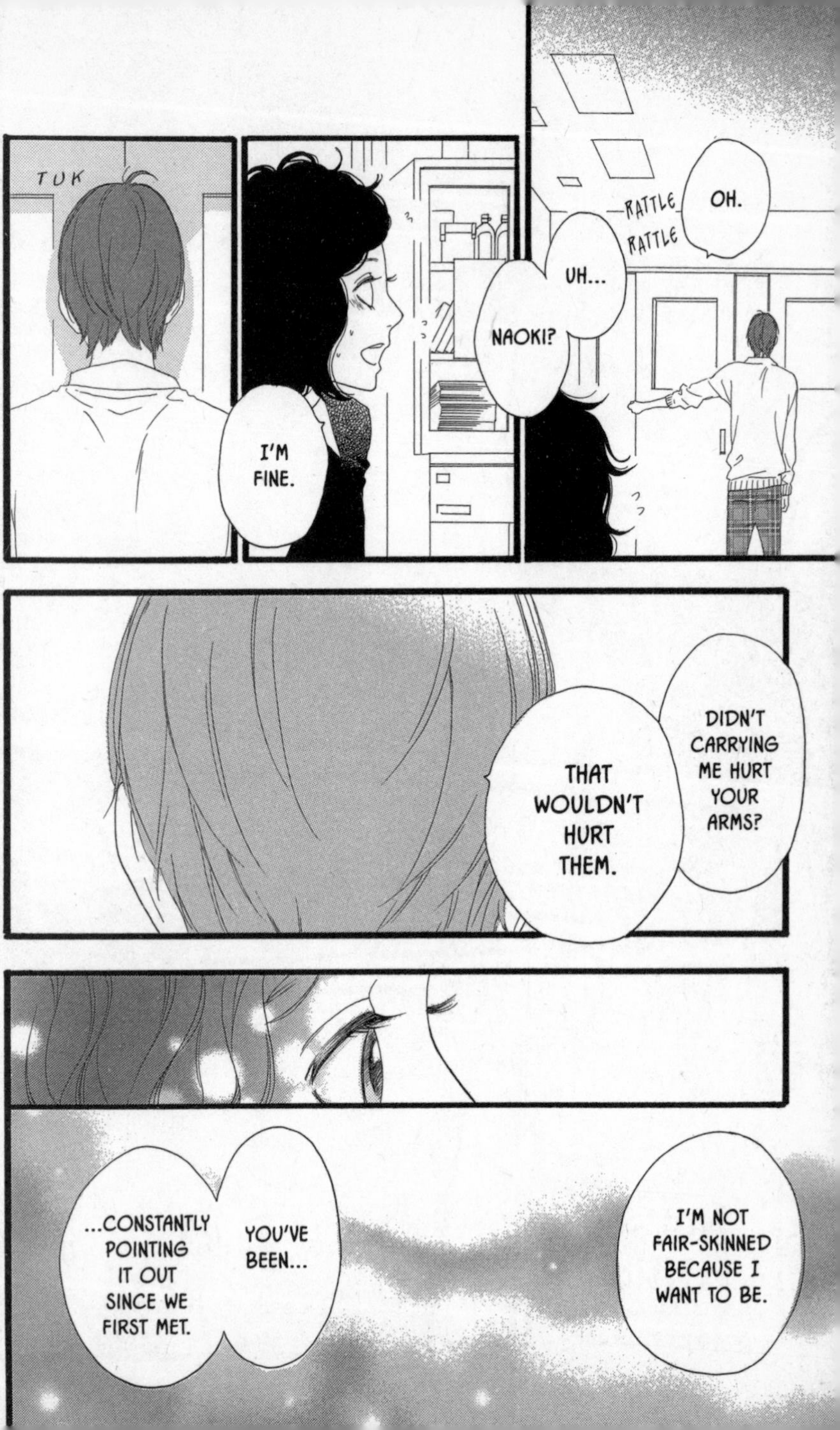
OH.
RATTLE RATTLE
UH...
NAOKI?
I'M FINE.
TUK
DIDN'T CARRYING ME HURT YOUR ARMS?
THAT WOULDN'T HURT THEM.
I'M NOT FAIR-SKINNED BECAUSE I WANT TO BE.
YOU'VE BEEN...
...CONSTANTLY POINTING IT OUT SINCE WE FIRST MET.

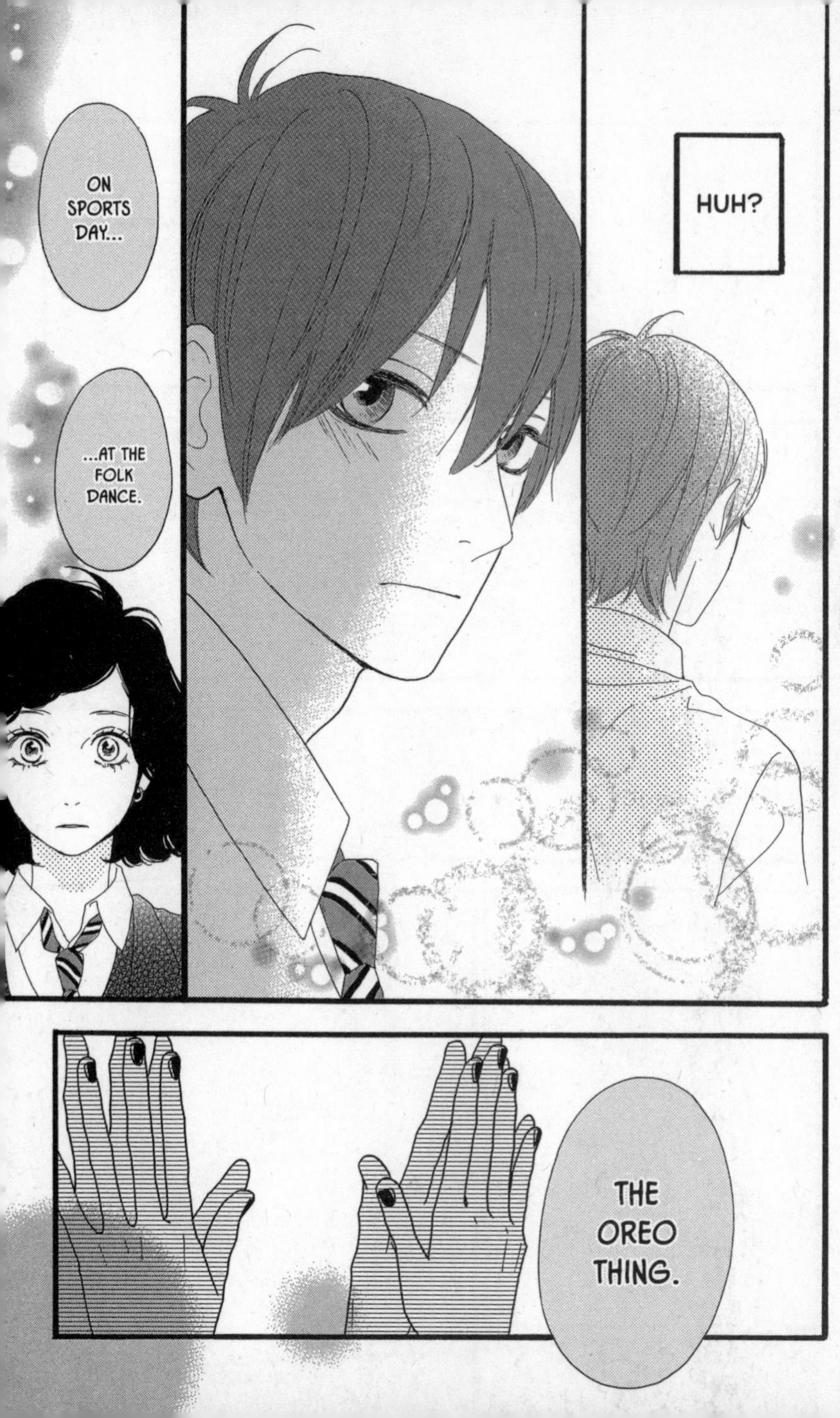
HUH?
ON SPORTS DAY...
...AT THE FOLK DANCE.
THE OREO THING.

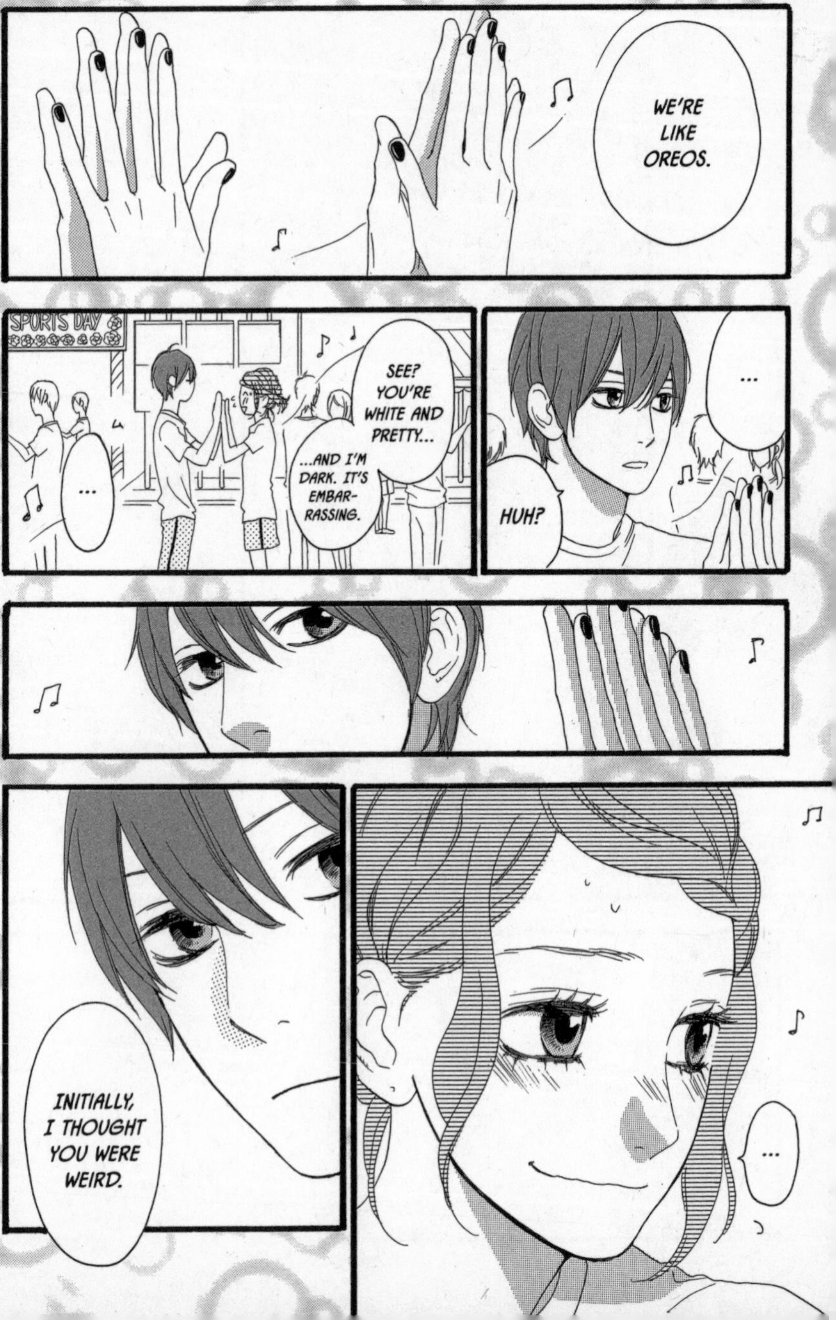
WE'RE LIKE OREOS.
...
HUH?
SPORTS DAY
SEE? YOU'RE WHITE AND PRETTY...
...AND I'M DARK. IT'S EMBARRASSING.
...
...
INITIALLY, I THOUGHT YOU WERE WEIRD.

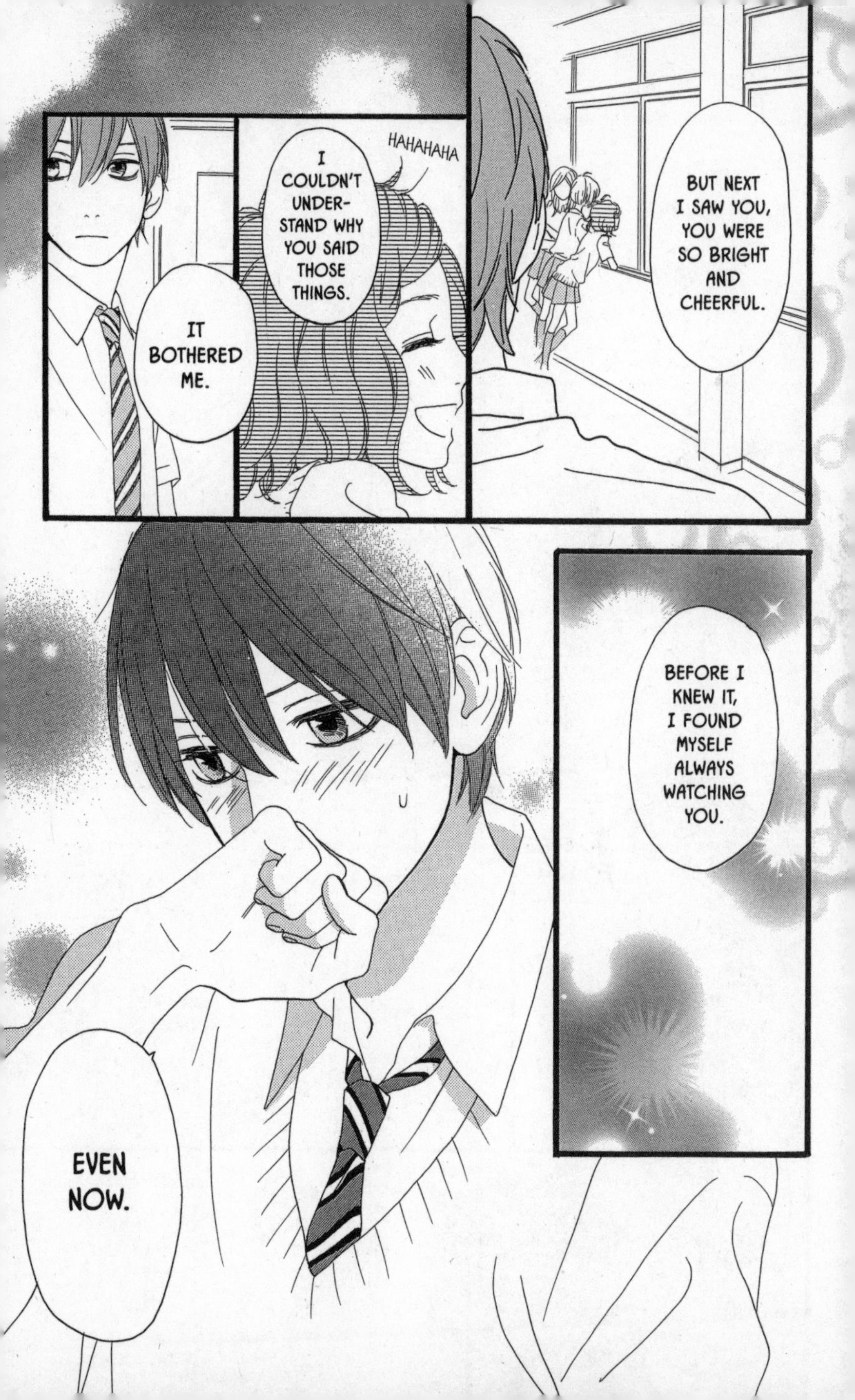
BUT NEXT I SAW YOU, YOU WERE SO BRIGHT AND CHEERFUL.
HAHAHAHA
I COULDN'T UNDER-STAND WHY YOU SAID THOSE THINGS.
IT BOTHERED ME.
BEFORE I KNEW IT, I FOUND MYSELF ALWAYS WATCHING YOU.
EVEN NOW.

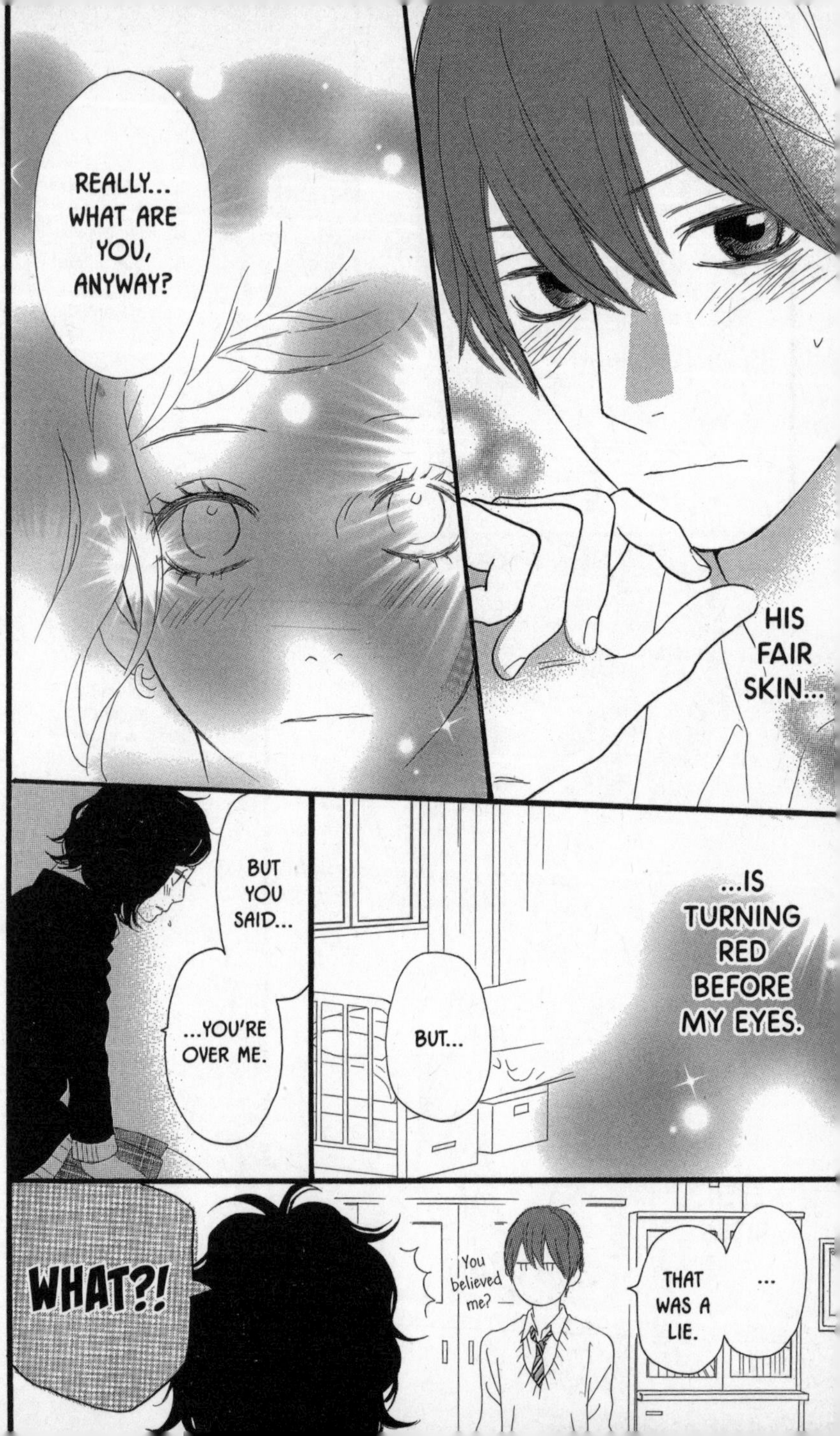
HIS FAIR SKIN...
REALLY... WHAT ARE YOU, ANYWAY?
...IS TURNING RED BEFORE MY EYES.
BUT...
BUT YOU SAID...
...YOU'RE OVER ME.
...
THAT WAS A LIE.
You believed me?
WHAT?!

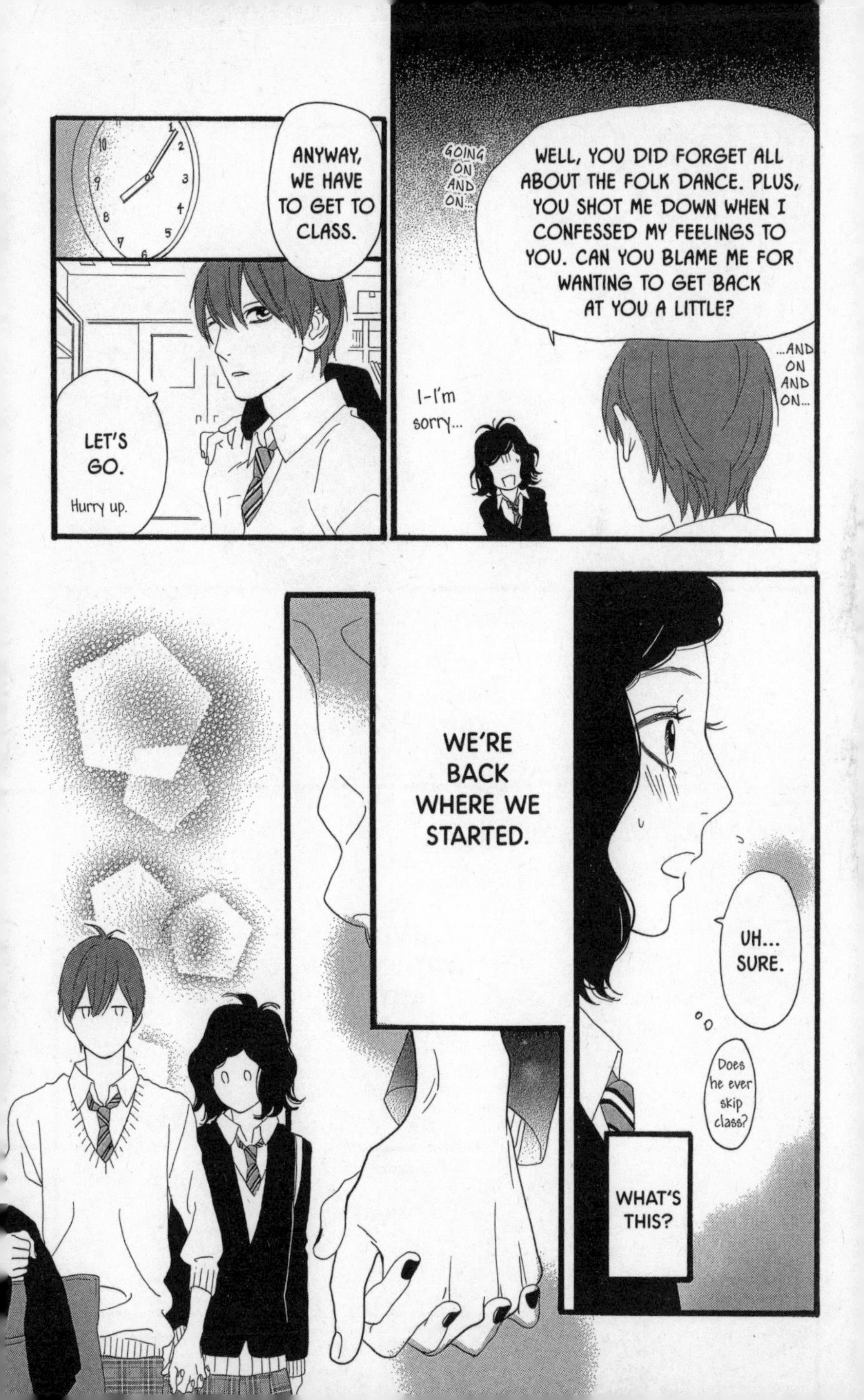
WELL, YOU DID FORGET ALL ABOUT THE FOLK DANCE. PLUS, YOU SHOT ME DOWN WHEN I CONFESSED MY FEELINGS TO YOU. CAN YOU BLAME ME FOR WANTING TO GET BACK AT YOU A LITTLE?
GOING ON AND ON...
...AND ON AND ON...
I-I'm sorry...
ANYWAY, WE HAVE TO GET TO CLASS.
LET'S GO.
Hurry up.
UH... SURE.
Does he ever skip class?
WHAT'S THIS?
WE'RE BACK WHERE WE STARTED.

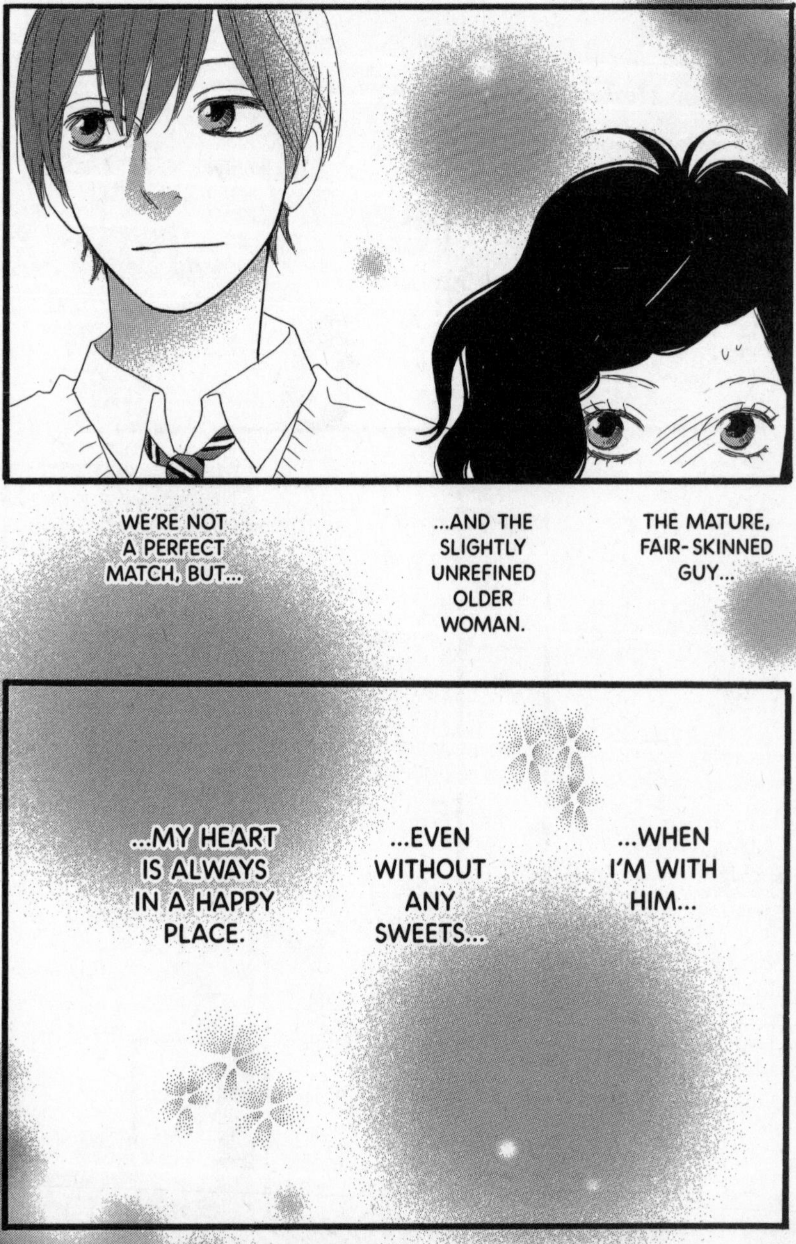
THE MATURE, FAIR-SKINNED GUY...
...AND THE SLIGHTLY UNREFINED OLDER WOMAN.
WE'RE NOT A PERFECT MATCH, BUT...
...WHEN I'M WITH HIM...
...EVEN WITHOUT ANY SWEETS...
...MY HEART IS ALWAYS IN A HAPPY PLACE.

The End

# About Cookie Girl, Cream Boy

This story is connected to my previous series, *Sugars*. It was printed in *Margaret Magazine*. To commemorate the end of *Sugars*, I was supposed to draw another 50 pages. However, because "it would be odd to end the series in *Margaret*," I reduced the number of pages meant to run in the magazine, and it was decided that the full story would be published separately as a *Sugars*-related story. The heroine is the younger sister of a character in "Jelly Beans," which is at the end of volume 5 of *Sugars*. I like this character's hair-style. This story was a rush job. That may be why I feel like I could've added another episode to it. But I kind of like these two characters. Plus, I got to do a cover for the first time.

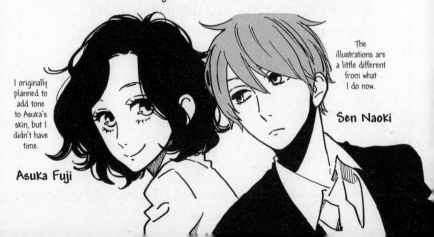

The illustrations are a little different from what I do now.
Sen Naoki
I originally planned to add tone to Asuka's skin, but I didn't have time.
Asuka Fuji

# About Rin Mikimoto

And so... Surprise! I had **Rin Mikimoto** draw some illustrations for me!! Yahoo!! I haven't seen the actual pictures (I'm having them sent directly to Shueisha), **but no way could they not be cute!!!**

When I was working on *Sugars*, one of my assistants told me about an artist who draws really cute pictures. That artist was Rin Mikimoto!! Back then, I was just another one of her fans, but now she's miraculously become a very good friend of mine. I will always remember how much fun I had with Momoko Koda, Rin and Ayu Watanabe last summer!! I hadn't laughed like that in a while. And the two girls were so cute—and sparkly!!

**"Kyou no Kira-kun" (Rin's book) volume 4 is in stores in Japan right now.** ♪

I wonder how the love between Nino and Kira will fare?! I hope Nino doesn't get hurt!! You'll find my illustrations of Nino and Kira in that volume. ☺

I hope you will buy it!!

# Rin Mikimoto

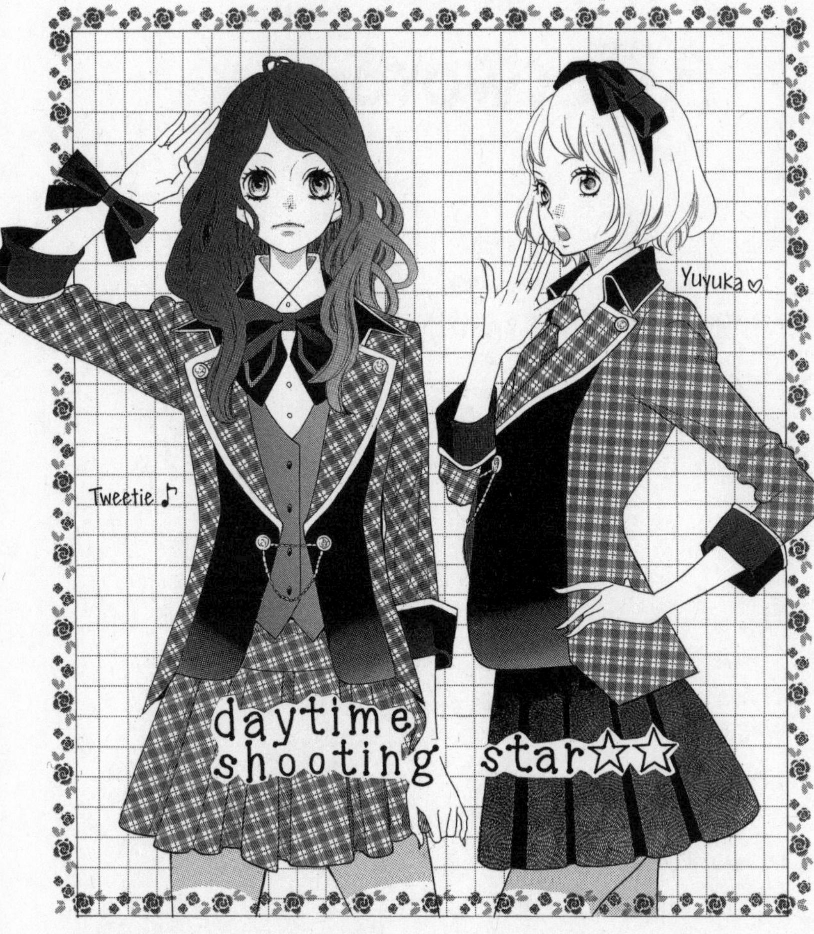
Yuyuka ♡
Tweetie ♪
daytime shooting star☆☆

I managed to draw these two characters! Oh, I was very nervous. (I'm sorry for dressing them up like idols. Forgive me, Mika.)
*Daytime Shooting Star* is a great story, isn't it? Of the girls, Yuyuka is my favorite. ♪ She has a sharp tongue, but you can tell she tries her best to be feminine. ♡ Without a doubt, when it comes to the guys, I love Mamura! Hurry up and get together with Tweetie! Ah, but then Yuyuka will be sad. But Miki will surely come up with a good ending for everyone!! The next time I see her, I wonder if I should ask her how the series will end. I want to know... Well, thank you very much for sharing such valuable space with me! I have great respect for you, Miki!

# And so... Afterword

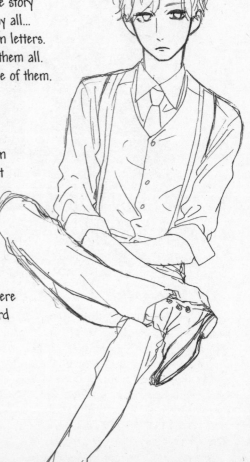

So, what did you think of this volume?
What? You think I've hit a rut?
I-I will do my best!! Please look forward to seeing how the story unfolds. Yes, I'll give it my all...
Thank you for all your fan letters.
I'm sorry I can't answer them all.
I read each and every one of them.

I hope to be able to begin answering them soon, but I don't know when that will be. So please be patient with me.

It's not important, but there sure are a lot of afterword pages in this volume.
I wonder why...?

Rejected draft of *Margaret* cover.

# ☆ Special ☆ Thanx ☆

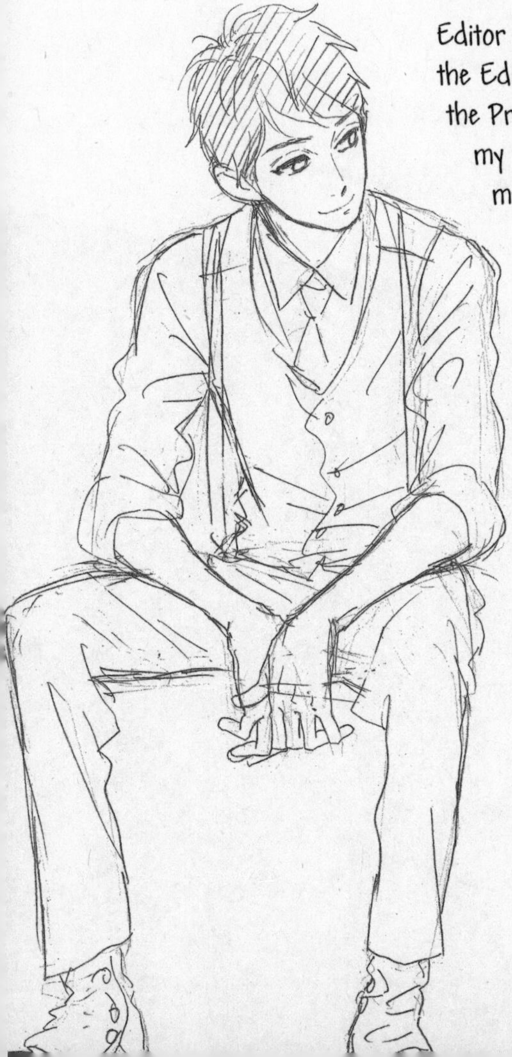

Editor U, my assistants,
the Editorial Department,
the Printer Staff, Ms. K,
my family, my friends, all of
my readers and to everyone
who supports me.

See you again in
volume 6.

*Shishio has gradually turned into a terrible grown-up, but I hope you won't give up on him.*

*—Mika Yamamori*

**Mika Yamamori** is from Ishikawa Prefecture in Japan. She began her professional manga career in 2006 with "Kimi no Kuchibiru kara Mahou" (The Magic from Your Lips) in *The Margaret* magazine. Her other works include *Sugars* and *Tsubaki Cho Lonely Planet*.

# ★DAYTIME★SHOOTING★STAR★ *5*

## SHOJO BEAT EDITION

Story & Art by
### Mika Yamamori

Translation ★ **JN Productions**
Touch-Up Art & Lettering ★ **Inori Fukuda Trant**
Design ★ **Alice Lewis**
Editor ★ **Karla Clark**

HIRUNAKA NO RYUSEI © 2011 by Mika Yamamori
All rights reserved.
First published in Japan in 2011 by SHUEISHA Inc., Tokyo.
English translation rights arranged by SHUEISHA Inc.

Printed in the U.S.A.

Published by VIZ Media, LLC
P.O. Box 77010
San Francisco, CA 94107

10 9 8 7 6 5 4 3 2 1
First printing, March 2020

viz.com                    shojobeat.com

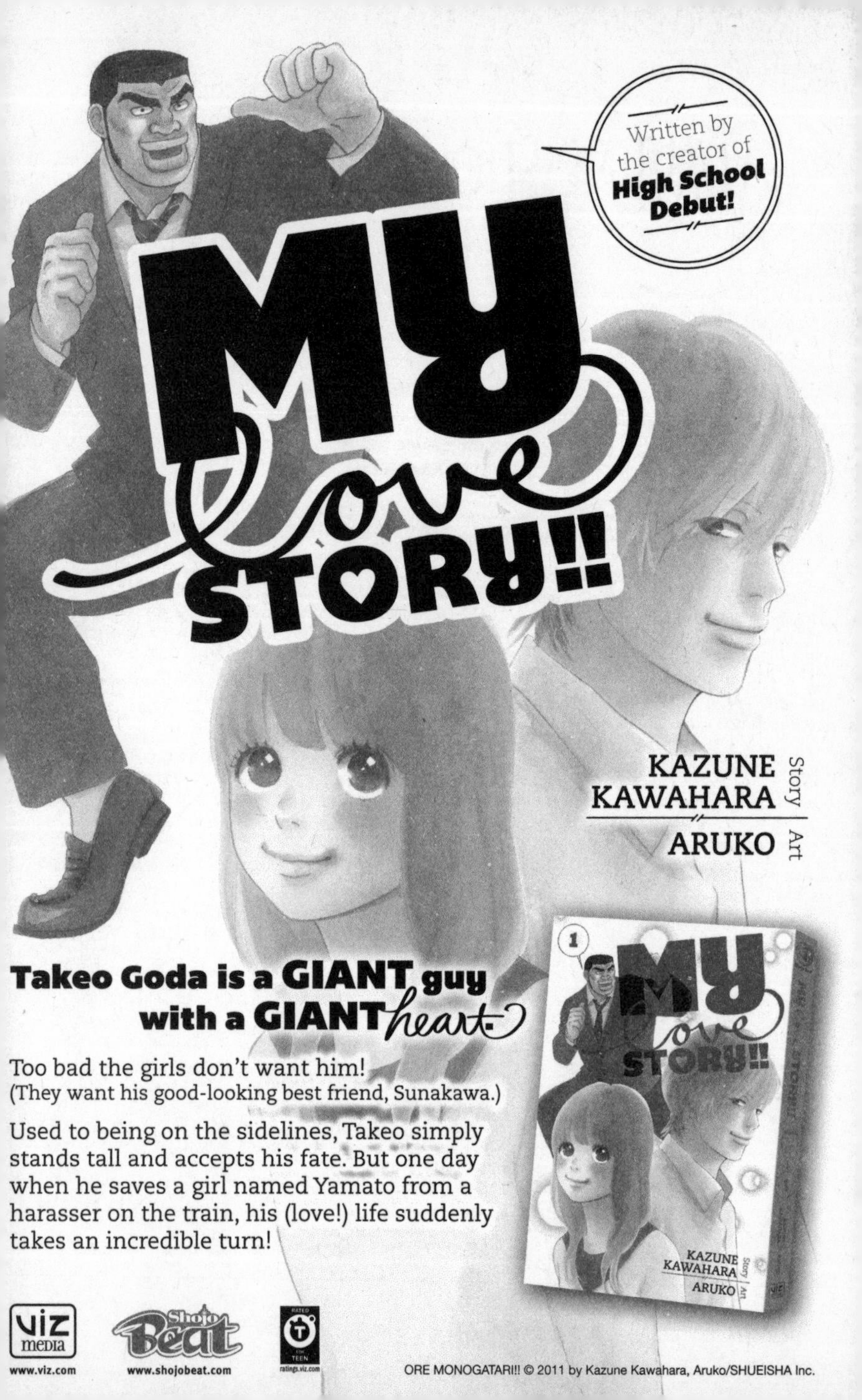
Written by the creator of High School Debut!
MY Love STORY!!
KAZUNE KAWAHARA Story
ARUKO Art
Takeo Goda is a GIANT guy with a GIANT heart
Too bad the girls don't want him!
(They want his good-looking best friend, Sunakawa.)
Used to being on the sidelines, Takeo simply stands tall and accepts his fate. But one day when he saves a girl named Yamato from a harasser on the train, his (love!) life suddenly takes an incredible turn!
1
MY Love STORY!!
KAZUNE KAWAHARA Story
ARUKO Art
VIZ media
www.viz.com
Shojo Beat
www.shojobeat.com
RATED T TEEN
ratings.viz.com
ORE MONOGATARI!! © 2011 by Kazune Kawahara, Aruko/SHUEISHA Inc.

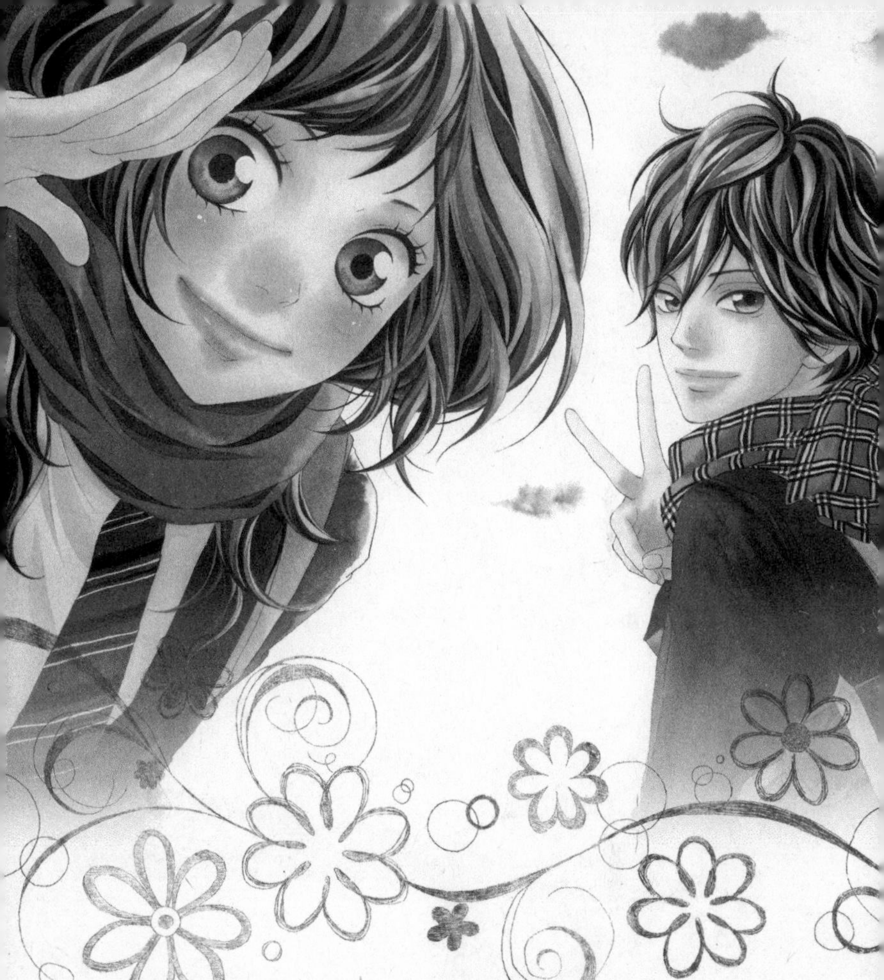



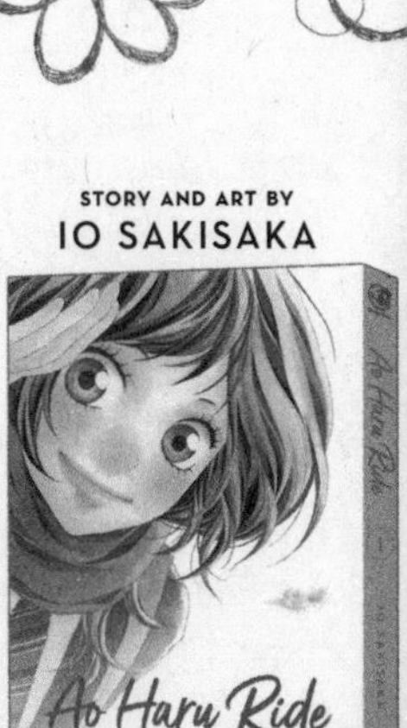

Ao Haru Ride
IO SAKISAKA
1

# STOP!

## You may be reading the wrong way!

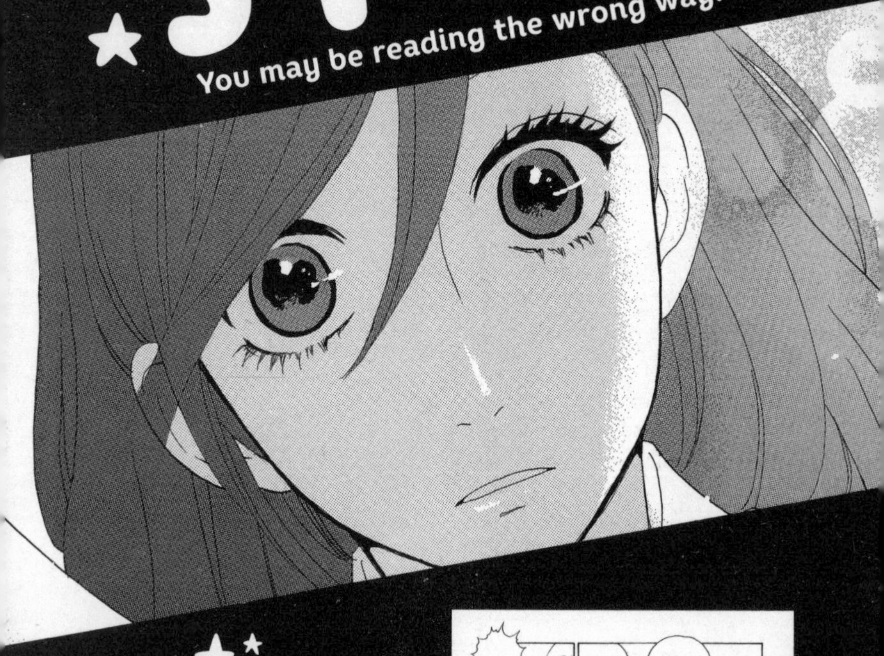

In keeping with the original Japanese comic format, this book reads from right to left—so action, sound effects and word balloons are completely reversed to preserve the orientation of the original artwork.

Check out the diagram shown here to get the hang of things, and then turn to the other side of the book to get started!

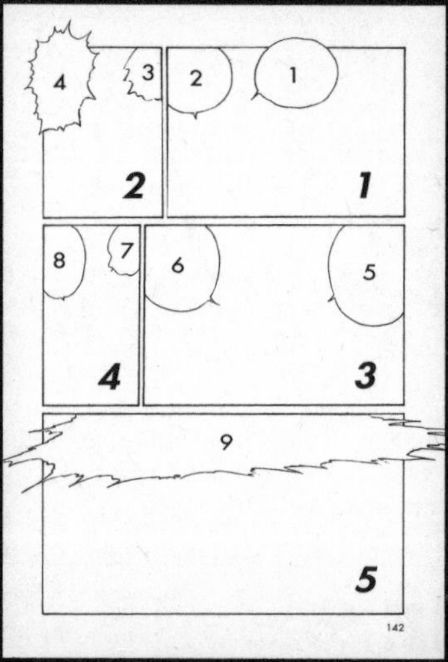
1
2
3
4
5
6
7
8
9
1
2
3
4
5
142